Tantric Techniques

Jeffrey Hopkins

Edited by Kevin Vose

Snow Lion Publications
Ithaca, New York

Snow Lion Publications
P.O. Box 6483
Ithaca, NY 14851 USA
(607) 273-8519
www.snowlionpub.com

Printed in USA on acid-free recycled paper.

ISBN-10: 1-55939-320-3
ISBN-13: 978-1-55939-320-1

Library of Congress Cataloging-in-Publication Data

Hopkins, Jeffrey.
Tantric techniques / Jeffrey Hopkins ; edited by Kevin Vose.
p. cm.
Includes bibliographical references and index.
ISBN-13: 978-1-55939-320-1 (alk. paper)
ISBN-10: 1-55939-320-3 (alk. paper)
1. Meditation--Tantric Buddhism. 2. Yoga--Tantric Buddhism. I. Vose, Kevin, 1970- II. Title.
BQ8938.H67 2009
294.3'4436--dc22

2008047799

Tantric Techniques

Contents

Technical Notes

Please notice that:

- Full bibliographical references are given in the footnotes at first citation.
- For translations and editions of texts, see the Bibliography.
- The names of Indian Buddhist schools are translated into English in an effort to increase accessibility for non-specialists.
- For the names of Indian scholars and systems cited in the body of the text, *ch, sh,* and *ṣh* are used instead of the more usual *c, ś,* and *ṣ* for the sake of easy pronunciation by non-specialists; however, *cch* is used for *cch,* not *chchh.* In parentheses the usual transliteration system for Sanskrit is used.
- Transliteration of Tibetan is done in accordance with a system devised by Turrell Wylie; see "A Standard System of Tibetan Transcription," *Harvard Journal of Asiatic Studies* 22 (1959): 261-267.
- The names of Tibetan authors and orders are given in "essay phonetics" for the sake of easy pronunciation.

Introduction

Across the vast reaches of the Tibetan cultural region in Inner Asia—stretching from Kalmyk Mongolian areas near the Volga River (in Europe) by the Caspian Sea and reaching through Outer Mongolia, Inner Mongolia, the Buriat Republic of Siberia, Bhutan, Sikkim, Ladakh, parts of Nepal, and what is currently called the "Tibetan Autonomous Region" but also most of Qinghai Province, and parts of the Gansu, Sichuan, and Yunnan Provinces which were included in greater Tibet before the Chinese remapped the area—Buddhism is practiced in many forms by a plethora of sects and sub-sects. Though their systems vary widely, they agree on dividing their practices into basically two styles, Sūtra and Mantra (also called Tantra), and all offer reasons why the Mantra system is superior. Based on Indian expositions of the greatness of Mantra, many scholar-practitioners catalogued and creatively developed these explanations, which came to be the means through which they perceived and ordered the otherwise overwhelmingly diverse forms of practice inherited from Buddhist India.

Most of the presentations of the distinctiveness of Mantra employ multiple formats for demonstrating its greatness, but one Tibetan scholar boils these down into a single central distinguishing feature—deity yoga, the meditative practice of imagining oneself to be an ideal being fully endowed with compassion and wisdom and their resultant altruistic activities. Whether or not one accepts that deity yoga is *the* central distinctive feature of Mantra, it is an important feature, and since meditation on emptiness is said to be the "life" of the Sūtra and Mantra paths and thus also of deity yoga, this book initially presents how Sūtra and Mantra describe the practice of reflecting on emptiness and then of relating to appearances. As a basic theme of Great Vehicle Buddhism, the compatibility of emptiness and appearance offers a window through which Sūtra and Mantra can be not just glimpsed but felt in imagination. Thus, although I have explained in two other books[a] the Sūtra style of meditation on emptiness, here, using a meditation manual by the Fifth

[a] Jeffrey Hopkins, *Meditation on Emptiness* (London: Wisdom Publications, 1983; rev. ed., Boston: Wisdom Publications, 1996) and *Emptiness Yoga* (Ithaca, N.Y.: Snow Lion Publications, 1987).

Dalai Lama, I will explore the process of this central meditation emphasizing its implications regarding its relation with appearances. It is in this issue that one of the prime differences between these two systems lies.

These two models—Sūtra and Mantra—are viewed by some Tibetan scholars as progressively more profound techniques of spiritual development in what, by the style of presentation, seems to be a *harmonious* development, much as histories of science often present developments as rational, step-by-step acquisitions of wider perspectives rather than a shifting of perspective. The gradualistic harmonious approach, while being valuable in showing the continuity between the two traditions, tends to obscure the innovative profundity of tantric meditation that may be experienced as a solution to a spiritual crisis centered around the appearance of phenomena. It strikes me as possible that the Sūtra model of meditation on emptiness, when it is implemented in effective practice, induces a problem-situation that is resolved in the tantric model of meditation.

In order to discuss that possibility, this book explores the Sūtra and Mantra models of meditation in considerable detail so that the discussion does not become an exercise in mere abstraction, for my points are founded not in abstract conceptualization but in practical implementation. Therefore, after the Sūtra model of meditation on selflessness and subsequent experience of appearances is given, the tantric model of meditating on oneself as an ideal being, a deity, is presented in detail in the second chapter through the example of a particular Action Tantra.

For comprehending the distinctiveness of the tantric practice of deity yoga, the theory of paradigm change—as enunciated by Thomas Kuhn in *The Structure of Scientific Revolutions*[a] and adapted by Hans Küng for theology[b]—offers insights that help to distinguish Sūtra and Mantra models of meditation by calling attention to a possible personal crisis to which the Sūtra model may lead. Thus, at the end of the second chapter the theory of paradigm change is introduced as a way to reveal the necessity for the development of the tantric model; my aim is not to use the data of this Asian tradition to support Kuhn's model but to use his model to make

---

[a] Second edition; Chicago: 1970.

[b] See "Paradigm Change in Theology and Science," in *Theology for the Third Millennium: An Ecumenical View* (New York: Doubleday, 1988), 123-169.

more accessible facets of the tradition that could easily be missed. The Sūtra and Mantra models of meditation are investigated with the aim of exposing a possible crisis that *requires* an individual to move to the tantric model; the analysis is "historical," not in the sense of charting and reflecting on centuries of development in schools of Buddhism, though undoubtedly such happened, but of an *individual's* progress in one life or over many lives.

In the third chapter, in order to convey a sense of the profundity of the tantric enterprise—the enormity of its claims of effectiveness—Carl Jung's exposition of the grave consequences of positive and negative inflation will be considered. His insights constitute warnings against doing just what the tantrics advise—identifying with a deity. Then, to present the full breadth of the path-structure of a tantric system, the next three chapters deal with the complicated series of practices following imagination of oneself as a deity in Action Tantra. Powerful techniques for concentrating the mind and inducing realization are implemented with the aim of de-autonomizing psychological and perceptual complexes.

In Part Two, presentations of the distinctiveness of Mantra from three Tibetan savants are considered, the underlying agenda being to highlight the plurality of approaches in two of these expositions in contrast to the emphasis on the sole feature of deity yoga found in the highly rationalistic writings of the late fourteenth- and early fifteenth-century founder of the Ge-luk-pa[a] order, Tsong-kha-pa Lo-sang-drak-pa.[b] His system is thereby put into historical context; the radical nature of his distilling the distinctive essence of Mantra down to the single central feature of deity yoga becomes clear through juxtaposing two earlier multifaceted approaches. First is a presentation on the difference between the Perfection and Mantra vehicles by Tsong-kha-pa's chief source, the prolific scholar Bu-tön Rin-chen-drup[c] (1290-1364), whose catalogue of traditional opinions provided the context for Tsong-kha-pa's analytical and critical delineation of which traditions could, in his mind, bear examination in the light of a larger coherent path-structure. Next is the creative and evocative presentation by the Nying-ma master Long-chen-rap-jam[d] (1308-1363). His multifaceted inspired

---

[a] *dge lugs pa.*

[b] *tsong kha pa blo bzang grags pa*, 1357-1419.

[c] *bu ston rin chen grub.*

[d] *klong chen rab 'byams dri med 'od zer.*

rendering is followed by a synopsis of Tsong-kha-pa's radically critical analysis of these traditions, with the First Paṇ-chen Lama's reformulation of Tsong-kha-pa's presentation also in an Appendix.

Part Three is concerned with Bu-tön's presentation of nine traditional ways of dividing the tantras into four groups—Action, Performance, Yoga, and Highest Yoga[a]—and Tsong-kha-pa's critical acceptance of only two of them. In conclusion I make the suggestion that these grids for organizing tantras in classes are self-aggrandizing and to a large extent obscure the psychological techniques employed to effect a transmutation of mind and body.

The issues at the heart of the exposition are: Is the progression from Sūtra-style meditation to Tantric meditation necessarily a smooth transition? Does deity yoga have safeguards against psychologically ruinous inflation? How are afflictive emotions[b] used in the path? Is Tantra for higher or lower types of practitioners?

---

[a] *bya ba, kriyā; spyod pa, caryā; rnal 'byor, yoga; rnal 'byor bla med, anuttarayoga.*

[b] *nyon mongs, kleśa.*

Part One: The Procedure of Deity Yoga

1. The Sūtra Mode of Meditation

Meditation on emptiness, discussed most vividly in Sūtra systems, is a powerful technique for transforming the ideational structures that underlie afflictive emotions, and, as such, it is said to be the very life of the tantric meditation of imagining oneself to be a deity, an ideal being. Therefore, both to communicate the importance of this facet of Sūtra meditation and to prepare the groundwork for an appreciation of tantric deity yoga, I will consider the Sūtra model of meditation on selflessness and subsequent reflection on appearances. To do this, I shall comment on the concise and lucid explanation of the perfection of wisdom in the Fifth Dalai Lama's *Sacred Word of Mañjushrī*.[a]

Sūtra model of meditation on selflessness and subsequent illusory-like appearance

The Fifth Dalai Lama presents the process of cultivating the perfection of wisdom in two parts: "the practice of the selflessness of persons and the practice of the selflessness of [other] phenomena."[b] He frames both practices around four essential steps:

1. ascertaining what is being negated

---

[a] *'jam dpal zhal lung*. Nga-wang-lo-sang-gya-tso (*ngag dbang blo bzang rgya mtsho*, 1617-1682), Fifth Dalai Lama, *Instruction on the Stages of the Path to Enlightenment, Sacred Word of Mañjushrī* (*byang chub lam gyi rim pa'i khrid yig 'jam pa'i dbyangs kyi zhal lung*) (Thimphu: kun-bzang-stobs-rgyal, 1976), 182.5-210.6. For an English translation, see Jeffrey Hopkins, "Practice of Emptiness" (Dharmsala: Library of Tibetan Works and Archives, 1974).

Though not cited, Tsong-kha-pa's five main texts on the Sūtra realization of emptiness form the background of the discussion. In order of composition these are his *Great Exposition of the Stages of the Path* (*lam rim chen mo*), *The Essence of Eloquence* (*legs bshad snying po*), *Explanation of (Nāgārjuna's) "Treatise on the Middle": Ocean of Reasoning* (*dbu ma rtsa ba'i tshig le'ur byas pa shes rab ces bya ba'i rnam bshad rigs pa'i rgya mtsho*), *Medium-Length Exposition of the Stages of the Path* (*lam rim 'bring*), and *Extensive Explanation of (Chandrakīrti's) "Supplement to (Nāgārjuna's) 'Treatise on the Middle'": Illumination of the Thought* (*dbu ma la 'jug pa'i rgya cher bshad pa dgongs pa rab gsal*).

[b] An earlier form of this exposition of emptiness yoga, without the Fifth Dalai's text, appeared as chapter four in my introduction to Tenzin Gyatso and Jeffrey Hopkins, *The Kālachakra Tantra: Rite of Initiation for the Generation Stage* (London: Wisdom Publications, 1985).

2. ascertaining the entailment of emptiness
3. ascertaining that the object designated and its basis of designation are not inherently one
4. ascertaining that the object designated and its basis of designation are not inherently different.

First essential: ascertaining what is being negated

With respect to the selflessness of a person, specifically of oneself, the first step is to identify the way we innately misconceive the "I" to exist inherently. As the Fifth Dalai Lama says:

> If both the self [that is the validly existent person] and [the self that is] the nonexistent object of negation are not intimately identified, it is like dispatching an army without knowing where the enemy is or like shooting an arrow without having sought out the target.

If we do not have a fairly clear sense of an inherently existent "I," we will mistake the refutation as negating the "I" itself rather than a specific reification of the "I." Shāntideva's *Engaging in the Bodhisattva Deeds* says:[a]

> Without contacting the superimposed existent,
> Its nonexistence cannot be apprehended.

If an image of the object of negation does not appear well to the mind, the meaning of the selflessness that negates it cannot be ascertained.

In what represents a shift of emphasis from Indian Buddhism and earlier forms of Tibetan Buddhism, the Ge-luk-pa school makes a *clear* differentiation between the existent self and the nonexistent self as it is posited in each of the four major Buddhist schools of tenets—Great Exposition School, Sūtra School, Mind-Only School, and Middle Way School.[b] The earlier lack of central emphasis on explicit identification of an existent self or person may have led to difficulties in the positing of moral responsibility, and thus a new approach of emphasizing the positing of an existent self emerged. The resolution comes through assuming a dual meaning to the term

---

[a] *byang chub sems dpa'i spyod pa la 'jug pa, bodhisattvacaryāvatāra*, IX.140.

[b] *bye brag smra ba, vaibhāṣika; mdo sde pa, sautrāntika; sems tsam pa, cittamātra; dbu ma pa, mādhyamika.*

"self"—the first, existent one is the person or "I" and the second, nonexistent one is a reification, an exaggeration, of the ontological status of any object, the reification here being inherent existence.[a] As the Fifth Dalai Lama says:

> Therefore, [when a selflessness of persons is presented, the word] "persons" refers to [nominally and validly existent] persons, that is, common beings, Superiors, and so forth within the six types of transmigrators [hell-beings, hungry ghosts, animals, humans, demigods, and gods] and the three vehicles [Hearer,[b] Solitary Realizer,[c] and Bodhisattva[d]]. The person's mode of abiding as if able to establish itself from its own side without being mentally imputed is called "self" or "inherent existence."

This distinction is upheld through the observation that when the "I" is apprehended, there are basically three possibilities with respect to how it is being conceived in relation to the other meaning of "self," inherent existence:

1. One may be conceiving the "I" to be inherently existent.
2. Or, if one has understood the view of the Middle Way School, one may conceive the "I" as only being nominally existent.
3. Or, whether one has understood the view of the Middle Way School or not, one may conceive the "I" without qualifying it with either inherent existence or an absence of inherent existence.

In this vein, the Fifth Dalai Lama says:

> Furthermore, consciousnesses innately apprehending "I"—which conceive an "I," or self, based on the [nominally existent] person—are of three types:
>
> 1. A conceptual consciousness [correctly] apprehending "I" that exists in a person who has generated the Middle Way view in his/her mental continuum. This consciousness [correctly] apprehends "I" taken to be qualified as being only designated in the context of its basis

---

[a] *rang bzhin gyis yod pa, svabhāvasat.*

[b] *nyan thos, śrāvaka.*

[c] *rang rgyal, pratyekabuddha.*

[d] *byang chub sems dpa'.*

of designation [mind and body].
2. An actual innate [consciousness mis]apprehending "I" taken to be qualified as being inherently existent. It is to be overcome through its antidote here on this occasion [of the path of wisdom].
3. A conventional validly cognizing consciousness that establishes [the existence of] "I." This consciousness exists [for example] in the continuums of those common beings whose mental continuums have not been affected by systems of tenets and who thus do not differentiate between nominal imputation and inherent existence. In this case, the "I" is not taken to be qualified as being either nominally imputed or inherently existent.

Though uneducated common beings do not *propound* either inherent existence or nominal imputation, the "I" appears to them to be inherently existent, and because they sometimes assent to that appearance—though without reasoning—they also have a conception of an inherently existent "I." Also, they, like all other beings, even including those who have been educated in wrong systems of tenets, have consciousnesses that do not engage in conceptions of inherent existence, such as when just conceiving of themselves without any particular attention. Therefore, it is not that all consciousnesses conceiving "I" in the continuum of a falsely educated person are wrong or that all consciousnesses conceiving "I" in the continuum of uneducated persons are right. Rather, both the uneducated and the falsely educated have the misconception of an inherently existent "I" as well as consciousnesses conceiving an "I" that is not qualified by being either nominally imputed or inherently existent.

Still, neither the falsely educated nor the uneducated can distinguish between an imputedly existent "I" and an inherently existent "I." Both must become educated in the Middle Way view of the absence of inherent existence and the presence of imputed existence in order to overcome their innate tendency to assent to the false appearance of the "I" as if inherently existent, existing from its own side, or existing under its own power. This is the immediate purpose of meditation on selflessness.

The first step in this meditation is to gain a clear sense of the reified status of the "I" as inherently existent. Even though such a misconception is subliminally always present, a condition of its obvious manifestation is required. Therefore, the meditator remembers a situation of false accusation that elicited a strong response or a situation of happiness that did the same, trying to watch the type of "I" that manifested and how the mind assented to its ever-so-concrete appearance. The Fifth Dalai Lama:

> A tight, firm mind thinking "I" exists in our mental continuums on all occasions of sleep and waking. However, like a mirror and an image of your face [in that the presence of the mirror yields a clear image of the face], when you encounter conditions of happiness and suffering, the mind [misconceiving "I"] manifests very strongly, but on occasions when such conditions are not encountered, it is a little unclear. Nowadays when most instructors on the view—not having analyzed whether such is manifest or not—speak about practice, they rely on impoverished words such as just saying, "The way that a consciousness innately conceiving "I" conceives "I." Such instruction does not at all get down to the essentials—like pointing an accusing finger at someone whose face is not well seen and saying, "This is yesterday's thief So-and-So."
>
> Therefore, you first need a clear notion of pleasure or pain that someone else actually caused you. If not [occurring now], you should recall a former occurrence of such to the point where it appears clearly to your mind. For example, if someone [falsely] accused you of being a thief even though the thought "I robbed So-and-So" was not in your mind, you could have strong hatred for the person, thinking, "He accused me of such a theft!" At that time, this "I," which is the object of the accusation of theft and which is held firmly and tightly in the center of the heart, seems even as if it can be seen with the eye and grasped with the hand.
>
> Similarly, if another person caused you to achieve a desired aim and you reflect that such and such help was rendered, the "I" that is the object helped appears vibrantly from the center of the heart. In reliance on your cultivating either of these two modes, this manifest mind thinking "I" causes other coarse thoughts to become dormant. You should allow the consciousness innately conceiving "I" to

increase in strength; then, analyze the way that the mind conceives "I."

Since watchfulness itself tends to cause this gross level of misconception to disappear, the first essential is said to be very difficult to achieve. You have to learn how to let the mind operate in its usual egoistic way and at the same time watch it, keeping watchfulness at a minimum such that the usual conception of a concrete and pointoutable "I" is generated. The Fifth Dalai Lama compares this dual functioning of the mind to simultaneously watching the path and your companion when walking:

> It is extremely difficult within a single consciousness to analyze both the conception of "I" and the way it is conceived [the first being identification of the "I" and the second being identification of its qualities of self-sufficiency and so forth]. If the force of the analytical consciousness is too strong, the strength of the mode of apprehension [of "I"] is destroyed and becomes unclear.
>
> *Question:* How should [the analysis] be done?
>
> *Answer:* Through the force of having cultivated calm abiding,[a] you have [gained an ability] to set [the mind] on any object of stabilizing or analytical meditation. Thus, in place of observing, for instance, the body of a Buddha, you should cause a manifest mind thinking "I" to appear. While the general consciousness remains on the "I" with distinct force, a corner of the mind should watch its mode of apprehension and analyze the way in which the "I" is being conceived. For instance, when you are walking with someone on a path, your eyes are mainly looking at the path, but with a corner of your eye you are watching your companion.

---

[a] *zhi gnas, śamatha.* The techniques for cultivating calm abiding were explained earlier in the Fifth Dalai Lama's text. For a detailed presentation see His Holiness the Dalai Lama, *How to See Yourself As You Really Are,* trans. and ed. by Jeffrey Hopkins (New York: Atria Books/Simon and Schuster, 2006), 87-119; Gedün Lodrö, *Calm Abiding and Special Insight,* trans. and ed. by Jeffrey Hopkins (Ithaca, N.Y.: Snow Lion Publications, 1998), 11-213; Lati Rinbochay, Denma Lochö Rinbochay, Leah Zahler, and Jeffrey Hopkins, *Meditative States in Tibetan Buddhism* (London: Wisdom Publications, 1983), 52-91; and Tsong-kha-pa, *The Great Treatise on the Stages of the Path to Enlightenment,* vol. 3, trans. and ed. Joshua W. C. Cutler and Guy Newland (Ithaca, N.Y.: Snow Lion Publications, 2002), 27-103.

The demand for watchfulness is mitigated by the need to allow what is usually unanalyzed to operate of its own accord; thus, the activity of introspection must be done subtly.

When success is gained, the meditator has found a sense of an inherently existent "I" that, far from seeming to be nonexistent, is totally convincing in its trueness. As the present Dalai Lama said while lecturing to Tibetan scholars in Dharmsala, India, in 1972, one has such strong belief in this reified "I" that upon identifying it, one has the feeling that if it is not true, nothing is. It would seem, therefore, that the first step in developing the view of the Middle Way is the stark and intimate recognition that for the meditator the opposite of that view is true.

Giving more detail about the sense of a concretely established "I," the Fifth Dalai Lama says:

> Previously, the "I" of the thought "I" seemed to exist in the center of the heart, but how it existed was not ascertained. From now on, a corner of awareness is to analyze it well. Sometimes it will seem to be in the context of the body; sometimes it will seem to be in the context of the mind; sometimes it will seem to be in the context of the other individual aggregates [feelings, discriminations, and compositional factors] and so forth. At the end of the arising of such a variety of modes of appearance, you will come to identify an "I" that exists in its own right, that exists inherently, that from the start is self-established, existing undifferentiatedly with mind and body, which are also mixed like milk in water.

In the face of this particular consciousness, mind and body are not differentiated and the "I" is not differentiated from mind and body. However, the "I" is seen to be self-established, self-instituting, under its own power, existing in its own right. It is not that one has the sense that mind, body, and "I" *cannot* be differentiated; rather, for this particular consciousness, mind, body, and "I" simply are not differentiated. For instance, for a consciousness merely apprehending a particular city, say, Chicago, the ground, buildings, and people of that city are not differentiated. These are the bases of designation of Chicago, which seems inextricably blended with these and yet has its own thingness.

Recognition of such an appearance with respect to the "I" and recognition of your assent to this appearance constitute the first essential step in realizing selflessness, emptiness. With this identification, analysis can work on that object; without it, analysis is undirected.

> This is the first essential [in the cultivation of wisdom]—ascertaining the object negated [in the view of selflessness]. You should analyze until deep experience of it arises. Having generated such in your mental continuum, you thereby crystallize an identification of the "I" conceived by an inborn consciousness conceiving "I" as self-instituting and as having a relation with your own five aggregates like that of water put in water. If such an identification crystallizes, analysis alone will cause you to attain ascertainment [of the absence of its inherent existence]. If you do not identify such an "I," analysis falls apart without ever getting started.

From the viewpoint of the scholar-practitioners of the Ge-luk-pa tradition of Tibetan Buddhism, most attempts to penetrate emptiness fail at this initial step, tending either to assume that the phenomenon itself is being refuted or that a superficial, philosophically constructed quality of the phenomenon, rather than one that is blended with the basic appearance of the object and is innately misconceived, is being refuted.

Second essential: ascertaining entailment of emptiness

Whereas in the first step the meditator allows an ordinary attitude to operate and attempts to watch it without interference, in the second step the meditator makes a non-ordinary, intellectual decision that must be brought gradually to the level of feeling. Here, you consider the number of possible relationships between a phenomenon designated and its basis of designation.

Phenomena designated are things such as a table, a body, a person, and a house. Their respective bases of designation are four legs and a top, five limbs (two arms, two legs, and a head)[a] and a trunk,

---

[a] In a culture such as that of pre-modern Tibet, where people think in their chests, the head is a limb and not an integral part of the trunk as it is often depicted in Europe, America, and so forth. Thus, here in this exposition there are *five* limbs and a trunk.

mind and body, and a number of rooms arranged in a certain shape. The meditator considers whether within the framework of inherent existence these two—phenomenon designated and basis of designation—must be either inherently the same or inherently different or whether there are other possibilities. If there seem to be other possibilities, can these be collapsed into the original two, being inherently the same or being inherently different?

Nāgārjuna lists five possibilities, and Chandrakīrti, two more beyond the five:

1. inherently the same
2. inherently different
3. the object designated (the "I") inherently depends on the basis of designation (mind and body)
4. the basis of designation (mind and body) inherently depends on the object designated (the "I")
5. the object designated (the "I") possesses the basis of designation (mind and body) either as a different entity in the way a person owns a cow or as one entity in the way a tree possesses its core
6. the object designated (the "I") is the special shape of the basis of designation (body)
7. the object designated (the "I") is the collection of the bases of designation (mind and body).

The last five can be collapsed into the first two as refinements of them: The third and fourth are forms of difference; the first aspect of the fifth is a form of difference; the second, a form of sameness of entity; the sixth and seventh are variations of sameness. Hence, it is held that all possibilities of inherent existence can be collapsed into the original two.

Conventionally, however, it is said that the "I" and its basis of designation, mind and body, are different but not different entities and that they are the same entity but not the same. This is technically called being one entity and different isolates[a]—essentially meaning that conceptuality can isolate the two within their being one entity. Why not consider this an eighth possibility?

The answer is that if the relationship of being one entity and different conceptually isolatable factors is within the context of

---

[a] *ngo bo gcig la ldog pa tha dad.*

inherent existence, then this possibility is internally contradictory, since within the context of inherent existence whatever is inherently the same is the same in all respects, making different isolates impossible. However, if the relationship of being one entity and different conceptually isolatable factors is within the context of conventional existence, then there is no need to include it here in this list of possibilities within inherent existence.

The list, therefore, does not include all possibilities for the mere existence of a phenomenon designated and its bases of designation because the examination here is concerned only with whether the "I" exists in the *concrete* manner it was seen to have during the first essential. If it does exist so concretely, one should be able to point concretely to it when examining it in relation to its basis of designation. As the Fifth Dalai Lama says:

> Chandrakīrti's *Clear Words*[a] says:
>
> > Consider whether the object of the conception of self has the nature of the [mental and physical aggregates] or is something different from the aggregates.
>
> The "I" appears as if established in the manner of being undifferentiable from the [mental and physical] aggregates which themselves are not differentiated [in the face of this particular consciousness]. However, though one thing such as a pot is not said to be separate or differentiable [from itself], in this context [with respect to the "I"] there arise the aspects of a basis of designation and a phenomenon designated, that is, "aggregates" and "I" [just as a pot can be considered as a phenomenon designated and the bottom, belly, and top of the pot as its bases of designation.]
>
> You should analyze whether the "I" that is inherently self-established in the context of the five aggregates has some way of existing other than a oneness with or separateness from the aggregates. Through taking other phenomena as examples, in the end you will realize that there is no third category [of existence]. The decision that [the "I" and the aggregates] are either one or different is the essential of ascertaining entailment. [If the "I" exists, it is

a *tshig gsal, prasannapadā.*

either one with or separate from the aggregates. Being either of those pervades, or occurs with every instance of, an existent "I."]

Since this decision—that inherent existence involves the necessity of the phenomenon designated being either one with or different from the basis of designation—is the anvil on which the sense of an inherently existent "I" will be pounded by the hammer of the subsequent reasoning, the second essential is not an airy decision to be taken lightly, despite its intellectual character. It must be brought to the level of feeling, this being done through considering that anything existent is either one or different. As the great eighteenth-century Mongolian scholar Jang-kya Röl-pay-dor-jay[a] says in his *Presentation of Tenets:*[b]

> You should consider whether this so-called person or self which is the basis of the conception thinking "I" is the same as your own [mental and physical] aggregates or different from them because, if it exists, it must be one of those two. For, in general it is seen in the world that if something is affirmed by the mind to have a counterpart, it is excluded from being without a counterpart; and, if something is affirmed as not having a counterpart, it is excluded from having a counterpart. Therefore, oneness and otherness are a mutually exclusive dichotomy.

A chair is one; a chair and a table are different; a chair and its parts are different; tables are different, and so forth. The yogi must decisively set standards that limit the possibilities so that the subsequent analysis can work, eventually causing disbelief in such an inherently existent "I."

Upon coming to this decision of logical limitations, you begin to question a little the existence of the self-instituting "I" identified in the first essential. The Fifth Dalai Lama says:

---

[a] *lcang skya rol pa'i rdo rje*, 1717-1786.

[b] *grub mtha'i rnam bzhag*. The full title is: *Clear Exposition of the Presentations of Tenets: Beautiful Ornament for the Meru of the Subduer's Teaching* (*grub pa'i mtha'i rnam par bzhag pa gsal bar bshad pa thub bstan lhun po'i mdzes rgyan*) (Varanasi: Pleasure of Elegant Sayings Printing Press, 1970), 435.20-436.5. For an English translation of part of the chapter on the Consequence School with commentary, see Jeffrey Hopkins, *Emptiness Yoga* (Ithaca, N.Y.: Snow Lion Publications, 1987), 264 (see also previous chapter) and 389.

> Previously, the I—the phenomenon designated in the context of the [mental and physical] aggregates which are the basis of designation—seemed to exist as if self-established and undifferentiable from the aggregates. Through having practiced this second essential, the former consciousness ascertaining [the appearance of "I"] cannot remain as it is, and there arises a little doubt about whether the "I" is the same as or different [from the aggregates.]

The late Geshe Rabten, a Ge-luk-pa scholar who served as abbot of a monastery in Switzerland,[a] compared the effect of this step to having doubts about an old friend for the first time. The emotionally harrowing experience of challenging your own long believed status has begun.

Third essential: ascertaining that the "I" and the aggregates are not one

The next step is to use reasoning to determine whether the "I" and the mental and physical aggregates could be inherently the same or inherently different. Reasoning here is a matter not of cold deliberation or superficial summation but of using various approaches to find one that can shake yourself to your being. Since this is the case, the seeming simple-mindedness and rigidity of the reasonings suggested must be transcended through gaining intimate experience with them.

The Fifth Dalai Lama lays out a *series* of approaches through reasoning, rather than just one, on the principle that certain reasonings would not work for some people. The first is a challenge from common experience: If I am one with body, how could I speak of "my body"? If I am inherently one with mind, how could I speak of "my mind"? Should we also speak of body's body? Or my I? He says:

> However, it is not sufficient just to doubt whether [the "I" and the aggregates] are the same or different; a decision must be reached. Therefore, you should analyze [first] whether the "I" which is conceived by an innate

[a] For an account of his life and a sample of his teachings, see *The Life and Teachings of Geshe Rabten*, trans. and ed. by Alan Wallace (London: George Allen and Unwin, 1982).

> [consciousness] conceiving true existence is one with body and mind. In that case, the "I" could not be anything but either one with the body or one with the mind. If the "I" were one with the body, it would not be sensible to say, "my body," from the viewpoint of associating an attribute, body, with a base, "I." Also, you would [absurdly] have to say, "my I," or "the body's body." Generate ascertainment that it is the same also if the "I" were one with the mind.

This reasoning alone may cut through to the heart of the matter, but on the assumption that it may not be sufficient for some persons, the Fifth Dalai Lama continues with a citation from Nāgārjuna on the same reasoning:

> If, having thought thus, [your attempt at understanding] is merely verbal and you do not gain strong conviction, contemplate the following. Nāgārjuna's *Treatise on the Middle* says:[a]
>
>> When it is taken that there is no self
>> Except the appropriated [aggregates],
>> The appropriated [aggregates] themselves are the
>> self.
>> If so, your self is nonexistent.
>
> Because the "I" and the aggregates would be inherently one, they would be one in all respects with utterly no division. Hence, the "I" and the aggregates would be none other than partless. Then you could not present—in the context of that partless unity—the two different things: the "I" that is the appropriator of the five aggregates and the "five aggregates" that are appropriated by it. In that case, an assertion of "my body" or "my aggregates" would be senseless.

Ge-luk-pa scholars do not hold that Nāgārjuna thought that beings commonly conceive the "I" to be one with body or one with mind. Rather, his thought is that *if* the "I" inherently exists, then oneness with its basis of designation would be one of two exhaustive possibilities. Nāgārjuna's reference is not to ordinary misconception but to a *consequence* of inherent existence, such concreteness requiring

---

[a] *rtsa shes / dbu ma'i bstan bcos, mūlaprajñā / madhyamakaśāstra,* XXVII.5.

a pointoutable identification under analysis.

The rules for inherent existence, therefore, are not the rules for mere existence. Within the context of inherent existence, sameness of entity requires utter oneness in all respects. Thus, the issue that is central to evaluating the soundness of this reasoning is not whether beings ordinarily conceive of such oneness (since it is not claimed that we do), but whether the logical rules that have been formulated for the concrete, pointoutable existence identified in ordinary experience in the first step are appropriate.

More reasonings

The Fifth Dalai Lama continues with permutations of the same reasoning; the mere presence of the reasoning is clearly not expected to be convincing. For these further reasonings to work, the meditator needs to believe in rebirth. They are: If the "I" and the body are one, after death when the body is burned, the "I" also would absurdly be burned. Or, just as the "I" transmigrates to the next life, so the body also would absurdly have to transmigrate. Or, just as the body does not transmigrate, so the "I" also would absurdly not transmigrate.

From meditating on such reasonings, you might come to think that probably the "I" is not the same as the body but is perhaps one with the mind, in which case you are asked to consider the following fallacies: Since it is obvious that the suffering of cold arises when the "I" is without clothes and it is obvious that the sufferings of hunger and thirst arise when the "I" lacks food and drink, these would—if the "I" were merely mental—be mental in origin, in which case one could not posit a reason why the same suffering would not be experienced in a life in a Formless Realm. Also, since the mind would be one with the "I," it would absurdly still have to make use of gross forms such as food and clothing which do not exist in the Formless Realm. About these, the Fifth Dalai Lama says:

> If this also does not get to the heart of the matter, think:
>
> > Because the "I" and the body are one, after death when the body is burned, the "I" would also be burned. Or, just as the "I" transmigrates to the next life, so the body also would have to transmigrate. Or, just as the body does not transmigrate, so the "I" also would not transmigrate.

Consider the application of such fallacies.

Through having meditated thus, you come to think, "The 'I' is probably not the same as the body." Then, if you think, "The 'I' is probably one with the mind," consider this fallacy:

> The suffering of cold arises when the "I" is without clothes, and the sufferings of hunger and thirst arise when the "I" lacks food and drink. Therefore, if after death the mind were born in a Formless Realm, then because the mind would be one with the "I," it would still have to make use of gross forms such as food and clothing.

If those absurd permutations of oneness do not clinch the matter, reflecting on a few more reasonings may allow you to reach a conclusion. First, the selves would have to be as many as mind and body, that is to say, two; or, put another way, the selves would have to be as many as the five aggregates (forms, feelings, discriminations, compositional factors, and consciousnesses), five.

> The above modes of reasoning are suitable and easy for beginners to develop. However, if you have been disciplined through discriminating wisdom, a little more elaboration will decide the matter. Therefore, consider the fallacy of the selves becoming many. Chandrakīrti's *Supplement to (Nāgārjuna's) "Treatise on the Middle"* says:[a]
>
> > If the self were the aggregates, then
> > Because they are many, there would be many
> > selves.
>
> Just as the aggregates are five, so the "I" would also become five, or just as the "I" is no more than one, so the aggregates could not be five.

This reasoning may seem extraordinarily simple-minded, but the requirements of such pointoutable, analytically findable existence—not the requirements of mere existence—are the anvil. The meditator is attempting through this analysis, not to describe how she or he ordinarily conceives such an inherently existent "I," but to subject it to the hammering of reasoning based on *consequences*

---

[a] VI.127ab.

of such inherent existence. Because the ordinary sense of concrete selfhood is the object on which the analysis is working, the experience is fraught with emotion.

The second additional reasoning revolves around entailment that the "I" would have inherently existent production and disintegration, in which case it would be discontinuous. The Fifth Dalai Lama's very brief description of this reasoning comes to life when teamed with the fourth reasoning below:[a]

> Similarly, Nāgārjuna's *Treatise on the Middle* says,[b] "If the self were the aggregates, it would have production and disintegration." Because the five aggregates would be inherently produced and would inherently disintegrate, you would have to assert that the "I" also is produced and disintegrates in that way.

The third additional reasoning also depends upon a belief in rebirth; for me, it reflects the type of reasoning in reverse that many use against rebirth. Its concern is not explicitly with the "I" and the mental and physical aggregates that are its bases of designation but the relationship between the "I" of this life and the "I" of the last life. It is: If they were one, then the sufferings of the former life would absurdly have to be present in this life.

> The "I" of the former birth and the "I" of this life can be only either one or different. If one, through the force of their being inherently one, the sufferings of the "I" in the former life as an animal—such as stupidity and enslavement for others' use—would also be experienced on the occasion of the "I" being a human in this birth. Also the human pleasures of this life would have been experienced as an animal in the former life. Contemplate such consequences.

The last additional reasoning expands on the fault of discontinuity between lives, suggested earlier in the second reasoning but not pursued. If they were different, which by the rules of inherent existence would make them totally, unrelatedly different, remembrance of former lives would become impossible. Moral retribution would be impossible. Undeserved suffering would be experienced.

---

[a] A longer explanation of this reasoning is given in Hopkins, *Meditation on Emptiness*, 183-185.

[b] XVIII.1.

Such difference would make a mere-I, the agent that travels from lifetime to lifetime, engaging in actions and experiencing their effects, impossible. The Fifth Dalai Lama says:

> Similarly, Chandrakīrti's *Supplement* says:[a]
>
> > Whatever are inherently separate are not
> > Suitable to be included in one continuum.
>
> If the "I" of the former life and the "I" of the next life were inherently different, they would be totally, unrelatedly different. Thereby it would be impossible to remember, "I was born in such and such a former birth," just as Devadatta does not remember that he was born in a former birth as [his contemporary] Yajñadatta.
>
> Furthermore, your accumulating actions for birth in a happy transmigration would be wasted because another would enjoy the fruition of the effects in a life of high status, and you yourself would not experience it. Why? The agent of the actions and the experiencer of the effects would not be included into the single base of a mere-I [that is to say, a nominally existent "I"] and would be unrelated.
>
> Therefore, if an action accumulated in a former life brought help or harm in this life, you would be meeting with [the effects of] actions not done [by yourself]. If help and harm did not arise [from deeds done], there would be no sense in abandoning ill deeds and adopting virtues in this life because their effects would not ripen for the future "I."
>
> Through contemplating such, you will gain ascertainment with respect to the third essential: ascertaining a lack of true oneness [of the "I" and the aggregates].

Oneness of the "I" and its bases of designation—the mental and physical aggregates—is impossible.

Fourth essential: ascertaining that the "I" and the aggregates are not inherently different

The meditator has been so disturbed by the analysis of oneness that he or she is ready to assume difference. However, the rules of

---

[a] VI.61cd.

inherent existence call for the different to be unrelatedly different, again the assumption being not that persons ordinarily consider the "I" and its bases of designation to be unrelatedly different but that within the context of inherent existence, that is, of such pointoutable, solid existence, difference necessitates unrelatedness. The Fifth Dalai Lama says:

> Now, you might think that the "I" and the five aggregates cannot be anything but different. Chandrakīrti's *Supplement* says:[a]
>
> > There is no self other than the aggregates because,
> > Apart from the aggregates, its conception does not
> > exist.
>
> The inherently different must be unrelated. Therefore, just as within the aggregates you can identify each individually—"This is the aggregate of form," and so forth—so after clearing away the five aggregates, you would have to be able to identify the "I:" "This is the 'I.'" However, no matter how finely you analyze, such an "I" is not at all to be found.

Many forms of Hinduism are seeking to find the self or ultimate reality that is left over when all else is removed; therefore, they would loudly exclaim the contrary: Something *is* found separate from mind and body. But would this be the "I" that goes to the store? Would this be the "I" that desires? Hates?

Still, the question is not easy to settle, and it does not appear that easy answers are wanted. Rather, the Fifth Dalai Lama emphasizes that deeply felt conviction is needed:

> It is not sufficient that the mode of non-finding be just a repetition of the impoverished phrase, "Not found." For example, when an ox is lost, one does not take as true the mere phrase, "It is not in such and such an area." Rather, it is through searching for it in the highland, midland, and lowland of the area that one firmly decides that it cannot be found. Here also, through meditating until a decision is reached, you gain conviction.

You have to bring the analysis to the point where there is an impressive non-finding.

---

[a] VI.120ab.

Realization of selflessness

With such conviction, the decision reached is that the "I" cannot be found under analysis. The decision is not superficially intellectual but a startling discovery of a vacuity upon having sought such an "I." This vacuity shows not that the "I" does not exist, but that it does not inherently exist as it was identified as seeming to in the first essential. This unfindability is emptiness itself, and realization of it is realization of emptiness, selflessness.

Incontrovertible inferential understanding, though not of the level of direct perception or even of special insight,[a] has great impact. For a beginner it generates a sense of deprivation, but for an experienced meditator it generates a sense of discovery, or recovery, of what was lost. The Fifth Dalai Lama conveys this with examples:

> When the "I," which previous to now seemed to be perceivable by the eye and graspable by the hand as truly existent, is not found and is just vacuous, this is said to be the initial finding of the view of the Middle Way.
>
> Moreover, as was explained before on the occasion of calm abiding, you should practice—with the wisdom arisen from thinking—what was found initially by the wisdom arisen from hearing, and eventually you will attain the wisdom arisen from meditation. Therefore, this initial generation of the Middle Way view is not actual special insight; however, like a moon on the second day of the month, it is a slight finding of the view. At that time, if you have no predispositions for emptiness from a former life, it seems that a thing that was in the hand has suddenly been lost. If you have predispositions, it seems that a lost jewel that had been in the hand has suddenly been found.

The perception of this vacuity, the absence of inherent existence, carries emotional force—first of loss, since our emotions are built on a false sense of concreteness, and then of discovery of a lost treasure that makes everything possible. From a similar point of view, the emptiness of the mind is called the Buddha nature, or Buddha lineage, since, like a valuable jewel, it is what allows for development of the marvelous qualities of Buddhahood. However,

---

[a] *lhag mthong, vipaśyanā.*

unless the meditator has predispositions from practice in a former life, the first experience of emptiness is one of loss; later, its fecundity and dynamism become apparent.

Space-like meditative equipoise

The realization of the absence of inherent existence needs to be increased through a process of alternating analytical meditation and stabilizing meditation. If the meditator has developed the power of concentration of the level of calm abiding, the analysis of the status of the "I" can be done within the context of this highly stable mind. However, too much analysis will induce excitement, reducing stabilization, and too much stabilization will induce an inability to analyze. Thus, analytical and stabilizing meditation must be alternated until the two are in such harmony that analysis itself induces even greater stabilization which, in turn, enhances analysis. At the point of harmony and mutual support between analysis and stabilization, special insight, which is necessarily a union of calm abiding and special insight, is achieved.

Leading to this state are several levels or stages; the Fifth Dalai Lama speaks of these with the technical vocabulary of the Buddhist delineation of the stages of meditation:

> After having settled the analysis of the four essentials through hearing and thinking, there arises during meditation distinct ascertainment that the "I"—as apprehended by the conceptual consciousness that conceives of "I" tightly, so tightly, in the center of the heart—does not inherently exist in the context of the mental and physical aggregates. When such ascertainment has arisen, the absence of inherent existence of the "I" is the actual object of meditation, and thus, retaining mindfulness of it, you should not forget it. Also, through introspection you should distinguish whether conceptuality conceiving an inherently existent "I" is interrupting or not. If it becomes necessary to revivify [realization of] the mode of the absence of inherent existence of the "I," then by means of a little analysis you should set [again] in meditative equipoise, thinking, "It does not exist that way."
>
> At this time, due to the force of past great familiarity with the conception of self [that is, inherent existence], the

> mind conceiving [an inherently existent] "I" is stronger and more frequent [than the realization of selflessness] even though you forcibly practice in accordance with [the initial among] the nine states of mind of calm abiding.[a] Therefore, the thought that the "I" does not truly exist comes only at intervals. Then, when you gradually become familiar [with selflessness], the conception of inherent existence [only] occasionally interrupts the consciousness of the view that the "I" does not truly exist. Then, just after the generation of a thought conceiving true existence, it can be overcome through just a little mindfulness; thereby, [the realization of selflessness] becomes uninterrupted. Then, in accordance with the ninth state of mind [preceding] calm abiding you no longer rely on any application [of antidotes to laxity and excitement] and relax the exertion [of introspection]; your meditation becomes a similitude—or small portion—of a union of calm abiding and special insight.

The four levels of increasingly steady realization correspond to four levels in the development of calm abiding called the four mental engagements[b]—forcible, interrupted, uninterrupted, and spontaneous engagement. Even though the meditator has previously passed through these four levels in developing calm abiding, at that time they were merely in the context of stabilizing, or fixating, meditation, and thus now that analytical mediation has been introduced, another progression through versions of these four (not as gross as before) must be made.

At the point when meditators have not yet reached the level of special insight but are close to it, they attain a similitude of special insight and a space-like meditative equipoise.

> Now you have one-pointed uninterrupted meditative equipoise on a nonaffirming negative.[c] This negative of the object negated [in the view of selflessness] is like, for example, the fact that "space" is posited as simply the absence of its object negated—obstructive contact—in the context of the clear appearance between things. This

---

[a] For a discussion of the nine levels leading to calm abiding see Hopkins, *Meditation on Emptiness*, 80-86.

[b] *yid byed bzhi, catvāramanaskāra.*

[c] *med dgag, prasajyapratiṣedha.*

> meditative equipoise [on the absence of inherent existence] is the actual way to sustain a space-like meditative equipoise. Just this is identified as the non-mindfulness of non-conceptuality that occurs when calm abiding is induced by the strength of analysis itself.

This meditative equipoise is called "space-like" because just as uncompounded space[a] is a mere absence—a mere negative—of obstructive contact, so emptiness is a mere absence, a mere negative, of inherent existence. Such steady reflection on emptiness, therefore, is called space-like meditative equipoise. Brought to the level of direct perception, it serves as the antidote to both the artificially acquired and innate afflictive emotions (though not all at once, except in Highest Yoga Mantra[b]).

Through prolonged training, the meditator develops a harmonious working of stabilizing and analytical meditation with the one increasing the other, such that the pliancy initially attained with mere calm abiding is exceeded by that induced by analysis at the level of special insight. The Fifth Dalai Lama describes the progression:

> At the point of nonapplication [when it no longer is necessary to apply the antidotes to laxity and excitement], a similitude of special insight is attained. Through meditation within sustaining its continuum you attain a superior pliancy, a serviceability of body and mind induced by analytical meditation. It greatly exceeds the bliss of physical pliancy induced earlier at the time of calm abiding through the power of meditative equipoise. When this superior pliancy is attained, actual special insight is attained, and thus you have gained a path consciousness that is an actual union of calm abiding and special insight.

The Fourth Paṇ-chen Lama, Lo-sang-pel-den-ten-pay-nyi-ma[c] describes the mind of space-like meditative equipoise from two points of view, in terms of appearance and in terms of

---

[a] *'dus ma byas kyi nam mkha', asaṃskṛtākāśa.*

[b] *sngags bla med, anuttarayogamantra.*

[c] *blo bzang dpal ldan bstan pa'i nyi ma*, 1781-1852/4. See Geshe Lhundup Sopa and Jeffrey Hopkins, *Cutting Through Appearances: The Practice and Theory of Tibetan Buddhism* (Ithaca, N.Y.: Snow Lion Publications, 1990), 98.

ascertainment. To that consciousness only an immaculate vacuity—an absence of inherent existence—*appears*, and that consciousness *ascertains* (that is, understands, comprehends, and realizes) the absence of inherent existence of the "I." Although reasoning has led to this state, the mind is not now reasoning; it is experiencing the fruit of reasoning in a state of continuous, one-pointed ascertainment of emptiness; the only thing appearing is an utter vacuity—an absence—of inherent existence. The Fourth Paṇ-chen Lama says:

> At that time you should sustain single-mindedly the following two facets of understanding emptiness. From the point of view of ascertainment, firm definite knowledge determines that the "I" does not inherently exist. Second, from the point of view of appearance there is an utter, clear vacuity that is only the absence of what is negated, that is, the true existence of "I." Sustaining these two single-mindedly is how to sustain the space-like meditative equipoise.

There is controversy within Ge-luk-pa over whether in an earlier stage the object being ascertained as empty of inherent existence appears to an inferential consciousness realizing emptiness; however, most monastic textbooks hold that even on that level all that appears is a vacuity, the non-finding of the object under such analysis. In any case, all agree that in space-like meditative equipoise only an immaculate vacuity that is a negative of inherent existence appears—nothing else. What is ascertained is also an absence of inherent existence. The same is also true for direct realization of emptiness, though any sense of duality, knower and known, has vanished.

Appearances subsequent to meditative equipoise

When the state of one-pointed concentration on selflessness is left, that is, when the meditator takes to mind any object other than emptiness, the object is viewed as *like* an illusion, appearing one way but existing another. Just as a magician's illusory elephant appears to be an elephant but in fact is not, so forms, sounds, and so forth appear to exist inherently but are understood as not existing inherently. The meaning of being like an illusion is not that the "I" or forms, sounds, and so forth appear to exist but actually do not; rather, their mode of existence appears to be concrete but is understood not to be so. The same is true for the "I." The Fifth Dalai

Lama addresses this issue directly:

> *Question:* Through having practiced the space-like meditative equipoise, what occurs after equipoise?
>
> *Answer:* The *King of Meditative Stabilizations Sūtra* says:[a]
>
> > Like a mirage, a city of Scent-Eaters,
> > A magician's illusions, and dreams,
> > Meditation on signs is empty of inherent existence.
> > Know all phenomena to be like that.
>
> After meditative equipoise, the appearance of a merely nominal "I" remaining after the negation of the object of negation should be like a magician's illusion.

The Fifth Dalai Lama proceeds to point out that mere realization that a magician's illusions or dream objects are not real does not constitute realizing phenomena to be like a magician's illusions, nor does realization of phenomena as like illusions mean that one merely desists from identifying appearances:

> Its mode of appearance in this system is not the realization

---

[a] *ting nge 'dzin rgyal po'i mdo, samādhirājasūtra,* stanza IX.11; Toh. 127, *sde dge* edition, *mdo sde,* vol. *da,* 26a.6; Sanskrit and Tibetan texts and English translation in Cristoph Cüppers, *The IXth Chapter of the Samādhirājasūtra: A Text-critical Contribution to the Study of Mahāyāna Sūtras,* Alt- und Neu-Indische Studien 41 (Stuttgart: Franz Steiner Verlag, 1990), 27: *yathaiva gandharvapuraṃ marīcikā yathaiva māyā supinaṃ yathaiva / svabhāvaśūnyā tu nimittabhāvanā tathopamāṃ jānatha sarvadharmān //.* The Tibetan is on 28, and an English translation on 93-94.

The *Four Interwoven Annotations on (Tsong-kha-pa's) "Great Exposition of the Stages of the Path"* (674.5) explains this stanza in detail:

> With respect to how all phenomena are signless, the *King of Meditative Stabilizations Sūtra* gives examples. Just as there is no water in a mirage but it appears to be water and just as a city of Scent-Eaters does not exist as the actualities of a city and so forth but appears to be a city and so forth and just as a magician's emanations do not exist as horses, elephants, and so forth but appear to be horses, elephants, and so forth and just as in a dream there are no men, women, and so forth but there appear to be (that is to say, just as mirages and so forth appear to be water and so on but are empty of water and so on), so forms and so forth, which are like signs of capacity to appear and manifest, are meditated on—that is to say, adhered to by way of taking them to mind—as manifestly evident (*mngon rtags*), are empty of inherent existence, and adherers to them are also empty of inherent existence. Know that this mode of emptiness is to be applied to all phenomena.

of the untruth of illusory horses and elephants or of appearances in dreams. If that were the case, even magicians and mature people who know language would know the Middle Way mode of illusory appearance. Also, the illusions referred to on this occasion are not the shimmering ephemeral appearances[a]—unidentified as being this and not that—which occur from having practiced analysis of the view.

Question: Then, what is needed?

Answer: Realizing that horses and elephants manifested by a magician are not horses and elephants does not damage the inherent existence of horses and elephants. The glorious Dharmakīrti in his *Commentary on (Dignāga's) "Compilation of Valid Cognition"* says:[b]

> Without refuting their objects, they cannot be abandoned.
> Desire, hatred, and so forth which are related to [perception
> Of] good qualities and defects [beyond what is actually there]
> Are abandoned by way of not seeing those in the object, not by an external means.

[To overcome an afflictive emotion] it is not sufficient to [try to] pull it out like a thorn; the misconceived object must be refuted.

It is undeniable that illusory horses and elephants are seen by an eye consciousness due to its being affected by a superficial cause of error [a magician's spell]. However, even mature worldly beings know that such horses and elephants do not exist as perceived. Just so, horses and elephants also undeniably appear to a conventional consciousness [to exist inherently] due to a deep cause of error [namely, the predispositions established by ignorance], but

---

[a] *snang ba ban bun.*

[b] *tshad ma rnam 'grel, pramāṇavārttika,* stanza II.222-II.223ab; Toh. 4210, *sde dge* edition, *tshad ma,* vol. *ce,* 116a.3; Yūsho Miyasaka, "*Pramāṇavarttika-kārikā:* Sanskrit and Tibetan," *Indo Koten Kenkyu (Acta Indologica)* 2 (1971-1772): 32-33: *adūṣite 'sya viṣaye na śakyaṃ tasya varjanaṃ / prahāṇir icchādveṣāder guṇadoṣānubandhinaḥ // tayor adṛṣṭir viṣaye na tu bāhyeṣu yaḥ kramaḥ /.*

> you must know that from the viewpoint of their own entities they are empty of inherent existence, like illusions.

The essential point is that the meditator first must realize that these objects do not inherently exist; there is no other method for inducing realization that phenomena are like illusions.

Tsong-kha-pa makes this point in his *Medium-Length Exposition of the Stages of the Path:*[a]

> *Question:* What has to be done for the meaning of illusion to dawn unerringly?
>
> *Answer:* For example, in dependence on the eye consciousness seeing illusory horses and elephants [conjured by a magician] and the mental consciousness ascertaining the nonexistence of those horses and elephants in accordance with how they appear, one generates ascertainment that the appearance of horses and elephants is an illusory, or false, appearance. Similarly, in dependence on the two—undeniable appearance of persons and so forth to a conventional consciousness and ascertainment of them by a rational consciousness[b] as empty of nature, that is, establishment by way of their own nature—one generates ascertainment of persons as illusory, or false, appearances. Due to this fact:
>
> - when in meditative equipoise one has become successful at meditating on space-like emptiness, [realizing that] the target aimed at by the apprehension of signs [that is, inherent existence,] does not exist, not even a particle,
> - then upon rising from [this meditative realization], when one views the dawning of objects, an illusory-like emptiness dawns subsequent to meditative equipoise.

---

[a] *lam rim 'bring / skyes bu gsum gyis nyams su blang ba'i byang chub lam gyi rim pa / skyes bu gsum gyi nyams su blang ba'i byang chub lam gyi rim pa bring po sa bcad kha skong dang bcas pa / lam rim chung ngu;* see Jeffrey Hopkins, *Tsong-kha-pa's Final Exposition of Wisdom* (Ithaca, N.Y.: Snow Lion Publications, 2008), 83. For Robert Thurman's translation of this passage see his "The Middle Transcendent Insight" in *Life and Teachings of Tsong Khapa,* Robert A. F. Thurman, ed. (Dharmsala: Library of Tibetan Works and Archives, 1982), 141.

[b] *rigs shes.*

> In that way, through analyzing phenomena frequently with the reasoning analyzing whether they are established by way of their own nature or not, strong ascertainment with respect to the absence of inherent existence is generated, and when, after that, one views the dawning of appearances, they dawn as like illusions. There is no separate way of delineating illusory-like emptiness.

Realization of the emptiness of inherent existence is the *only* method for gaining the subsequent realization that phenomena are like illusions.

The Fourth Paṇ-chen Lama speaks similarly but also addresses the issue of the substance of the appearances that are left over. He calls for viewing them as the sport[a] of emptiness:[b]

> Subsequent to meditative equipoise, all phenomena—the "I" and so forth—should be meditated on as the sport [of emptiness] like a magician's illusions. In other words, rely on developing a strong conviction of truthlessness [that is to say, the knowledge that phenomena do not inherently exist] during meditative equipoise and afterwards learn to view all that appears, even though appearing [to exist inherently], as the sport [of emptiness] like a magician's illusions, truthless and false.

Since the emptiness of inherent existence makes appearance possible, phenomena are, in a sense, the sport of emptiness. It may even be said that their basic substance is emptiness. However, emptiness is a nonaffirming negative, a mere absence or mere elimination of inherent existence, which does not imply anything in place of inherent existence even though it is compatible with dependently arisen phenomena. Hence, emptiness is not a positive substance giving rise to phenomena, even if it is their ground.

The vocabulary of sport or play is reminiscent of various Hindu identifications of phenomena as the sport of God. Emptiness is what makes cause and effect possible; the emptiness of the mind is called the Buddha nature, the causal lineage of Buddhahood, even though it is not itself an actual cause. As the mere negative of inherent existence, it makes enlightenment possible.

---

[a] *rnam rol, līla.*

[b] Sopa and Hopkins, *Cutting Through Appearances*, 98.

Summation of the sūtra model of meditation on selflessness and appearance

Including the steps of setting the basic motivation for meditation as well as the subsequent state of realizing appearances to be like illusions, the Sūtra process of meditating on the selflessness of the person is in seven movements:

preliminary: adjustment of motivation by taking refuge and developing an altruistic intention to become enlightened

1. ascertaining what is being negated—inherent existence
2. ascertaining entailment of emptiness
3. ascertaining that the "I" and the aggregates are not inherently the same
4. ascertaining that the "I" and the aggregates are not inherently different
5. realizing the absence of inherent existence of the "I" in space-like meditative equipoise

concluding: emerging from space-like meditative equipoise and viewing all phenomena as like a magician's illusions.

All activities are to be done within realization that phenomena are like illusions, understanding that space-like meditative equipoise negates only a false sense of *inherent* existence and not the very existence of objects. Tsong-kha-pa's *Medium-Length Exposition of the Stages of the Path* emphasizes this practical point:[a]

> Consequently, even when engaging in the class of behavioral practices, such as prostration, circumambulation, and so forth, you should do them within being affected by the force of analytical ascertainment as [explained] above and thereby train in illusory-like appearance. They should be done within this. Through having become proficient in this, even by merely becoming mindful of the view those will dawn as like illusions.

It is important to understand that space-like meditative equipoise reveals only the nature of phenomena and negates only a false sense of inherent existence and not the very existence of objects.

---

[a] See Hopkins, *Tsong-kha-pa's Final Exposition of Wisdom,* 84. This passage is also translated in Thurman, "The Middle Transcendent Insight" in *The Life and Teachings of Tsong Khapa,* 141.

The Fifth Dalai Lama stresses this point:

> Also, it is known that a lion manifested by a magician does not exist in fact, but through having manifestly seen an illusory lion kill an illusory elephant, utter certainty that an illusory lion killed an illusory elephant is induced. Just so, a person, who does not inherently exist but appears [to exist inherently] like an illusion, accumulates wholesome and unwholesome actions[a] and experiences their fruition. My lama said that inducement of deep conviction about this is a distinguishing feature of this [Middle Way] doctrine.
>
> When inherently existent horses and elephants are refuted by reasoning, for such a conventional consciousness the apprehension of horses and elephants as being established as their own reality is mistaken, like apprehending illusory horses and elephants [as real]. However, from the viewpoint of a worldly consciousness, a consciousness that apprehends horses and elephants as established as [their own] reality is nonmistaken, and a consciousness that apprehends illusory horses and elephants is mistaken. It is with such fine distinctions that the example of magician's illusions is drawn.
>
> If, having thought that horses and elephants are not inherently existent, you take horses and elephants and illusory horses and elephants to be similar even conventionally, then you would contradict the meaning of Chandrakīrti *Supplement* which says:[b]
>
> > Those objects realized by the world
> > And apprehended with the six unimpaired senses
> > Are true from [the viewpoint of] just the world.
>
> You would be deprecating conventionalities.
>
> Mañjushrī told the Foremost Lama [Tsong-kha-pa] that it was necessary to value the varieties of appearances. His thought was based on a qualm that in the future trainees who did not understand such an essential would fall into a view of nihilism. Thus, many modes of establishing the existence of appearances are [presented] in Tsong-kha-pa's

---

[a] *las, karma.*

[b] VI.25abc.

> great and small expositions of the *Stages of the Path* and in his commentaries on Nāgārjuna's *Treatise on the Middle* and Chandrakīrti's *Supplement*. However, the lion of proponents, the translator Tak-tsang[a] [criticizes Tsong-kha-pa] saying, "Upon analyzing with many forms of reasoning, he asserts that impure mistaken appearances are validly established." [This criticism] is seen to arise from the same source of error.

The change from the historically earlier model of merely refuting self without emphasizing the distinction between a self that validly and effectively exists to refuting a meaning of self that is explicitly limited to a reification of inherent existence with a validly established effective self left over is justified in moral terms. For delimiting the object of negation in emptiness allows for a basis for agency of deeds and a continuity of experience of their fruitions within a context, not just of worldly renown, but of valid establishment. The change is also given the authority of the god of wisdom, Mañjushrī, who is said to have been Tsong-kha-pa's supra-human teacher and who advised him to maintain valid establishment of appearances.[b] That the physical manifestation of the wisdom of all Buddhas prompted this move in Tsong-kha-pa's thought makes the point that this shift of emphasis is a return to a basic undying truth and not a new creation.

Comments

The Sūtra model of meditation on selflessness and subsequent relation with appearance is built around an analytical search for the seemingly concrete existence of an object, such as oneself, the existence of which has hitherto been largely uncontested. Though the mode of search is analytical, the examination of the object is intensely emotional since emotions such as desire and hatred are built on a perceived status of objects that is now being challenged. The analysis is neither cold nor superficially intellectual but

---

[a] *stag tshang shes rab rin chen*, born 1405. For his criticisms of Tsong-kha-pa and Ge-luk-pa responses, see Jeffrey Hopkins, *Maps of the Profound: Jam-yang-shay-ba's Great Exposition of Buddhist and Non-Buddhist Views on the Nature of Reality* (Ithaca, N.Y.: Snow Lion Publications, 2003), 527-694.

[b] Despite the oft-repeated claim of relying *only* on reasoning, the Ge-luk-pa order makes frequent claims of divine authorization.

an expression of the intellect in the midst of the clatter of emotional rearrangement and unreasoned re-assertion of the concrete findability of the object. The analysis is by no means a rote run-through of a prescribed ritual, nor is it merely aimed at refuting other philosophical systems; rather, it is aimed at the heart of one's emotional and intellectual life, at the ideational underpinnings of our self-conceptions, our relations with others, our conceptions of subject and object, and our ideologies.

At the end of successful analysis, what is experienced is merely a non-finding—a void, a vacuity—of the object in which one originally so intensely believed. That very object, in all of its seeming concreteness, has literally disappeared from mind; the very type of awareness that believed in it has now sought for it according to rules of analysis that have been seen to be not just appropriate but binding. It has not found this object, even though so many emotions have been built in dependence on its seemingly verifiable status. The experience of not finding this previously reliable underpinning is earth-shattering.

The meditator does not immediately rush back to perception of appearances but remains with this vacuity, a mere absence of such an inherently existent object, appreciating its implications, letting the ramifications of the analytical unfindability of object affect her mind, letting it undermine the emotional frameworks of countless lives in a round of suffering induced by ignorance of this fact. After such immersion, the meditator again returns to the world of appearance, at which point objects dawn as like a magician's illusions, seeming to exist in their own right but known to be empty of such concrete existence. The world—oneself, others, and objects such as chairs and tables—is seen in a new way, falsely seeming to have a status that it actually does not have, but now unmasked.

But what do objects appear from? What is their substance? What is its relation to one's own mind? These are issues that the tantric model of meditation goes on to face, not so much through conceptual presentation but through a mode of experiencing objects after realizing emptiness that bridges the gap between emptiness and appearance in an even more vivid way. Let us turn to the Mantra model of meditating on emptiness and subsequent relation with appearance.

2. The Tantric Mode of Meditation

Deity yoga, as is made clear in Tsong-kha-pa's lengthy treatment of the difference between Sūtra and Mantra in his *Great Exposition of Secret Mantra*,[a] is the distinctive essence of tantric meditation. It provides a unique combination of method (compassion) and wisdom (realization of selflessness) in one consciousness and thus an additional mode of meditating on selflessness. Let us consider the process of cultivating deity yoga in meditation through the example of Action Tantra as presented by Tsong-kha-pa's students, Dül-dzin-drak-pa-gyel-tsen and Ke-drup Ge-lek-pel-sang.[b] The process is structured around successively more profound stages of meditative stabilizations of exalted body, speech, and mind. Our concern in this chapter is with the first.

---

[a] See H.H. the Dalai Lama, Tsong-kha-pa, and Jeffrey Hopkins, *Tantra in Tibet* (London: George Allen and Unwin, 1977; reprint Ithaca, N.Y.: Snow Lion Publications, 1987), 81-169. A condensed version of this chapter and the next has appeared in my article "The Ultimate Deity in Action Tantra and Jung's Warning Against Identifying with the Deity," *Buddhist-Christian Studies* 5 (1985): 159-172.

[b] For exposition of the procedure of meditation on selflessness and on appearance in Tantra I shall use short explanations of Action Tantra yoga by two of Tsong-kha-pa's students, Dül-dzin-drak-pa-gyel-tsen (*'dul 'dzin grags pa rgyal mtshan*, 1374-1434) in his *Presentation of the General Rites of Action and Performance Tantra and Their Application to the Three Lineages, Set Down by Dül-dzin According to the Foremost [Tsong-kha-pa's] Practice* (*bya spyod kyi spyi'i cho ga'i rnam par bzhag pa rigs gsum la sbyor tshul rje'i phyag bzhes bzhin 'dul ba 'dzin pas bkod pa*), Collected Works of Rje Tsoṅ-kha-pa Blo-bzaṅ-grags-pa, vol. 17 (*na*), 437-449.6, and by Ke-drup Ge-lek-pel-sang (*mkhas grub dge legs dpal bzang*, 1385-1438) in his *Extensive Explanation of the Format of the General Tantra Sets* (*rgyud sde spyi'i rnam par gzhag pa rgyas par brjod pa*). With respect to the latter, the edition used is that published by Ferdinand D. Lessing and Alex Wayman in their *Mkhas Grub Rje's Fundamentals of the Buddhist Tantras* (The Hague: Mouton, 1968), 158-163; see the same pages for their translation. Tsong-kha-pa's own exposition of the difference between Sūtra and Mantra in general (found in his *Great Exposition of Secret Mantra* which I have translated in H.H. the Dalai Lama, Tsong-kha-pa, and Hopkins, *Tantra in Tibet*) and the procedure of Action Tantra in particular (found in H.H. the Dalai Lama, Tsong-kha-pa, and Jeffrey Hopkins, *The Yoga of Tibet* [London: George Allen and Unwin, 1981; reprinted as *Deity Yoga* with minor corrections, Ithaca, N.Y.: Snow Lion Publications, 1987]) are very much the foundation even if not cited.

Meditative stabilization of exalted body

There are basically two types of deity yoga, generation in front and self-generation—imagining a deity in front of oneself as a visitor and imagining oneself as a deity. Preliminary to this are extensive preparations (to be described in chapter four),[a] after which the meditator begins the four-branched repetition which basically is in two parts—first the four branches and then repetition. The meditator enacts four distinct stages, these being the four branches, or members, that make repetition possible:

1. generating a deity in front called "other-base"
2. generating oneself as a deity called "self-base"
3. a step called "mind"
4. a step called "sound."

These four are included within the meditative stabilization of exalted body; the repetition done after succeeding in visualizing these four is included in the meditative stabilization of exalted speech.

The practice of visualizing an ideal being in front of oneself and making offerings and so forth, although a form a deity yoga, is not the deity yoga that distinguishes Sūtra from Mantra. The distinctively tantric practice is *self*-generation, imagining oneself as a deity, the second of the four branches, and thus we shall consider this first, leaving the other Action Tantra meditations for chapters four, five, and six.

Imagining oneself as a deity

In Action Tantra the process of imagining, or generating, oneself as a deity is structured in six steps called six deities, which supply a basic tantric paradigm for meditation on selflessness and subsequent relation with appearance. This process is referred to but not described in the *Concentration Continuation Tantra* (to be cited in chapter four) and is known from the *Extensive Vidāraṇa Tantra*,[b] available only in citation in Buddhaguhya's commentary, which is extant only in Tibetan. The *Extensive Vidāraṇa Tantra* says:

> Having first bathed, a yogi

---

[a] For details on these preparatory stages see *Deity Yoga*, 79-101 and 215.

[b] *rdo rje rnam 'joms kyi rgyud rgyas pa*, **vajravidāraṇāvaipūlya*. For the citation, see *Deity Yoga*, 109.

> Sits on the vajra cushion
> And having offered and made petition
> Cultivates the six deities.
> Emptiness, sound, letter, form,
> Seal, and sign are the six.

The six deities are:

1. ultimate deity (also called emptiness deity or suchness deity)
2. sound deity (also called tone deity)
3. letter deity
4. form deity
5. seal deity
6. sign deity.

Let us consider these six steps in detail, using the commentaries mentioned above.

Ultimate deity. Dül-dzin-drak-pa-gyel-tsen describes the ultimate deity very briefly:[a]

> The ultimate deity is meditation on emptiness:
>
> > *Oṃ svabhāva-śuddhāḥ sarva-dharmāḥ svabhāva-śuddho 'haṃ* (*Oṃ* naturally pure are all phenomena; naturally pure am I.) Just as my own suchness is ultimately free from all the proliferations [of inherent existence], so also is the deity's suchness. Therefore, in terms of nonconceptual perception [of the final mode of subsistence of phenomena] the suchness of myself and the suchness of the deity are undifferentiable, like a mixture of water and milk.

The brevity of his description of this initial and crucial step of meditation on emptiness is due to the fact that although realization of emptiness is obviously integral to Mantra, descriptions of how to do it, though present in tantras such as the *Concentration Continuation Tantra*,[b] are found in far more detail in the Sūtra systems.[c] The

---

[a] Collected Works of Rje Tsoṅ-kha-pa Blo-bzaṅ-grags-pa, vol. 17 (*na*), 447.2-447.3.

[b] See *Deity Yoga*, 104-106, 168-171.

[c] See Gung-tang (*gung thang dkon mchog bstan pa'i sgron me*, 1762-1823), *Beginnings of a Commentary on the Difficult Points of (Tsong-kha-pa's) "Differentiation of the Interpretable and the Definitive," the Quintessence of "The Essence of Eloquence"* (*drang nges

meditator is expected to bring such knowledge to this practice.

The description of the ultimate deity by Ke-drup in his *Extensive Explanation of the Format of the General Tantra Sets* speaks to this point directly:[a]

> Meditation within settling well—in dependence upon a Middle Way reasoning such as the lack of [being] one or many and so forth—that one's mind is empty of inherent existence is the suchness of self. Then, meditation [on the fact] that the suchness of whatever deity is being meditated and the suchness of oneself are undifferentiably without inherent existence is the suchness of the deity. That two-fold suchness is the suchness deity from among the six deities. It is the equivalent of meditating on emptiness within saying *svabhāva* [that is, *oṃ svabhāva-śuddhāḥ sarva-dharmāḥ svabhāva-śuddho 'haṃ*: "*Oṃ* naturally pure are all phenomena; naturally pure am I"] or *śūnyatā* [*oṃ śūnyatājñānavajra-svabhāvātmako 'haṃ*: "I have a nature of indivisible emptiness and wisdom"] in higher tantra sets.

A Middle Way reasoning such as the lack of being an inherently existent one or an inherently existent plurality is used for the sake of realizing first that oneself (or, alternately, one's own mind) does not inherently exist. Thus, this first step in imagining oneself as a deity incorporates the Sūtra style meditation described in the previous chapter (14 ff.):

1. ascertaining what is being negated—inherent existence
2. ascertaining entailment of emptiness
3. ascertaining that the "I" and the aggregates are not inherently the same
4. ascertaining that the "I" and the aggregates are not inherently different
5. realizing the absence of inherent existence of the "I" in space-like meditative equipoise.

Tsong-kha-pa and his followers emphasize over and over again that

---

rnam 'byed kyi dga' 'grel rtsom 'phro legs bshad snying po'i yang snying) (Guru Deva: Sarnath, no date), 21.7-21.11.

[a] The text is Lessing and Wayman, *Fundamentals*, 158.16ff; for their translation, see the same.

the view of emptiness in Sūtra and in Mantra is the same,[a] this preferably being as explained by what is considered to be the final philosophical system, the Middle Way Consequence School.[b] Thus, these five steps are to be brought into the tantric meditation in toto.

The difference is that tantric practitioners, after meditating on their own lack of inherent existence, proceed to reflect on the emptiness of the deity as whom they will appear and then reflect on the sameness of themselves and the deity in terms of their own and the deity's ultimate mode of subsistence, an absence of inherent existence. The ultimate reality of oneself and the ultimate reality of the deity are viewed as like "water and milk" which mix so completely that they cannot be distinguished. Thus, the first step in meditating on oneself as a deity is to realize that, from the viewpoint of the perception of suchness, oneself and the deity are the same; this realization serves to break down the conception that either oneself or the deity inherently exists.

Tsong-kha-pa refers to the conception of sameness of ultimate nature as "pride":[c]

> Just as the suchness of oneself is ultimately free from all proliferations [of inherent existence], so is the suchness of the deity. Therefore, create the pride of the sameness of oneself and the deity in terms of nonconceptual perception of the undifferentiability of those two, like a mixture of water and milk. Concentrate without appearance [of the two as different] until your knowledge is very definite. This is the ultimate deity.
>
> Meditating thus on the emptiness of all [coarse and subtle] selves of persons and [other] phenomena is the same essential as when in other tantras, prior to meditating on a deity, one says a mantra, such as *svabhāva* [that is, *oṃ svabhāva-śuddhāḥ sarva-dharmāḥ svabhāva-śuddho 'haṃ*: "Oṃ naturally pure are all phenomena; naturally pure am I"] , and meditates on its meaning.[d]

---

[a] See *Tantra in Tibet,* 110.

[b] *dbu ma thal 'gyur pa, prāsaṅgikamādhyamika.*

[c] *Tantra in Tibet,* 106.

[d] Since both Tsong-kha-pa and Ke-drup speak of the ultimate deity as the *equivalent* of meditation on the meaning of the mantra in the higher tantra sets,

That the meditator takes *pride* in ultimately having the same nature as the deity suggests that the meditator develops a conscious willingness to identify himself or herself with the deity in terms of their final nature. The word "pride" suggests the boldness of making the identification—a force of will being required to overcome the reluctance to make such a grand identification in the face of analytical unfindability which is commonly associated with diminution in a beginning stage, since, as the Fifth Dalai Lama says (see 31), the initial experience of unfindability is of losing something.

This additional step of conscious identification of the sameness of final nature of oneself and of the deity drastically alters the space-like meditative equipoise which is a state of concentration solely on a nonaffirming negative, a mere absence of inherent existence. Now, one comes to meditate on an affirming negative[a]—that is, on the *sameness* in final nature of oneself and the deity as being without inherent existence. Even though this is done through the route of an initial space-like meditative equipoise meditating on the nonaffirming negative of first one's own and then the deity's inherent existence, the conclusion of the first step in self-generation is a positive affirmation of the *sameness* of oneself and the deity in terms of a pure final nature, itself a mere absence of inherent existence.

The relation between the emptiness realized and the being who appears subsequent to space-like meditative equipoise is made more explicit through this conscious identification. The passage from space-like meditative equipoise to taking cognizance of other objects is now no longer, as in the Sūtra system, a matter of merely letting other objects appear to the mind within the context of seeing them as like illusions. The meditator now consciously takes the ultimate deity as the basic stuff of the appearances yet to come. A bridge is made between emptiness and appearance—going beyond realization of their compatibility as in the Sūtra systems.

---

that Dül-dzin-drak-pa-gyel-tsen puts the mantra at the head of this Action Tantra meditation is clearly a case of bringing a practice from other Tantras to this one. Still, since he claims in the title of his work, *Presentation of the General Rites of Action and Performance Tantra and Their Application to the Three Lineages, Set Down by Dül-dzin According to the Foremost [Tsong-kha-pa's] Practice,* to be presenting Tsong-kha-pa's system of practice, the suggestion is that Tsong-kha-pa advised him to use the mantra in the actual practice of Action Tantra, perhaps because of its familiarity.

[a] *ma yin dgag, paryudāsapratiṣedha.*

Appearances are no longer just *allowed* to re-appear; instead, the meditator deliberately reflects on her own final nature as being the stuff out of which they will appear.

The fact that emptiness (and the mind fused with it in realization) is called a deity is similar to calling the emptiness of the mind the Buddha nature, Buddha lineage, or naturally abiding lineage[a] in that it is all-powerful in the sense of being that which makes everything possible. As Nāgārjuna's *Treatise on the Middle* says:[b]

> For whom emptiness is possible
> For that [person] all is possible.

Due to the emptiness of inherent existence, change and transformation are possible, whereas without it everything is frozen in substantial existence. Here in this first step of deity yoga the meditator identifies himself, in terms of ultimate nature, with this basic stuff.

Sound deity. In the second through fifth steps the mind of wisdom, fused with and realizing emptiness, is used as a basis of emanation—the mind itself appearing in form. Rather than merely letting phenomena appear as is done after space-like meditative equipoise in the Sūtra system, the yogi uses the mind of wisdom as the stuff out of which and within which first sounds and then visible forms and so forth will appear. About the sound deity Dül-dzin-drak-pa-gyel-tsen says:

> The tone or sound deity is the contemplation:
>
> > From within emptiness [the wisdom realizing the ultimate deity appears] in the aspect of the tones of the mantra resounding in space.

Within continuously realizing the emptiness of inherent existence, the mind of wisdom itself first appears as the sounds of the mantra of the deity whom the meditator will become, resounding in space. Ke-drup indicates that the sounds of the mantra are, in entity, the deity:

> Then from within emptiness contemplate what, in entity, is just whatever deity is being meditated but, in aspect, is resounding in the aspect of the sounds of the mantra to be

---

[a] *rang bzhin gnas rigs, prakṛtiṣṭhagotra.*

[b] XXIV.14ab.

> repeated. One-pointed mental observation of this is the sound deity.

Out of emptiness comes mantra—word—which itself is the deity. It is clear that the meditator is not to think of the deity as only appearing when the god with a face, arms, legs, and so forth manifests. Everything that appears from this point on is made from the ultimate deity and is essentially the deity.

Letter deity. The meditator's mind realizing the sameness of ultimate nature of oneself and the deity transforms into a white, flat moon disc shining in space on which the letters of the mantra appear standing around its edge (facing inward, according to oral explanations). Dül-dzin-drak-pa-gyel-tsen says:

> The letter deity is the contemplation:
>
> > My mind having the subjective aspect of [realizing] the undifferentiable suchness of myself and the deity becomes a moon disc. The aspects of the mantra tones resounding in space are set on it in the aspect of written letters like very pure mercury adhering to [or completely mixing with] grains of gold.

In an explanation of the example by Ye-shay-gyel-tsen,[a] the sounds of the mantra are compared to mercury that mixes with grains of the gold, the written letters. Hence, in his stimulating explanation, the upright letters are not just color and shape but are fused with their respective sounds.

Ke-drup simplifies the example, suggesting that, at least to him, Tsong-kha-pa did not emphasize this fusion of sound and visible form:

> Then, meditate on what in entity is just whatever deity is being meditated but in aspect is the letters of the mantra to be repeated in the aspect of the color of refined gold [standing] on one's own mind which has transformed into a moon in space. This is the letter deity.

Despite Ke-drup's not mentioning the mixture of sound and visible

---

[a] Ye-shay-gyel-tsen (*ye shes rgyal mtshan*, 1713-1793), *Illumination of the Meaning of Action Tantra* (*bya rgyud don gsal*), Collected Works, vol. 9 (New Delhi: Tibet House, 1976), 487.3.

form, it seems to me to be an important connecting link in the gradual evolution from emptiness to sound to visible form.

Form deity. The next step is the transformation of this moon disc with upright letters into the usual physical form of the deity with a face, arms, legs, and so forth. Prior to that, however, there is an intermediary step of emitting from the moon a multitude of compassionately beneficent forms of the deity, through which active compassion is established as the precursor of one's own bodily appearance. As Dül-dzin-drak-pa-gyel-tsen says:

> The form deity is creation of the pride that the deity is not different from yourself within meditating on the deity:
>
> > [The moon and mantra letters] are transformed such that the hand symbol of the deity [appears on the moon] with the mantra letters. Variegated rays of light are emitted from the moon, hand symbol, and mantra. From the points of the light rays innumerable forms of the deity emerge, pervading the entire sphere of space. Through emanating great clouds of offerings they make splendid offerings to all the Conquerors. Also, they emanate great clouds from which a rain-stream of ambrosia descends, extinguishing the fires of the sufferings of all transmigrators—hell-beings and so forth—as well as satisfying those [beings with whatever they want]. Then, the rays of light as well as the divine bodies return and enter the moon disc, hand symbol, and mantra which are my mind, whereupon I emerge in the full form of the deity.

The moon and mantra letters transform such that a hand-symbol—a vajra or wheel, for instance—also appears on the moon. Then, from all of these emanate rays of light from which, in turn, myriad forms of the deity emerge. These deities then emanate great clouds piled with offerings which they offer to already enlightened beings. The deities also emanate great clouds from which a rain-stream of ambrosia descends, cleansing and satisfying all other beings. The Dalai Lama movingly describes this phase of the meditation:[a]

[a] *Deity Yoga,* 23.

> Imagine that from the moon and the mantra letters light rays are emitted, from the points of which emerge forms of the deity to be meditated. These deities emanate clouds of offerings to the Buddhas, Bodhisattvas, and so forth, as well as clouds with a rain of nectar. It falls on the beings in cyclic existence[a] and purifies them, giving a good body to those who need it, coolness to those suffering from heat, the warmth of the sun to those suffering from cold, food and drink to the hungry and thirsty—emanating to each just what he or she needs, affording beings the basis for practicing the path as well as teachers to instruct them in the essential paths of the four truths, the two truths, and so forth. They are caused to ascend the paths and attain the final happiness of Buddhahood.

The activity of offering to high beings fortifies the basic motivation toward enlightenment by associating the purpose of worthwhile material things and pleasures with Buddhahood. The activity of cleansing those trapped in suffering makes the very essence of physical appearance be compassionate activity for the welfare of the world.

Psychologically, the meditator must confront and transform many untamed contents of mind which appear as the deprived and depraved beings who receive the bountiful blessings of the rain of ambrosia. One can speculate that a prime reason for the vivid descriptions of the hells and other unfortunate existences found in other texts[b] is to make manifest to oneself unconscious tendencies of mind and spirit so that such meditative confrontation and transformation can be enacted.

According to Tibetan explanations, imitating the deeds of Buddhahood through raining down this ambrosia establishes patterns and predispositions to be fulfilled after one's own enlightenment. In addition, an internal transformation is enacted in a process that begins with a step much like Jung's description of assimilation of unconscious complexes, not through identification,

---

[a] *'khor ba, saṃsāra.*

[b] See, for example, H.V. Guenther's *Jewel Ornament of Liberation* (Berkeley, Calif.: Shambhala, 1971), 56-62, and Khetsun Sangbo's *Tantric Practice in Nyingma* (London: Rider/Hutchinson, 1982; Ithaca, N.Y.: Snow Lion Publications, 1983), 65-72.

but through confrontation. Jung says:[a]

> The supreme aim of the *opus psychologicum* is conscious realization, and the first step is to make oneself conscious of contents that have hitherto been projected.

Recognition of the needy and unpleasant beings to be helped by the beneficent rain constitutes confrontation with one's own tendencies and predispositions. It is interesting to note that the transformation is not an instantaneous transmutation into divinity but begins with first *satisfying* the needs of the deprived and depraved contents.[b] Also, oral explanations from lamas indicate that the rain of ambrosia *gradually* leads these beings (psychological contents) to higher and higher levels through providing opportunities for practice, teachings, and so forth. The sense of quasi-otherness under the guise of which this practice is done has, as its basis, the same wisdom as Jung's warning to assimilate unconscious contents through confrontation, not through identification, in order to avoid being taken over by them, as will be discussed in the next chapter. The step of healingly transforming these contents after recognizing them proceeds a step beyond Jung's confrontational assimilation in that these forces, once confronted, not only lose much of their autonomous power but also are transformed.

Although only Highest Yoga Mantra mirrors in its deity yoga the afflicted processes[c] of (1) death, (2) intermediate state, and (3)

---

[a] *The Collected Works of C.G. Jung* (Princeton: Princeton University Press, 1971, second printing 1974), vol. 16, para. 471 (the last number refers not to the page number but to the paragraph number, which is used for coordination between editions).

[b] See the description of a similar practice done in the Vajrasattva meditation and repetition of mantra in Khetsun Sangpo, *Tantric Practice in Nyingma,* 149-150.

[c] Tsong-kha-pa gives this opinion in his explication of Yoga Tantra in the *Great Exposition of the Stages of Secret Mantra:*

> Cultivation of deity yoga in the pattern of the stages of production of [a life] in cyclic existence [mimicking the process of death, intermediate state, and rebirth]—the thoroughly afflicted class [of phenomena]—is not set forth in any reliable text of the three lower tantra sets; consequently, such is a distinguishing feature of Highest Yoga Mantra. However, [in the three lower tantra sets] there is a cultivation of deity yoga in the pattern of the very pure class [of phenomena], for the cultivation of the five manifest enlightenments [in Yoga Tantra, for instance] is said to be meditation within assuming the pride of such and such [stage] in

rebirth by (1) mimicking the eight signs of death,[a] appearing (2) as a seed syllable, and then (3) as a deity with a physical body, it strikes me that these stages of gradual appearance as a deity in Action Tantra mirror, in pure form, an ordinary, uncontrolled process of appearance—the imitation being for the sake of gaining control over it. Given the selfishness of ordinary life, there must be a phase in the process of awakening after sleep opposite to the compassionate emanation of myriad helpful forms. In ordinary, selfish life, the corresponding psychological structuring of our relation to the environment would be the emanation of forms similar to ourselves for the sake of warding off anyone who would interrupt our pleasure, making sure that disease visits others and not ourselves, wreaking havoc on others for the sake of control, and so forth. It also may be that this process in ordinary life is so out of control that one emanates forms that destroy one's own welfare, much like dream beings that pursue us or a paranoiac's attackers.

In this transmutory practice, after the enactment of such compassionate activity, the rays and deities return with actualized (not just potential) compassion to dissolve with all their power and experience into the moon, letters, and hand-symbol which turn into the deity. The meditator now could not view the deity as just a neutral appearance of light in a certain form but must see and feel it as an active expression of compassion and wisdom. Ke-drup says:

> Then, from those letters innumerable rays of light are emitted, at the points of which innumerable aspects of the body of just that deity being meditated are emitted. These purify all ill deeds, obstructions, and sufferings of all sentient beings and delight all the Buddhas as well as their children [that is, Bodhisattvas] with offerings. Then the rays of light together with the deities again gather, dissolving into the letters, due to which the moon together

accordance with the stages of full purification of Bodhisattvas in their last lifetime.

See H.H the Dalai Lama, Tsong-kha-pa, and Jeffrey Hopkins, *Yoga Tantra: Paths to Magical Feats* (Ithaca, N.Y.: Snow Lion Publications, 2005), 76.

[a] Mirage, smoke, fireflies, flame of a butter lamp, mind of vivid white appearance, mind of vivid red or orange increase, mind of vivid black near attainment, and mind of clear light. See Lati Rinbochay and Jeffrey Hopkins, *Death, Intermediate State, and Rebirth in Tibetan Buddhism* (London: Rider/Hutchinson, 1980; Ithaca, N.Y.: Snow Lion Publications, 1980), 15-19 and 32-46.

> with the letters thoroughly transforms into the body of whatever deity is being meditated. Observation of the full generation of this divine body is the form deity. When doing approximation upon cultivating self-generation, except for just the principal [figure] it is not necessary to meditate on the surrounding [figures], inestimable mansion, and so forth.

The rays of light emitted from the moon, which itself is a manifestation of the mind realizing the ultimate deity, are endowed with compassionate potential for appearance in forms working the weal of sentient beings. One has appeared in divine form, the essence of which is the wisdom of emptiness and active compassion.

Still, self-generation is not complete. The imagined deity must be further enhanced.

Seal deity. Enhancement is accomplished through uttering mantra at the same time as physically touching important places on one's imagined divine body with a hand-gesture called a seal.[a] Dül-dzin-drak-pa-gyel-tsen says:

> The seal deity is to construct the pledge seal of the particular lineage and to bless into a magnificent state the heart, point between the brows, the neck, and the shoulders through touching them with the seal and repeating the pledge mantra.

The one pledge seal of the particular lineage may be used or individual seals for each of the places may be used. Ke-drup speaks of touching not five (counting the shoulders as two) but nine places:

> Then, touch the crown protrusion, hair-treasury [a single coiled hair in the middle of the brow], eyes, the two shoulders, neck, heart, and navel with the individual mantras and seals if you know them. If you do not know that much, do it with the single mantra and seal of whatever the general lineage is from among the three lineages [One-Gone-Thus,[b] lotus, and vajra lineages]. Touching and blessing those places into a magnificence is the seal deity. It is the equivalent of blessing the [six] sense spheres [that is, sense

---

[a] *phyag rgya, mudrā.*

[b] *de bzhin gshegs pa.*

> organs] in the higher tantras.

The word for "blessing"[a] means to transform into a magnificent state. Thus, with each mantra and touch the meditator imagines a heightening of the particular area of the divine body in terms of its brilliance and magnificence. This is a further sanctifying of an appearance that is already sacred due to being a manifestation of wisdom and compassion.

Sign deity. Now that all the signs of a full-fledged deity are present, the meditator, based on clear appearance of pure mind and body, can gain a sense of divine personhood or selfhood. Dül-dzin-drak-pa-gyel-tsen says:

> The sign deity is, within observing just that deity that has been generated, to perform analytical meditation—visualizing it [more clearly] and so forth—as well as the stabilizing meditation of mental one-pointedness.

Two types of meditation are used, *analytical,* which involves particular attention to details or brightening of the object, and *stabilizing,* which is one-pointed attention on just one aspect.

For deity yoga to succeed, two prime factors are needed—clear appearance of a divine body and pride in being that deity. Ke-drup says:

> Then, clearly visualizing the aspect of the deity and making the pride [of being the deity] firm, mentally observe it one-pointedly. This is the sign deity.

With success in visualizing the deity, both mind and body appear to be pure; hence, the sense of self that the meditator has in dependence upon purely appearing mind and body is of a pure self, a divine self. About such divine pride, the Fourteenth Dalai Lama says in *Tantra in Tibet:*[b]

> ...initially one meditates on an emptiness, and then, within the context of the mind's continuous ascertainment of emptiness, the meditator believes that he/she is using this mind as the basis [or source] of appearance. At that time, the sense of a mere "I" designated in dependence on the

---

a *byin gyis rlobs pa, adhiṣṭhāna.*

b *Tantra in Tibet,* 64.

> pure resident—the deity—and residence—the palace and surroundings—is a fully qualified divine pride. As much as one can cultivate such pride, so much does one harm the conception of inherent existence that is the root of cyclic existence.

Divine pride itself is said to harm or weaken the conception of inherent existence, which is at the root of all other afflictions including afflicted pride. Due to the initial and then continuous practice of realizing the emptiness of inherent existence, the meditator realizes that the person is merely designated in dependence upon pure mind and body and is not analytically findable among or separate from those bases of designation. Thereby, divine pride itself serves as a means for eliminating exaggerated conceptions of the status of phenomena including the person; this is how it prevents afflicted ego-inflation.

With success at deity yoga at the level of the meditative stabilization of exalted mind (discussed in chapter six, 153ff.), the practitioner has the factors of wisdom and compassionate method in one consciousness at one time. The "ascertainment factor"[a] of this consciousness realizes the emptiness of inherent existence at the same time as the "appearance factor"[b] appears in ideal, compassionate form acting to help beings. This is said to be superior to the Sūtra version of the union of method and wisdom in which method (cultivation of compassion) merely affects wisdom with its force and in which wisdom (realization of emptiness) merely affects compassionate activities with its force, the two not actually being manifest at one time. In Mantra the presence of compassionate method and wisdom in a single consciousness is said to quicken progress toward Buddhahood—a state of nondual realization of the nature of phenomena within spontaneous dualistic appearance for the benefit of others.

A profound development has occurred when a practitioner becomes capable of deity yoga. After realizing emptiness, appearances are no longer just allowed to re-emerge within understanding that there is a conflict between how they appear to exist in their own right and their actual lack of such concreteness; rather, the practitioner's own mind realizing emptiness

---

[a] *nges cha.*

[b] *snang cha.*

and understanding that one's own and a deity's final nature are the same becomes the stuff out of which phenomena appear. The relation between emptiness and appearance, the gap between an experience of unfindability and re-emergence, is bridged.

Paradigm change

Tsong-kha-pa and his followers present the Perfection and Mantra vehicles as an integrated progression; the very foundations of Perfection Vehicle practice, altruism and wisdom, are reformulated in the Mantra Vehicle in the practice of deity yoga. As will be clear in chapter nine on his delineation of the tantric difference—this being the meditative use of a mind of wisdom to appear in compassionately active form—he stresses the continuity between the two vehicles, two models or paradigms of the relation of the fundamental emptiness (or the wisdom realizing emptiness) with appearance. But is the progression from the Sūtra to the Mantra model of relation with appearance necessarily a smooth transition, a harmonious, incremental putting together of two models, or could it also be fraught with tension?

In preparing for a Buddhist-Christian Encounter conference in Hawaii in 1984 in which Hans Küng's theological adaptation of Thomas Kuhn's theory of paradigm change in the sciences was used as the focus, I was struck by Kuhn's and Küng's emphasis on crisis in the development and movement from one paradigm to another. For me, Küng's description of a critical period during which inadequacies and discrepancies of the old paradigm lead to uncertainty such that conviction in the adequacy of the old paradigm is shaken rang true with my own experience of the transition from Sūtra practice to tantric practice. Thus, I have found it helpful to use the language of paradigm change—of an initial period of crisis, then a new formation, and finally a sense of continuity with the old paradigm—to appreciate the distinctiveness of tantric deity yoga and the issues remaining from the Sūtra model of meditation that it resolves.

My suggestion is that an individual practitioner's change from the Sūtra to the Mantra model may not, in some cases, be a harmonious gradual acquisition of a new technique but may be fraught with psychological crisis. Despite the structural harmony that Tsong-kha-pa presents with such brilliance and clarity, the history of a particular practitioner's personal incorporation of this paradigm change may not be a smooth transition. I recognize the autobiographical nature of these reflections and offer them only as a stimulus to appreciation of the profundity of deity yoga.

From one model to another

In that the content to be understood through the meditations of both the Sūtra and Mantra models is the nature and basis of appearance, we are dealing with two macro models,[a] for they are both experientially oriented explanations of the very phenomena of life. Despite being taught by the same school (in this case, the Ge-luk-pa order of Tibetan Buddhism), they are purposely kept distinct, not just to preserve schools of teachings from India, but, I would contend, to induce—through initial practice of the Sūtra model of meditation on selflessness—the crisis that will lead to appreciation of the tantric. Some Ge-luk-pa scholar-practitioners choose only to follow the Sūtra model, resisting the change to the tantric model. This can occur (1) by refusing to engage in tantric practice, (2) by engaging in tantric ritual but not believing it, (3) or by incorporating an external show of the practice of both Sūtra and Mantra but actually not penetrating either.

The change, or evolution, from the Sūtra to the Mantra model cannot actually be made until one learns in meditative *experience* to use the mind "realizing" emptiness and the emptiness—with which it is fused—as a basis of imaginative appearance, in imitation of a Buddha's ability to do this in fact. Thus, the change cannot be made superficially merely through using the tantric descriptions or through sitting through a ritual that incorporates this process.

A somewhat successful Sūtra practitioner, who is able to experience something resembling space-like meditative equipoise, may arrive at a point of hiatus during which he/she is not satisfied with merely letting objects re-appear after reflecting on emptiness. The question, the crisis, of comprehending the stuff of appearances may be sufficiently pressing that he or she becomes increasingly dissatisfied with the break between the space-like realization and the subsequent plethora of appearances, despite appearances being marked with realization of the emptiness of inherent existence

[a] In this section I am using the vocabulary of paradigm change as found in the chapter "Paradigm Change in Theology," in Hans Küng, *Theology for the Third Millennium: An Ecumenical View* (New York: Doubleday, 1988), 123-169.

through the force of the earlier cognition. There is a retraction of mind when moving from space-like meditative equipoise—in which the mind is fused with the emptiness of inherent existence of all phenomena—to a condition in which the meditator's mind only affects those appearances in the sense of marking or sealing them with this realization.

There can be a period of transitional uncertainty during which the Sūtra model is challenged for its inability to address the problem of the relation of this deep mind realizing emptiness to appearances. The problem of the relation of one's own mind to those appearances can assume crisis proportions, creating openness to drastic change. The breakdown of the Sūtra model at this point and the crisis, induced not only by this breakdown but also by the difficulty of comprehending the tantric model despite its availability, leads to new thinking seeking a way to solve the puzzle, a withdrawal of sole commitment to the Sūtra model even though the practitioner might not express it this way. The crisis—the breakdown of the available rules—cracks and softens the rigidity of the devotion to the old model.

The new paradigm candidate, the tantric model, was in a sense always at hand in the form of lectures and ceremonies but was hardly *available* since only through considerable experience with searching for objects, not finding them, and then practicing illusory-like appearance can the additional technique of using this mind realizing emptiness as the basis that itself appears in physical form be appreciated. This is partially due to the general Buddhist analytic tendency, breaking things down to basic parts and those, in turn, to smaller and smaller units since, in the face of this basic perspective, such a grandly synthetic view as is presented in the tantric model might seem even non-Buddhist. A version of the synthetic view is present in the Sūtra system in that all appearances are viewed as the sport of emptiness in the sense that the emptiness of inherent existence makes them possible; however, this does not take account of the relation of mind to those appearances as the tantric system does.

The change to the new paradigm constitutes a revolution in outlook, lending an entirely new sense to the meaning of mind-only[a] beyond the one rejected earlier, as a "lower view," in

---

[a] *sems tsam, cittamātra.*

the progress toward the view of the Middle Way School. When the mind realizing emptiness is itself used as that from which phenomena are emanated, the practitioner's orientation toward the world of appearances undergoes a fundamental reorganization; the model of understanding appearance changes. As I have suggested, this is not done without opposition and struggle both from within and from without, the latter being from concern with teachers and members of the monastic community in the old camp. A period of doubt, loss of faith, and uncertainty due to the pressing inadequacy of the old model is transcended through conversion to a model that copes better with the relation between mind and appearance on an experiential, practical level. The conversion could be prompted by attending a rite where the tantric model is used or by one's own daily rehearsal of a rite that previously did not have much meaning.

The new, tantric model absorbs the old, preserving in its procedures an important place for the space-like meditative equipoise in the first phase of cultivation of deity yoga, the ultimate deity. Hence, the meditator experiences, after the conversion, a continuity with his or her earlier practice through enactment (at least six times daily) of a ritual that also incorporates the old model. Due to the continuing, and even essential, importance of realization of the absence of inherent existence and of altruism, a *fundamental continuity* is experienced: the very structure of the old model, wisdom and compassion, is literally reshaped to appear in ideal form, wise and compassionate.

Mantra, in this light, can be seen as a *new formation* of the Buddhist tradition, not a new invention of a tradition; the primordial importance of wisdom and compassion remains the basis. In the progression I have outlined, the process of moving from one model to the other, at least for some persons, may not be a simple matter of the incorporation of a new technique, deity yoga, as the Ge-luk-pa tradition in its emphasis on the integration of two vehicles gives the impression that it is. Crisis and shift may better describe the person's progression from the Sūtra vehicle to the Mantra vehicle; still, from the new perspective the continuity can be seen. Perhaps, the deity yoga that constitutes the difference between the two vehicles according to Tsong-kha-pa and his followers is not merely a distinctive, important factor of the tantric path not found in Sūtra but also a difficult one the comprehension of which is fraught with developmental crisis.

3. Jung's Warnings Against Inflation

As we have seen, in deity yoga compassion and wisdom are combined in a single consciousness such that the mind of wisdom realizing emptiness is used as the basis from which oneself emanates as, or appears as, a deity. The mind of wisdom itself appears compassionately as a deity; the "ascertainment factor"[a] of the consciousness realizes emptiness while the "appearance factor"[b] appears as an ideal being, whose very essence is compassion and wisdom.

Tsong-kha-pa singles out this practice of deity yoga as the central (but not the only) distinctive feature of Mantra. The Sūtra systems involve meditation that is similar in aspect to a Buddha's Body of Attributes in that in meditative equipoise directly realizing emptiness the Bodhisattva's mind realizing emptiness is similar in aspect to a Buddha's exalted knowledge of the mode of being of phenomena in its aspect of perceiving only the ultimate, emptiness. However, the Sūtra systems do not involve meditation similar in aspect to a Buddha's form body, in that the meditator does not imagine himself or herself to have a Buddha's physical form, whereas such does occur in Mantra. Thus, for Tsong-kha-pa, visualizing oneself as a deity and identification with that deity comprise the central distinguishing feature of tantric meditation. In descriptions of the distinctiveness of Mantra in other orders of Tibetan Buddhism also, deity yoga is a distinguishing feature of Mantra but is not singled as out as the *central* difference.

On the surface, Carl Jung's warning that inflation necessarily attends identifying oneself with an archetypal motif would seem completely applicable to the practice of deity yoga. His cautions are profound and serve to highlight the enormity of the task that the tantric systems are attempting. Jung frequently warns against the inflation attendant upon assimilation of autonomous complexes and identification with their content, as, for instance, when he says:[c]

---

[a] *nges cha.*

[b] *snang cha.*

[c] *Collected Works*, vol. 7, para. 243 (the last number refers not to the page number but to the paragraph number, which is used for coordination between editions).

> It will be remembered that in the analysis of the personal unconscious the first things to be added to consciousness are the personal contents and I suggested that these contents which have been repressed, but are capable of becoming conscious, should be called the *personal unconscious*. I also showed that to annex the deeper layers of the unconscious, which I have called the *collective unconscious,* produces an extension of the personality leading to the state of inflation.

Jung feared the perils of inflation that he found in Westerners who attempted Eastern yoga. To counteract this, he stressed assimilation of contents of the collective unconscious, not through identification, but through confrontation, wisely avoiding equation with either the lowest or highest aspects of one's own psyche.

This Tibetan system, however, stresses the importance of "divine pride,"[a] in which the practitioner seeks to develop such clear imagination of herself or himself as a deity that the sense of *being* a deity occurs strongly (though not to the point of utter conviction). As we have seen in the previous chapter, in Action Tantra this practice begins with emptiness yoga, called the "ultimate deity," and the deity is an appearance of the wisdom realizing the emptiness of inherent existence—the deity being merely the person designated in dependence upon purely appearing mind and body. Because the empty status of the person is being realized, it is said that deity yoga serves even to counteract the conception of oneself as inherently existent and thereby to prevent afflicted pride, a version of ego-inflation which Jung sought to avoid by advising against identifying with assimilated contents.

In exploring these issues, let us first consider Jung's very sensible and profound warnings and then whether any of the specific steps in the practice of deity yoga in Buddhist Tantra could serve to prevent inflation. I find Jung's framing of the issue to be profoundly stimulating, serving as a foil for appreciating the significance of deity yoga.

Jung's warnings

To Carl Jung it is by no means so simple. This can be seen when he

---

[a] *lha'i nga rgyal.*

speaks of great dangers in Westerners' attempting the Eastern yoga which, for him, is amoral but is misinterpreted in the West as a pretext for immorality:[a]

> Anyone who affects the higher yoga will be called upon to prove his professions of moral indifference, not only as the doer of evil but, even more, as its victim. As psychologists well know, the moral conflict is not to be settled merely by a declaration of superiority bordering on inhumanity. We are witnessing today some terrifying examples of the Superman's aloofness from moral principles.
>
> I do not doubt that the Eastern liberation from vices, as well as from virtues, is coupled with detachment in every respect, so that the yogi is translated beyond this world, and quite inoffensive. But I suspect every European attempt at detachment of being mere liberation from moral considerations. Anybody who tries his hand at yoga ought therefore to be conscious of its far-reaching consequences, or else his so-called quest will remain a futile pastime.

Such misapplication of yoga leads to positive and negative inflation and all their attendant ills of which Jung speaks repeatedly and eloquently throughout his works. For instance:[b]

> In projection, he vacillates between an extravagant and pathological deification of the doctor, and a contempt bristling with hatred. In introjection, he gets involved in a ridiculous self-deification, or else a moral self-laceration. The mistake he makes in both cases comes from attributing to a *person* the contents of the collective unconscious. In this way he makes himself or his partner either god or devil. Here we see the characteristic effect of the archetype: it seizes hold of the psyche with a kind of primeval force and compels it to transgress the bounds of humanity. It causes exaggeration, a puffed-up attitude (inflation), loss of free will, delusion, and enthusiasm in good and evil alike.

Positive inflation of the religious sort can lead to assumptions of grandeur, viewing oneself as having the universal panacea:[c]

---

[a] *Collected Works,* vol. 11, para. 825-826.

[b] *Collected Works,* vol. 7, para. 110.

[c] *Collected Works,* vol. 7, para. 260.

> The second possible mode of reaction is identification with the collective psyche. This would be equivalent to acceptance of the inflation, but now exalted into a system. In other words, one would be the fortunate possessor of *the* great truth that was only waiting to be discovered, of the eschatological knowledge that means the healing of the nations. This attitude does not necessarily signify megalomania in direct form, but megalomania in the milder and more familiar form it takes in the reformer, the prophet, and the martyr.

Just as the prophet convinced that he/she has *the* final truth is inflated through identification with the forces of deep contents, so is the humble disciple, affecting the posture of only following the master's dictums:[a]

> But besides the possibility of becoming a prophet, there is another alluring joy, subtler and apparently more legitimate: the joy of becoming a prophet's disciple....The disciple is unworthy; modestly he sits at the Master's feet and guards against having ideas of his own. Mental laziness becomes a virtue; one can at least bask in the sun of a semidivine being....Naturally the disciples always stick together, not out of love, but for the very understandable purpose of effortlessly confirming their own convictions by engendering an air of collective agreement....[J]ust as the prophet is a primordial image from the collective psyche, so also is the disciple of the prophet.
>
> In both cases inflation is brought about by the collective unconscious, and the independence of the individuality suffers injury.

In a similar vein:[b]

> These few examples may suffice to show what kind of spirit animated these movements. They were made up of people who identified themselves (or were identified) with God, who deemed themselves supermen, had a critical approach to the gospels, followed the promptings of the inner man, and understood the kingdom of heaven to be within. In a

---

[a] *Collected Works*, vol. 7, para. 263-265.

[b] *Collected Works*, vol. 9.ii, para. 140.

> sense, therefore, they were modern in their outlook, but they had a religious inflation instead of the rationalistic and political psychosis that is the affliction of our day.

Jung's description of his own time as being under the sway of a "rationalistic and political psychosis" in which gathered libido is invested in rationalism as a cure-all and is invested in politics as a panacea for all ills prompts me to add that today such inflation is also found in excessive concentration on economics, such that the focus of improvement is on the level of personal income and the gross national product with personal fulfillment being almost forgotten.

Too much attention is turned to externals, as if proper social, political, and economic arrangements would cure our situation. Jung advises against identifying with offices and titles since such excludes the richness of our situation:[a]

> A very common instance is the humorless way in which many men identify themselves with their business or their titles. The office I hold is certainly my special activity; but it is also a collective factor that has come into existence historically through the cooperation of many people and whose dignity rests solely on collective approval. When, therefore, I identify myself with my office or title, I behave as though I myself were the whole complex of social factors of which that office consists, or as though I were not only the bearer of the office, but also and at the same time the approval of society. I have made an extraordinary extension of myself and have usurped qualities which are not in me but outside me.

And:[b]

> There is, however, yet another thing to be learnt from this example, namely that these transpersonal contents are not just inert or dead matter that can be annexed at will. Rather they are living entities which exert an attractive force upon the conscious mind. Identification with one's office or one's title is very attractive indeed, which is precisely why so many men are nothing more than the decorum

[a] *Collected Works,* vol. 7, para. 227.

[b] *Collected Works,* vol. 7, para. 230.

> accorded to them by society. In vain would one look for a personality behind the husk. Underneath all the padding one would find a very pitiable little creature. That is why the office—or whatever their outer husk may be—is so attractive: it offers easy compensation for personal deficiencies.

The basic problem is that one has lost a healthy respect for the need to mediate between the conscious and the unconscious, thereby (in one version) inflating the importance of the ego:[a]

> To the extent that the integrated contents are *parts of the self*, we can expect this influence [of assimilation] to be considerable. Their assimilation augments not only the area of the field of consciousness but also the importance of the ego, especially when, as usually happens, the ego lacks any critical approach to the unconscious. In that case it is easily overpowered and becomes identical with the contents that have been assimilated....I should only like to mention that the more numerous and the more significant the unconscious contents which are assimilated to the ego, the closer the approximation of the ego to the self, even though this approximation must be a never-ending process. This inevitably produces an inflation of the ego, unless a critical line of demarcation is drawn between it and the unconscious figures.

The problem of inflation occurs whether the ego is drowned in the larger self or the larger self is pretentiously assimilated to the ego:[b]

> It must be reckoned a psychic catastrophe when the *ego is assimilated by the self*. The image of wholeness then remains in the unconscious, so that on the one hand it shares the archaic nature of the unconscious and on the other finds itself in the psychically relative space-time continuum that is characteristic of the unconscious as such....Hence it is of the greatest importance that the ego should be anchored in the world of consciousness and that consciousness should be reinforced by a very precise adaptation. For this, certain virtues like attention, conscientiousness, patience and so

[a] *Collected Works*, vol. 9.ii, para. 43-44.

[b] *Collected Works*, vol. 9.ii, para. 45-46.

> forth, are of great value on the moral side, just as accurate observation of the symptomatology of the unconscious and objective self-criticism are valuable on the intellectual side.
>
> However, accentuation of the ego personality and the world of consciousness may easily assume such proportions that the figures of the unconscious are psychologized and the *self consequently becomes assimilated to the ego.* Although this is the exact opposite of the process we have just described it is followed by the same result: inflation.

Correspondingly, inflation is of two varieties, negative and positive, the former being when the ego is subsumed in the collective unconscious and the latter when the ego takes too much to itself. Jung says:[a]

> With the integration of projections—which the merely natural man in his unbounded naïveté can never recognize as such—the personality becomes so vastly enlarged that the normal ego-personality is almost extinguished. In other words, if the individual identifies himself with the contents awaiting integration, a positive or negative inflation results. Positive inflation comes very near to a more or less conscious megalomania; negative inflation is felt as an annihilation of the ego.

Jung frequently makes clear his position that one must negotiate the passage between the Scylla and Charybdis of the needs of unconscious contents to manifest and the imperative of effective individuation. For example, he says,[b] "The unconscious can only be integrated if the ego holds its ground," and:[c]

> If our psychology is forced, owing to the special nature of its empirical material, to stress the importance of the unconscious, that does not in any way diminish the importance of the conscious mind. It is merely the one-sided over-valuation of the latter that has to be checked by a certain relativization of values. But this relativization should not be carried so far that the ego is completely fascinated and overpowered by the archetypal truths. The ego lives in

[a] *Collected Works,* vol. 16, para. 472.

[b] *Collected Works,* vol. 16, para. 503.

[c] *Collected Works,* vol. 16, para. 502.

> space and time and must adapt itself to their laws if it is to exist at all. If it is absorbed by the unconscious to such an extent that the latter alone has the power of decision, then the ego is stifled, and there is no longer any medium in which the unconscious could be integrated and in which the work of realization could take place....Against the daemonism from within, the church offers some protection so long as it wields authority. But protection and security are only valuable when not excessively cramping to our existence; and in the same way the superiority of consciousness is desirable only if it does not suppress and shut out too much life. As always, life is a voyage between Scylla and Charybdis.

He identifies the two perils eloquently:[a]

> Even when the conscious mind does not identify itself with the inclinations of the unconscious, it still has to face them and somehow take account of them in order that they may play their part in the life of the individual, however difficult this may be. For if the unconscious is not allowed to express itself through word and deed, through worry and suffering, through our consideration of its claims and resistance to them, then the earlier, divided state will return with all the incalculable consequences which disregard of the unconscious may entail. If, on the other hand, we give in to the unconscious too much, it leads to a positive or negative inflation of the personality.

Without such care, a person is subject to psychological disaster, primarily the loss of the powers of discrimination:[b]

> An inflated consciousness is always egocentric and conscious of nothing but its own existence. It is incapable of learning from the past, incapable of understanding contemporary events, and incapable of drawing right conclusions about the future. It is hypnotized by itself and therefore cannot be argued with. It inevitably dooms itself to calamities that must strike it dead. Paradoxically enough, inflation is a regression of consciousness into

[a] *Collected Works*, vol. 16, para. 522.

[b] *Collected Works*, vol. 12, para. 563.

> unconsciousness. This always happens when consciousness takes too many unconscious contents upon itself and loses the faculty of discrimination, the *sine qua non* of all consciousness....It seems to me of some importance, therefore, that a few individuals, or people individually, should begin to understand that there are contents which do not belong to the ego-personality, but must be ascribed to a psychic non-ego. This mental operation has to be undertaken if we want to avoid a threatening inflation.

Jung's view is that certain contents, although associated with the ego merely by the fact of being in the collective unconscious, are definitely non-ego and must be left so. Otherwise, one is swallowed up and destroyed by them:[a]

> ...they are meant to fulfill their earthly existence with conviction and not allow themselves any spiritual inflation, otherwise they will end up in the belly of the spider. In other words, they should not set the ego in the highest place and make it the ultimate authority, but should ever be mindful of the fact that it is not sole master in its own house and is surrounded on all sides by the factor we call the unconscious.

One can approach only with caution:[b]

> The victory over the collective psyche alone yields the true value, the capture of the hoard, the invincible weapon, the magic talisman, or whatever it be that the myth deems most desirable. Therefore, whoever identifies with the collective psyche—or, in terms of the myth, lets himself be devoured by the monster—and vanishes in it, is near to the treasure that the dragon guards, but he is there by extreme constraint and to his own greatest harm.

From this, it can be seen that there is no question that, for Jung, identification with the ultimate deity would be a horrendous mistake. In his introduction to the *Tibetan Book of the Dead* he suggests that it is only Westerners who would take literally an injunction to

---

a *Collected Works*, vol. 10, para. 673.

b *Collected Works*, vol. 7, para. 261.

identify with the clear light:[a]

> The soul is assuredly not small, but the radiant Godhead itself. The West finds this statement either very dangerous, if not downright blasphemous, or else accepts it unthinkingly and then suffers from a theosophical inflation. Somehow we always have a wrong attitude to these things. But if we can master ourselves far enough to refrain from our chief error of always wanting to *do* something with things and put them to practical use, we may perhaps succeed in learning an important lesson from these teachings, or at least in appreciating the greatness of the *Bardo Thödol*, which vouchsafes to the dead man the ultimate and highest truth, that even the gods are the radiance and reflection of our own souls.

It is clear from the presentations of Action yoga given above that, contrary to Jung's warnings, the injunctions for identification are to be taken literally, to be implemented in practice. For Jung, this would be all the worse unless there were a means for mitigating the problems, which are by no means little:[b]

> According to the teachings of the *Bardo Thödol,* it is still possible for him, in each of the *Bardo* states, to reach the *Dharmakāya* by transcending the four-faced Mount Meru, provided that he does not yield to his desire to follow the "dim lights." This is as much as to say that the individual must desperately resist the dictates of reason, as we understand it, and give up the supremacy of egohood, regarded by reason as sacrosanct. What this means in practice is complete capitulation to the objective powers of the psyche, with all that this entails; a kind of figurative death, corresponding to the Judgment of the Dead in the Sidpa Bardo. It means the end of all conscious, rational, morally responsible conduct of life, and voluntary surrender to what the *Bardo Thödol* calls "karmic illusion." Karmic illusion springs from belief in a visionary world of an extremely irrational nature, which neither accords with nor derives from our rational judgments but is the exclusive product of

[a] *Collected Works,* vol. 11, para. 840.

[b] *Collected Works,* vol. 11, para. 846.

> uninhibited imagination. It is sheer dream or "fantasy," and every well-meaning person will instantly caution us against it; nor indeed can one see at first sight what is the difference between the fantasies of this kind and phantasmagoria of a lunatic.

The problems with identification—loss of essential rationality and perspective—are so great that even the alchemical model of a successful union, in which Jung invested much interest, is for him only suggestive, far from the truth. Although on the one hand he says,[a] "...the alchemist's endeavour to unite the *corpus mundum*, the purified body, with the soul is also the endeavour of the psychologist once he has succeeded in freeing the ego-conscious from contamination with the unconscious," he also holds that the aim of such grand transmutation of the collective unconscious is partly an illusion:[b]

> I hold the view that the alchemist's hope of conjuring out of matter the philosophical gold, or the panacea, or the wonderful stone, was only in part an illusion, an effect of projection; for the rest it corresponded to certain psychic facts that are of great importance in the psychology of the unconscious. As is shown by the texts and their symbolism, the alchemist projected what I have called the process of individuation into the phenomena of chemical change.

Autonomous complexes. The theoretical underpinning of Jung's caution is his estimation, based on experience both with his own quest and with patients, that complexes are autonomous:[c]

> This points also to the complex and its association material having a remarkable independence in the hierarchy of the psyche, so that one may compare the complex to revolting vassals in an empire.

Though autonomous complexes may and, in fact, *must* be approached, they never come under conscious control:[d]

> What then, scientifically speaking, is a "feeling-toned

[a] *Collected Works,* vol. 16, para. 503.

[b] *Collected Works,* vol. 12, para. 564.

[c] *Collected Works,* vol. 2, para. 1352.

[d] *Collected Works,* vol. 8, para. 201.

> complex"? It is the *image* of a certain psychic situation which is strongly accentuated emotionally and is, moreover, incompatible with the habitual attitude of consciousness. This image has a powerful inner coherence, it has its own wholeness and, in addition, a relatively high degree of autonomy, so that it is subject to the control of conscious mind to only a limited extent, and therefore behaves like an animated foreign body in the sphere of consciousness. The complex can usually be suppressed with an effort of will, but not argued out of existence, and at the first suitable opportunity it reappears in all its original strength.

Autonomous complexes seem even to have their own consciousness:[a]

> We have to thank the French psychopathologists, Pierre Janet in particular, for our knowledge today of the extreme dissociability of consciousness....These fragments subsist relatively independently of one another and can take another's place at any time, which means that each fragment possesses a high degree of autonomy....whether such small psychic fragments as complexes are also capable of a consciousness of their own is a still unanswered question. I must confess that this question has often occupied my thoughts, for complexes behave like Descartes' devils and seem to delight in playing impish tricks....As one might expect on theoretical grounds, these impish complexes are unteachable.

They have the character of splinter psyches:[b]

> But even the soberest formulation of the phenomenology of complexes cannot get round the impressive fact of their autonomy, and the deeper one penetrates into their nature—I might almost say into their biology—the more clearly do they reveal their character as splinter psyches.

And:[c]

> I have frequently observed that the typical traumatic affect

---

[a] *Collected Works,* vol. 8, para. 202.

[b] *Collected Works,* vol. 8, para. 203.

[c] *Collected Works,* vol. 16, para. 267.

> is represented in dreams as a wild and dangerous animal—a striking illustration of its autonomous nature when split off from consciousness.

Furthermore, since autonomous complexes are the very structure of even normal psychic life, they remain autonomous and cannot be fully assimilated:[a]

> I am inclined to think that autonomous complexes are among the normal phenomena of life and that they make up the structure of the unconscious psyche.

For Jung, it seems that almost everything is an autonomous complex. The soul is an autonomous complex:[b]

> Looked at historically, the soul, that many-faceted and much-interpreted concept, refers to a psychological content that must possess a certain measure of autonomy within the limits of consciousness. If this were not so, man would never have hit on the idea of attributing an independent existence to the soul, as though it were some objectively perceptible thing. It must be a content in which spontaneity is inherent, and hence also partial unconsciousness, as with every autonomous complex.

Objects of an ordinary consciousness are autonomous complexes, overvalued with psychic force, and religion seeks to collect back the libido that has been over-invested in the external:[c]

> To be like a child means to possess a treasury of accumulated libido which can constantly stream forth. The libido of the child flows into things; in this way he gains the world, then by degrees loses himself in the world (to use the language of religion) through a gradual over-valuation of things. The growing dependence on things entails the necessity of sacrifice, that is, withdrawal of libido, the severance of ties. The intuitive teachings of religion seek by this means to gather the energy together again; indeed, religion portrays this process of re-collection in its symbols.

---

[a] *Collected Works,* vol. 8, para. 218.

[b] *Collected Works,* vol. 6, para. 419.

[c] *Collected Works,* vol. 6, para. 422.

Even when this overvaluation is withdrawn, God (or let us substitute the mind of clear light or ultimate deity) becomes an autonomous complex:[a]

> If the 'soul' is a personification of unconscious contents, then, according to our previous definition, God too is an unconscious content, a personification in so far as he is thought of as personal, and an image of expression of something in so far as he is thought of as dynamic. God and the soul are essentially the same when regarded as personifications of an unconscious content. Meister Eckhart's view, therefore, is purely psychological. So long as the soul, he says, is not only in God, she is not blissful. If by "blissful" one understands a state of intense vitality, it follows from the passage quoted earlier that this state does not exist so long as the dynamic principle "God," the libido, is projected upon objects. For, so long as God, the highest value, is not in the soul, it is somewhere outside. God must be withdrawn from objects and brought into the soul, and this is a "higher state" in which God himself is "blissful." Psychologically, this means that when the libido invested in God, that is, the surplus value that has been projected, is recognized as a projection, the object loses its overpowering significance, and the surplus value consequently accrues to the individual, giving rise to a feeling of intense vitality, a new potential. God, life at its most intense, then resides in the soul, in the unconscious. But this does not mean that God has become completely unconscious in the sense that all idea of him vanishes from consciousness. It is as though the supreme value were shifted elsewhere, so that it is now found inside and not outside. Objects are no longer autonomous factors, but God has become an autonomous psychic complex. An autonomous complex, however, is always only partially conscious, since it is associated with the ego only in limited degree, and never to such an extent that the ego could wholly comprehend it, in which case it would no longer be autonomous.

Even the ego, the mediator, is an autonomous complex:[b]

---

[a] *Collected Works,* vol. 6, para. 421.

[b] *Collected Works,* vol. 2, para. 1352.

> Researches have shown that this independence is based upon an intense emotional tone, that is upon the value of the affective elements of the complex, because the 'affect' occupies in the constitution of the psyche a very independent place, and may easily break through the self-control and self-intention of the individual....For this property of the complex I have introduced the term *autonomy*. I conceive the complex to be a collection of imaginings, which, in consequence of this autonomy, is relatively independent of the central control of the consciousness, and at any moment liable to bend or cross the intentions of the individual. In so far as the meaning of the ego is psychologically nothing but a complex of imaginings held together and fixed by the coenesthetic impressions, also since its intentions or innervations are *eo ipso* stronger than those of the secondary complex (for they are disturbed by them), the complex of the ego may well be set parallel with and compared to the secondary autonomous complex.

Remarks

As we have seen, Jung's estimation of the nature of the mind does not allow for complete transformation; it is of the nature of the mind for elements to remain unconsciously imbedded in its framework, assimilatable into consciousness only in the sense of the ego's confronting them and then only in a never-ending, piecemeal way. We can speculate that, for him, identification with an ideal being—a deity—would exalt to the grandiose level of a systematic religious practice the self-inculcation of inflation and all its attendant ills. Having lost respect for and a critical attitude toward unconscious contents and their powerful influence on mental life, one would have pretentiously assimilated too much to the ego in "positive inflation," and also, due to denying the powerful autonomous contents that can wreak havoc with those who neglect them, one would eventually be overpowered by those autonomous contents—drowned in the larger self in "negative inflation."

The ideal being as whom the practitioner would be masquerading would be unable to negotiate between the needs of unconscious contents to manifest and the imperative of effective individuation, drowned in a sea of a pretension of grand, merely public affectations of compassion, love, generosity, and so forth. Self-hypnotized, closed to criticism, bloated from feeling that the very structure of pure reality is his or her own basic nature, the practitioner would lose the faculty of discrimination, the essence of a healthy psychological life. The basic problem would be the failure to recognize that since the structure of the psyche is to be found in autonomous complexes—ranging from unconscious contents in the personal unconscious, to those in the collective unconscious, to the ego itself—the primary need is to learn that these autonomous factors need to be negotiated; nothing could be worse than a pretension of grandiose control.

Possible amelioration of autonomous complexes in deity yoga

Jung's cautions are based on considerable therapeutic experience, and it should be clear that I not only do not take them lightly but am considerably impressed with his insights. Still, several provocative questions can be raised in light of the description of deity yoga in Action Tantra:

1. The use of rationality in the initial step, the ultimate deity, to penetrate the appearance of objects as if they inherently exist or exist under their power suggests that recognition and realization of emptiness, even in a nondual manner, is not a surrender to irrationality but to be done only by a highly discriminative mind. It is likely that emptiness yoga—which is aimed at overcoming the sense that phenomena, mental and otherwise, exist under their own power, autonomously—could de-autonomize complexes.
2. Much as Jung emphasizes not just the appearance of feeling-toned complexes to the conscious mind but also the conscious mind's adopting a posture of confrontation, the Buddhist division of the mind of deity yoga into an appearance factor appearing as an ideal being and an ascertainment factor realizing emptiness suggests how discrimination is maintained in the face of a profoundly different type of appearance—in this case an ideal being—despite identification with that appearance. Identification has assumed a different meaning, for the meditator merely is identifying himself or herself as that pure person designated in dependence upon purely appearing mind and body and not findable either among or separate from mind and body.

3. Admittedly, the assumption of ultimate pride—the recognition that the deity's final nature and one's own are the same—may be a compensation for the negative inflation of being overly absorbed in emptiness and thus may be an expression of positive inflation. However, it is likely that identifying that one's final nature is an absence of inherent, or autonomous, existence and that this emptiness is compatible with dependently arisen appearances counteracts positive inflation. Also, even though the final nature of a person is his or her emptiness of inherent existence, a person is not his or her emptiness of inherent existence. Similarly, even though the fundamental innate mind of clear light taught in Highest Yoga Mantra is the final basis of designation of a person, since a person is not his or her basis of designation, a person is not his or her fundamental innate mind of clear light. Furthermore, the fundamental innate mind of clear light is individual to each person. Hence, the meditation is neither that one is ultimate reality in general or the fundamental innate mind of clear light in general.

4. Just as Jung emphasizes the virtues of attention, conscientiousness, and patience as countermeasures to negative inflation—identified as too great absorption in the deeper self—so the compassionately active emanations at the point of the form deity in Action Tantra meditation establish altruism as the basic motivation and inner structure of individuation, re-appearance in ideally compassionate form, thereby establishing this practice as highly moral. The practice of transmuting depraved and deprived contents under the guise of quasi-otherness and the continuous recognition of the emptiness of inherent existence may provide a means for "teaching" even what Jung calls "impish" complexes despite his claim of their unteachability.

5. Though I have found no doctrinal injunctions corresponding to Jung's call for more than public virtues, specifically for a connection with one's own earthy self, the biographies of masters emphasize personalized feelings and reactions.[a] Also, I have

[a] For instance, five visions of Tsong-kha-pa appeared to his student Ke-drup after Tsong-kha-pa's death "during periods of (1) tearful sadness about the level of trainees he was encountering, (2) tearful sadness from his inability to penetrate the meaning of difficult points in texts, (3) tearful mindfulness of the greatness of his teacher's service to the world, (4) tearful wishfulness to be in his teacher's pres-

> observed in Tibetan monastic communities how the community serves to exert pressure on persons who have become too grandly public in their virtues—through teasing, mild derision, mimicry, and so forth. Still, the danger of retreating into a persona of fatuous, unfounded, "good character" while at the same time wreaking havoc on all those around oneself is great.

In conclusion, the transmutation sought through deity yoga involves a constellation of techniques: (1) development of positive moral qualities, (2) confrontation with neurotic contents and gradual education of them, (3) identification with the sublime, and (4) de-autonomizing objects and consciousnesses through realization of the status of phenomena and through taking emptiness and wisdom as the stuff of appearance. Jung's cautions, nevertheless, need to be heeded; his insights make it clear that deity yoga, *if* it is possible, is no easy matter.

Given its built-in safeguards and moral tone, there is the suggestion that deity yoga could actually succeed in overcoming inflation, despite the enormity of the task. Still, anyone who made such a proclamation would, most likely, be reeking with the stink of inflation.

With a sense of humility in the face of the issue that we are considering, let us take a detailed look at other elements in the Action Tantra path in the next three chapters.

---

ence given the fragility of Tsong-kha-pa's teaching remaining in the world, and (5) intense longing to rejoin his teacher." See the brief account in Tenzin Gyatso and Jeffrey Hopkins, *The Kālachakra Tantra: Rite of Initiation for the Generation Stage,* 145.

4. The Path in Action Tantra: Divine Body

In order to appreciate how tantric systems could possibly claim to bring about radical purification of defilement, it is necessary to comprehend the full breadth of the path that deity yoga encompasses. Tantric practices came to be absorbed in a highly systematized culture of internal development that reached acmes of development in Tibet and Japan, and since we are concerned with claims of efficacy, in this chapter we will continue the examination, begun in chapter two, of a highly developed tradition within Tibetan Buddhism.

Research into the historical origins of such systems would take us in a different direction that in the end would indeed enrich our understanding of the meditative cultivation that is our focus, but, in the infant stage of knowledge of these traditions outside of Asia, each inquiry must define its own field in order to avoid attempting too much and achieving nothing. Thus, here we shall not be looking backward to origins but will examine a path-structure within a developed tradition. To do this, the context of a spiritual path-structure that, within Tibet, provides the background for appreciating the significance of these practices must be made explicit. To accomplish this, I will synthesize these elements, not out of the arrogance of assuming possession of an all-encompassing, superior perspective but with considerable trepidation at attempting to communicate a meaningful portion of a highly complex, multifaceted spiritual culture that provides a context of reverberation of nuance and value.

Deity yoga in Action Tantra is not just imagination of oneself as an ideal being but, as was mentioned briefly at the beginning of chapter two, is organized in an increasingly profound series of multiphased meditations called the meditative stabilizations of exalted body, speech, and mind. Imagination of oneself as a deity (described in chapter two) is the heart of the first of these, the meditative stabilization of exalted body. One of the problems in understanding the steps of these meditations is that there exists a plethora of vocabulary for the stages of the path even just in Action Tantra that must have developed over centuries and was co-opted and amalgamated under a single system. For instance, mention has been made of the meditative stabilizations of exalted body, speech, and mind which provide a basic framework for the entire path, but another framework, "concentration with repetition [of mantra]" and "concentration without repetition [of mantra]" is also used. One would expect that repetition of mantra would be confined to the meditative stabilization of exalted speech and that "concentration without repetition [of mantra]" would not involve mantra sounds, but neither of these seemingly innocuous assumptions is true, as will be detailed below.

Also, how do these rubrics fit together with other ones such as the cultivation of calm abiding and special insight? Or yoga with signs and yoga without signs? Or prior approximation, effecting achievement of feats, and activities? Or the five paths and ten grounds? These sets of vocabulary, which seldom involve equivalent terms, offer a variety of intertwining approaches for viewing the path of Action Tantra that enrich and foster appreciation of its complex structure. By immersing ourselves in the detail of this path with its intricate and overlapping terminology, the boundaries of which are often in question,[a] we will advance discussion of the issues raised at the end of the last chapter.

As sources for an exposition of Action Tantra, I am primarily using texts stemming from the delineation of the path of Action Tantra found in Tsong-kha-pa's *Great Exposition of Secret Mantra*. There, he presents the general mode of procedure of Action Tantra, applicable to deities of all three Action Tantra lineages—One-Gone-Thus, lotus, and vajra. This division into general and specific modes of procedure mirrors a division of the tantras in this class into two types, general ones that present the path and surrounding activities in a manner that is suitable for all three lineages and specific ones that are concerned with a particular deity and lineage.

Tsong-kha-pa draws his exposition of the general meditation from what his student Ke-drup[b] identifies as the four general Action Tantras—the *General Secret Tantra*,[c] the *Questions of Subāhu Tantra*,[d]

---

[a] For a chart of this Action Tantra meditation as well as a meditation manual extracted from Tsong-kha-pa's text see chapter 7.

[b] Lessing and Wayman, *Mkhas Grub Rje's Fundamentals of the Buddhist Tantras*, 134.23. Ke-drup reports that the list is in terms of their respective lengths, the first being the longest.

[c] *spyi'i cho ga gsang ba'i rgyud, sāmānyavidhīnām guhyatantra;* P429, vol. 9.

[d] *dpung bzang gis zhus pa'i rgyud, subāhuparipṛcchātantra;* P428, vol. 9.

the *Susiddhi Tantra*,[a] and the *Concentration Continuation Tantra*.[b] As the late-fifteenth- and early-sixteenth-century Ge-luk scholar Paṇ-chen Sö-nam-drak-pa[c] says:[d]

> [The Action Tantras of the three lineages in general] are the *General Secret Tantra*, the *Susiddhi*, the *Questions of Subāhu*, and the *Concentration Continuation*. The first of these teaches the maṇḍala rites of Action Tantra in general, ranging from the rite for the place [where initiation will be conferred] through the bestowal of initiation. It also sets forth the three thousand five hundred maṇḍalas related with the three lineages.
>
> The *Susiddhi Tantra* teaches the approximation and the achievement related with the fierce Susiddhi, the details of his activities, and those topics in the presentation of initiation in the *General Secret Tantra* that need supplement. The *Questions of Subāhu* teaches the measure of [having completed] approximation of the deities indicated in the *General Secret Tantra* and the *Susiddhi* as well as how to achieve limitless activities.
>
> The Action Tantra *Concentration Continuation* teaches the mode of progressing on the paths in Action Tantra in general—the concentrations of the four branches of repetition, abiding in fire, abiding in sound, and bestowing liberation at the end of sound as well as what to do before and after those, rites for [achieving] yogic feats, rites of burnt offering, how to practice, in what sort of place, and so forth.

Tsong-kha-pa briefly cites the *General Secret Tantra* in connection with initiation, which is the main topic of that tantra, and cites the *Questions of Subāhu* only a few times—with regard to how to repeat mantra, qualities of calm abiding, and achieving feats—but his presentation is mainly structured around copious usage, cited and

---

[a] *legs grub kyi rgyud, susiddhitantra;* P431, vol. 9.

[b] *bsam gtan phyi ma rim par phye pa, dhyānottarapaṭalakrama;* P430, vol. 9.

[c] *paṇ chen bsod nams grags pa*, 1478-1554.

[d] *Presentation of the General Tantra Sets: Captivating the Minds of the Fortunate* (*rgyud sde spyi'i rnam par bzhag pa skal bzang gi yid 'phrog*), as cited in *Deity Yoga*, 246-247. See also the translation in Panchen Sonam Dragpa, *Overview of Buddhist Tantra*, trans. by Martin J. Boord and Losang Norbu Tsonawa (Dharmsala, India: Library of Tibetan Works and Archives, 1996), 28-29.

uncited, of the *Concentration Continuation* and the *Susiddhi*, with their commentaries by Buddhaguhya[a] and Varabodhi[b] respectively. The *Concentration Continuation* and Buddhaguhya's commentary present the actual meditations very clearly but do not detail the preliminary rites, the pledges, and so forth, which Tsong-kha-pa takes from the *Susiddhi* and Varabodhi's formulation of it into a daily practice rite called a "means of achievement."[c] Almost all of Tsong-kha-pa's presentation can be found in these two tantras and two commentaries. His creative innovation was to interweave them into a complete system of practice of this class of Tantra.

Structure of the Action Tantra path

The practice of deity yoga is employed in order to become close to, or approximate, the state of a deity—a pure, ideal being—and hence it is found, but not exclusively, in a phase called "prior approximation"[d] within the triad of prior approximation, effecting achievement of feats, and activities. "Prior approximation" is a prerequisite to techniques, such as making offerings in fire or performing special series of repetitions of mantra, to induce achievement of unusual yogic feats.[e] These feats are in three categories:[f]

1. *pacification*[g] such as avoiding untimely death, illnesses, epidemics, harmful influences, and contagion
2. *increase*[h] such as lengthening life span, youth, magnificence, power, qualities of realization, and resources
3. *ferocity*[i] such as killing, expelling, or confusing harmful beings.

These accomplishments—which also include clairvoyance, the

---

[a] *sangs rgyas gsang ba;* eighth century. His commentary is *bsam gtan phyi ma rim par phye ba rgya cher bshad pa, dhyānottarapaṭalaṭīkā;* P3495, vol. 78.

[b] In Tibetan, his name is usually *byang chub mchog,* but Dül-dzin-drak-pa-gyel-tsen calls him *ye shes mchog.* Also called Vilāsavajra, he flourished in roughly the same period as Buddhaguhya, the eighth century, and his commentary is *legs par grub par byed pa'i sgrub pa'i thabs bsdus pa, susiddhikarasādhanasaṃgraha;* P3890, vol. 79.

[c] *sgrub thabs, sādhana.*

[d] *sngon du bsnyen pa.*

[e] *dngos grub, siddhi.*

[f] *Deity Yoga,* 174.

[g] *zhi ba.*

[h] *rgyas pa.*

[i] *drag po/ drag shul.*

capacity to understand all treatises immediately upon reading them, and so forth—are sought in order to enhance the power of the yoga that comprises prior approximation. Thus, although the triad of prior approximation, effecting achievement of feats, and engaging in altruistic activities suggests a movement from the first to the last, the yoga that constitutes the first phase is the most important. The feats that allow a practitioner to perform special activities for the benefit of others bring about merit that further enhances the capacity of this same yoga so that Buddhahood can be achieved. Let us turn to the many steps of the yoga of prior approximation.

Prior approximation

As Tsong-kha-pa's student Ke-drup clearly says in his *Extensive Explanation of the Format of the General Tantra Sets,*[a] the phase of prior approximation is divided into two parts—concentration with repetition and concentration without repetition. The first also is called the "four-branched repetition," the four branches being (1) imagination of a deity in front of oneself, (2) imagination of oneself as a deity, (3) imagination of a moon disc sometimes at the heart of the deity in front and sometimes at one's own heart, and (4) imagination of the written letters of the mantra, set upright around the edge of the moon disc. Repetition of mantra is *eventually* performed within constant maintenance of these four elements, and thus the entire first phase, much of which does not involve repetition of mantra, is called the "four-branched repetition."

The concentration with repetition is preceded by many activities that serve as preparations for it, conveniently included within the concentration with repetition by dividing it into two parts—preliminaries and the actual four-branched repetition. Since the actual yoga is our main concern, the preliminaries will be discussed only briefly here.

Preliminaries to concentration with repetition

The preliminaries are in four parts, concerned with establishing the motivational and the physical context in which the yoga will be conducted. They precede imagination of a deity in front of oneself

[a] Lessing and Wayman, *Mkhas Grub Rje's Fundamentals of the Buddhist Tantras,* 158.1.

and involve extensive preparation for the visit of a deity, who is treated like a guest. Practitioners establish themselves in humility, altruism, self-sacrifice, and pure perception in the first phase and then bathe and enter the sacred place of yoga. Offerings are cleansed of obstructors (including autonomous complexes) and then blessed into a state of magnificence. The practitioners themselves as well as the place are similarly protected from the interfering influence of obstructors. The overall structure is that first mostly *mental* adjustments in motivation, attitude, and perception are made, after which *external* adjustments, enacted both physically and mentally, are taken.

Tantric systems often treat as external forces what many other psychologies would consider internal; in Jungian terms, the wisdom behind this tantric externalization is that autonomous complexes are thereby confronted in a manner preventing identification with them and thus being overpowered by them. Also, the contemporary psychological exaggeration in which complexes are considered to be "mine" as if they were somehow within one's sphere of control becomes impossible. On the negative side, excessive projection onto the environment could lead to misidentifying as external the source of what are actually internal problems with the result that one becomes paranoically concerned with outside forces—be these beings on a different plane or just other people in one's environment—which are actually projections of one's own afflictive emotions. Indeed, some practitioners seem caught in a process of external projection that they seek to relieve through the performance of rites. Still, I do not want to fall into the arrogance of the assumption that *only* projection is involved; I by no means feel justified in assuming that there are not harmful (or helpful) external entities on a subtle level.

Let us list the preliminaries to concentration with repetition:[a]

What to do initially in the place of dwelling

Making the seal and reciting the mantra of the general lineage
Homage to the Buddhas and Bodhisattvas
Offering oneself
Refuge and altruistic mind generation
Protection through mantra and seal
Reflection on purity

[a] For detail see below, 167ff., and *Deity Yoga*, 79-101.

Going outside

How to bathe outside and enter the place of practice

Bathing

Picking up earth

Self-protection

Expelling obstructors in the body

Creating vajra armor

Dispelling obstructors

Casting mantra into the water

Mantrafying the earth

Ablution

Protecting and tying up the hair

Mantrafying, circling, and rubbing earth on the body

Stirring the water

Offering to the Three Jewels

Pouring water on the head

Inviting the deity and bathing his/her body

Entering the temple and engaging in the pledges

Having dressed and sat on the cushion, blessing the offerings

Removing contamination

Sprinkling the cushion and sitting

Putting on the circlet, *kusha* grass sprinkler, head binder, and image of the crown protrusion

Dispelling obstructors

Generating magnificence

Protecting oneself and the place

Self-protection

Making a seal and reciting a mantra for expelling obstructors in the body

Repeating the mantra for all activities into scented water and sprinkling it on yourself, dispelling obstructors

Place-protection

Sprinkling

Creating the ritual dagger

Fumigating

Binding obstructors

Creating a fence

Creating a latticework

Closing off the area

Many of the steps are concerned with cleansing the environment and oneself of "obstructors"—these being protection through mantra and seal, self-protection, expelling obstructors in the body, creating vajra armor, dispelling obstructors, removing contamination, again dispelling obstructors, self-protection, and the seven steps of place-protection. The number of times that such rituals are performed suggests that we live in a world bombarded with counterproductive forces, whether their source be external or internal, and that ordinary life is buffeted and swayed by them. When these are understood to include autonomous complexes (as I think they should be), the picture is of a mind subject to a continuous barrage of influences of its own making, much like Freud's depiction of the unconscious as a seething cauldron of repressed impulses seeking expression, necessary to be held in check, constantly afflicting one's perceptions and interactions but, for the most part, working unseen havoc. The practitioners themselves, their place of practice, the water with which they bathe, the dirt (like a soap) they use to wash their bodies, their hair, the deity to be invited, and the offerings to be given to the deity are cleansed of the contamination of these forces. At the end of the preparations, all obstructors in the area are bound, and then in what would be redundant were it not for the near uncontrollability of such contents (remember Jung's reference to their "impishness"), a fence is erected to keep out obstructors. This not being enough, a roof of interlaced vajras is erected on the fence, and a blazing mass of fire outside all of this closes off the area. Now that elements causing interference and interruption have been put at bay, the meditation can begin.

It is said that on the night before the dawn of his enlightenment Shākyamuni Buddha conquered with the meditative stabilization of love a host of demons, attractive and unattractive, that appeared to him. At this point in tantric meditation, however, a massive defense-structure to keep demons away is erected, albeit within a motivation of love and compassion. Perhaps these defenses are used to create a space in which a basically diseased mind can begin to create positive mental forces, but it is also possible that they are used within a context of projection and denial and are aimed at forestalling recognition of their origin within oneself. It is not difficult to imagine that someone attempting this yoga could become a rather nasty person to live with, constantly projecting inner impulses onto the environment and fighting against others in order to ward off evil forces that actually are that person's own afflictive emotions. Still, the quasi-otherness with which these forces are treated constitutes recognition that despite the basic Buddhist doctrine that contamination is from within, the extent of this contamination is so great, so difficult to face, so intimately associated with our being and, when it becomes close to consciousness, so liable to overpower the personality, that it is necessary to treat them under the guise of otherness. Earlier, we saw how Jung's descriptions of the problems attendant upon inflation revealed the enormity of the enterprise of deity yoga; here, from within this traditional system itself, we gain a sense of the condition of the ordinary mind as swamped in a sea of karmically created forces. Again, a picture of the enormity of the task of purification that is at the heart of deity yoga is painted.

Actual concentration with repetition

"Concentration with repetition" refers to meditation that eventually involves repetition of mantra but does not necessarily do so at all times. Repetition is performed within continuous and intense concentration on oneself as a deity and a similar deity in front of oneself. As was mentioned earlier, it is called "four-branched" because it requires maintenance of four factors:

1. imagination of a deity in front of oneself, called "other-base"
2. imagination of oneself as a deity, called "self-base"
3. imagination of a moon disc sometimes at the heart of the deity in front and sometimes at one's own heart, called "mind"
4. imagination of the written letters of the mantra, set upright around the edge of the moon disc, called "sound."

The forms of the mantra letters standing around the edge of the moon are not sounds but are called "sound." The Action Tantra that Buddhaguhya uses as the prime source for the mode of meditation, the *Concentration Continuation* (which Ke-drup[a] says is called this because it is a continuation of or supplement to the Action Tantra called the *Vajroṣhṇīṣha*),[b] refers to these four by condensing the two

---

[a] Lessing and Wayman, *Mkhas Grub Rje's Fundamentals of the Buddhist Tantras*, 136.18.

[b] Buddhaguhya (P3495, vol. 78, 73.2.5) also says that it is called "*Concentration Continuation*" because of presenting the later concentrations, that is, those following the initial practices explained earlier in the *Vajroṣhṇīṣha* (*rdo rje gtsug tor gyi rgyud*). Thus, in my translation of the title, the word "Continuation" can refer either to

"bases" into one and reversing their order, most likely for the sake of euphony: "Flow to sound, mind, and base."[a] The *Concentration Continuation* itself does not explain what these four are, since they were explained earlier in the *Vajroṣhṇīṣha Tantra* (which is no longer extant in the original and was not translated into Tibetan but is known through Buddhaguhya's commentary on the *Concentration Continuation*). As Buddhaguhya says:[b]

> The characteristics of the branches of repetition and so forth, such as sound, mind, and base, are not explained here because they were explained in this Tantra [the *Vajroṣhṇīṣha*] at the beginning. The characteristics that were explained there are these: "Sound" is [the forms of] mantra letters. "Mind" is the manifestation of a moon disc that is the base of the mantra. One "base" is the entity of a One-Gone-Thus's body. The second base is one's own [appearance in the] form of a deity.

The same format of four branches is used in what has come to be considered the chief Performance Tantra, the *Vairochanābhisambodhi*:[c]

> "Letter" is the mind of enlightenment [appearing as a moon].
> The second ["letters"] are called "sounds" [the forms of the letters on the moon].
> "Base" is to imagine one's own body
> As that of one's deity.
> That called the second base
> Is a perfect Buddha [imagined

---

this tantra's being a continuation of the earlier tantra or to the concentrations that are continuations of those explained in the earlier tantra; the two meanings are indeed compatible. According to the latter etymology, it could be translated as the "*Later Concentrations.*" As Buddhaguhya says (*Deity Yoga,* 55), the *Vajroṣhṇīṣha* explains the four branches, and the *Concentration Continuation* explains the remaining steps.

[a] *sgra dang sems dang gzhi la gzhol;* P430, vol. 9, 55.3.4. Buddhaguhya's commentary is P3495, vol. 78, 73.2.7 and 73.4.1. In *Deity Yoga* (55 and 141), I have made the line more accessible by translating it in the order of meditation, "Flow to the bases, mind, and sound."

[b] *Deity Yoga,* 55.

[c] Ibid., 56 and 192. Buddhaguhya cites the passage in his commentary on the *Concentration Continuation,* P3495, vol. 78, 73.3.3.

> In front], the best of the two-legged.

The deity imagined in front and the deity as whom one imagines oneself are called "bases" because they are the places where the mantra letters are imagined on a moon disc—they are bases for the moon and the mantra letters.

When the central activity is meditation, the imagination of a deity in front is performed first, at least by beginners. This is because it involves a *variety* of activities related with inviting the deity and thus would be distracting to *one*-pointed meditation on one's own divine body that is to be done within stopping even the breath.[a] As the *Concentration Continuation Tantra* says:[b]

> The intelligent who dwell in yoga
> Contemplate the presence of a One-Gone-to-Bliss[c]
> Only having first made offerings
> To the image of a deity's body.

First, offerings and so forth are made to a deity imagined in front of oneself, and then one meditatively imagines oneself to be a deity, that is to say, contemplates oneself as being a Buddha. "Offerings" are just illustrative; all of the other preliminary practices are to be done prior to self-generation by those "intelligent," that is to say, competent, practitioners who are fully capable of deity yoga.

First branch: other-base—a deity in front [d]

A principal reason for inviting a deity is to serve as a recipient of virtuous activities such as making offerings, praising, and worshipping the deity as well as to witness the virtuous activity of one's cultivating an altruistic attitude. Thus, the external deity—not oneself imagined as a deity—is called a field, or basis, for the accumulation of merit, that is to say, a context for the development of internal power producing beneficent effects. A basic Buddhist perspective is that all pleasurable and painful circumstances and feelings are produced through the force of internal potencies established by former actions; here one is exerting influence on one's own future experiences by intentionally engaging in positive activities of body,

---

[a] Tsong-kha-pa's explanation in *Deity Yoga,* 113.

[b] Stanza 8; P430, vol. 9, 53.3.2; see *Deity Yoga,* 103.

[c] *bde bar gshegs pa, sugata.*

[d] In *Deity Yoga,* this stage is described on 19-20, 115-138, and 215.

speech, and mind. To heighten the force of these activities, one imagines that they are done in the presence of a divine being, the enhanced force probably coming both from increased attention (such as when receiving a high official) and also from the fact that the deity subsists in accordance with reality, and thus the deity's existence is founded, not on the distortions of desire, hatred, and ignorance, but on wisdom and compassion. Also, imagining a deity separate from oneself aids in the process of imagining oneself with divine body, speech, and mind, much as merely perceiving our companions (or actors in a movie) has an influence on how we perceive ourselves.

Neither the *Concentration Continuation Tantra* nor Buddhaguhya's commentary on it describe the practices involved in imagining a deity in front of oneself; therefore, Tsong-kha-pa draws his explanation of these from the *Susiddhi Tantra* and Varabodhi's formulation of it into a rite of daily practice called a Means of Achievement.[a]

Imagining a divine residence.[b] The deity will arrive with his or her own palace magically coming together with the resident, but one imagines such a residence in front of oneself into which the actual palace of the deity will merge when the deity arrives. To help in imagining the residence and the deity, practitioners often hang up a painting or set up a statue in front of their place of meditation. They meditate on emptiness and then imagine that all the features of the divine residence appear from within emptiness.

The divine residence is not just a palace but also a land of jewels of cosmic proportions covered with grains of gold, in the middle of which is an ocean, white like milk, adorned with flowers. Birds that are as if made of jewels fly over the ocean. In the middle of the ocean is the great square Mount Meru with stairs on all four sides, made respectively of gold, silver, sapphire, and topaz. The mountain is covered with wish-granting trees, themselves adorned with thousands of flapping victory banners. On top of the mountain is a huge lotus—its stalk adorned with jewels, petals made of jewels, a gold corolla, and topaz anthers. On the lotus is an empty inestimable mansion, a palace imagined either as appearing together with the land and so forth, or as emerging from the

---

[a] *sgrub thabs, sādhana.*

[b] *Deity Yoga,* 19 and 115-117.

transformation of the Sanskrit syllable *bhrūṃ,* standing upright in the middle of the lotus. In the middle of the palace is another lotus, this one serving as a seat for the deity, yet to appear. Instantaneously, a huge canopy appears over the palace.

If done sequentially, practitioners imagine this grand setting in four phases—first the ground, then the ocean with flowers and birds, then the mountain with lotus and residence, and finally the canopy. After the first three phases, the practitioner makes what have been imagined more magnificent by blessing them with mantra—*oṃ calavī hūṃ svāhā* recited once for the ground, *oṃ vimaladhaha hūṃ* recited once for the ocean with flowers and birds, and *namaḥ sarvatathāgatānāṃ sarvathā udgate spharaṇahimaṃ gaganakhaṃ svāhā* recited a hundred times for the mountain with lotus and residence. With the mantra recitation, the objects imagined become even brighter. (One need only do this to recognize its value as a technique for enhancing visualization.)

From a Jungian point of view, practitioners are being asked to utilize not creative imagination but the results of another person's creative imagination, in which a certain visionary content has appeared, reflecting that person's own psychic situationality. The effectiveness of the visualization could be questioned from the viewpoint that it does not allow a meditator to develop his or her own particular expressiveness, essential to unlocking the passageway to deeper layers of mind. This qualm is difficult to answer, but it seems to me that this type of meditation with its grand dimensions, its reliance on basic elements—land, ocean, mountain, flower, and palace—as well the richness of imagery ranging from its size to the substances are evocative of basic psychic forms, archetypes. Also, there is room for much personal adaptation of the imagery, but indeed not of the basic variety that Jung's depiction of creative imagination would yield.

The formality of this Action Tantra system of meditation also stands in stark contrast to the Nying-ma practice of the Great Completeness in which, in a phase called "spontaneity," the mind is allowed to display appearance upon appearance to the point where, as the Nying-ma lama Khetsun Sangpo said, the whole cosmos becomes like a giant movie screen. Though this Nying-ma practice has similarities with Jungian creative imagination, it is markedly different in that the meditator is not seeking to become involved in the imagery but is, instead, using the practice to allow the latent fecundity of the mind to develop in manifest form. The aim is to bring this display of appearances to its fullest peak by not getting involved with it, after which the display naturally subsides, leaving direct perception of reality. The meditator of the Great Completeness is looking not for a central image to develop as in creative imagination but for the imagistic power of the mind to completely ripen into manifest perception of the the noumenon (ultimate reality). Here in Action Tantra visualization practices, on the other hand, the mind is being gradually opened to new levels through systematically proceeding through carefully framed steps.

Inviting the deity.[a] The meditator has previously prepared an oblation, like a drink to be offered a visitor; the substance of the vessel (gold, silver, stone, wood, and so forth) and the contents (barley and milk, sesame and yogurt, cow urine and rice, and so forth) are determined by the feat that one is seeking to receive from the deity after completing the meditations. Now the practitioner blesses the oblation into a magnificent state and is ready to invite the deity.

In his commentary on Tsong-kha-pa's text, the Dalai Lama[b] explains that form bodies of Buddhas can appear instantaneously to a faithful person and thus do not have to come from one place to another but that for persons bound by the conception of inherent existence it is helpful to imagine inviting a deity from a Pure Land and to treat the deity in a manner modeled after the reception of a special visitor. That actual divine beings can appear anywhere at any time suggests that our minds are closed—by the conception that objects exist solidly from their own side—to the fecundity of reality, that we are bound, closed, and shut off from the richness of our own situation. In the process of breaking out of the prison of oversolidified conception, we may need to use the rules of the confines, inviting a deity to come, with palace and full retinue filling space, from a distant land.

The invitation is done through making a beckoning gesture with the hands, called a "seal of invitation" (such gestures are called "seals" most likely because, like a seal that guarantees a promise, they do not deviate from their specific symbolization, which in this case is to invite the deity). The practitioner says:

---

[a] *Deity Yoga,* 20 and 117-122.

[b] Ibid., 20.

Due to my faith and [your compassionate] pledges[a]
Come here, come here, O Supramundane Victor.
Accepting this oblation of mine,
Be pleased with me through this offering.

A mantra appropriate to the invited deity is recited, and the practitioner assumes a posture corresponding to that of the deity—standing, sitting, bent to one side, and so on—and holds up the oblation to entice the deity to come. If the proper ingredients have not been obtained, the practitioner begs the deity's pardon, much as we do when we have not been able to provide the full complement of food and drink at a dinner party.

The deity arrives and is offered a seat either with the appropriate hand-gesture and mantra or by reciting:[b]

It is good that the compassionate Supramundane Victor has come.
I am meritorious and fortunate.
Taking my oblation,
Please pay heed
[To me] and grant [my request].

The guest is clearly not an equal but a superior powerful being who can grant favors. Practitioners curry favor with the deity, who is an appearance of a superior level of their own minds projected externally. That such projective techniques are used indicates the difficulty of achieving enlightenment—that the conscious mind must be manipulated out of its adherence to a limited state.

Displaying hand-gestures. The mind has been heightened through imagining the arrival of an ideal being, and it is probably for the sake of making this firm that the practitioner now recites once the mantra *śaṃkare samaye svāhā,* displaying the pledge vajra seal and then the hand-gesture appropriate to the lineage of the practitioner along with the lineage essence-mantra—*jinajik* for the One-Gone-Thus lineage, *ārolik* for the lotus lineage, and *vajradhṛk* for the vajra lineage, the three lineages corresponding to three levels of practitioners. The hand-gestures at this point seem a bit like the private handshakes of fraternal clubs, indicating recognition of the other

[a] Deities have made pledges, previously while training, to be available to serve sentient beings; the practitioner is calling on such a pledge.

[b] *Deity Yoga,* 122.

person and identifying oneself as being of the same club, as well as being means of keeping interlopers away.

The invitation to a divine being has provided an avenue for the practitioner to come into contact with positive forces deep in his or her mind, but it also has opened the way for obstructive contents to appear; so, one drives them away by circling the great pledge hand-gesture of one's lineage. As Tsong-kha-pa says:[a]

> This is said to afford great protection from all evil deeds by obstructors who arrive after [the achievement of deities due to one's own karma and conceptions], and so forth.

That when one's mind has become opened, both greater good and greater evil arrive suggests that a prime reason for an ordinary person's being shut off from the amazing potential of the mind is that we employ dullness as a defense mechanism to keep evil tendencies at bay. We are locked within a stultified mode of operation of mind, not just out of inattention to our potential but out of fear and a need to control forces lurking within.

Here in this ritual, by imagining a pure being the current psychological system-level is enlarged; a higher system-level is tapped, requiring a different type of defense against corresponding forces of evil. This is the problem with gradualistic expansion and development; it is not a mere adjustment of perceptions but an opening up of previously unused layers of mind not under one's control; one arrives like a vassal in a kingdom with new and different rulers. Unlike the manifestation of the fundamental innate mind of clear light in Highest Yoga Mantra which is beyond the combat between good and evil and which itself is the resolution of all conflict, the gradualistic opening up of the mind *toward* that level (for those who cannot immediately manifest the most profound level of mind) requires that the present system-level become gradually re-educated and re-organized in order to handle the forces unleashed with each enhancement. As the tantric abbot Ngawang Lekden[b] put it, "With each advancement, there is a corresponding strengthening of bad forces."

Offering to the deity. Not only is evil thwarted with various techniques, but also the good is reinforced with devotional acts. Offerings are presented, most likely to strengthen one's

---

[a] Ibid., 122.

[b] *ngag dbang legs ldan,* 1900-1971.

commitment to the right and the pure through committing resources to it.

The practitioner rids the offerings of obstructors, cleanses them, and blesses them into a magnificent state, these ritual activities again suggesting that objects of common perception are overlain with autonomous images obstructing perception of their actual nature. The false solidity of objects into which our perceptions are mired is composed of imagistic overlays incited by correspondences with past perceptions and eliciting places for suppressed and repressed contents to find expression. The ritual removal of these encrustations is a forerunner of the force of wisdom realizing the absence of inherent existence that first makes afflictive emotions impossible and then removes the appearance of objects as if they existed concretely from their own side. As a precursor of wisdom through a correspondence of activity, the repeated performance of such ritual cleansing and enhancement must also help to induce wisdom.

The articles offered are the oblation already mentioned, a foot-bath, a bath through pouring water on an image of the deity in a mirror, clothing, adornments, music, perfume, flowers, incense, food, and lamps. These are performed with hand-gestures and recitation of a stanza appropriate to the particular article as well as a mantra at the end. For instance, the flower-offering is made with:

> I offer with faith these flowers
> Of auspicious divine substance,
> Grown from the clean, most clean.
> Receiving them, be pleased with me.
> *Āhara āhara sarvavidyādhari pūjite svāhā.*

As the Dalai Lama says:[a]

> The offerings prescribed are distinctly Indian, being geared to receiving a guest in a hot country—cool water for the feet, a cool drink, a garland for the head, fragrant perfume for the feet, sprinkling of water, and so forth.

The process of visualizing a visit by a special being in his/her palace is reminiscent of a child's imagining a doll-house and then engaging in all sorts of marvelous activities that teach the child how to act—family roles and so forth.

---

[a] Ibid., 20.

Praising. The practitioner raises up songs of praise, first for the Three Jewels—Buddha, his doctrine, and the spiritual community—and then for the lords of the three lineages, these being Mañjushrī who is the physical manifestation of the wisdom of all Buddhas, Avalokiteshvara who is the physical manifestation of the compassion of all Buddhas, and Vajrapāṇi who is the physical manifestation of the power of all Buddhas. This triad of wisdom, compassion, and power mirrors the three principal qualities of Buddhahood, the character-traits that practitioners are seeking to develop. Praising the three deities with lines extolling these very qualities serves to strengthen the practitioner's commitment to their development.

> Homage also to Mañjushrī,
> Bearer of the appearance of a youth,
> Vividly adorned with the lamp of wisdom,
> Dispeller of the three worlds' darkness.
>
> Homage to the always merciful,
> Whose name is Avalokiteshvara,
> Composite of all excellent qualities,
> Strongly praised by all the Buddhas.
>
> Homage to Vajrapāṇi,
> Powerful and fierce,
> Virtuous king of knowledge-mantra,
> Tamer of the hard to tame.

By imagining in front of oneself beings who have wisdom, compassion, and power to their fullest degree, practitioners mix their minds with states currently beyond them, thereby exerting a pull toward these qualities.

The directionality suggested by this practice is a far cry from the abject, amoral submission to unconscious forces that Jung warned Westerners against in undertaking "Eastern yoga." We can see that this system is replete with techniques, positive and negative, for developing what Jung sought—a strong ego that can mitigate the demands of expression of the unconscious and the requirement that one's conscious mind not become enslaved by the contents that manifest.

Worship. These techniques take quintessential form in the seven-branched service—disclosure of ill deeds; taking refuge in Buddha, his doctrine, and the spiritual community; generating altruism; admiration of one's own and others' virtues; entreaty of the Buddhas to remain teaching; supplication to them not to withdraw physical appearance so beneficial to the world; and prayer-wishes. The first is to confess or, more literally, to *disclose* previous ill deeds, to cease hiding them, for it is wisely said that when ill deeds are hidden, their force increases daily, no doubt due to identifying with them. Fear of disclosure usually comes from not wanting to have to identify with one's deeds, but actually it appears that disclosure allows one, after the pain of open identification, to cease identifying with those deeds.

The practice involves being regretful for what has been done and being committed not to repeat the activity in the future and is accompanied by the enactment of a specific virtuous action aimed at atoning for the misdeed. It is a technique for releasing oneself from the sway, the autonomous force, of past negative actions. The *Susiddhi Tantra,* from which Tsong-kha-pa takes his text for the seven-branched service, prescribes disclosure this way:

> Ones-Gone-Thus residing in all
> Directions of the worlds,
> Foe Destroyers,[a] and Bodhisattvas,

---

[a] *dgra bcom pa, arhan.* With respect to the translation of *arhan* (*dgra bcom pa*) as "Foe Destroyer," I do this to accord with the usual Tibetan translation of the term and to assist in capturing the flavor of oral and written traditions that frequently refer to this etymology. Arhats have overcome the foe which is the afflictive emotions (*nyon mongs, kleśa*), the chief of which is ignorance, the conception (according to the Consequence School) that persons and phenomena are established by way of their own character.

The Indian and Tibetan translators were also aware of the etymology of *arhant* as "worthy one," as they translated the name of the purported founder of the Jaina system, Arhat, as *mchod 'od,* "Worthy of Worship" (see Jam-yang-shay-pa's *Great Exposition of Tenets, ka,* 62a.3). Also, they were aware of Chandrakīrti's gloss of the term as "Worthy One" in his *Clear Words:*

> *sadevamānuṣāsurāl lokāt pūnārhatvād arhannityuchyate* (Poussin, 486.5), *lha dang mi dang lha ma yin du bcas pa'i 'jig rten gyis mchod par 'os pas dgra bcom pa zhes brjod la* (409.20, Tibetan Cultural Printing Press edition; also, P5260, vol. 98, 75.2.2): "Because of being worthy of worship by the world of gods, humans, and demigods, they are called Arhats."

Also, they were aware of Haribhadra's twofold etymology in his *Illumination of the Eight Thousand Stanza Perfection of Wisdom Sūtra;* in the context of the list of epithets qualifying the retinue of Buddha at the beginning of the Sūtra (see Unrai Wogihara, ed., *Abhisamayālaṃkārālokā Prajñā-pāramitā-vyākhyā, The Work of Haribhadra*

I ask you to heed me.

Whatever ill deeds
I have committed in any lifetime,
Or, disturbed by the power of desire,
Stupidity, or anger in cyclic existence
In former lives or in this life,
Whatever ill deeds I have done,
Asked others to do, or admired even a little,
Even slight ones unconscientiously done
With body, speech, or mind
To Buddha, doctrine, or spiritual community,
Or gurus, father and mother,
Foe Destroyers, Bodhisattvas,
Or any object of giving,
Or to other sentient beings—
Educated or uneducated—
Having mentally collected all these,
I bow down in great respect

[Tokyo: The Toyo Bunko, 1932-5; reprint ed., Tokyo: Sankibo Buddhist Book Store, 1973], 8.18), Haribhadra says:

> They are called *arhant* [=Worthy One, from root *arh* "to be worthy"] since they are worthy of worship, of religious donations, and of being assembled together in a group, and so forth (Wogihara, 9.8-9.9: *sarva evātra pūjā-dakṣiṇā-gaṇa-parikarṣādy-ārhatay**ārhantaḥ**;* P5189, 67.5.7: *'dir thams cad kyang mchod pa dang // yon dang tshogs su 'dub la sogs par 'os pas na dgra bcom pa'o*).

Also:

> They are called *arhant* [= Foe Destroyer, *arihan*] because they have destroyed (*hata*) the foe (*ari*). (Wogihara, 10.18: *hatāritvād* ***arhantaḥ;*** P5189, 69.3.6: *dgra rnams bcom pas na dgra bcom pa'o*).

(My thanks to Gareth Sparham for the references to Haribhadra.) Thus, we are not dealing with an ignorant misconception of a term, but a considered preference in the face of alternative etymologies—"Foe Destroyer" requiring a not unusual *i* infix to make *ari-han*, *ari* meaning enemy and *han* meaning to kill, and thus "Foe Destroyer." Unfortunately, one word in English cannot convey both this meaning and "Worthy of Worship"; thus, I have gone with what clearly has become the predominant meaning in Tibet. (For an excellent discussion of the two etymologies of *arhat* in Buddhism and Jainism, see L.M. Joshi's "Facets of Jaina Religiousness in Comparative Light," L.D. Series 85 [Ahmedabad: L.D. Institute of Indology, May 1981], 53-58.)

To the perfect Buddhas and their children[a]
Manifest before me now
And disclose individually
And repeatedly my mistakes
With pressed palms and saddened mind.

Just as the perfect Buddhas know
The ill deeds that I have committed,
I make individual disclosure.
Henceforth I will not do such.

The meaning of the last stanza is that, not being omniscient, one does not know all the ill deeds that one has done over the beginningless course of lifetimes, and thus one also makes a general disclosure of all the ill deeds that omniscient beings know one has done. Implicitly, the important message is communicated that it is impossible to hide ill deeds.

Given that one of the most pernicious defenses against inner forces is denial, the general Buddhist notion that over the course of lifetimes we have committed every possible misdeed and have, in our mental continuums, forces predisposed to committing these again provides a healthy perspective, certainly not preventing denial on all levels (since the depths of our own depravity are not easy to recognize) but opening the way to conscious recognition of what lies beneath the surface. To disclose, to confess all of these ill deeds is to affirm their presence, thereby weakening the force of denial and strengthening the ego as the arbiter, rather than the victim, of these forces.

To speak of these seven practices in brief: *Refuge* in the Three Jewels establishes the long-term perspective that help will be sought by incorporating the doctrine through practice. *Altruistic mind generation* makes compassion the basis of relationships with others. *Admiration* of one's own and others' virtues reinforces commitment to those activities; unlike pride which shuts off development of further qualities, admiration of virtues (or nonvirtues) promotes their continuance and development. *Entreaty* for continued teaching and *supplication* for spiritual teachers to remain in the world reinforces connection with the sources of doctrines that when attempted in practical implementation, conflict with

[a] That is, Bodhisattvas.

tendencies acquired over lifetimes and thus are uncomfortable, causing counterproductive wishes that the teachings and teachers of such doctrine not remain. These counterproductive wishes are countered through praying that the Buddhas and their teachings remain forever in the world. Complexes are being put on notice that one will persist in practices that compromise their autonomy.

In the last phase of the seven-branched service, *prayer-wishes* are made or, more literally, planted. Wishes, as a form of meditation, are powerful techniques for influencing the unfolding of the future, for they direct the course of one's mind—they shape, they order the future. Wishes for the well-being of all persons, oneself included, are to be made within what Tsong-kha-pa[a] calls "one-pointed attention to the meaning"; thus, wishes are not mere whims, mere passing fancies of what might be, but are cultivated repeatedly and concentratedly. The prayer-wishes that Tsong-kha-pa draws from the *Susiddhi Tantra* are:[b]

> Just as the earlier Buddha children
> Made prayer-wishes,
> I also with a virtuous mind
> Plant prayer-wishes in that way.
>
> May all beings have happiness,
> Peace, and freedom from disease.
> May I be capable in all activities
> And also possess all good qualities.
>
> May I be wealthy, generous,
> Intelligent, and patient,
> Having faith in virtue, memory
> Of former births in all lives, and mercy.

Since wishes shape the manifestation of virtuous forces, one makes them both for others' prosperity and for one's own. In addition, because both consciously and unconsciously our perceptions of others serve as models for our own development, wishes for others' success also have an advantageous effect on our own future.

Cultivating altruism in the presence of the deity. Prayer-wishes are followed by cultivation of the four immeasurables—compassion,

---

[a] *Deity Yoga*, 136.

[b] Ibid., 136.

love, joy, and equanimity.[a] Nāgārjuna speaks of the great power of love in his *Precious Garland:*[b]

> Even three times a day to offer
> Three hundred cooking pots of food
> Does not match a portion of the merit
> In one instant of love.
>
> Though [through love] you are not liberated
> You will attain the eight good qualities of love,
> Gods and humans will be friendly,
> Even [nonhumans] will protect you,
>
> You will have mental pleasures and many [physical] pleasures,
> Poison and weapons will not harm you,
> Without striving you will attain your aims,
> And be reborn in the world of Brahmā.

Love has the power not only to make others be friendly but to grant protection even from poison and weapons. During lectures at Harvard University in 1981, the Dalai Lama similarly spoke of the power of love when asked about the meaning of a certain class of demon:[c]

> Devaputra demons are classified among the six categories of gods in the Desire Realm, specifically in the class called "Those Enjoying Control over Others' Emanations." We ourselves have formerly been born in that type of life within cyclic existence. All of us have acted as horrible demons, all of us! With regard to techniques that can be employed if one is being bothered by such a demon, in the Mantra

---

[a] The more usual order is with equanimity last; however, Kensur Ngawang Lekden, abbot of the Tantric College of Lower Lhasa (*rgyud smad*) before escaping Tibet in 1959, frequently taught that equanimity is practiced first among the four immeasurables in Great Vehicle practice. Tsong-kha-pa (*Deity Yoga*, 136) has a different order—compassion, love, joy, and equanimity—with equanimity meaning cultivation of the thought, "May they [all creatures stricken with suffering] pass from sorrow with the unsurpassed nirvāṇa of a Buddha."

[b] Stanzas 283-285; see Jeffrey Hopkins, *Buddhist Advice for Living and Liberation: Nāgārjuna's Precious Garland* (Ithaca, N.Y.: Snow Lion Publications, 1998), 130-131.

[c] His Holiness the Dalai Lama, *The Dalai Lama at Harvard*, trans. and ed. by Jeffrey Hopkins (Ithaca, N.Y.: Snow Lion Publications, 1989), 153.

> system there are meditations of a wheel of protection, but the best of all techniques is to cultivate love. When Shākyamuni Buddha, from among the twelve great deeds of his lifetime, performed the deed of taming demons the night before his enlightenment, he did it by way of cultivating the meditative stabilization of love.
>
> Sometimes, when one has a bad dream or nightmare and awakens, even if one repeats mantra or meditates on a wheel of protection, these will not help, but when one cultivates love, it cures the situation. This is the best technique.

Altruism has such great power probably because love and compassion—wishing for all *equally* to attain happiness and overcome suffering—as well as the ability to take joy in others' achievement of happiness do not separate one off from others, but through sympathy and empathy bond one to them. This bonding takes from unfriendly objects such as the ghouls of nightmares the autonomous power that fear has granted them.

The stanzas drawn from the *Susiddhi Tantra* that Tsong-kha-pa uses for this practice are rich with wishes for bringing beneficence to all beings:[a]

> In order to pacify the suffering
> Of limitless realms of sentient beings,
> To release them from bad transmigrations,
> Liberate them from afflictive emotions,
> And protect them completely
> From the varieties of sufferings
> When the discomforts of cyclic existence crowd in,
> I will generate an altruistic intention to become enlightened.
>
> May I always be a refuge
> For all destitute sentient beings,
> A protector of the protectorless,
> A support of those without support,
> A refuge for the unprotected,
> Maker of the miserable happy.
>
> May I cause the pacification

[a] *Deity Yoga*, 136-137.

Of all sentient beings' afflictive emotions.
May whatever virtuous actions
I have accumulated in this and other lives
Assume the aspects of the collections
That are called merit and wisdom.

May whatever effort I make
By way of the six perfections
Be of benefit to all beings
Without there being any exception.

Making effort until enlightenment,
I will strive at actions temporarily
And limitlessly over lives so that, in short,
All the afflictive emotions of all sentient beings
May be pacified and they be freed.

This single-pointed dedication to the welfare of others comes not from a Sūtra practice brought over to Mantra but from the *Susiddhi Tantra* itself. Still, the techniques for the practice of altruism are laid out in greater detail in the Sūtra system, and to get a sense of their impact the Dalai Lama advises readers to turn to a description of them.[a] Without intimate exposure to one's own hatreds that these practices force and a clear perception of the value of persisting at the development of positive attitudes, it is impossible to understand how the tantric enterprise could succeed. Tsong-kha-pa emphasizes the need for the development of such altruism prior even to attainment of tantric initiation.[b]

With cultivation of the four immeasurables, the practices of the first of the four branches of repetition, called "other-base," are now complete. It is clear that a deity is invited into one's presence in order to heighten virtuous activities by moving the mind to another level. The extensive cleansing of the place before the practice and the high reception of the guest serve to heighten the mind, generating a sense of the unusual, of the special, of awe, with the result that succeeding activities are done with more intensity, more

---

[a] See, for instance, His Holiness the Dalai Lama, *How to Expand Love: Widening the Circle of Loving Relationships,* trans. and ed. by Jeffrey Hopkins (New York: Atria Books/Simon and Schuster, 2005) and Jeffrey Hopkins, *The Tantric Distinction* (London: Wisdom Publications, 1984), 58-74.

[b] See *Tantra in Tibet,* 165-168.

feeling.

This first branch from among the four branches of repetition is the tantric equivalent of the first step mentioned earlier (40) in relation to meditating on selflessness in the Sūtra system—taking refuge and re-adjusting the motivation in an altruistic direction. The fact that practice begins with cultivation of a compassionate motivation is evidence that this Tantra system is by no means a turn away from the high altruism of the Sūtra systems but is founded on such altruism in its own right. In this formulation of tantric practice following the *Susiddhi Tantra* and the *Concentration Continuation Tantra* and the commentaries by the Indian scholars Buddhaguhya and Varabodhi, altruism is integral to Mantra.

Second branch: self-base—oneself as a deity

It will be remembered that we are describing the phase of prior approximation and, from within that, the meditative stabilization of exalted body. Now that the many activities involved in imagining a deity in front of oneself have been completed, the practitioner can imagine him/herself as a deity. The *Concentration Continuation Tantra* says:[a]

> Afterwards, freed from the limbs,
> [Suchness is] not discriminated,
> Thoroughly devoid of discrimination, and subtle.
> Unmoving and clear, mental analysis remains in its presence.

"Afterwards," that is, after making offering and so forth to the deity invited in front of oneself, one meditatively cultivates the ultimate deity, the first of the six steps involved in self-generation. One reflects on one's own suchness, which is "freed from the limbs," or senses, in that the senses do not ultimately exist. Also, one's own suchness, being formless, is not apprehended by others and thus is not "discriminated" by others, and it itself does not apprehend forms and so forth and thus is "Thoroughly devoid of discrimination." One's own suchness is an absence of inherent existence, and this absence also does not inherently exist; hence, it is "subtle." "Mental analysis," or examination with wisdom, reveals one's own emptiness of inherent existence and in this sense "remains in the

---

[a] P430, vol. 9, 53.3.2; *Deity Yoga,* 105 and 168-171.

presence" of one's final nature; this analysis should be "unmoving"—endowed with stability free from excitement—and "clear," that is to say, free from laxity.

The six-step process of imagining oneself as a deity, called the six deities, is described in detail above in chapter two, and thus, here I will merely list the six with brief identifications.

1. Ultimate deity: meditation on oneself and the deity as the same in terms of being empty of inherent existence.
2. Sound deity: the appearance of the mind of wisdom—realizing emptiness—as the sounds of the mantra reverberating in space.
3. Letter deity: the appearance of the forms of the mantra letters around the edge of a flat moon disc in space.
4. Form deity: the moon and mantra letters transform such that a hand-symbol also appears on the moon. Then, from all of these emanate rays of light from which myriad forms of the deity emerge. The deities emanate great clouds piled with offerings that they offer to already enlightened beings. The deities also emanate great clouds from which a rain-stream of ambrosia descends, cleansing and satisfying all other beings. The rays of light, as well as the myriad forms of the deity, return and enter the moon disc, hand symbol, and mantra, which transform into the full form of the deity.
5. Seal deity: blessing into a heightened state important places in the divine body with hand-gestures.
6. Sign deity: meditation on the divine body with clear appearance and divine pride.

Let us consider two points of terminology:

- In the second step, the sound deity, the mind of wisdom realizing the sameness of oneself and a deity in terms of final nature appears as the sounds of the mantra of the deity as whom one will emerge later in the fourth step, but the sound deity does not involve what is termed "repetition of mantra," even though the mantra is resounding repeatedly in space. This is because none of these six steps involves any voiced, whispered, or mental repetition. Still, the meditations of the six deities are part of what is called the "concentration with repetition" not because they themselves involve repetition of mantra but because they form the foundation of eventual repetition, as will be seen in the next chapter.

- During the cultivation of "self-base" through the rite of the six deities, the mind is mainly held to one's own body imagined as a deity. Thus, up through the first two of the four branches—these four being the causal conditions that form a base for the repetition of mantra—the meditations are called the "meditative stabilization of exalted body."

Practitioners have imagined a deity in front and then themselves as a deity; at this point, they repeat the rites of offering and praising but this time to themselves, since they are now deities.[a] To imagine that oneself is being made offerings and is being praised might seem to be egregious self-aggrandizement (positive inflation in Jung's terms), and indeed one of the purposes is to heighten and enhance one's sense of a pure self acting in relation to other beings *but* within the context of an emptiness of inherent existence. Offering and praising oneself bring home the point that emptiness, far from implying nonexistence or nonfunctionality, is the key for existence and functionality. Offering and praising vivify the mind, awakening potential in the face of emptiness yoga, which, when not understood in its fullness, can lead to self-abasement and even stultification (negative inflation in Jung's terms).

One might expect the meditation to proceed with imagining the other two of the four branches—mind (moon) and sound—but, since those are concerned with mantra repetition and thus with the meditative stabilization of exalted speech, one does not continue on to imagine a moon disc and the "sounds," the latter actually being the letters of the mantra set around the edge of the moon disc at the heart. Rather, one remains meditating on one's own divine body. As Dül-dzin-drak-pa-gyel-tsen says:[b]

> After having cultivated the six deities—the form deity and so forth as explained above—you should one-pointedly take cognizance of the firm pride of being a deity and observe the clear divine form and also bind the inhalation and exhalation of breath, [thereby] achieving a firm meditative stability free from laxity and excitement.

Let us consider this pithy statement of the process of meditation in detail, but first, what is to be done with the deity imagined in front

---

[a] Ibid., 114.

[b] 467.4.

of oneself? Tsong-kha-pa[a] indicates that one possibility is to cause the invited deity (who, being the actual deity, is called a "wisdom-being") to enter oneself (who, being only an imagined deity until this point, is called a "pledge-being").

With the entry of the wisdom-being, one becomes the actual deity, in the context of which one meditates on the clear appearance of one's body as an actual divine body. Then, from time to time, one again visualizes the deity in front and holds the mind on that divine body, within maintaining a less emphasized observation of oneself as a deity.[b] Tsong-kha-pa does not say why switching to meditating on the deity in front is done, but it can be extrapolated from later explanations that it is for the sake of keeping the mind alert. It also brings the increasingly strong perception of purity into a relationship with another being.

For the meditation to be successful, two factors are needed—clarity and the stability of being able to stay on the object. Clear appearance is achieved through a style of meditation called here "concentration" (*bsam gtan, dhyāna*),[c] which involves observing *many* aspects, either the six deities themselves or the specifics of the divine body—the color, the hand symbol, the shape of particular parts of the body—and correcting their appearance by adjusting clarity and so forth. Then, stability is achieved through a style of meditation called "meditative stabilization" (*ting nge 'dzin, samādhi*), which involves dwelling one-pointedly either on the divine body in general or on a particular part.

This usage of the term "meditative stabilization" is not to be confused with that in the term "meditative stabilization of exalted body," for even the phase called "concentration" is included within the meditative stabilization of exalted body. Similarly, this usage of the term "concentration" is not to be confused with that in the term "concentration with repetition," for even the style of meditation called "meditative stabilization" is included within

---

[a] *Deity Yoga*, 137-138.

[b] Tsong-kha-pa implicitly suggests that a meditator could forego the step of causing the deity in front to enter oneself, and proceed with reflecting on one's own divine body within the sense that the deity in front is present but not as an object of attention; then, after a considerable period of meditating on one's own divine body, one would switch to putting the emphasis on the deity in front.

[c] See *Deity Yoga*, 25 and 110-113.

concentration with repetition.[a]

The *Concentration Continuation Tantra* describes these two types of meditation:[b]

> Having set oneself thus,
> Meditate with the mantra minds.
> Restrained, dwell in meditative stabilization.
> Thoroughly restrain vitality and exertion.

The "mantra minds" are the six deities. "Meditate" means that one's mental continuum is to be suffused with these six through the style of meditation called "concentration," which is to contemplate in series the various aspects of the divine body, adjusting their shape, color, and so forth. "Dwell in meditative stabilization" indicates the other style of meditation, which is to fixate on either the divine body in general or one aspect of it within restraining "vitality" (breath) and "exertion" (distraction).

Thus, first a meditator scans through the entire divine body in the phase called "concentration"; since one is noticing and adjusting the appearance of the various parts of the divine body, this is called "analytical meditation."[c] Then, when one fixes one-pointedly on either the general body or a particular part in "meditative stabilization," the type of meditation is called "stabilizing meditation."[d] As Tsong-kha-pa says:[e]

> Concerning this, initially it is necessary to generate a composite of *clarity* of the divine body and *dwelling* for a long time on it. Therefore, clear appearance must be achieved by means of concentration having many aspects because it arises from repeatedly putting in mind the aspects with which one is familiarizing, as is the case with conditioning to desire or fright [whereupon their objects appear vividly to the mind. Also,] if [the mind] is not set one-pointedly [on the divine body], then even though clear appearance arises, one cannot remain on a single object of observation as

---

[a] It will be remembered that the concentration with repetition does not involve repetition of mantra at this point.

[b] P430, vol. 9, 53.3.3; *Deity Yoga,* 109 and 110.

[c] *dpyad sgom.*

[d] *'jog sgom.*

[e] *Deity Yoga,* 164.

> much as one wishes. Thus, it is [also] necessary to fixate by means of one-pointed meditative stabilization.

The examples given for the way that "concentration"—which is repeatedly to put in mind the various aspects of an object—brings about clear appearance of the object are the processes that occur when becoming desirous or fearful; in both cases, features of the object, be they attractive or repulsive, are taken to mind again and again, whereupon the object stands, so to speak, in front of oneself, compelling attention.

Once the object appears clearly, it is necessary to fixate on it, considering not many aspects but only one, which can be either the divine body in general or a particular part such as the head. To assist in this, a meditator employs breath control. Even though both "concentration" and "meditative stabilization" require the "binding of the inhalation and exhalation of breath" as Dül-dzin-drak-pa-gyel-tsen words it, "meditative stabilization" requires an intense form of the practice of breath control, and thus *prāṇāyāma*[a]—the restraining of vitality[b] (which means breath or wind) and exertion[c] (which means distraction)—is usually explained in the context of "meditative stabilization."[d]

In the term *prāṇāyāma, prāṇa* is taken to mean vitality, which means not just breath but also the wind (or energy) that enters and emerges through the eyes, ears, nose, mouth, navel, sex organ, anus, and hair-pores. The wind or energy on which consciousness rides moves through these openings, and thus to control the mind, the wind that moves through these pathways is to be reversed and held inside. Also, *yāma*[e] is taken to mean "exertion," which, in turn, is glossed as mindfulness, not in the good sense of keeping in mind a virtuous object but in the bad sense of distractedly taking something else to mind (it seems to me the tradition is enjoying playing with the vocabulary); distraction also must be restrained. Putting Buddhaguhya's description of this process into his own words,

---

[a] *srog rtsol.*

[b] *srog.*

[c] *rtsol ba.*

[d] *Deity Yoga,* 112.

[e] *Āyāma* means stretching, extending, restraining, stopping, which yield etymologies for *prāṇāyāma* in other contexts as "extending life" (*srog sring ba*) and "stopping breath" (*srog dgag pa*); here, my guess is that the etymology is drawn from *yāma* as in *vyāma* (*rtsol ba*), "exertion."

Tsong-kha-pa says:[a]

> Bind these two in this way: Stop the exhalation and inhalation of breath; withdraw inside movements of the breath throughout the body like a turtle's retracting its limbs and like like drinking water drawn up with the tongue by means of the upwards-moving wind.[b] Also, withdraw inside the usual intense movement of the nonequipoised mind out through the senses. Nevertheless, leave your eyes a little open, raise your face a little, and set yourself in one-pointed meditative equipoise, observing your own body clarified as a deity. The observation should be done like that of a person dwelling in a cave and looking outside.

The meditator withdraws the winds that travel throughout and outside the body, like a turtle withdrawing its limbs or like drinking water with your tongue, sucking it inward—the images giving a sense of what it feels like to withdraw these energies. The meditator has the sense of being within the divine body, most likely at the heart region, viewing the divine body much like a person in a cave looking outside, not outside the body but at the insides of the body from a vantage point—the image of looking from a cave conveying a sense of containment but not utter withdrawal as into sleep.

This etymology of *prāṇāyāma* with *prāṇa* being taken as wind and *yāma* as mindfulness, with the implicit understanding that these are to be stopped, accords with a passage in the *Vairochanābhisambodhi Tantra* that says:[c]

> "*Prāṇa*" is explained as wind,
> "*Yāma*" as mindfulness.

In another etymology, however, *prāṇa* is taken as wind, and *āyāma* is taken as meaning "stopping"; the compound *prāṇāyāma* is thus taken to mean "stopping wind," or ceasing exhalation and inhalation.[d] Despite the different etymologies, the term comes to have the

---

[a] *Deity Yoga*, 111.

[b] *gyen rgyu'i rlung.*

[c] Ibid., 56 and 192. The actual passage is cited in P3495, vol. 78, 78.3.3.

[d] The term has, in general, been translated into Tibetan as *srog rtsol* in accordance with the first etymology. My usage of "vitality and exertion" as a translation equivalent can create difficulties in those instances when an author views it as meaning "stopping wind" (*srog dgag pa*).

same meaning. In Highest Yoga Mantra, however, *prāṇāyāma* has a different meaning, for it refers to stopping the movement of the winds in the right and left channels in order to cause them to enter, remain, and dissolve in the central channel, whereupon subtler levels of consciousness dawn. The form of *prāṇāyāma* specific to Highest Yoga Mantra is performed during its second and last stage, the completion stage, whereas here in Action Tantra it is performed during the early stages of holding the mind on the divine body. This type of *prāṇāyāma,* as opposed to that specific to Highest Yoga Mantra, is also required during early phases of the practice of Highest Yoga Mantra when meditation on a divine body is performed.

Here in this Action Tantra practice, meditators hold the breath while observing one part of the divine body, and then when no longer able to hold the breath, let it out gently, relaxing by viewing their general divine body,[a] and then they return to viewing the same specific aspect within holding the breath. Viewing the general body when exhaling is a technique of resting within intense meditation; it differs from other forms of resting done when tired, a principal technique there being to repeat mantra[b] (though still not to be confused with later, more advanced phases of meditation in the concentration with repetition that call for repetition of mantra within specific visualizations). The process of holding the breath while viewing a specific part of the body and of exhaling while viewing the general body is continued until immovable clear perception of the divine body in all situations, both in and out of formal meditation, is gained along with the firm sense of the "pride" of being the deity. One is seeking to stop the "pride" of ordinariness—that is to say, taking pride in being ordinary, the sense of having an ordinary mind and body and the sense of being an ordinary person designated in dependence upon ordinary mind and body.

Imagination is used in order to replace limited and stultified mind and body with superior forms of these, whereby a new sense of selfhood develops—compassionate, wise, and pure. Realization of emptiness clearly is not seen as a way to obliterate the self; it is just the opposite; it is a means to unleash the innate capacity for pure

---

[a] If the object of "meditative stabilization" has been the general divine body instead of a specific part, then with exhalation one views the general body more loosely. See the Dalai Lama's explanation in *Deity Yoga,* 26.

[b] Ibid., 138.

motivation and expression. This can only be done if the meditation is clear and steady, "a firm meditative stability free from laxity and excitement," as Dül-dzin-drak-pa-gyel-tsen says. This requires a level of meditative one-pointedness called "calm abiding,"[a] which is achieved in complete form in the meditative stabilization of exalted speech, to be discussed in the next chapter, but is begun during the meditative stabilization of exalted body. As a technique aimed toward achieving calm abiding, meditators employ the stopping of breath and distraction, dwelling as much as possible on the appearance of divine form and the sense of being an ideal person.

From within prior approximation, we have now finished discussing cultivation of the meditative stabilization of exalted body, which comprises the first two of the four branches of concentration with repetition: other-base, self-base, mind, and sound.

[a] *zhi gnas, śamatha.*

5. Mantra Repetition

When meditators gain the capacity to remain within visualization of their own body as a deity's, they proceed to cultivate the meditative stabilization of exalted speech. The stated general purpose of cultivating the meditative stabilizations of exalted body and exalted speech is to achieve calm abiding, a powerfully focused mind that, when teamed with wisdom and brought to the level of direct perception of emptiness, can overcome—from the root—afflictive emotions such as desire and hatred. At that point, afflictive emotions are not just replaced through thinking about something else, not merely suppressed through thinking about their faults, not merely repressed through defense mechanisms, and not merely sublimated through becoming conscious of them. They are totally and forever removed in a gradual process that extirpates increasingly subtle levels of desire, hatred, and ignorance until they are entirely uprooted. This is the claim that we are exploring through gaining a comprehensive picture of the path in Action Tantra; it would be difficult to come to a conclusion on whether the practices could be *this* effective, but detailing the complexity and profundity of this religious culture will tease our minds into considering the possibility.

A question that needs first to be settled is just when a meditator is to proceed from cultivating the meditative stabilization of exalted body to cultivating that of exalted speech. It is clear that actual calm abiding is achieved at the end of the meditative stabilization of exalted speech,[a] but when, during the well laid out process of cultivating calm abiding, does one switch from mainly concentrating on divine body to concentrating on mantra? To appreciate speculation on this question and gain a sense of one of the chief purposes of the meditative stabilizations of exalted body and speech, let us consider briefly the process of developing calm abiding from Sūtra system presentations, since even though calm abiding is integral to Mantra, it is described in more detail in the Sūtra systems.

---

[a] In his introduction to Tsong-kha-pa's text, the Dalai Lama (*Deity Yoga*, 29) says, "The concentration of abiding in sound is the time of achieving a fully qualified calm abiding (*śamatha*), an effortless and spontaneous meditative stabilization induced by physical and mental pliancy."

Tibetan descriptions of the process of achieving calm abiding often combine two Indian presentations—Maitreya's depiction of five faults and eight antidotes in his *Differentiation of the Middle and the Extremes*[a] and Asaṅga's depiction of nine states called "mental abidings" and of four mental engagements in his *Grounds of Hearers* and *Summary of Manifest Knowledge*. I will give a brief synopsis of this combined exposition.

Calm abiding

About achieving calm abiding, Maitreya's *Differentiation of the Middle and the Extremes* says:[b]

> It arises from the cause of implementing
> The eight activities[c] abandoning the five faults.

"Activities" here are antidotes counteracting the five faults, which are:

1. laziness
2. forgetting the instruction on the object of meditation
3. laxity and excitement—the mind's being too loose or too tight
4. nonapplication of antidotes when laxity and excitement arise
5. overapplication of antidotes when laxity and excitement are no longer present.

Laziness includes not only the *indolence* of attachment to sleeping and so forth, *procrastination,* and a *sense of inadequacy* in which one thinks, "How could someone like myself accomplish calm abiding!" but also *attachment to bad activities* such as those of desire or hatred.

---

[a] *dbus dang mtha' rnam par 'byed pa, madhyāntavibhaṅga.* The exposition of calm abiding is drawn to a great extent from Hopkins, *Meditation on Emptiness,* 67-88. For lengthy treatments of calm abiding, see Gedün Lodrö, *Calm Abiding and Special Insight,* trans. and ed. by Jeffrey Hopkins (Ithaca, N.Y.: Snow Lion Publications, 1998), 11-213, and Lati Rinbochay, Denma Lochö Rinbochay, Leah Zahler, and Jeffrey Hopkins, *Meditative States in Tibetan Buddhism* (London: Wisdom Publications, 1983), 52-91.

[b] IV.3b. The Sanskrit is: *pañcadoṣaprahāṇā 'ṣṭasaṃskārā 'sevanā 'nvayā.* See Ramchandra Pandeya, ed., *Madhyānta-Vibhāga-Śāstra* (Delhi: Motilal Banarsidass, 1971), 129. For English translations see the Bibliography.

[c] That is to say, antidotes.

Chart 1: Faults of Meditative Stabilization and Their Antidotes

Faults	*Antidotes*
laziness	faith aspiration exertion pliancy
forgetting the object of meditation	mindfulness
[nonidentification of] laxity and excitement	introspection
nonapplication	application
application	desisting from application

Of the eight antidotes, four are prescribed as counteragents to laziness—faith, aspiration, exertion, and pliancy. In this context, faith refers to being *captivated* with the advantages of meditative stabilization as well as *wishing* to attain those qualities and *being convinced* of those advantages. The cultivation of faith calls for reflecting on the disadvantages of not having meditative stabilization—namely, the faults of distraction—as well as the beneficial results of being endowed with meditative stabilization, such as being able, when teamed with wisdom, to remove afflictive emotions from their root. In dependence upon such faith, aspiration seeking meditative stabilization arises. This, in turn, induces the exertion necessary to achieve it. Eventually, exertion at the process of meditative stabilization yields pliancy which makes laziness impossible; however, since pliancy comes only after long experience, it is not relevant at the beginning, except in that reflection on the advantages of meditative stabilization induces enthusiasm for practice.

The fifth antidote, mindfulness, is prescribed as an antidote to the fault of forgetting the object. As cited by Tsong-kha-pa in his presentation of Yoga Tantra, Shākyamitra quotes Bhāvaviveka's graphic description of the process of bringing the mind under control. Tsong-kha-pa says:[a]

> With regard to the way to hold the mind, Shākyamitra[b] cites Bhāvaviveka's *Heart of the Middle*[c] and says to do it that

[a] H.H the Dalai Lama, Tsong-kha-pa, and Hopkins, *Yoga Tantra: Paths to Magical Feats*, 94.

[b] Toh. 2503, *sde dge* edition, vol. *yi*, 154b.4.

[c] *dbu ma'i snying po, madhyamakahṛdaya;* P5255, vol. 96, 4.1.7.

way:

> The crazy elephant of the mind behaving wildly
> Is tied to the pillar of an object of observation
> With the rope of mindfulness.
> By degrees it is brought under control with the
> hook of wisdom.

"Wisdom" here is introspection.[a] Hence, the example of taming an elephant indicates the achievement of a serviceable mind by way of the two—mindfulness and introspection. The subtle vajra that is the base on which the mind is being set is like the stable pillar to which the elephant is tied. The unserviceable mind is like an untamed elephant. Causing the mind not to be distracted from its object of observation through relying on mindfulness is like using a rope to tie an elephant. Setting [the mind] free from fault—when it does not hold the object of observation as [originally] set—through immediately recognizing such by means of introspection is like a herder's hitting an elephant with his hook and correcting it when it strays from the tie-up.

The elephant of the mind is being tied to the pole of an object of observation—in this case, one's own divine body—with the rope of mindfulness so that it can be brought under control by the hook of introspection. Mindfulness is a faculty that, in increasing degrees, keeps the mind from losing its object; it is gained by constantly returning the mind to the object. The sixth antidote, introspection, inspects from time to time to determine whether laxity and excitement (the third fault) are present.

Laxity primarily refers to the mind's being too loose; in its worst form, one has as if entered into darkness, losing the object of meditation entirely. A middling form of laxity occurs when the mind stays on the object but without clarity—"clarity" here referring to a quality of mental alertness; a subtle form occurs when the mind stays on the object and with clarity but without *intense* clarity. Thus, it is possible for meditators to be deceived into thinking they have achieved meditative stabilization when they are actually stuck in subtle laxity because the object appears clearly and the mind remains clearly and stably on it, but they have not recognized that

---

[a] *shes bzhin, saṃprajanya.*

the clarity of mind lacks intensity.

Excitement, on the other hand, is primarily a scattering of the mind to an object of desire, although, by extension, it includes all types of scattering, whether the object be virtuous, nonvirtuous, or neutral. Again, there are levels of excitement; in the worst version, the object is entirely captivated with something else, but in the subtler version the mind remains on its object with a tendency to fast-moving thought underneath. The latter is compared to water moving about under a frozen river.

The sixth antidote, introspection, is a counteragent to *nonrecognition* of laxity and excitement. The actual antidote to these two is the application of techniques to rid the mind of whichever of these faults is present; thus, the seventh antidote is called "application" of the antidotes, which serves to counteract the fourth fault, nonapplication.

The techniques for removing laxity and excitement are presented in series beginning with the least intrusive. (As will be seen, in Action Tantra the meditative stabilizations of exalted body and speech contain important factors enhancing these techniques.) For laxity, there are five levels of counteragents to apply. Since laxity is a looseness in the mind's mode of holding the object, the first and least intrusive method is merely to tighten the mode of apprehension of the mind a little. The process is compared to tightening the strings on a musical instrument; how much to tighten can be known only through experience. If this does not work, the next level is to increase the object's brightness or to notice the details of the object, or to move it higher. (In the Action Tantra system of meditation that we have been considering, the technique of blessing parts of the body into a state of magnificence, this being during the "seal deity," helps in this regard as does the very process of the style of meditation called "concentration" in which the practitioner reviews the appearance of the various parts of the deity's body, adjusting for color, brightness, and so forth—the act of attention to detail itself being a way of making the mode of apprehension of the mind more taut. Also, the spreading out of light rays removes laxity.)

Then, if that does not work, since laxity must nevertheless be removed, one leaves the main object of observation—here, one's own divine body—and invigorates the mind by reflecting on something joyous, such as the marvelous fortune of having attained a human life, the wonderful qualities of the Three Jewels, the benefits of altruism, or the benefits of meditative stabilization. This level of technique requires that the meditator has previously engaged in analysis of these topics so that, as soon as they are considered, their respective impact manifests, thereby invigorating the mind. Otherwise, a neophyte at these contemplations would have to engage in multifaceted analytical meditation in order to generate the requisite feelings, in which case the attempt at creating one-pointedness of mind would become diverted. The Dalai Lama, speaking about applying this level of antidote to laxity and excitement, says:[a]

> A person who is cultivating calm abiding needs to be in a state where such reflections will move the mind immediately. Therefore, prior to working at achieving calm abiding, it is necessary to have become convinced about many topics—such as those involved in the four establishments in mindfulness—through a considerable amount of analysis. In an actual session of cultivating calm abiding, one is performing stabilizing meditation, not analytical meditation, but if one has engaged in considerable analysis of these topics previously, the force of the previous reflection remains with the mind and can be recalled. Thus, when you switch to such topics in order either to elevate or to lower the mind, the mind will be immediately affected. In this way, if ascertainment has been generated previously, then reflecting on the value of meditative stabilization or the value of a human lifetime will immediately heighten the mind, and reflection on sobering topics such as the nature of the body or the ugliness of objects of desire will immediately lower its mode of apprehension.

Considerable prior reflection is needed is order to make use of the force of such attitudes when they are needed. Then, as soon as the mind heightens, one returns to the original object, so as not to become distracted.

Similarly, one could take to mind a particularly luminous object or imagine great acts of charity (one could imagine putting groceries on every table, for instance). However, if even these do not

---

[a] *The Dalai Lama at Harvard,* 148.

work, there is what is called a "forceful method," which is to imagine one's mind as a drop of white light at the heart and, with the sound *phaṭ,* imagine that it exits from the crown of the head high into the sky and mixes with the sky. (It is said that the technique is not dangerous, but I nevertheless wonder whether it is suited for all.) If laxity is still not overcome, then the only recourse is to leave the meditative session, since to remain in the session would mean that one is cultivating laxity, and this would have the counterproductive effect of promoting general dullness of mind. It is recommended that one walk about, throw cold water on the face, look far off into the distance, and so forth.

With respect to corresponding techniques to counteract excitement, the first level is to loosen the mode of apprehension of the mind. Then, if that does not work, the object can be lowered and imagined as being heavy (dense) and oily in nature. If that does not work, then since one has not been able to remove excitement within staying on the object, one temporarily switches objects, reflecting on a topic that sobers the mind, such as impermanence, death, the sufferings of the various levels of cyclic existence, and so forth. As before, it is said that unless the meditator has previous acquaintance with these topics, it is hard for them to be effective, although with acquaintance they are very effective. Still, if this does not remove excitement, the forceful method is to observe the breath, thinking, "Inhaling, exhaling," or counting to ten and back to one. If this does not work, the only choice is to leave the session.

If, in applying these antidotes, they are successful, then to keep applying them when they are no longer needed is counterproductive, and thus the fifth and last fault is overapplication of the antidotes, which is countered by the eighth antidote, desisting from application of them.

When meditators successfully work at removing these five faults through the eight antidotes, they gradually pass through nine states, culminating in a tenth, which is calm abiding itself. The states are called the "nine mental abidings."[a] (See the chart on the next page.)

[a] *sems gnas dgu, navākārā cittasthiti.*

Chart 2: States and Factors in Achieving Calm Abiding

(Read from bottom to top.)

<table>
<tr><th>Six Powers</th><th>Nine Mental Abidings</th><th>Four Mental Engagements</th></tr>
<tr><td rowspan="2">familiarity</td><td>9. setting in equipoise</td><td>spontaneous engagement</td></tr>
<tr><td>8. making one-pointed</td><td>uninterrupted engagement</td></tr>
<tr><td rowspan="2">effort</td><td>7. thorough pacifying</td><td rowspan="5">interrupted engagement</td></tr>
<tr><td>6. pacifying</td></tr>
<tr><td rowspan="2">introspection</td><td>5. disciplining</td></tr>
<tr><td>4. close setting</td></tr>
<tr><td>mindfulness</td><td>3. resetting</td></tr>
<tr><td>thinking</td><td>2. continuous setting</td><td rowspan="2">forcible engagement</td></tr>
<tr><td>hearing</td><td>1. setting the mind</td></tr>
</table>

At the first level, called "setting the mind,"[a] through the power of having heard about the value of meditative stabilization, one tries to set the mind on the object of observation. During this state, distraction far exceeds periods of remaining on the object, and, due to the fact that one is trying to keep the mind on the object and thus is noticing that the mind wanders from topic to topic, there is the sense that thought is increasing. Then, the second level, "continuous setting"[b] is achieved when, through the power of thinking about the object over and over, one can extend the continuum of attention a little, even though distraction still exceeds being able to stay on the object. With the third state, called "resetting,"[c] mindfulness is able to re-tie the mind to the object, like putting a patch on clothing, through recognizing distraction. At this level, the ability to remain on the object exceeds the periods of distraction, and thus one has risen to the level of "meditating" from among the triad of hearing, thinking, and meditating. This level of mind is required for actual analytical meditation, although that is not its usage here.

The description of these stages may make it seem as if progress is gradual and also sure of success if one only keeps at it, but this is not the case, as is made clear by Geshe Gedün Lodrö when he points to the need for employing analytical techniques to counteract afflictive emotions. The problem is that, with the channeling of

---

[a] *sems 'jog pa, cittasthāpana.*

[b] *rgyun du 'jog pa, saṃsthāpana.*

[c] *slan te 'jog pa, avasthāpana.*

mental energies thereby strengthening the mind, one's problems become more manifest. He says:[a]

> During the first three mental abidings, or placings of the mind on the object of observation, the greatest faults are laziness and forgetfulness. Thus, as we have said, it is very important to rely on the antidotes to these during this time. If, during these three mental abidings, you are so beset by laziness or forgetfulness that even though you rely on the antidotes—faith, aspiration, exertion, and mindfulness—you do not succeed in overcoming the faults, you must analyze the situation. There are many such cases in which meditators cannot conquer the difficulties and cannot go on. A very sharp person can do her or his own analysis at this time. Otherwise, as in the Ka-gyu-pa tradition, you offer your realization[b] to your teacher—that is, you tell her or him about your meditation. Your teacher will then tell you what to do. The practice of offering one's realization to a spiritual guide comes at this point in the nine mental abidings. Thus, if you arrive at the third mental abiding and, because of a predominant afflictive emotion such as hatred, are unable to progress to the fourth mental abiding, you ask for advice.
>
> In cultivating meditative stabilization, one must draw the mind inside. At that time, whatever is strongest in the mind will become manifest. For example, a person much accustomed to hatred is unable to advance because hatred becomes manifest when she or he cultivates calm abiding. When this person is not cultivating meditative stabilization, however, hatred does not become manifest because the mind is distracted.
>
> Most people have a particular afflictive emotion, and some also have unusual diseases which impede progress at this time; thus, it is necessary to reduce these. To do so, it is necessary to set aside the previous cultivation of calm abiding and engage in the cultivation of love, for instance, by way of analytical imputed special insight. There is no

---

[a] Gedün Lodrö, *Calm Abiding and Special Insight*, 74.

[b] *rtogs pa phul ba.*

> stabilizing meditation[a] here, just analytical meditation[b] to reduce the force or vibrancy of the hatred. One must rely on the antidotes to hatred from the viewpoint of many reasonings. No stabilizing meditation is permitted at this juncture because it would only cause the afflictive emotion to return. Thus, the meditator must analyze.

The great danger I see is that because the mind has become much more powerful than usual, one could mistake this for profound spiritual realization such that when, within this state, afflictive emotions manifest strongly, one could mistake them for expressions of spirituality. This may be one avenue leading to systems of corrupt ethics in which "gurus" have unlimited sex, greed, and even rage. Rather than agreeing with the manifestations of one's afflictive emotions, one needs the full force of the tradition, either in the presence of a competent guide or in knowledge of techniques transmitted in the tradition, to counteract the situation. The process is clearly fraught with dangers, such as in Jung's calling for confronting contents but not identifying with them.

Many of the preliminary practices in Action Tantra yoga that place the practice within an ethical tradition make one accountable to that tradition and thus provide a context in which peer-pressure can operate to prevent aberrations. Also, the intense altruism cultivated in the presence of the deity imagined in front of oneself frames relationships with others, thereby creating an effective counterforce when previously unmanifest afflictive emotions come to the surface. In addition, it may be that the techniques of expelling and binding obstructors provide a more forceful method of controlling these impulses, given that the prime technique is to melt them into the clear light. However, as mentioned earlier, the dangers of suppression and distorted manifestation that could attend such techniques should not be belittled. Over and over again, the tradition in general praises compassion and realization of emptiness as powerful techniques for restoring balance to the mind; thus, it makes a great deal of sense to attempt the practice of calm abiding *after* gaining some progress in developing compassion and rough knowledge of the emptiness of inherent existence. This may be the astuteness behind the frequent call for a practitioner to have

---

[a] *'jog sgom.*

[b] *dpyad sgom.*

developed recognition of suffering, realization of the imminence of death, experience of compassion, and some understanding of emptiness before being considered a suitable receptacle for tantric initiation. Tsong-kha-pa's student Gyel-tsap[a] speaks eloquently about the need for such practices prior to receiving initiation:[b]

> It is necessary to practice the common path, ranging from contemplating the difficulty of gaining the leisure and fortune [that in a human lifetime provide conditions for practicing the doctrine] and their meaningfulness through to generating your mind altruistically toward the supreme of enlightenments as well as the deeds of the six perfections—giving, ethics, patience, effort, concentration, and wisdom.
>
> If your [mental] continuum has not been well trained by means of those paths, you will not have eliminated attached involvement in this lifetime, whereby your wish to practice the doctrine will not be firm. Since nothing more than verbal faith will have been generated, a full entrusting of your mind to the sources of refuge will not come.
>
> Since firm ascertainment with respect to actions and their effects will not have been gained, you will become a coarse practitioner, without the refinement of keeping even any vow. Since an actual sense of reversal of attitude away from cyclic existence will not have been generated, your seeking liberation will be merely intellectual. Since you will not have generated a nonartificial aspirational intention to become enlightened, which has love and compassion as its roots, your being a person of the Great Vehicle will be merely in name.
>
> Since a strong wish to train in the general deeds of Bodhisattvas will not have arisen, the actual form of the vow of the practical intention to become enlightened will not be generated. Since pure understanding of general calm abiding and special insight will not have formed, you will err with respect to subtle meditative stabilization and will

---

[a] *rgyal tshab dar ma rin chen*, 1364-1432.

[b] *How to Practice the Two Stages of the Path of the Glorious Kālachakra: Quick Entry to the Path of Great Bliss* (*dpal dus kyi 'khor lo'i lam rim pa gnyis ji ltar nyams su len pa'i tshul bde ba chen po'i lam du myur du 'jug pa*), Collected Works of Rgyal-tshab Dar-ma-rin-chen, vol. 1 (Delhi: Guru Deva, 1982), 2a.2/91.2.

> not generate ascertainment of the view of selflessness.
>
> In particular, your assumption of the general and specific vows of the five lineages will also have become a mere verbal repetition of [what] the master [said when giving the vows], and thus a strong wish to keep the pledges without deterioration and a strong wish to attain the state of Vajradhara will not have arisen. Therefore, purification of the mental continuum through the paths common to Mantra and the Perfection Vehicle is a necessary prerequisite....Understanding this, [a master] should not in any form bestow the profound initiations on a beginner whose mind has not been purified in the least.

Gyel-tsap's admonitions make clear that this form of "Eastern yoga" at least is not amoral, as Jung thought (above, p. 67).

It seems to me that a similar admonition to cultivate the basic paths would be appropriate before attempting to achieve calm abiding, whether in the Sūtra or the Mantra systems. Such paths provide a foundational framework of techniques for avoiding problems. They bring with them a greater possibility of success when faced with manifestations of inner turmoil brought out by the practice of meditation itself, since greater concentration strengthens a mind embedded in distortion.

Through drawing on the resources of the tradition and of personal knowledge, one's uncommon afflictive emotion is sufficiently conquered so that progress can again be made, at which point one returns to the original meditation. Now, mindfulness can reach maturity, due to which the object is no longer lost, and the fourth level, called "close setting,"[a] is achieved. At this point, coarse laxity and excitement do not occur, but subtle versions persist. Since the factor of stability has greatly increased, this is likely the point at which a person cultivating the meditative stabilization of exalted body switches to cultivating the meditative stabilization of exalted speech, since Tsong-kha-pa says,[b] "Prior to repetition it is very important to achieve a firm meditative stabilization observing a deity." He is not indicating that one switches to mantra repetition *after* achieving actual calm abiding, since calm abiding is gained during the meditative stabilization of exalted speech in the phase called

---

[a] *nye bar 'jog pa, upasthāpana.*

[b] *Deity Yoga,* 164-165.

"concentration of abiding in sound." The inception of mantra repetition must be at a time of considerable but not complete stability, this likely being the fourth mental abiding.

Since, to achieve such stability, the mind has been strongly withdrawn from scattering to outside objects, the mind tends to become overly withdrawn, at which point powerful introspection is required to recognize subtle laxity. Thus, the fifth mental abiding, called "disciplining,"[a] is achieved when introspection and application of the antidotes to laxity are able to relieve the mind of this fault.

Then, since the mind was revivified through tightening its mode of apprehension, the danger on the fifth mental abiding comes from subtle excitement; through introspection that has matured to full force, one recognizes subtle excitement and applies the antidotes, thereby achieving the sixth level, called "pacifying."[b]

Through this process, one eventually arrives at a point when even subtle laxity and excitement cannot interrupt meditative stabilization to any significant degree; this seventh level, therefore, is called "thorough pacifying."[c] At this time it is difficult for any sort of laxity or excitement to create problems, but because strong effort is needed, it is said that this level is achieved through the power of effort, though indeed effort has been required all along.

When a meditator is able to remain on the object for an entire session without interference by laxity and excitement, either coarse or subtle, this is the mark of having achieved the eighth mental abiding called "making one-pointed."[d] At the beginning of the session, the practitioner initiates a little effort directed at maintaining mindfulness of the antidotes to laxity and excitement, and this alone is sufficient to keep these faults away. Then, through having become accustomed to this state, meditative stabilization dawns of its own accord, without requiring effort, this being the ninth level, called "setting in meditative equipoise."[e] Now, the object is engaged spontaneously, whereas on the eighth level, though uninterrupted, it was not spontaneous.

Still, one has not yet achieved calm abiding which requires—in

---

[a] *dul bar byed pa, damana.*

[b] *zhi bar byed pa, śamana.*

[c] *nye bar zhi bar byed pa, vyupaśamana.*

[d] *rtse gcig tu byed pa, ekotīkaraṇa.*

[e] *mnyam par 'jog pa, samādhāna.*

addition to being able spontaneously to remain on the chosen object free from laxity and excitement and endowed with both clear appearance of the object and intense clarity of the subject—a full complement of mental and physical serviceability called "pliancy." Pliancy is attained by becoming used to the state of spontaneous placement on the object, whereby a series of experiences occurs:

- Gradually the "winds" (currents of energy) that are involved in unhealthy physical states are calmed and leave the body through the top of the head, where a tingly sensation is created.
- Thereupon, a *mental pliancy,* which is a pacification of unhealthy states making the mind heavy and preventing its usage in virtue according to one's will, is generated; this makes the mind serviceable.
- Through its force, a "wind" of serviceability moves throughout the body, inducing a *physical pliancy* that causes separation from physical states of roughness and heaviness, whereupon one is able to use the body at will in virtuous actions (including meditation) without any sense of hardship. This physical pliancy itself is an internal object of touch, an internal smoothness and lightness; the body is light like cotton and as if filled with this serviceable wind.
- Experiencing this special internal object of touch, one has a *bliss of physical pliancy,* and due to the mental consciousness paying attention to this bliss accompanying the body consciousness, a *bliss of mental pliancy* is generated. At this point, one's body seems to have dissolved, and nothing but the object of observation appears—in this case, one's divine body. The mind is so buoyantly joyous that it is as if it is now almost unable to remain on its object.
- The excessive buoyancy is gradually removed, at which point one attains an immovable pliancy, in which the mind remains stably and joyously on the object of observation. This is calm abiding.

The *Questions of Subāhu,* one of the four general Action Tantras, speaks of the immovable, serviceable, and clear nature of this state:[a]

---

[a] Cited in *Deity Yoga,* 164.

> Look at the tip of the nose and abandon thought.
> When, though moving about, one is immovable,
> And a purity from states of unclarity is attained,
> The mind is certain to become serviceable.

It also speaks of pliancy and bliss:[a]

> In a person having a one-pointed mind
> Mentally arisen joy is strongly produced.
> Through joy, physical pliancy is attained.
> Through suppleness of body, one has the fortune of bliss.
> Through physical bliss, one-pointed mind, and meditative stabilization,
> Repetition is then unobstructed.

Putting this passage together with the process outlined above, we could say that the "one-pointed mind" refers to the eighth and ninth mental abidings; "mentally arisen joy is strongly produced" refers to excessively buoyant joy; "through joy physical pliancy is attained" refers to the generation of physical pliancy; and "through suppleness of body one has the fortune of bliss" refers to the generation of the blisses of physical and mental pliancy. As with Tsong-kha-pa's statement cited above, the last lines misleadingly seem to indicate that repetition is begun *after* the attainment of calm abiding, since "meditative stabilization" most likely refers to calm abiding. However, it is clear that actual calm abiding is achieved during the meditative stabilization of exalted speech since the new objects of observation of that phase are especially geared to removing laxity and excitement, as will be detailed below.

A mind of calm abiding has many advantages; the Dalai Lama describes them vividly:[b]

> When such mental meditative stabilization has been achieved, external good and bad objects, such as visible forms and so forth, that generate desire, hatred, and obscuration do not appear to be as solid as they usually do; through the force of having familiarized with meditative stabilization, they appear to be less concrete. When, from the perspective of experiencing meditative stabilization, one views such objects, they seem to dissolve of their own

---

[a] Ibid., 165.

[b] *The Dalai Lama at Harvard*, 156.

> accord, and the mind immediately withdraws inside. Consequently, at this time there is no danger at all from the usual scattering of the mind outside. Again, as external distractions lessen, one's mind remains experiencing its natural entity of mere luminosity and knowing; due to this, the internal generation of good and bad conceptions lessens. Even when conceptions are generated, they are like bubbles produced from water—they are not able to keep their own continuums going, they disappear immediately.

Actual calm abiding has such qualities, and Tsong-kha-pa is concerned that it be properly identified, lest it be confused with lower levels of mental stability:[a]

> In all four tantra sets the time of initially achieving a fully qualified calm abiding is chiefly when being instructed in deity yoga. Therefore, if you do not distinguish between fully qualified calm abiding and a similitude of it and do not finely differentiate the time of achieving calm abiding in accordance with how it appears in the great texts, you will not know the extent to which you must be led when initially being instructed in deity yoga.

("Deity yoga" at the end of the passage refers not just to the meditative stabilization of exalted body but includes the meditative stabilization of exalted speech.) Tsong-kha-pa is concerned with the proper identification of calm abiding not only so that a lower state is not mis-identified as calm abiding but also so that it is not confused with the greater bliss of Highest Yoga Mantra. As the Dalai Lama says about the bliss of calm abiding:[b]

> Though it is indeed blissful, it has no connection with the bliss described in [Highest Yoga] Mantra; it does not involve concentrated emphasis on important points in the body but is merely due to withdrawing the mind onto an object of observation—it is due to the power of just such meditative stabilization.

Calm abiding is a powerful tool to be used in the service of enhancing the force of the wisdom realizing the emptiness of inherent

---

[a] *Deity Yoga*, 165.

[b] *The Dalai Lama at Harvard*, 156.

existence so that it can overcome intellectually acquired and innate conceptions of inherent existence. The aim is to undo the ideational process behind afflictive emotions and then to remove even the *appearance* of inherent existence that prevents Buddhahood.

The details of the process of achieving calm abiding yield a picture of how the human condition is viewed in these traditions. Humans are trapped in a situation of repeated suffering not just by false assent to the seeming solidity of objects but also by a mind that is so mired in the extremes of either being too loose or too tight that attempts at correction push the mind between these two extremes. Also, the very structure of the ordinary mind prevents manifestation of certain chronic psychic problems, such that when this structure is disturbed by attempting to focus it and develop powers of concentration, deeply seated problems appear with greater force and others newly manifest.

Also, the mere fact that mindfulness and introspection need to be developed means that even though at present we have small versions of these, we have little idea of their potential—we are in a state of deprivation, sometimes arrogantly convinced of our wholeness and sometimes disparagingly reluctant to take cognizance of our potential. The system points to attainable states of mind that dramatically enhance the quality of life and that, of themselves, eliminate a host of problems, but whose attainment requires exposure to psychological pressures fraught with danger.

In one way, the systematic layout of stages gives the impression that mere application of the prescribed techniques would yield definite incremental results, but, in another way, examination of the complex techniques prescribed in the process of training yields a far different view of a mind that balks at improvement and enhancement, erects barriers, and places pitfalls in one's path. In such a context, we can appreciate the plethora of techniques employed in the tantric systems to attempt to counteract and undermine these forces. Whether they could be successful is no easy matter to determine; a claim that they definitely are would be superficial and do disservice to the complex vision of the human situation that a system such as that found in Action Tantra evinces.

Meditative stabilization of exalted speech

We have been discussing the meditative stabilization of exalted body from within the concentration with repetition. (It is important to remember that "repetition" means repetition of mantra but there has been no repetition of mantra until this point except as a technique for resting.) Now meditators pass from the meditative stabilization of exalted body to the meditative stabilization of exalted speech, which itself has many phases that span not only the remaining half of the concentration *with* repetition but also the first two of the three phases of the concentration *without* repetition. This means that the meditative stabilization of exalted speech does not necessarily involve repetition of mantra, as will be explained below.

Having achieved stable appearance of their own bodies as divine and having established a stable sense of themselves as deities designated in dependence upon pure mind and body, practitioners move to a more subtle level—the three meditative stabilizations of exalted body, speech, and mind being a series of increasingly more subtle levels of meditation. As Tsong-kha-pa says:[a]

> Here [with respect to the concentrations of Action Tantra] three meditative stabilizations are to be generated: observing divine body, observing divine speech mantra, and observing suchness—the divine mind. The first is a "very gross" or very coarse meditative stabilization. The second is subtler than that, and the third is very subtle. Hence, the order is definite, since they must be generated in the mental continuum in stages, beginning with the coarse.

Within the meditative stabilization of exalted speech itself, there are levels of coarseness and subtlety structured around the objects being observed, meditators always beginning with the more coarse. Also, mantra repetition is done first in whispered form, which is coarser, and then mentally, which is subtler.[b] Success with the former undoubtedly opens possibilities for greater success with the latter, even if it appears that one could perform the latter right away.

The part of the meditative stabilization of exalted speech that is included within the concentration with repetition is basically in two sections—repetition of mantra within observing the *form* of the letters and repetition of mantra within observing the *sound* of the letters. In the first, the practitioner observes the form of the letters

---

[a] *Deity Yoga*, 164.

[b] Ibid., 146.

(or syllables) of the mantra initially in the heart of the deity in front and then the letters are moved to the practitioner's own heart where the meditation continues. Let us consider these stages.

Repetition of mantra within observing the form of the letters at the heart of the deity in front

In the first stage, the mantra letters are set on a flat brilliantly white moon disc at the heart of the deity in front, the moon and the letters being the remaining two branches of the four-branched repetition. "Branch" (*yan lag, aṅga*) sometimes has the sense of prerequisite, and perhaps here also it suggests four factors that must be brought together prior to repetition of mantra. The first branch, it will be remembered, is the deity in front which is "not too distant and a little higher than yourself";[a] the second branch is oneself imagined as a deity; the third branch is the moon disc imagined at the heart of the deity in front; and the fourth is the form of the mantra letters set around the edge of the moon standing upright and facing inward.

About this phase of the meditative stabilization of exalted speech, the *Concentration Continuation Tantra* says:[b]

> Flow to sound, mind, and bases.
> Dwell on the immutable secret mantra base [the deity].
> Repeat secret mantra without losing the branches.
> If becoming tired, rest yourself.

One "base" is the deity in front; the second "base" is oneself imagined as a deity.[c] "Mind" is a moon disc at the heart of the deity in front. "Sound" is the forms of the letters of the mantra set on the moon disc. "Flow" means to adhere to these (especially the deity in front with moon and mantra letters) with uninterrupted observation. Because a meditator *continuously* and *without deviation* imagines the deity in front, which is the *base* where the moon and letters are placed, the text says, "Dwell on the *immutable* secret mantra *base*." "Immutable" here has the sense that the base—in observation of which repetition is performed—should not deviate from appearance as a deity. Since repetition is to be done within

---

[a] Ibid., 144.

[b] Stanza 11; P430, vol. 9 53.3.4; cited in *Deity Yoga*, 55 and 141.

[c] The explanation is drawn from *Deity Yoga*, 141-142.

constant imagination of the four branches (three in front: the *letters* on the *moon* at the heart of the *deity in front* which are the focus; and *oneself as a deity* but not as a central part of the meditation), the tantra says, "Repeat secret mantra *without losing the branches.*"

Tsong-kha-pa[a] reports that although neither the *Concentration Continuation Tantra* nor Buddhaguhya mentions it, other Indian masters advise that one imagine beams of light streaming from the mantra letters, making offerings to Buddhas and bringing about the welfare of sentient beings. According to the process described earlier during the "form deity" in self-generation, from the light rays innumerable forms of the deity emerge, pervading all of space, and the deities, in turn, emanate great clouds of offerings through which they make splendid offerings to all the Conquerors. Also, they emanate great clouds from which a rain-stream of ambrosia descends, extinguishing the fires of the sufferings of all beings—hell-beings, hungry ghosts, animals, humans, demigods, and gods—satisfying those beings with whatever they want. This technique enhances considerably the therapeutic power of the meditation, although it would have to be done in a secondary way so that it did not interfere with the central concentration on the forms of the letters at the heart of the deity in front. It seems likely that the curative influence of this additional highly moral visualization (quite contrary to Jung's depiction of amoral yoga) would indeed help to remove some of the emotional obstacles to developing a strongly focused mind and would dispel laxity.

About repetition of mantra, the *Questions of Subāhu Tantra* says:[b]

> Reversing quickly from the objects to which
> A lazy, desirous, and nonvirtuous mind
> Is distracted and runs, apply the mind well
> To the supreme letters of secret mantra.

The *Susiddhi Tantra* warns against being distracted even to virtuous objects:[c]

> When reciting with repetition,

---

[a] Ibid., 146.

[b] Ibid., 147.

[c] P431, vol. 9, 64.1.2. This is cited in Varabodhi's *Clear Realization of Susiddhi* (P3890, vol. 79, 272.1.7). Cited in *Deity Yoga*, 50, and explained on 147; cited in Ye-shay-gyeltsen, *Illumination of the Meaning of Action Tantra*, 504.2.

> Except for knowledge-mantra and deity
> Do not apprehend in thought at all
> [Other] meditations though cherished as supreme.

The process begins with whispered repetition of the mantra, about which the *Questions of Subāhu Tantra* says:[a]

> When performing repetition be not fast nor slow,
> Be not loud nor very soft.
> Do it not while speaking nor while distracted.
> Lose not the vowels, *anusvāra,* or *visarga.*

When, through becoming familiar with whispered repetition, one becomes able to remain single pointedly on mainly the form of the mantra letters, one switches to more subtle, mental repetition within still mainly focusing on the form of the mantra letters on the moon disc at the heart of the deity in front. Throughout the many phases of the concentration with repetition, when mental repetition of mantra is done, one is as if listening to one's own recitation, whereas later during the first two phases of the concentrations without repetition called the concentrations of abiding in fire and in sound, the meditator is as if listening to mantra recited by someone else[b]—this being why, even if mantra is still present, the concentrations of abiding in fire and in sound are classed as concentrations *without* repetition.

With mental repetition, it is possible to engage in the practice of holding the breath, *prāṇāyāma*—the restraining of vitality (breath or wind) and exertion (distraction). Therefore, after inhaling, one holds the breath, mentally repeating the mantra while focusing on the letters standing upright around the edge of the moon at the heart of the deity in front, while also maintaining the sense of oneself as a deity but not focusing on that. With exhalation, one views one's own divine body without repeating the mantra. Then, with inhalation, the same procedure is reenacted.

When whispered repetition is performed within observing the form of the letters of the mantra standing on a moon at the heart of the deity in front, one is as if reading the letters[c]—neither swiftly

---

a *Deity Yoga,* 147.

b Ibid., 28, 145, and 160.

c The Dalai Lama's commentary in *Deity Yoga,* 28.

nor slowly and such that only oneself can hear it. Buddhaguhya[a] describes the meditation as having three objects of observation—(1) the deity in front, (2) the moon at the deity's heart, and (3) the letters of the mantra that stand along the rim of the moon disc. Still, during this period one does not lose the appearance of one's own body as a divine body, since a capacity for continual imagination of oneself as a deity has been gained through previous cultivation of the meditative stabilization of exalted body. Also, during exhalation one switches from observing the letters at the heart of the deity in front to viewing one's own divine body without reciting the mantra.

Gradually, as the mind stays more and more on its object, one desists from whispered repetition and, holding the breath, repeats the mantra mentally. This is the only change in procedure between whispered and mental repetition of mantra, the objects of observation being the same, and when exhaling, one views one's own divine body without repeating the mantra.

Resting

As the *Concentration Continuation Tantra,* cited above, says, "If becoming tired, rest yourself." Buddhaguhya[b] explains how, at the end of the session, meditators should rest so as to avoid becoming excessively distracted by discursiveness. The process reenacts the steps of all the meditations so far but in reverse order:

- First, one ceases repeating the mantra.
- Then, one ceases visualizing the forms of the mantra letters and observes the moon on which they stood at the heart of the deity in front of oneself; one thereby has moved backwards from the sound branch to the moon branch.
- Then, one ceases visualizing the moon and observes the deity in front—the branch called "other-base."
- Next, one ceases visualizing the deity in front and observes one's own divine body—the branch called "self-base" which is the sixth deity, called the "sign deity," as well as the fourth deity, called the "form deity."
- Next, one ceases visualizing one's divine body and observes the letters on the moon disc in space—the second part of the third

[a] Ibid., 146.

[b] P3495, vol. 78, 74.1.4-74.1.8. See *Deity Yoga,* 142-143.

deity, the "letter deity."

- Then one ceases visualizing the letters on the moon and observes the moon disc in space—the first part of the letter deity.
- Then one ceases visualizing the moon disc and observes the sounds of the mantra reverberating in space—the second deity, called the "sound deity."
- Then one ceases observing the sounds of the mantra and observes the pride of the sameness of the nature of oneself and the deity—the last part of the first deity, called the "ultimate deity."
- Then one ceases observing the pride of the sameness of the nature of oneself and the deity and observes the suchness of self, one's own emptiness of inherent existence, this being the first part of the ultimate deity.
- The meditator remains in meditative equipoise on his/her own emptiness and then all at once rises in a divine body, which is the same as that visualized earlier though in simpler form.

Even between sessions practitioners remain within deity yoga, albeit not as complete as before, going about daily activities. In this way, the periods between sessions and actual meditative sessions are mutually supportive.

Repetition of mantra within observing the form of the letters at one's own heart

In the next phase of concentration with repetition, the meditator inhales the moon disc, together with the mantra letters standing at its edge into his/her own heart from the heart of the deity in front. Again, whispered repetition is performed first, but when the mind becomes steady, one holds the breath and recites the mantra mentally, as if one's mind is in the center of the moon disc and is reading the letters of the mantra on it facing inward. When exhaling, repetition of mantra is stopped, and the moon and letters move with the breath back to the deity's heart, and then with inhalation the moon and mantra letters again move to one's own heart, and repetition is resumed.

The *Concentration Continuation Tantra* indicates this phase with:[a]

> Likewise contemplate a mental purity [that is, a moon

[a] Stanza 12; P430, vol. 9, 53.3.4; *Deity Yoga*, 144.

> disc],
> Possessing immutability and letters,
> Which is imagined for your mantra.
> It moves from the base [in front] to the base [yourself].

"Likewise" indicates that this is another mode of observation in which a "mental purity," a moon disc, is contemplated. The moon disc is called "mental" because it is a manifestation of the mind realizing the emptiness of inherent existence; it is a "purity" in the sense that it is unpolluted by the stains of desire and so forth, is complete in all respects, and appears without any taint. The moon "possesses" (in the sense of having on it) the mantra "letters," which are endowed with "immutability" since they do not deviate from vivid appearance because of the thoroughness of the yogi's meditation. In another way, the mind realizing emptiness that appears as a moon disc has "immutability" in the sense that it does not become separated from the mantra letters.

Since, as before, the moon disc is the base on which the mantra is set, it "is imagined for your mantra." With the inhalation of breath, the moon "moves from the base to the base," that is to say, it moves from one of its bases, the deity in front who is a little higher and not far from oneself, to its other base, which is the meditator. With exhalation, it moves from oneself back to the deity in front. Repetition is performed when the moon disc and letters are at one's own heart, but then during exhalation repetition of mantra is stopped. With inhalation, the process begins again. As before, whispered repetition is performed first, and then mental repetition.

Repetition of mantra within observing the sound of the letters

In the next phase, the *sounds* of the mantra become the principal object of observation. This does not mean that the four branches of repetition—the deity in front, oneself as a deity, the moon, and form of the letters—disappear; rather, the meditator *focuses* on the sounds of the letters. Initially whispered and then mental repetition is performed; with the latter, the breath is held, as before. Neither the Tantra, nor Buddhaguhya, nor Tsong-kha-pa mentions what to do when exhaling; perhaps one observes the forms of the mantra letters.

About this phase, the *Concentration Continuation Tantra* says:[a]

> Having again retracted the mind through withdrawal
> And restrained vitality and exertion,
> Join the mind of secret mantra to the mantra
> And begin mental repetition.
>
> Otherwise, by means of just this rite
> Whispering is also suitable.
> One wishing feats of mantra knowledge
> Should not perform other repetition.

"Having again retracted the mind through withdrawal" refers to the process, described in the previous chapter, of withdrawing inside the movements of the breath throughout the body, like a turtle's retracting its limbs and like drinking water with the tongue. Also, the usual intense movement of the nonequipoised mind out through the senses is withdrawn inside. The four branches of repetition are to be visualized, and then the meditator's mind is to concentrate principally on the *sounds* of the mantra as is indicated by "Join the mind of secret mantra to the *mantra*."

Although the *Concentration Continuation Tantra* mentions breath control and mental repetition first and then speaks of whispered repetition as also suitable to be done through "just this rite" of observing the sounds of the mantra, Buddhaguhya's commentary[b] makes it clear that whispered repetition is coarser and to be done first, after which mental repetition induces a subtler meditative stabilization. He also makes the point that indeed it is impossible to practice breath control when whispering mantra. Moreover, although whispered and mental repetition as well as the restraining of breath and distraction are explicitly prescribed for this phase, Buddhaguhya emphasizes that they are also to be performed during the earlier phases of observing the form of the mantra letters at the heart of the deity in front and in one's own heart.

When this meditative stabilization becomes firm, the concentration of the four-branched repetition is complete, as is the first part of the meditative stabilization of exalted speech. The meditation has proceeded in three phases from coarser to subtler objects of observation. Even though the four branches of repetition—deity

[a] Stanzas 13-14; P430, vol. 9, 53.3.5; *Deity Yoga*, 145.

[b] P3495, vol. 78, 75.2.3 and 75.1.2.

in front, oneself as a deity, moon, and the form of the letters—always provide the context of the meditation and thus never entirely disappear, Buddhaguhya[a] describes the first phase—repetition of mantra within observing the form of the letters at the heart of the deity in front—as having three objects of observation, these being the deity in front, the moon, and the forms of the mantra. Similarly, the second phase—repetition of mantra within observing the form of the letters at one's own heart—is said to have two objects of observation, just the moon and the forms of the letters at one's own heart. The last is said to have only one object of observation, the sounds of the mantra. However, these counts refer only to the *main* objects of meditation, for as the Dalai Lama says in commentary:[b]

> These refer to the *main* objects of observation on which the mind focuses and should not be taken as meaning that the other factors do not remain vividly appearing to the mind. One must remain undistractedly on whatever the object is at that point.

Similarly, Tsong-kha-pa says:[c]

> When meditative stabilization observing a [divine] body becomes firm, you leave that and train in meditative stabilization observing a speech mantra. "Leaving" should be understood as setting aside the training of continuously holding the mind on the [divine] body and mentally apprehending another object of observation. It does not preclude the later [continued] clear appearance of the deity because there are many descriptions of observing a deity during the three repetitions [observing the form of the letters at the heart of the deity in front and at one's own heart and observing the sounds of the letters] as well as during [the concentrations of] abiding in fire and in sound.

It might seem to be extremely difficult to simultaneously keep so much in mind, but for someone who has become thoroughly accustomed to the clear appearance of, for instance, one's own body as a deity's, it must be easy to shift the focus to something else and yet

---

[a] P3495, vol. 78, 75.2.3.

[b] *Deity Yoga*, 29.

[c] Ibid., 165-166.

not lose the earlier appearance, much as we can think of a street that we know well and focus on a particular building on that street without losing the appearance of the general locale.

6. Concentration Without Repetition

The meditative stabilization of exalted speech has two more phases, both of which involve mantra but not accompanied by the sense that one is listening to one's own repetition. In these phases, the meditator concentrates on the mantra tones as if resounding of their own accord or as if being recited by someone else; therefore, these steps—the concentrations of abiding in fire and of abiding in sound—constitute the first part of the concentration *without* repetition and yet are still part of the meditative stabilization of exalted speech. The remaining part of the concentration without repetition—the concentration bestowing liberation at the end of sound—constitutes the meditative stabilization of exalted mind.

In this way, the concentration without repetition itself has three phases called the three principles,[a] these being the concentration of abiding in fire, the concentration of abiding in sound, and the concentration bestowing liberation at the end of sound. As just mentioned, the first two are included in the meditative stabilization of exalted speech, whereas the last constitutes the meditative stabilization of exalted mind. About these, the *Concentration Continuation Tantra* says:[b]

> The secret mantra abiding in fire bestows feats.
> That abiding in sound bestows yoga.
> The end of sound bestows liberation.
> These are the three principles.

From among the three principles, the first—"The secret mantra abiding in fire," or concentration of abiding in fire—is said to "bestow feats," not in the sense that it alone is sufficient for the achievement of major yogic feats but in the sense that, through causing the concentration on mantra to become more powerful and causing the mind to become more stable,[c] one comes considerably closer to the achievement of feats.

The concentration of abiding in sound "bestows yoga" in that it is the time of achieving a fully qualified calm abiding.[d] The

---

a *de nyid gsum.*

b Stanza 17; P430, vol. 9, 53.3.8; cited in *Deity Yoga*, 155.

c Ibid., 29 and 158.

d Ibid., 29 and 166.

concentration bestowing liberation at the end of sound brings about achievement of a union of calm abiding and special insight realizing the emptiness of inherent existence, which, when cultivated over time, brings direct realization of emptiness and eventually leads to the great liberation of Buddhahood.[a] Let us consider these three concentrations in detail.

Concentration of abiding in fire

When meditators have firm success with the many levels of the concentration with repetition, they pass to a subtler level, the concentration of abiding in fire. As just mentioned, this also is a meditation observing a divine speech mantra, but "repetition" is not involved because in this case when one's own mind appears in the aspect of the sounds of mantra it is not as if oneself is reciting them, but as if one is hearing them resounding of their own accord or hearing another's repetition. Because it is free from the aspect of one's own recitation of mantra, it is called a concentration *without* repetition. It is called "abiding in fire" because the sounds of mantra are heard as if resounding within a tongue of flame on a moon disc at the heart of one's own body visualized as that of a deity. As the Dalai Lama says in commentary:[b]

> Previously, during the repetition of mantra while observing the sound of the letters, it was as if you were listening to the reverberation of the sounds of your own recitation, whether whispered or mental. However, here you are to listen to the mantra sounds as if someone else were reciting them. Therefore, that the concentration of abiding in fire is said to be without mantra repetition means that it is free from the aspect of *one's own* repetition, not that it is free from mantra sounds altogether.
>
> These sounds are "heard" from within a tongue of flame imagined at the heart—all this within the clear appearance of your own body as a deity's. Your own mind is as if inside the tongue of flame, appearing in the form of the mantra sounds resounding as if by their own power. This is like the practice on other occasions of the mind's taking the mind as its object of observation—a factor of the mind

---

[a] Ibid., 29-30.

[b] Ibid., 30-31.

> taking the general mind as its object. Here the mind is appearing as the sounds of someone else's repetition and is simultaneously listening to those sounds.
>
> In the previous meditations all forms and sounds were appearances of the mind realizing suchness; thus, all forms seen and sounds heard were appearances of the mind. Within that, one was as if listening to the mantra repeated by oneself; hence, there still was a sense of a listener and the listened. However, here in the concentration of abiding in fire one's own basis of designation is as if dwelling inside the tongue of flame, and it itself is appearing as the sounds being listened to in that same place.

One's mind, which is the basis in dependence upon which oneself is designated, is imagined as dwelling within the fire and as appearing as the mantra sounds. The brightness of the fire helps to remove laxity, and the placement of one's own mind *within* the small space of the flame helps to remove excitement, the scattering of the mind to other objects. With proficiency, the sounds of the mantra are "heard" as if in continual reverberation. Buddhaguhya[a] explains that meditation at this point becomes one's own sustenance such that there is no sense of hunger or thirst.

The unusual practice of causing one's own mind to appear as sounds that have the aspect of being recited by someone else or reverberating of their own accord brings about a diminishment of the sense of subject and object, the bifurcation of the world into what is on this, the subject's, side and what is on that, the object's, side. The diminishment of duality mimics the lack of dualistic conception in the realization of emptiness and thus helps to induce such realization through familiarity with a psychological counterpart of a central feature of that realization.

The *Concentration Continuation Tantra* describes the concentration of abiding in fire with three stanzas:[b]

> Māntrikas with intelligence bind to the self [that is, the mind]
> The phenomena arisen from the nondistinguished [mental consciousness].

[a] P3495, vol. 78, 77.1.7. Cited in *Deity Yoga*, 158.

[b] Stanzas 18-20; P430, vol. 9, 53.3.8; cited in *Deity Yoga*, 156.

Dwelling on what transcends the branches [that is, the eyes
and so forth],
They concentrate without adherence.

When they contemplate within adhering
To the immutable letters [that is, sounds] strung together,
Continual like the sounds of bells
And set in a series called "sound,"

[The sounds] should be contemplated as abiding in fire—
Quiescent, free from words, having the branches [that is,
the mantra letters]
With a nature also of having stopped vitality and exertion
As well as having forsaken sleep.

The first stanza describes the initial cultivation of one's own final nature, the suchness of self, the equivalent of the ultimate deity from among the six deities. Practitioners of Mantra ("Māntrikas") are to "concentrate without adherence," meaning that they are to meditate within ceasing the conception of inherent existence. They "dwell on" the emptiness of inherent existence, which "transcends the branches"—"branches" here referring not to the four branches of repetition but to conventional phenomena in general, such as eyes, ears, nose, and so forth. They do this by "binding to the self"—that is, to the mind—the mental factors that accompany it. These mental factors are "phenomena arisen from the nondistinguished" in that they are associated with an internal consciousness that cannot be distinguished, or apprehended, by another's eye consciousness and so forth. The mental factors involved with the entanglements of the afflictive emotions are "bound" to the mind in the sense that due to strongly contemplating the emptiness of inherent existence, afflictive emotions do not arise. Such Māntrikas are endowed with "intelligence," for they have the wisdom capable of investigating their own suchness, their own final nature.

Having concentrated on suchness, practitioners rise from solely contemplating the emptiness of inherent existence and, within appearing in the form of a deity and conceiving of themselves to be deities, their own mind of wisdom appears in the aspect of the mantra as if one were hearing another's recitation of them or resounding of their own accord. Because the mind of wisdom itself is appearing as sound, the sounds of the mantra and one's own final nature are completely mixed like water and milk.

The practitioner "adheres" in mind to the sounds of the letters, which are "immutable" in that they uninterruptedly appear without any fluctuation "strung together" in a series such that, with proficiency, they become "continual like the sounds of a bell," the earlier sounds not disappearing with the appearance of the later ones. The sounds are imagined "as abiding in fire," that is to say, in a tongue of flame at one's heart; the fire is "quiescent" in the sense that it does not burn, even though once proficiency is gained, there is a sense of warmth. Also, the sounds of the mantra are "free from words" as they are neither whispered nor mentally repeated in the aspect of one's reciting them. Moreover, the mantra is endowed with "the branches," which here means all of its individual letters. "Vitality and exertion," or breath and distraction, are stopped in order to avoid excitement and scattering of the mind. "Having forsaken sleep" indicates that laxity and slackness in the mode of apprehension of the mind are to be stopped.

Concentration of abiding in sound

When proficiency is achieved in concentrating on the sounds of the mantra in a tiny flame on a moon disc at the heart of one's own divine body, the meditator proceeds to cultivate the concentration of abiding in sound. This phase involves placing a tiny deity within the flame and then imagining a flame on a moon disc at the heart of the small deity.[a] When this visualization becomes firm, one's own mind appears as the mantra sounds within the flame at the heart of the tiny inner deity; the smallness of the flame and the withdrawal of the basis of one's sense of self within a body that is within another body bring about a more intense withdrawal of consciousness but without much danger of laxity because of the brightness of the object of observation, fire. As the Dalai Lama says in commentary:[b]

> These unusual objects of observation in the concentrations of abiding in fire and abiding in sound are for the sake of achieving clear appearance and thereby avoiding laxity. For even if the earlier meditations involved the appearance of bright mantra letters and so forth, here one imagines fire

---

[a] Tsong-kha-pa does not explicitly mention the tongue of flame inside the small deity, but the Dalai Lama (*Deity Yoga,* 31) does. Most likely, it would, as before, be on a moon disc like the flame at the heart of the larger divine body.

[b] *Deity Yoga,* 31.

> itself, even the name of which evokes a bright appearance, thereby helping in relieving the mind of laxity—any looseness in the mode of apprehension of the object.

When the mind is able to remain stably and alertly on this new visualization, the meditator takes the sounds of the mantra as the principal object of observation.

The *Concentration Continuation Tantra* describes two alternative ways of cultivating the concentration of abiding in sound:[a]

> Place [a divine body which is] the base of the immutable [mantra letters]
> In the very peaceful tongue
> Of flame with brilliant pure light
> That is on a subtle stainless moon disc dwelling at the heart.
>
> Then contemplate the sounds while abiding in bliss.
> Or, having set the [written] letters
> On the immutable [moon disc],
> Contemplate only the sounds themselves.

Here, it is emphasized that the "moon disc dwelling at the heart" of the practitioner who is visualizing his or her body as a divine body is "subtle" because the smallness of the object helps to eliminate excitement and scattering of the mind. The meditator "places" a small divine body—which is the "base" of a moon on which the mantra letters are set—in the tongue of flame (as imagined in the concentration of abiding in fire) on the small moon at the heart of one's larger divine body. As earlier, the mantra letters are called "immutable" because they uninterruptedly appear without any fluctuation in a series that is continual like the sounds of a bell.

Then, the meditator leaves off observing these forms and "contemplates the sounds," which, although the text does not explicitly say so, are viewed as being in the midst of a tiny tongue of flame on a tiny moon at the heart of the tiny deity on the very small moon at the heart of one's larger divine body. The emphasis here, however, is on just the sounds, which become the principal object of observation and even the *sole* object of observation in that the other parts only provide context.

The tantra offers a second way to cultivate the concentration of

---

[a] Stanzas 21 and 22; P430, vol. 9, 53.4.2; cited in *Deity Yoga*, 159.

abiding in sound that dispenses with the second deity and even with the flame on the moon. In this version, the meditator "sets the letters," that is, the written letters, on the edge of "the immutable," this being the moon disc which is called immutable because it symbolizes the mind of enlightenment realizing the emptiness of inherent existence that abides solely, and thus immutably, in an aspect devoid of dualistic appearance. In this version, the meditator first observes the written letters of the mantra on the moon disc and then, leaving the written letters, "contemplates only the sounds themselves."

With success at this meditation, a fully qualified calm abiding is achieved—a state of meditative stabilization conjoined with the bliss of mental and physical pliancy. The meditations to this point have employed many techniques to concentrate the mind—to withdraw it from the usual sweep of distraction but without the accompanying dullness and drowsiness that ordinary withdrawal of the senses involves.

In the Sūtra system style of cultivating calm abiding, only one object is the focus of meditation, with other objects used only when techniques to counteract laxity and excitement do not work and either sobering reflection on, for instance, impermanence and death, or revivifying imaginations such as imagining vast acts of charity are needed. Except for such circumstances, the meditator is advised to remain with one and only one object, not switching from it to another. Here in this Action Tantra, however, a series of meditations that involve switching from object to object upon gaining proficiency with the former serves as a means of keeping the mind alert. Also, the individual meditations themselves call for considerable activity and change; for instance, the reading of mantra letters in a circular fashion on the moon at the heart of the deity in front not only collects the mind in one place but also keeps the mind lively by the very fact of movement, as is similarly the case with moving the moon and letters to one's own heart with inhalation and then exhaling them back into the deity in front. Furthermore, the progression from listening to one's own recitation of mantra, either whispered or mental, to listening to sounds that are like someone else's recitation or a natural reverberation but which are still an appearance of one's own consciousness helps to remove distraction in that outside and inside become blended.

All of these factors help to induce the withdrawn and intensely focused mind of calm abiding, but their effects are not limited to building one-pointedness of mind. The very act of imagining one's own body to be composed not of ordinary substances such as flesh, blood, and bone but of an appearance of consciousness interferes with a basic self-perception—one's own body—that is usually taken as a given. Such givenness runs counter to dependent-arising and its consequent emptiness of inherent existence, and thus the undermining of the sense that one's body is "just there as it is" radically alters a basic self-perception, preparing the way for increased understanding of emptiness. In this fashion Bu-tön Rin-chen-drup (below, 217) says:

> Through mindfulness of Buddhas and having faith upon recognizing Buddhas and making offerings with resources, collections of merit are always produced. Also, when meditation of a divine body has become manifest, all phenomena are understood as just appearances of one's own mind, and moreover, understanding that even the mind is not established arises. Through this and since pristine wisdom is generated in the mental continuum of one with merit, such serves as a cause of pristine wisdom.

At minimum, the meditator, to this point, has been imagining his/her body as composed of an appearance of consciousness, or at least of light, and this process has not just been entertained intellectually but imagined over such a long period of time that one's new body appears *clearly* and *continually* as like that of a deity, and one's mind similarly manifests in a state far superior to the usual. In dependence upon such enhanced mind and body, one also gains an enhanced sense of self, again undermining perceptions taken in the past to be givens set in place.

Beyond this, the technique of causing the mind to appear as body and as sounds of mantra upsets the division of classes of objects, and the technique of causing one's mind to appear as sounds that are as if recited by someone else further upsets the ingrained sense of subject and object. Factors of body, mind, self, and subject and object—assumed to be in the warp and woof of appearance—are thereby challenged by substitution meditations that themselves induce a sense of the implications of the emptiness of inherent existence. Thus, even though the tradition subsumes the meditative stabilizations of exalted body and speech (and thus the concentration with repetition and the first two phases of the concentration without repetition) under the rubric of developing calm abiding and thereby points to an important process being accomplished during these phases, the impact is by no means limited to achieving calm abiding. Practitioners' world-views are being challenged in such a way that internal potential for a new way of life is revealed, and groundwork is laid for greater comprehension of the ramifications of emptiness—the refutation of objects' existing from their own side. The suggestion is that meditation on emptiness through reasonings such as the sevenfold reasoning is not sufficient; it is necessary to coax out its significance by disturbing basic patterns of perception. These techniques assist in the process of overcoming the sense that phenomena exist under their own power and thereby shake up autonomous complexes, including even the appearance of self-subsisting phenomena such as one's own body.

Concentration bestowing liberation at the end of sound

When the meditative stabilization of exalted speech is complete, practitioners proceed, still within the concentration without repetition, to cultivate the even more subtle meditative stabilization of exalted mind, called the concentration bestowing liberation at the end of sound. Prior to this point, namely, during the four-branched repetition and the concentrations of abiding in fire and in sound, the main style of meditation was stabilizing meditation, since a principal aim of those phases was to generate a mind of calm abiding—a one-pointed highly alert and joyous mind spontaneously remaining on its object. During that phase, analytical meditation employing analytical reasoning would have been counterproductive, since it would have interfered with developing one-pointedness of mind. However, now that calm abiding has been achieved, stabilizing meditation can be alternated with analytical meditation in such a way that the power of stability is brought to one's analysis.[a]

The object now is the emptiness of inherent existence. Even though realization of emptiness was cultivated earlier during the

---

[a] Earlier there was alternation with a different type of analytical meditation, which at that time was to pay attention to details and so forth, in order to remove laxity.

first step of self-generation, the ultimate deity, and even though it was involved in all subsequent steps in that the mind realizing emptiness was used (at least in pretend) as the basis of emanation of the various divine appearances, emptiness was not the *central* object of meditation. Now, during cultivation of the meditative stabilization of exalted mind, that is, the concentration bestowing liberation at the end of sound, it is the main focus. The aim is to develop a mind that is a union of calm abiding and special insight realizing emptiness.

Earlier, analysis would have caused the mind to become unstable, and now even though calm abiding has been achieved, too much analysis still tends to promote excitement and reduce the mind's factor of stability, and thus analysis must be alternated with nonanalysis, setting the mind on its object—the emptiness of inherent existence—without analyzing. Again, when performing stabilization, too much stabilization will harm the factor of analysis, causing one not to want to analyze, and thus, when sufficiently stable, one alternates back to analytical meditation.

At this and preceding levels, stabilizing and analytical styles of meditation work against each other, the one undermining the other. Calm abiding and analysis are like two ends of a scale, the one lowering in force when the other becomes higher. However, this incompatibility is viewed not as being due to the nature of stability and of analysis themselves but as being due to distortions in one's own mind. The aim in alternating the two styles of meditation is to bring them to the point where they are in such great harmony that the one, far from harming the other, increases the other; analysis induces even more stability which, in turn, induces greater analytical ability, eventually without any need for alternation. In time, analysis itself induces levels of physical and mental pliancy even greater than those experienced during calm abiding. As the Dalai Lama says:[a]

> Gradually, the power of analysis itself is able to induce physical and mental pliancy similar to those explained earlier with respect to calm abiding, but to a greater degree. The generation of the bliss of physical and mental pliancy, induced through the power of analysis, marks the attainment of fully qualified special insight, and from this

---

[a] *The Dalai Lama at Harvard*, 160.

> point on, one has a union of calm abiding and special insight. One now has powerful weapons for realizing the coarser and subtler levels of emptiness in order to overcome obstructions.

Special insight is defined as a wisdom of thorough discrimination of phenomena conjoined with special pliancy induced by the power of analysis.[a] Etymologically, special insight (*lhag mthong, vipaśyanā*) is so called because it is sight (*mthong, paśya*) that exceeds (*lhag, vi*) that of calm abiding in that analysis induces a clarity surpassing the clarity experienced during calm abiding.[b]

The purpose of the concentration bestowing liberation at the end of sound is to generate such special insight realizing emptiness, which is subsequently brought to the level of direct perception so that obstructions preventing liberation from cyclic existence and preventing omniscience can be overcome. About the concentration bestowing liberation at the end of sound, the *Concentration Continuation Tantra* says:[c]

> A Conqueror knows the abandonment of [four] branches [or states]
> Of the lords [that is, deities] of knowledge-mantra—
> (1) Dependent appearance with the limbs [of a deity], (2) the one called "sound" [whispered repetition],
> (3) The mental one [mental repetition], and (4) what are pure of words [the concentrations of abiding in fire and in sound].

A "Conqueror," a Buddha, "knows" the stage of liberation when emptiness is meditated after the gradual "abandonment of the branches"—that is to say, after gradually leaving four states of meditation, called "branches" (not to be confused with the four branches of repetition or any of the other meanings of "branches"). These are four states "of the lords of knowledge-mantra," that is to say, of the deities of knowledge-mantra and of secret mantra who are being meditated. The four states of deities that are left or forsaken in the sense that they no longer are the focus of attention are:

---

[a] Jam-yang-shay-pa's *Great Exposition of the Concentrations and Formless Absorptions*, 81b.3.

[b] Ibid., 83b.7.

[c] Stanza 24; P430, vol. 9, 53.4.4; cited in *Deity Yoga*, 161.

1. "appearance with the limbs" of a deity—that is to say, in a complete divine body—that appears "dependent" upon a style of meditation involving serially reviewing the various aspects of the divine body and adjusting color, shape, and so forth (this being called concentration) and a style of meditation in which one fixes on just one particular aspect of the divine body or just the general body (called meditative stabilization) and which involves binding the breath and stopping distraction
2. "sound," which here specifically refers to whispered repetition of mantra
3. "the mental one," that is, mental repetition of mantra
4. "what are pure of words," these being the concentrations of abiding in fire and in sound in which, even though they involve concentration on mantra, the mind itself appears as the mantra as if recited by someone else or reverberating of its own accord, and thus the concentrations of abiding in fire and in sound are "pure of words," or free from repetition in the aspect of one's own words.

These four states are left in the sense that each of the steps is cultivated in meditation until it becomes firm, at which point the next, more subtle level is begun. Leaving or abandoning states, therefore, does not mean that these factors cease to appear; rather, the *focus* of attention shifts to a more subtle level. Due to having thoroughly trained in the lower levels to the point where their facets appear stably to the mind, it is possible to add something else to the meditation without the former factors disappearing.

What becomes the focus of attention here is the "end" or final nature of "sound," its emptiness of inherent existence. "Sound" here refers to all four states listed above, since all four involve sound in important respects:

1. The first state, appearance in a divine body, is the place, or basis of mantra sound since the practitioner who is appearing as a deity is the repeater of mantra.
2. The second state is itself "sound" or whispered repetition.
3. The third state, "the mental one," is mental repetition of the sounds of mantra.
4. The fourth state, "what are pure of words," these being the concentrations of abiding in fire and in sound which involve the appearance of the sounds of mantra, as if recited by

someone else or reverberating of their own accord.

These four are left in the sense that even though they may still appear to the *appearance* factor of the meditator's consciousness, they no longer appear to the *ascertainment* factor of that consciousness, which is concerned only with the emptiness of inherent existence.

The meditator has so trained in these appearances that it is possible for them to remain appearing without effort; this allows the meditator simultaneously and explicitly to realize the absence of these same factors' being established from their own side, their emptiness of inherent existence.

Realization of emptiness was cultivated earlier at the time of the ultimate deity, the first of the six deities in self-generation, at the point of meditating on the suchness of self—one's own emptiness of inherent existence—and on the suchness of the deity, after which one reflected that one's own and the deity's final nature are the same. Also, a sense of the emptiness of inherent existence was maintained throughout the subsequent phases of meditation; however, the main focus of these meditations was on developing the ability to cause these various elements to appear and thus it was impossible for the meditator to focus on emptiness. Instead, the realization of emptiness, though not manifestly present, *affected* the practices in the sense that those yogas were conjoined with the force of emptiness yoga. Now, however, emptiness itself becomes the main object of a powerfully focused mind that is so trained that these various appearances continue even while focusing on emptiness.

The description of such a state is facilitated by making a distinction between what appears and what is being ascertained—a divine body and so forth appear, but what is being ascertained is the emptiness of inherent existence. In his *Terminology Arising in Secret Mantra, the Scriptural Collections of the Knowledge Bearers,*[a] Long-döl Nga-wang-lo-sang[b] (1719-1794) uses the evocative example of a double moon appearing to someone with defective eyesight (such as nearsightedness) who, all the while, understands that the moon is single. Similarly, to the appearance factor of the

---

[a] *gsang sngags rig pa 'dzin pa'i sde snod las byung ba'i ming gi grang,* The Collected Works of Longdol Lama, Part 1 (New Delhi: International Academy of Indian Culture, 1973), 101.3.

[b] *klong rdol ngag dbang blo bzang.*

consciousness forms and so forth appear, but to the ascertainment factor only emptiness appears and is realized. The Dalai Lama, in commentary on Action Tantra, speaks clearly to this point:[a]

> One is no longer mainly concerned with developing clear appearance but is mainly meditating on emptiness. Still, this does not mean that the divine body, sounds, and so forth necessarily no longer appear. Rather, to the *ascertainment factor* of the concentration on the end of sound only emptiness—a negative of inherent existence—appears. However, sounds and so forth may still appear to what is called the appearance factor of that consciousness. This means that although the sounds and so forth may appear, the mind is ascertaining or realizing only emptiness. This is the union of the two truths in Mantra—one consciousness appearing in the form of divine body or speech and simultaneously realizing emptiness.

Thus, the difference between the concentration bestowing liberation at the end of sound and all those preceding is that the earlier deity yoga was merely *affected* by the force of previously realizing emptiness, whereas now the one consciousness that appears as the mantra sounds, divine body, and so forth also actually and explicitly realizes emptiness. When one consciousness is capable of these two activities, the yoga of the nonduality of the profound (realization of the emptiness of inherent existence) and the manifest (compassionate appearance) is complete. Until this point, the meditator has only been imitating such an ability, and thus the deity yoga of nondual profundity and manifestation, which according to Tsong-kha-pa is the central distinctive feature of tantra (see chapter 10), begins only from this point.

Through gradually cultivating the concentration bestowing liberation at the end of sound by alternating analytical and stabilizing meditation, the capacity of the mind increases to the point where analysis itself induces an even greater calm abiding than experienced previously. This enhanced calm abiding, in turn, serves as a basis for even greater penetration of the nature of phenomena. This state is called special insight, which necessarily is a union of calm abiding and special insight.

---

[a] *Deity Yoga*, 34.

It is evident from this progression of practices that the use of rationality to undermine the appearance of objects as if they inherently existed or existed under their power is aimed at overcoming the sense that phenomena, mental and otherwise, exist under their own power, autonomously. Autonomous complexes are being undermined, not just weakened or accommodated as was Jung's aim. This Buddhist division of the mind of deity yoga into an appearance factor appearing as an ideal being and an ascertainment factor realizing emptiness suggests how discrimination is maintained in the face of a profoundly different type of appearance, an ideal being, despite identification with that appearance. Identification has assumed a different meaning, for the meditator merely is identifying himself or herself as that pure person designated in dependence upon purely appearing mind and body and not findable either among or separate from mind and body. This may be how the tantric procedure of deity yoga can go beyond Jung's emphasis on the conscious mind's adapting a posture of confrontation of feeling-toned complexes.

In sum, we have seen how the transmutation sought through deity yoga involves development of positive moral qualities, confrontation with neurotic contents and gradual education of them, identification with the sublime, and de-autonomizing objects, consciousnesses, and dysfunctional tendencies through realization of the status of phenomena and through taking emptiness and wisdom as the stuff of appearance. In particular, Jung's brilliant descriptions of positive and negative inflation have provided an avenue for appreciating the possibility that in deity yoga:

- identification that one's final nature is an absence of inherent, or autonomous, existence may counteract positive inflation, and
- appearance of the wisdom of emptiness itself as an ideal pure being may counteract negative inflation.

However, as mentioned earlier, his cautions need to be heeded; his insights make it clear that deity yoga, *if* it is possible, is no easy matter. Given its built-in safeguards and moral tone, deity yoga may actually succeed in overcoming double-edged inflation, despite the enormity of the task. Nevertheless, I will try not to fall into the trap of claiming to have found the universal panacea.

Five paths and ten grounds

In order to illuminate how the path procedure of Action Tantra fits into the course of spiritual training, the Mongolian scholar Nga-wang-pel-den juxtaposes the standard Great Vehicle way of presenting the path in terms of five levels—the paths of accumulation, preparation, seeing, meditation, and no more learning—with these Action Tantra meditations.[a] His relating these two systems is typical of the synthetic nature of the religious culture in the Tibetan cultural region. Such juxtaposition not only absorbs a particular system into a grand world-view and thus fulfills a need for coherence and harmony but also enriches understanding of a particular system by intertwining it with a familiar set of vocabulary. Although the fitting together of the two systems can at times become mechanistic, it is both challenging in terms of the attempt to align the two as if they seamlessly were that way from the start and revealing in the sense that, when seen in the context of the larger system, the emphasis of this particular system becomes apparent.

Nga-wang-pel-den explains that, related to those practicing Action Tantra, the first, the path of accumulation, is attained when (1) the practitioners generate a nonartificial aspiration to highest enlightenment for the sake of others, thinking to accomplish this in dependence upon the path of Action Tantra, (2) enter an Action Tantra maṇḍala, and (3) receive initiation. At that point, practitioners become Mantra Bodhisattvas. Then, during the path of accumulation, they achieve calm abiding by way of the four-branched repetition and the concentrations of abiding in fire and abiding in sound and begin training in the concentration bestowing liberation at the end of sound. When, in dependence upon this, they generate special insight realizing emptiness, they pass to the Action Tantra path of preparation. In this way, the attainment of a full-fledged concentration bestowing liberation at the end of sound—a meditative stabilization that is a union of calm abiding and special insight realizing emptiness—marks the beginning of the second of the five paths, the path of preparation.

The *Concentration Continuation Tantra* itself says nothing more about the remainder of the path, and thus the remainder of Nga-wang-pel-den's description enriches the path-procedure of this tantra through superimposing the remainder of the Sūtra path on

---

[a] Ibid., 229-234.

the concentration bestowing liberation at the end of sound. He explains that on the four levels of the path of preparation—called heat, peak, forbearance, and supreme mundane qualities—through further cultivation of the concentration bestowing liberation at the end of sound, the sense of duality between the mind of wisdom and its object, emptiness, gradually diminishes, eventually culminating in direct perception of emptiness, this marking the beginning of the third path, the path of seeing, and the first of the ten Bodhisattva grounds. The mind of meditative equipoise on the path of seeing is totally nondualistic, devoid of the five types of dualistic appearance:[a]

1. There is no conceptual appearance.
2. There is no sense of subject and object; subject and object are like fresh water poured into fresh water, indistinguishable.
3. There is no appearance of inherent existence.
4. There is no appearance of conventional phenomena; only emptiness appears.
5. There is no appearance of difference; although the emptinesses of all phenomena in all world systems appear, they do not appear to be different.

Because of the utterly nondualistic nature of this state, it is impossible for a divine body or any appearance other than emptiness to occur. However, it is not that emptiness blots out or cancels phenomena; rather, the limitations of the unenlightened mind make it impossible for emptiness to be *directly* realized and for phenomena qualified by emptiness to appear at the same time.

At this point, practitioners begin to overcome obstructions from the root. The initial period of the path of seeing acts as the antidote to intellectually acquired afflictive obstructions, these being (1) forms of ignorance conceiving inherent existence gained by way of incorrect teachings and scriptures and (2) resultant afflictive emotions. Innate afflictive emotions begin to be overcome when the concentration bestowing liberation at the end of sound becomes capable of acting as an antidote to the grossest level of innate afflictive emotions, at which point the fourth path, the

---

[a] The source for this list is the late Kensur Yeshi Thupten, abbot of the Lo-sel-ling College of Dre-pung Monastic University, re-established in Mundgod, Karnataka State, South India. The contents of the list are common knowledge among Ge-luk-pa scholars.

path of meditation, begins. During this period, Action Tantra Bodhisattvas pass through the remaining nine Bodhisattva grounds, gradually purifying the mind of the innate afflictive emotions and the obstructions to omniscience. The innate afflictive emotions are divided into three levels—big, middling, and small—which in turn are divided into big, middling, and small, making a total of nine levels. When the concentration bestowing liberation at the end of sound becomes capable of acting as the antidote to the big of the big innate afflictive emotions, the second Bodhisattva ground is attained. Then, when it becomes capable of acting as the antidote to the middling of the big innate afflictive emotions, the third Bodhisattva ground is attained. When it becomes capable of acting as the antidote to the small of the big innate afflictive emotions, the fourth Bodhisattva ground is attained. Similarly, when the concentration bestowing liberation at the end of sound becomes capable of acting as the antidote to the three levels of middling innate afflictive emotions, the fifth, sixth, and seventh Bodhisattva grounds are attained. This pattern is broken with the next step, since the eighth ground is attained when the concentration bestowing liberation at the end of sound *simultaneously* becomes capable of acting as the antidote to all three grades of small innate afflictive emotions. (It surely seems that numerological concerns and devotion to roundness of system dictate the breaking of the pattern.)

Then, during a second phase of the eighth ground, the concentration bestowing liberation at the end of sound becomes capable of acting as the antidote to the first of four degrees of obstructions to omniscience, these being the "big" level. Then, when it becomes capable of acting as the antidote to the middling level of obstructions to omniscience, the ninth Bodhisattva ground is attained. Similarly, the tenth is attained when the concentration bestowing liberation at the end of sound becomes capable of acting as the antidote to the coarse small level of obstructions to omniscience. During a second phase of the tenth ground, it becomes capable of acting as the antidote to the subtle of the small obstructions to omniscience, immediately after which Buddhahood and the last of the five paths, the path of no more learning, are simultaneously attained.

Since through cultivating the concentration bestowing liberation at the end of sound over a long period of time a meditator is eventually freed from the afflictive obstructions preventing liberation from cyclic existence and from the obstructions to omniscience, earlier the *Concentration Continuation Tantra* said that "The end of sound bestows liberation." When put in the context of such a path-structure, "liberation" here is seen to refer not just to release from cyclic existence but also to the great liberation of Buddhahood, free from what prevents simultaneous cognition of all objects of knowledge—both phenomena themselves and their final nature, emptiness.

For the concentration bestowing liberation at the end of sound to accomplish the task of removing the obstructions to omniscience, it must be enhanced in force, this being accomplished not only through the usual Great Vehicle means of activities of compassion but also through the particularly tantric means of utilizing special feats in order to promote others' welfare.[a] Ge-luk-pa scholars explain that this process of abandoning the innate afflictive emotions and obstructions to omniscience takes two periods of countless eons.

---

[a] For a brief discussion of the feats, see below, 202; for a presentation of the purpose of these feats, see my supplement in *Deity Yoga*, 207-212; for discussion of feats in the context of Yoga Tantra, see H.H the Dalai Lama, Tsong-kha-pa, and Hopkins, *Yoga Tantra: Paths to Magical Feats*, 64-66 and 110-119.

7. The Practice

As explained in the preceding five chapters, Tsong-kha-pa presents in the second chapter of his *Great Exposition of Secret Mantra* the meditative procedure of Action Tantra mainly through interweaving the *Susiddhi Tantra*, the *Concentration Continuation Tantra*, and their respective commentaries by Varabodhi and Buddhaguhya. While not itself a ritual manual, Tsong-kha-pa's presentation offers almost all of the contents of such a ritual, which can be extracted to make just such a formulation. Thus, as a way to both summarize the material presented in the above chapters and to flesh out many of the details of actual practice, the present chapter is devoted to providing a means of achievement (*sgrub thabs, sādhana*) around the deity Avalokiteshvara, based on the *Great Exposition of Secret Mantra* with supplementary material drawn from his student Dül-dzin-drak-pa-gyel-tsen's *Presentation of the General Rites of Action and Performance Tantra and Their Application to the Three Lineages, Set Down by Dül-dzin According to the Foremost [Tsong-kha-pa's] Practice* and from the eighteenth-century Ye-shay-gyel-tsen's *Illumination of the Meaning of Action Tantra*, along with His Holiness the Dalai Lama's commentary to Tsong-kha-pa's text in *Deity Yoga*.[a]

First the structure of the meditative ritual is given in outline form for the sake of getting a handle on how the five overarching formats of the practice relate to each other:

- prior approximation, effecting the achievement of yogic feats, and activities
- yoga with signs and yoga without signs
- concentrations with repetition and concentration without repetition
- meditative stabilizations of exalted body, speech, and mind
- calm abiding and special insight.

---

[a] I have also added descriptions of how to cultivate altruism and how to meditate on emptiness, which an experienced Tibetan practitioner would bring to the practice, these being from His Holiness the Dalai Lama, *How to Expand Love: Widening the Circle of Loving Relationships*, translated and edited by Jeffrey Hopkins (New York: Atria Books/Simon and Schuster, 2005) and *How to See Yourself As You Really Are*, translated and edited by Jeffrey Hopkins (New York: Atria Books/Simon and Schuster, 2006). I was stimulated to put together this means of achievement by a request from Tibet House Guatemala in 2008.

Outline

I. Prior approximation: approaching the state of a deity

YOGA WITH SIGNS

A. Concentration with repetition

MEDITATIVE STABILIZATION OF EXALTED BODY

1. Preliminaries to the four-branched repetition
2. Actual concentration with repetition
    a. Concentration on the four branches of repetition
        (1) First branch: Other-base
        (2) Second branch: Self-base

MEDITATIVE STABILIZATION OF EXALTED SPEECH

        (3) Third branch: Mind/Moon
        (4) Fourth branch: Sound
    b. Repetition in dependence upon the four branches (deity in front, yourself as a deity, moon, and letters)
        (1) Repeat mantra within observing the form of the letters
            (a) Repeat mantra within observing the form of the letters at the heart of the deity in front
            (b) Repeat mantra within observing the form of the letters at your own heart
        (2) Repeat mantra within observing the sound of the letters
    c. Concluding the concentration of four-branched repetition

B. Concentration without Repetition

1. Concentration of Abiding in Fire
2. Concentration of Abiding in Sound

YOGA WITHOUT SIGNS

MEDITATIVE STABILIZATION OF EXALTED MIND

3. Concentration Bestowing Liberation at the End of Sound

II. Effecting the achievement of yogic feats

A. Analyzing dreams

B. Performing the above meditation in modified form and burnt offerings or repetitions of mantra and so forth

III. Activities

Action Tantra Means of Achievement

Prior Approximation: approaching the state of a deity

YOGA WITH SIGNS

A. Concentration with repetition

MEDITATIVE STABILIZATION OF EXALTED BODY

1. Preliminaries to the four-branched repetition

What to do initially in your place of dwelling

Daily, when you rise from bed in the early morning for the first session and at the beginning of other sessions, construct the pledge seal of the lotus lineage (seal 2[a]) and, holding it at your heart, say:

> ***Oṃ padma-udbhavaye svāhā.***

Make homage to the Buddhas and Bodhisattvas: putting your palms together, observe all the Buddhas in the ten directions and bow down at their feet, saying:

> ***Oṃ sarva-tathāgata kāya-vāk-citta-vajra-praṇamena sarva-tathāgata-vajra-pāda-vandanaṃ karomi.***

Offering yourself, offer your body, saying:

> **If until I am in the essence of enlightenments,[b] I totally and thoroughly offer myself at all times to all Buddhas and Bodhisattvas abiding in the ten directions, may the great Buddhas and Bodhisattvas please take hold of me. Please bestow upon me the unsurpassed feat of Buddhahood.**

Go for refuge and generate an altruistic intention to become enlightened:

> **To Buddha, Doctrine, and Supreme Community**
> **I go for refuge until enlightenment.**
> **To achieve the welfare of myself and others**
> **I will generate the mind of enlightenment.**
>
> **Listen, O Buddhas and Bodhisattvas**
> **Abiding in the ten directions,**

---

[a] For descriptions and pictures of the seals (*phyag rgya, mūdrā*), see *Deity Yoga*, 80-152.

[b] The "essence of enlightenments" is the highest form of enlightenment among the three types, those of a Hearer, a Solitary Realizer, and a Buddha.

I now for the sake of perfect enlightenment
Will generate the mind of enlightenment.

Create protection by making the seal (seal 4) of the Fierce Unobscured One (*mnol ba med pa*), saying the mantra:

Oṃ vajra-krodha mahābālā hana daha pacha vidhvaṃsaya ucchuṣma-krodha hūṃ phaṭ.

(Create protection with this mantra also when eating, drinking, urinating, and defecating.)

Reflecting on purity, think:

The two syllables—*ma,* the entity of Vairochana, on a moon at my heart and *ha,* the entity of Achala, at my head—with interconnecting flames—are stirred up.

and say:

Oṃ svabhāva-śuddhāḥ sarva-dharmāḥ svabhāva-śuddho 'haṃ. (Oṃ naturally pure are all phenomena; naturally pure am I.)

and imagine:

All phenomena have become naturally pure.

Then, leaving the house, brush your teeth and so forth. Collect and remove the dirt and dust in the temple and so forth.

Bathing outdoors and entering the place of practice

Go to a shore where beings do not gather and where there is nothing frightful. Construct the pledge seal of the lotus lineage (seal 2) and, holding it at your heart, say:

Oṃ padma-udbhavaye svāhā.

With seal 5, touch clean earth, saying:

Oṃ nikhanavasude svāhā.

Picking up the earth, divide it into three portions, and put them in a clean place. Protect yourself through Amṛitakuṇḍali by constructing seal 6, pressing the lower lip with the upper teeth, looking with a fierce gaze, and saying:

Namo ratnatrayāya, namaṣcaṇḍa-vajrapāṇaye, mahāyakṣasena-pataye, namo vajra-krodhāya, tadyathā oṃ hulu hulu tiṣṭha tiṣṭha bandha bandha hana hana amṛte hūṃ phaṭ.

To expel obstructors in your body, construct seal 7, and say:

Oṃ hana hana amṛte hūṃ phaṭ.

To put on vajra armor, construct seal 8, and put on vajra armor to prevent obstructors from entering. Then construct the vajra armor seal (seal 9), and touching it to the head, tops of both shoulders, heart, and neck, make (that is, imagine) the armor, saying:

Namo ratnatrayāya oṃ khakiḷ hūṃ phaṭ.

To dispel obstructors, construct seal 10, and touching it to earth and water, say:

Namo vajrāya hūṃ, hana dhuna matha vidhvaṃsaya udsarāya phaṭ.

Cast this mantra into the water:

Namo ratnatrayāya, namaṣcaṇḍa-vajrapāṇaye, oṃ hana hana, vajra vajraṇaha.

Constructing seal 11, touch this seal of Kīlikīla to the water, and sprinkle the earth with the water, saying:

Oṃ kīlikīla hūṃ phaṭ.

Mantrafy the earth seven times with:

Oṃ vajra hara hūṃ.

and pick up one portion of the earth. Wearing a bathing cloth, enter into the water just to the disappearance of the navel, and bathe, washing below the navel with the first portion of earth. Then, wash your hands with the second portion of earth, and construct the seal of Sarasvatī (seal 12), saying:

Oṃ śruti smṛti dhaṛani hūṃ ha.

The seal and mantra can serve as ablution. Or:

Squat, stop talking, and put your two hands between your knees. Bend a little the middle and ring fingers of the right hand with the palm turned upwards, and hold this towards your mouth. Wipe your mouth many times with water in which anthers have been soaked, and having touched the two ear-holes, two eyes, nose, mouth, hands, navel, and heart two or three times, drink three gulps of the water, wiping your lips twice.

Tying up the hair on your head, create protection by saying:

Oṃ susiddhikari svāhā.

Pick up the third portion of earth, mantrafy it with:

Oṃ bhūr jala hūṃ phaṭ.

and circling it to the right, face it to the sun, and rub it on the entire body.

Construct the water-stirring seal (seal 13), and with it stir the water, saying:

Namo ratnatrayāya, namaṣcaṇḍa-vajrapāṇaye, mahāyakṣasenāpataye, namo vajra-krodhāya ḍaṃṣṭokaṭa bhairavāya, tadyathā, oṃ amṛtakuṇḍali, khakha, khāhi khāhi, tiṣṭa tiṣṭa, bandha bandha, hana hana, garja garja, visphoṭāya, sarva-vighnāṃ vinayakāna, mahāgaṇa-pati, jīvita-antakarāya svāhā.

Then, offer three handfuls of water to the Three Jewels, saying:

Oṃ rate rate buddhāya svāhā.

Saying:

Oṃ amṛte hūṃ phaṭ.

cup your hands together, and pour three handfuls of water on your head, and wash your hands. With that very mantra confer initiation on yourself with three handfuls of water:

Oṃ amṛta hūṃ phaṭ.

Mentally invite Avalokiteshvara and ask him to reside on a lotus imagined in front of you. Bathe his body, saying:

Oṃ sarva-tathāgata-amṛte svāhā.

Then, if repetition is to be done in the temple, repeat the mantra twenty-one times while in the water:

Oṃ sarva-tathāgata-avalokiteśvare svāhā.

Go up to the temple, and wash your feet; facing east or north, do ablution:

Squat, stop talking, and put your two hands between your knees. Bend a little the middle and ring fingers of the right hand with the palm turned upwards, and hold this towards your mouth. Wipe your mouth many times with water in which anthers have been soaked, and having touched the two ear-holes, two eyes, nose, mouth, hands, navel, and heart two or three times, drink three gulps of the water, wiping your lips twice.

Enter the place of practice, and visualizing the deities vividly, make homage, bowing down at their feet, saying:

Oṃ sarva-tathāgata kāya-vāk-citta-vajra-praṇamena sarva-tathāgata-vajra-pāda-vandanaṃ karomi.

Repeat this engagement in the pledges:

Oṃ viraja viraja, mahāvajri sata sata, sarate sarate, trayi trayi, vir-dhamani saṃbhañjani taramati siddha-agretaṃ svāhā.

Putting on the robe, sitting on the cushion, and blessing the offerings

Put on the robe, and having sat on the cushion, bless the offerings by removing contamination from yourself through pouring scented water in the palm of your hand, repeating the essence mantra three times:

Ārolik ārolik ārolik.

and sprinkling the water on top of your head, thereby clearing away defects of contamination and so forth. Sprinkle the cushion made of kusha grass or other material while reciting the mantra of Kuṇḍali:

Namo ratnatrayāya, namaşcaṇḍa-vajrapāṇaye, mahāyakṣasena-pa-taye, namo vajra-krodhāya, tadyathā oṃ hulu hulu tiṣṭha tiṣṭha bandha bandha hana hana amṛte hūṃ phaṭ.

and sit on the cushion in either the lucky, lotus, or vajra cross-legged posture. Then, anoint with incense a bracelet made from an uneven number of threads spun by a girl and wound and tied in an uneven number of knots and with one rosary bead of the lotus lineage set in the center; repeat a hundred times into the bracelet the knowledge-mantra of the lotus lineage, the mantra of the lineage mother:

> Homage to the Three Jewels. Homage to the Bodhisattva, the great being, the Superior Avalokiteshvara.
>
> May I cure all illness
> Of all sentient beings
> Through their seeing, hearing,
> Touching, or remembering me.
>
> *Tadyathā kaṭe vikaṭe kaṃkaṭe kaṭa vikaṭe, kaṃkaṭe bhagavati vijaye svāhā.*

and tie the bracelet to the wrist of the right hand. Repeating the lotus lineage essence-mantra:

> *Ārolik.*

put a sprinkler made of kusha grass on the ring finger of your right hand. Into the *ze'u kha,* the skull binder made from red silk or cotton, cast the mantra:

> *Oṃ rakṣa rakṣa mānā sarva-buddha-adhiṣṭhana ātma civara svāhā.*

and tie it on your head. Also, put on clothing into which this very mantra has been cast. Tie up your hair as an image of the crown protrusion:

> *Oṃ susiddhikari svāhā.*

Go for refuge and generate an altruistic intention to become enlightened, as before, saying:

> To Buddha, Doctrine, and Supreme Community
> I go for refuge until enlightenment.
> To achieve the welfare of myself and others
> I will generate the mind of enlightenment.
>
> Listen, O Buddhas and Bodhisattvas
> Abiding in the ten directions,
> I now for the sake of perfect enlightenment
> Will generate the mind of enlightenment.

Clear away obstructors in the flowers and so forth through repeating into scented water either the mantra of Kuṇḍali:

Namo ratnatrayāya, namaṣcaṇḍa-vajrapāṇaye, mahāyakṣasena-pataye, namo vajra-krodhāya, tadyathā oṃ hulu hulu tiṣṭha tiṣṭha bandha bandha hana hana amṛte hūṃ phaṭ.

or the mantra of all activities of the lotus lineage:

Oṃ namo mahā-śrīyāyai, sau me siddhi siddha sādhaya, śivi śivaṃkari, abhaha, sarva-artha-sādhani svāhā.

Putting scented water into the left hand, repeat into the water the lineage essence:

Ārolik.

and sprinkle the flowers and so forth. From the seal of dispelling obstructors (seal 10) construct the seal of generating magnificence (seal 14), and with it distribute magnificence on top of the perfume, flowers, and so forth and repeat the mantra of generating magnificence:

Oṃ divya divya dhipaya, avesha mahāśrīye svāhā.

thinking that thereby:

The offerings turn into perfect divine substances.

Then, bless them into magnificence with the mantra of Kuṇḍali:

Namo ratnatrayāya, namaṣcaṇḍa-vajrapāṇaye, mahāyakṣasena-pataye, namo vajra-krodhāya, tadyathā oṃ hulu hulu tiṣṭha tiṣṭha bandha bandha hana hana amṛte hūṃ phaṭ.

and repeat the essence mantra of the lotus lineage:

Ārolik.

Self-protection

Make seal of expelling obstructors in the body (seal 7) and repeat the mantra of expelling obstructors:

Oṃ hana hana amṛte hūṃ phaṭ.

Then repeat into the scented water either the mantra for all activities of the lotus lineage:

Oṃ namo mahā-śrīyāyai, sau me siddhi siddha sādhaya, śivi śivaṃkari, abhaha, sarva-artha-sādhani svāhā.

or the mantra of Kuṇḍali:

Namo ratnatrayāya, namaṣcaṇḍa-vajrapāṇaye, mahāyakṣasena-pataye, namo vajra-krodhāya, tadyathā oṃ hulu hulu tiṣṭha tiṣṭha bandha bandha hana hana amṛte hūṃ phaṭ.

and sprinkle it on yourself, dispelling obstructors.

Place-protection

Repeat into scented water seven times:

Oṃ kīlikīla vajri vajri bhur bandha bandha hūṃ phaṭ.

and sprinkle the scented water in all directions. Making the ritual dagger seal (seal 15), and reciting:

Oṃ kīlikīlvajri vajri bhur bandha bandha hūṃ phaṭ.

think:

Through implanting the obstructors with the Fierce Vajra Daggers they have become immovable.

Repeating this general mantra for the three lineages into the fumes of powdered incense:

Oṃ susiddhikara jvalita, ananta-murtaye jvala jvala, bandha bandha, hana hana hūṃ phaṭ.

and this mantra for the lotus lineage:

Oṃ padmini bhagavati mohaya mohaya, jagad mohani svāhā.

think:

The upper demonic gods are bound.

Then, repeating the essence mantra into scented water:

Ārolik.

sprinkle the environs with scented water. Repeating the secret mantra of the knowledge kings of the three lineages:

Bhrūṃ oṃ amṛtodbhava udbhava hūṃ phaṭ, namo ratnatrayāya, namaṣcaṇḍa-vajrapāṇaye, mahāyakṣasena-pataye, oṃ sumbha nisumbha hūṃ, gṛhṇa gṛhṇa hūṃ, gṛhṇāpaya gṛhṇāpaya hūṃ, ānayaho bhagavān vidyā-rāja hūṃ phaṭ svāhā.

think:

All directional obstructors have been bound.

From the dagger seal (seal 15) make the fence seal (seal 16), and saying:

Namo ratnatrayāya, namaṣcaṇḍa-vajrapāṇaye, mahāyakṣasena-pataye, tadyathā oṃ sara sara vajra-prakara hūṃ phaṭ.

think:

A vajra fence has circled the area without break.

Displaying the fence seal itself (seal 16) upside down, move it in a circle (seal 17), and saying:

Namo ratnatrayāya, namaṣcaṇḍa-vajrapāṇaye, mahāyakṣasenapataye, oṃ bhisphu-rakṣa-vajrapāṇi hūṃ phaṭ.

think:

A vajra tent has come to be on top of the vajra fence.

To bless the fence and tent into magnificence, recite the mantra of Kuṇḍali:

Namo ratnatrayāya, namaṣcaṇḍa-vajrapāṇaye, mahāyakṣasena-pataye, namo vajra-krodhāya, tadyathā oṃ hulu hulu tiṣṭha tiṣṭha

bandha bandha hana hana amṛte hūṃ phaṭ.

and making the dagger seal (seal 15), say:

Oṃ kīlikīla vajri vajri bhur bandha bandha hūṃ phaṭ.

To close off the area make seal 18, and say:

Namaḥ samanta-vajraṇāṃ, oṃ tara tara, turu turu, maṭa maṭa, bandha bandha, sarvatra apratihate, sasime samabandha, kuru kuru tara tara samanta-vajre, samanta-vajre, kuru amale kuruṇa, maye tutaye tutaye, bara bara, kara kara, sumima samanta, vidhvaṃsaye, jvalāya svāhā.

2. Actual concentration with repetition

a. Concentration on the four branches of repetition

First branch: Other-base[a]

Imagining a deity in front of yourself

Imagine the ground for a divine residence:

In front is a ground of many precious substances covered with grains of gold.

Bless it into magnificence by reciting once:

Oṃ calavī hūṃ svāhā.

Imagine:

On top of it is an ocean, white like milk, adorned with flowers such as lotus and utpala. Flocks of birds as if made of jewels fly overhead.

Bless these into magnificence by reciting once:

Oṃ vimaladhaha hūṃ.

Imagine Mount Meru with lotus and divine residence:

In the middle is the great square Mount Meru adorned on all four sides with stairs, made respectively of gold, silver, sapphire, and topaz. The mountain is covered with well-grown wish-granting trees, themselves adorned with thousands of flapping victory banners. On top of the mountain is a huge lotus; its stalk, rising out of the center of Mount Meru, is adorned with jewels, petals made of jewels, a gold corolla,

[a] Tsong-kha-pa indicates (*Deity Yoga,* 103-104) that it is easier for beginners to meditate on the deity in front first and then oneself as a deity, since meditation on a deity in front requires many activities whereas self-generation is aimed at developing *steady* concentration on oneself in divine form. Thus, the order of the first two of the branches could be reversed.

and topaz anthers with silver lines surrounding the top at its center. From the lotus stalk hundreds, thousands, ten thousands, and millions of lotus latticeworks emerge. The syllable *bhrūṃ*, standing upright in the middle of the lotus, transforms into an empty inestimable mansion. In the middle of the palace is another lotus, the deity's seat.

With seal 19 bless the imagined residence into magnificence by reciting a hundred times:

Namaḥ sarvatathāgatānāṃ sarvathā udgate spharaṇahimaṃ gaganakhaṃ svāhā.

Imagine a canopy over the divine residence:

Instantaneously, a canopy appears over the residence.

Inviting the deity

You have previously prepared an oblation; the substance of the vessel (gold, silver, stone, wood, and so forth) and the contents (barley and milk, sesame and yogurt, cow urine and rice, and so forth) are determined by the feat that you are seeking to receive from the deity after the meditations are completed. Infuse the oblation with incense, and bless it into a magnificent state by reciting the appropriate mantra seven times.

Oṃ namo mahā-śrīyāyai, sau me siddhi siddha sādhaya, śivi śivaṃkari, abhaha, sarva-artha-sādhani svāhā.

Facing in front where a painting, or the like, of the deity is placed, bow down, saying the mantra:

Oṃ sarva-tathāgata kāya-vāk-citta-vajra-praṇamena sarva-tathāgata-vajra-pāda-vandanaṃ karomi.

Then, kneeling, invite the deity through making the seal of invitation (seal 20), which is a beckoning gesture, saying:

Due to my faith and your compassionate pledges,
Come here, come here, O Supramundane Victor.
Accepting this oblation of mine,
Be pleased with me through this offering.
Ārolik, ehyahi.

Assuming the same posture as Avalokiteshvara, that is, sitting, hold up the oblation at the level of your head, and offer it, saying:

Oṃ avalokiteśvara arghaṃ pratīccha svāhā.

If the proper ingredients have not been obtained, beg the deity's pardon:

Whatever even slightly has been done wrongly

Out of the obscuration in my mind,
Please, O Protector, bear with it all
Since you are the refuge of all the embodied.

Whatever has been done here
Due to non-acquisition, lack of thorough knowledge,
Or not having the capacity,
It is right for the Chief to bear with it all.

Then:

The Supreme Superior, the Great Compassionate One, Avalokiteshvara—with white body bedecked with various jewel adornments, having one face with an affectionate smiling aspect and two eyes, with four arms, the two upper hands holding a wish-granting jewel at the heart, the other right hand holding a pearl rosary, and the other left hand holding a white lotus, with an antelope skin draped over the left shoulder, sitting in the adamantine cross-legged posture on a lotus seat—arrives together with his inestimable mansion which fuses with the imagined mansion.

Offer a seat while reciting:

It is good that the compassionate Supramundane Victor has come.
I am meritorious and fortunate.
Taking my oblation,
Please pay heed and grant my request.

From compassion for myself and transmigrators
As long as I make offering
May the Supramundane Victor please remain here
Through your powers of magical creation.

Displaying the pledge vajra seal (seal 24), recite once:

Śaṃkare samaye svāhā.

Make seal 26, and say the essence-mantra for the lotus lineage:

Ārolik.

Make the great pledge seal of the lotus lineage (seal 2) and revolve it to protect against obstructors. Dispel obstructors from the articles of offering, saying:

To Buddha, Doctrine, and Supreme Community
I go for refuge until enlightenment.
To achieve the welfare of myself and others
I will generate the mind of enlightenment.

Listen, O Buddhas and Bodhisattvas
Abiding in the ten directions,
I now for the sake of perfect enlightenment
Will generate the mind of enlightenment.

and repeating into scented water:

Namo ratnatrayāya, namaṣcaṇḍa-vajrapāṇaye, mahāyakṣasena-pataye, namo vajra-krodhāya, tadyathā oṃ hulu hulu tiṣṭha tiṣṭha bandha bandha hana hana amṛte hūṃ phaṭ

and sprinkle the flowers to clear away obstructors. Putting scented water in the left hand, repeat the mantra for the lotus lineage into the water and dispel obstructors with it:

Ārolik.

With the seal of generating magnificence (seal 14), spread magnificence on top of the offerings and say the appropriate mantra for generating magnificence:

Oṃ divya divya dhipaya, aveśa mahāśrīyaye svāhā. (Lotus lineage)

With the oblation seal (seal 28), offer oblation, saying:

You have come blissfully, Supramundane Victor.
Come here and please be seated.
Receiving my oblation also,
Please take pleasure mentally from this.
I have respect for you.

Oṃ sarva-tathāgata-avalokiteśvara-saparivāra arghaṃ pratīccha svāhā.

With the foot-bath seal (seal 29), offer a foot-bath, saying:

You have come blissfully, Supramundane Victor.
Come here and please be seated.
Receiving my foot-bath also,
Please take pleasure mentally from this.
I have respect for you.

Oṃ sarva-tathāgata-avalokiteśvara-saparivāra pravarasatkaraṃ pratīccha svāhā.

With the seal of washing the body (seal 30), imagine washing the deity's body with great clouds of perfumed water which have risen from many precious gold vases and so forth filled with fragrant perfumes; say:

You have come blissfully, Supramundane Victor.
Come here and please be seated.
Receiving my bath also,
Please take pleasure mentally from this.

I have respect for you.

Oṃ sarva-tathāgata-avalokiteśvara-saparivāra sarvadevatā-acinta-amṛta svāhā.

Mentally offer clothing and adornments; offer music, and mentally raise up melodies of praise.

With the perfume seal (seal 31), offer perfume, saying:

With faith I offer these perfumes
Of wholesome divine substances
Arisen from the clean, most clean.
Receiving them, be pleased with me.

Oṃ sarva-tathāgata-avalokiteśvara-saparivāra āhara āhara sarva-vidyādhari pūjite svāhā.

With the flower seal (seal 32), offer flowers, saying:

With faith I offer these flowers
Of auspicious divine substance,
Grown from the clean, most clean.
Receiving them, be pleased with me.

Oṃ sarva-tathāgata-avalokiteśvara-saparivāra āhara āhara sarva-vidyādhari pūjite svāhā.

With the incense seal (seal 33), offer incense, saying:

With faith I offer divine substances
Made with perfume,
Pleasant essences of the forest.
Receiving them, be pleased with me.

Oṃ sarva-tathāgata-avalokiteśvara-saparivāra āhara āhara sarva-vidyādhari pūjite svāhā.

With the seal of divine food (seal 34), offer food, saying:

With faith I offer
These foods of mantra,
Pleasant medicinal essences.
Receiving them, be pleased with me.

Oṃ sarva-tathāgata-avalokiteśvara-saparivāra āhara āhara sarva-vidyādhari pūjite svāhā.

With the lamp seal (seal 35), offer lamps, saying:

With faith I offer these dispellers
Of darkness, conquering harmers,
Auspicious and virtuous.
I beg you to receive these lamps.

Oṃ sarva-tathāgata-avalokiteśvara-saparivāra ālokāya ālokāya vidhādhare pūjite svāhā.

Repeat one hundred times the mantra of blessing the place into magnificence:

Namaḥ sarvatathāgatānāṃ sarvathā udgate spharaṇahimaṃ gagana-khaṃ svāhā.

Praise the Three Jewels—Buddha, his doctrine, and the spiritual community:

Homage to the One-Gone-Thus,
Protector with great compassion,
Omniscient teacher,
Oceanic field of merit and attainments.

Homage to the pacifying doctrine,
Through purity separating from desire,
Through virtue liberating from bad transmigrations,
In all ways the supreme ultimate.

Respectful homage to the spiritual community,
Liberated, teaching the path of liberation,
Completely dwelling in the precepts,
Excellent field of merit, endowed with attainments.

Praise the lords of the three lineages—Mañjushrī, who is the physical manifestation of the wisdom of all Buddhas; Avalokiteshvara, who is the physical manifestation of the compassion of all Buddhas; and Vajrapāṇi, who is the physical manifestation of the power of all Buddhas:

Homage also to Mañjushrī,
Bearer of the appearance of a youth,
Vividly adorned with the lamp of wisdom,
Dispeller of the three worlds' darkness.

Homage to the always merciful,
Whose name is Avalokiteshvara,
Composite of all excellent qualities,
Strongly praised by all Buddhas.

Homage to Vajrapāṇi,
Powerful and fierce,
Virtuous king of knowledge-mantra,
Tamer of the hard to tame.

Make praises specifically of Avalokiteshvara, and repeat one hundred times the mantra of bringing forth praise:

Namaḥ sarva-buddha-bodhisattvānāṃ, sarvatra saṃkurumita avijñā-rāśini namo stute svāhā.

Disclose ill deeds with an attitude of contrition and future restraint:

Ones-Gone-Thus residing
In all directions of the worlds,
Foe Destroyers, and Bodhisattvas,
I ask you to heed me.

Whatever ill deeds
I have committed in any lifetime,
Or, disturbed by the power of desire,
Stupidity, or anger in cyclic existence
In former lives or in this life,
Whatever ill deeds I have done,
Asked others to do, or admired even a little,
Even slight ones unconscientiously done
With body, speech, or mind
To Buddha, doctrine, or spiritual community,
Or gurus, father and mother,
Foe Destroyers, Bodhisattvas,
Or any object of giving,
Or to other sentient beings—
Educated or uneducated—
Having mentally collected all these,
I bow down in great respect
To the perfect Buddhas and their children
Manifest before me now
And disclose individually
And repeatedly my mistakes
With pressed palms and saddened mind.

Just as the perfect Buddhas know
The ill deeds that I have committed,
I make individual disclosure.
Henceforth I will not do such.

Take refuge in Buddha, his doctrine, and the spiritual community with strong intent:

So that the sufferings of beings might be pacified
I respectfully go for true refuge
To Buddha, Doctrine, and Spiritual Community
As long as I remain alive.

Admire your own and others' virtues:

Set in equipoise, I take admiration
In the varieties of practical implementation of doctrine.

Entreat the Buddhas to remain teaching and supplicate them not to withdraw physical appearance so beneficial to the world:

To generate nonconceptual pristine wisdom
I entreat you to turn the wheel of doctrine
And not to pass away from sorrow
Until trainees are satisfied.

Make prayer-wishes:

Just as the earlier Buddha-children
Made prayer-wishes,
I also with a virtuous mind
Plant prayer-wishes in that way.

May all beings have happiness,
Peace, and freedom from disease.
May I be capable in all activities
And also possess all good qualities.

May I be wealthy, generous,
Intelligent, and patient,
Having faith in virtue, memory
Of former births in all lives, and mercy.

Cultivate the four immeasurables—compassion, love, joy, and the equanimity that is devoid of the conceptions of subject and object as inherently existent:

May all sentient beings be free from all suffering.
May all sentient beings be endowed with all happiness.
May all sentient beings be blissful with the bliss of Buddhahood.
May all sentient beings pass from sorrow with the unsurpassed nirvāṇa of a Buddha.

Generate an altruistic intention to become enlightened such that it definitely suffuses your mental continuum:

Foundational Step: Equality

1. **From their own point of view, friends, enemies, and neutral beings equally want happiness and do not want suffering.**
2. **From my own point of view, each and every one of them has been my friend limitless times over beginningless cyclic existence and will definitely help me again in the future; each**

has equally been my enemy; and each has equally been neutral.

3. Thus from whatever side it is considered, my own or others, there is no point in exaggerating feelings of intimacy or alienation. I should not value one person as basically good and another as bad, even though their present actions may be good or bad, helpful or harmful. There is no reason to be nice at heart to one person and not nice to another. Though it is true that people are friends or enemies temporarily—helpful or harmful—it is a mistake to use this fluid state as the basis for an inflexible attraction or hatred.

First Step: Recognizing Friends

1. My births in cyclic existence have no beginning.
2. When I was born from a womb as an animal or human, or when I was born from an egg, I required a mother. Since my births are innumerable, I must have had innumerable mothers over the course of those many lifetimes. The implication is that every living being has been my mother at some time. See whether there is a reason why any sentient being has not been my mother; such a conclusion is impossible.
3. The times I took birth from a womb or an egg are unlimited in number, and therefore my mothers are also unlimited in number.
4. Each sentient being has to have been my mother many times.

Second Step: Appreciating Kindness

Visualize your prime nurturer, vividly in front, and think:

> This person was my mother many times over the continuum of lives; in just this present lifetime she has bestowed on me a body that supports an auspicious life in which I am able to progress spiritually. She sustained me in her womb for nine months, during which she could not behave as she wished but had to pay special attention to this burden that she carried in her body, making it difficult to move about. Even though my movements would cause her pain, she would take delight in them, thinking how strong her child was, rather than becoming angry and concentrating on her pain. Her sense of closeness and dearness was great.

If you use as a model a person other than your mother, recall in detail the kindnesses he or she extended.

Having understood the kindness of your prime nurturer of this lifetime, extend this understanding gradually to other friends, then neutral persons, and finally enemies.

Third Step: Returning Kindness

Think:

> **If my mother (or best friend) of this lifetime was blind and, not in her right mind, was proceeding along the edge of a frightful cliff without a guide, and if I, her own child, did not pay attention and take on the task of helping her, it would be awful.**

Extend the example:

> **All sentient beings throughout space have been my mother and have protected me with great kindness; they do not know what in their behavior to discard and what to adopt in order to promote their own long-term interests. Without a spiritual guide, they are walking along the edge of a cliff of frightful sufferings in cyclic existence. If, knowing this, I did not consider their welfare but only my own freedom, it would be awful.**

In response to being cared for by others in this and other lifetimes, develop a determination to help them in whatever way is appropriate:

> **I will do whatever I can for these beings—my own nurturing friends—stricken by such suffering.**

Commit to their welfare.

Fourth Step: Love

Starting with your best friend, think:

> **This person wants happiness but is bereft. How nice it would be if she or he could be imbued with happiness and all the causes of happiness!**

Continue the same meditation with respect to more and more friends until this wish for happiness and all the causes of happiness is equally strong for all of them, and then consider neutral beings and finally enemies.

Then intensify the feeling, starting with friends, with:

> **This person wants happiness but is bereft. May she or he be imbued with happiness and all the causes of happiness!**

Extend the same wish to neutral beings, and enemies.

Then intensify the feeling, starting with friends, with:

> **I will do whatever I can to cause her or him to be imbued with happiness and all the causes of happiness!**

Extend the same wish to neutral beings, and enemies.

Fifth Step: Compassion

Bring to mind a friend who has obvious pain, and think:

> **Like me, this person wants happiness and does not want suffering, yet is stricken with such pain. If this person could only be free from suffering and the causes of suffering!**

Visualize a friend who, even though not blatantly suffering, will suffer in the future due to substantial counterproductive actions of the kind that we all have committed over the course of beginningless time. Think:

> **Like me, this person wants happiness and does not want suffering, yet is stricken with such pain. If this person could only be free from suffering and the causes of suffering!**

Slowly extend this meditation person by person, first with more friends, then with neutral persons, and finally with enemies, eventually including all sentient beings throughout space.

Then intensify the feeling, starting with friends, then neutral persons, and then enemies:

> **Like me, this person wants happiness and does not want suffering, yet is stricken with such pain. May this person be free from suffering and the causes of suffering!**

Extend the same wish to neutral beings, and enemies.

Then intensify the feeling, starting with friends, then neutral persons, and then enemies:

> **Like me, this person wants happiness and does not want suffering, yet is stricken with such pain. I will help this person be free from suffering and all the causes of suffering!**

Extend the same wish to neutral beings, and enemies.

Sixth Step: Total Commitment

1. **Afflictive emotions do not dwell in the nature of the mind; therefore, they can be removed.**
2. **Since afflictive emotions can be separated from the mind, it is realistic for me to work to achieve enlightenment and to help others do the same.**
3. **Even if I have to do it alone, I will free all sentient beings**

from suffering and the causes of suffering, and join all sentient beings with happiness and its causes.

Seventh Step: Seeking Altruistic Enlightenment

Analyze whether in your present state you have the capacity to bring about the welfare of all beings by freeing them from suffering and joining them with happiness.

Though I can help others on a limited level, I cannot yet do so on a vast level. In addition to giving food, clothing, and shelter it is necessary to educate people so that they can take care of their own lives. Teaching what should be adopted and discarded is crucial, and therefore I must know their dispositions and interests and have full knowledge of beneficial practices. Thus it is necessary for me to achieve enlightenment, in which the obstacles keeping me from realizing everything knowable are completely removed and I gain total realization of the nature of persons and things.

Think:

I will attain Buddhahood in order to liberate stricken transmigrating beings.

and say:

To pacify the suffering
Of limitless realms of sentient beings,
Release them from bad transmigrations,
Liberate them from afflictive emotions,
And protect them completely
From the varieties of sufferings
When the discomforts of cyclic existence crowd in,
I will generate an altruistic intention to become
enlightened.

May I always be a refuge
For all destitute sentient beings,
A protector of the protectorless,
A support of those without support,
A refuge for the unprotected,
One who makes the miserable happy.

May I cause the pacification
Of all sentient beings' afflictive emotions.
May whatever virtuous actions

I have accumulated in this and other lives
Assume the aspects of the collections
That are called merit and wisdom.

May whatever effort I make
By way of the six perfections
Be of benefit to all beings
Without there being any exception.

Making effort until enlightenment,
I will strive at actions temporarily
And limitlessly over lives so that, in short,
All the afflictive emotions of all sentient beings
May be pacified and they be freed.

Second branch: Self-base

Imagining Yourself as a Deity: Meditation of the Six Deities

1. Ultimate Deity (also called emptiness deity or suchness deity): meditate on yourself and the deity as the same in being empty of inherent existence

Ascertain what is being negated—inherent existence:

Imagine, for instance, that someone criticizes you for something you actually have not done, saying, "You ruined such and such," pointing a finger at you.

Watch your reaction. How does the "I" appear to your mind?

In what way are you apprehending it?

Notice how that "I" seems to stand by itself, self-instituting, established by way of its own character.

Ascertain the entailment of emptiness:

Analyze whether the "I" that is inherently self-established in the context of the mind-body complex could have a way of existing other than being part of or separate from mind and body.

Take other phenomena, such as a cup and a table, or a house and a mountain, as examples. See that there is no third category of existence. They are either the same or different.

Decide that if the "I" inherently exists as it seems to, then it must be either one with or separate from mind and body.

Ascertain that the "I" and the aggregates are not inherently the same by considering the consequences if the "I" is the same as mind-body and if the "I" is established in and of itself in accordance with how it appears to your mind:

Since mind and body are plural, a person's selves also would be plural!

Since I am just one, mind and body also would be one!

Ascertain that the "I" and the aggregates are not inherently different by considering the consequences if the "I" is inherently different from mind-body and if the "I" is established in and of itself in accordance with how it appears to your mind:

I and mind-body would have to be completely separate!

In that case, I would have to be findable after clearing away mind and body!

I would not have the characteristics of being produced, abiding, and disintegrating!

I would have to be just a figment of the imagination or permanent!

I would not have any physical or mental characteristics!

Not finding yourself either of these ways, realize the absence of inherent existence of the "I" in space-like meditative equipoise.

Reflect on the sameness of yourself and the deity in terms of your final nature:

Just as my own suchness is ultimately free from all the proliferations of inherent existence, so also is the deity's suchness. Hence, in nonconceptual perception of the final mode of subsistence of phenomena, the suchness of myself and of the deity are undifferentiable, like a mixture of water and milk.

2. Sound Deity (also called tone deity)

From within emptiness my wisdom realizing the ultimate deity manifests as the tones of the mantra resounding in space.[a]

Oṃ maṇi padme hūṃ.

3. Letter Deity

My mind having the aspect of realizing the undifferentiable suchness of myself and the deity becomes a moon disc. The mantra tones resounding in space are set upright on the edge of the moon disc in the aspect of written letters, like very pure

[a] Alternatively, this step can include the appearance of a moon disk above which the tones of mantra resound.

mercury adhering to or completely mixing with grains of gold. (The letters are not just color and shape but are fused with their respective sounds.)

4. Form Deity

The moon and mantra letters transform such that variegated rays of light are emitted from the moon and mantra letters. From the points of the light rays innumerable forms of the deity emerge, pervading the entire sphere of space. Through emanating great clouds of offerings they make splendid offerings to all the Buddhas and Bodhisattvas. Also, they emanate great clouds from which a rain of ambrosia descends, extinguishing the fires of the sufferings of all transmigrators, hell-beings and so forth, as well as satisfying beings with whatever they need—giving a good body to those who need it, coolness to those suffering from heat, the warmth of the sun to those suffering from cold, food and drink to the hungry and thirsty—emanating to each just what he or she needs, providing beings with the basis for practicing the spiritual path as well as teachers to instruct them in the four truths, the two truths, and so forth, whereby they ascend the five paths and ten Bodhisattva grounds and attain the final happiness of Buddhahood.

Then, the divine bodies dissolve back into the rays of light with all their magnificent qualities of body, speech, and mind and return and enter the moon disc and mantra letters, whereupon I emerge in the full form of Avalokiteshvara, the Supreme Superior, the Great Compassionate One, with white body bedecked with various jewel adornments, having one face with an affectionate smiling aspect and two eyes, with four arms—the two upper hands holding a wish-granting jewel at the heart, the other right hand holding a pearl rosary, and the other left hand holding a white lotus—with an antelope skin draped over the left shoulder, sitting in the adamantine cross-legged posture on a lotus seat.

5. Seal Deity

Construct the pledge seal of the lotus lineage (seal 2) and bless into a magnificent state the heart, the point between the brows, the neck, and the shoulders[a] through touching them with the seal and

[a] Or, alternatively, the crown protrusion, hair-treasury (a single coiled hair in the

repeating the pledge mantra:

Oṃ padma-udbhavaye svāhā.

With the oblation seal (seal 28), offer oblation to yourself as the deity, saying:

Arghaṃ pratīccha svāhā.

With the foot-bath seal (seal 29), offer a foot-bath, saying:

Oṃ pravarasatkaraṃ pratīccha svāhā.

With the seal of washing the body (seal 30), imagine washing the deity's body with great clouds of perfumed water which have risen from many precious gold vases and so forth filled with fragrant perfumes; say:

Oṃ sarva-devatā-acinta-amṛta svāhā.

Mentally offer clothing and adornments; offer music, and mentally raise up melodies of praise.

With the perfume seal (seal 31), offer perfume, saying:

Āhara āhara sarva-vidyādhari pūjite svāhā.

With the flower seal (seal 32), offer flowers, saying:

Āhara āhara sarva-vidyādhari pūjite svāhā.

With the incense seal (seal 33), offer incense, saying:

Āhara āhara sarva-vidyādhari pūjite svāhā.

With the seal of divine food (seal 34), offer food, saying:

Āhara āhara sarva-vidyādhari pūjite svāhā.

With the lamp seal (seal 35), offer lamps, saying:

Ālokāya ālokāya vidhādhare pūjite svāhā.

Offer praise:

Homage to the always merciful,
Whose name is Avalokiteshvara,
Composite of all excellent qualities,
Strongly praised by all Buddhas.

6. Sign Deity

Within observing just that deity that has been generated, develop clear appearance of your divine body and develop pride in being that deity.

To do this:

Stop the exhalation and inhalation of breath; withdraw inside movements of the breath throughout the body like a turtle's retracting its limbs and like drinking water drawn up with the

---

middle of the brow), two eyes, two shoulders, neck, heart, and navel.

tongue by means of the upwards-moving wind. Also, withdraw inside the usual intense movement of the nonequipoised mind out through the senses. Nevertheless, leave your eyes a little open, raise your face a little, and set yourself in one-pointed meditative equipoise, observing your own body clarified as a deity. Like a person dwelling in a cave and looking outside, you are as if inside the divine body observing it from within.

Hold your breath as much as you can, all the while observing one aspect of the divine body.

Then, let the breath out gently; relax, viewing yourself clarified as a deity.

Again hold your breath and observe the same one aspect of your divine body.

Do this until you gain the capacity to stop—by means of the clear appearance of the deity and by means of the pride of being a deity—the pride of ordinariness. Both clear appearance and divine pride divine pride are necessary.

Resting

Ceasing to visualize your divine body, observe the letters on the moon disc in space (which is the second part of the third deity, the "letter deity").

Ceasing to visualize the letters on the moon, observe the moon disc in space (which is the first part of the letter deity).

Ceasing to visualize the moon disc, observe the sounds of the mantra reverberating in space (which is the second deity, the "sound deity").

Ceasing to observe the sounds of the mantra, observe the pride of the sameness of the nature of yourself and the deity (which is the last part of the first deity, the "ultimate deity").

Ceasing to observe the pride of the sameness of the nature of yourself and the deity, observe the suchness of self, your own emptiness of inherent existence (which is the first part of the "ultimate deity").

Remain in meditative equipoise on your own emptiness.

All at once rise in a divine body, which is the same as that visualized earlier.

Between sessions

Between sessions remain within deity yoga, albeit not as complete as before, going about daily activities.

MEDITATIVE STABILIZATION OF EXALTED SPEECH

Third branch: Mind/Moon

A moon disc appears at the heart of the deity in front.

Fourth branch: Sound

The written letters of the mantra are set upright and facing inward around the edge of the moon disc at the heart of the deity in front.

Rays of light are emitted from the moon and mantra letters. From the points of the light rays innumerable forms of the deity emerge, pervading the entire sphere of space. Through emanating great clouds of offerings they make splendid offerings to all the Buddhas and Bodhisattvas. Also, they emanate great clouds from which a rain of ambrosia descends, extinguishing the fires of the sufferings of all transmigrators, hell-beings and so forth, as well as satisfying beings with whatever they need—giving a good body to those who need it, coolness to those suffering from heat, the warmth of the sun to those suffering from cold, food and drink to the hungry and thirsty—emanating to each just what he or she needs, providing beings with the basis for practicing the spiritual path as well as teachers to instruct them in the four truths, the two truths, and so forth, whereby they ascend the five paths and ten Bodhisattva grounds and attain the final happiness of Buddhahood.

b. Repetition in dependence upon the four branches (deity in front, yourself as a deity, moon, and letters)

(1) Repeat mantra within observing the form of the

letters[a]

(a) Repeat mantra within observing the form of the letters at the heart of the deity in front

[a] Dül-dzin-drak-pa-gyel-tsen (549.4-550.3) structures the repetition of mantra within observing the form of the letters differently. Instead of performing both whispered repetition and mental repetition first within observing the form of the letters at the heart of the deity in front and then both whispered repetition and mental repetition within observing the form of the letters at one's own heart, he performs whispered repetition within observing the form of the letters at the heart of the deity in front and then within observing the form of the letters at one's own heart, after which he performs mental repetition within observing the form of the letters at the heart of the deity in front and then within observing the form of the letters at one's own heart. In his version, the steps of meditation are:

(1) Repeat mantra within observing the form of the letters

(a) Repeat mantra in whisper within observing the form of the letters

(i) At the heart of the deity in front

Focusing on the three—the front deity, moon, and letters—repeat mantra in whisper, as if reading the letters, while exhaling.

While inhaling, switch to observing yourself as a deity without repetition.

Repeat the above.

(ii) At your own heart

Inhale—indto your own heart from the heart of the deity in front—the moon disc together with the mantra letters standing at its edge.

Perform whispered repetition, focusing on the moon and letters.

At the end of exhaling, emit the moon and letters back to the deity in front, focusing on moon and letters, without repetition.

Repeat the above.

(b) Repeat mantra mentally within observing the form of the letters

(i) At the heart of the deity in front

Holding your breath after inhalation and focusing on the three—the front deity, moon, and letters—repeat mantra mentally as if listening to your own recitation.

While exhaling, switch to observing yourself as a deity without repetition.

Repeat the above.

(ii) At your own heart

Inhale—into your own heart from the heart of the deity in front—the moon disc together with the mantra letters standing at its edge without repetition.

Stop your breath and recite mantra mentally, focusing on moon and letters, as if your mind is in the center of the moon disc and is reading the letters of the mantra standing on the edge of the moon disc facing inward.

When exhaling, stop repetition of mantra, and move the moon and letters with your breath to the deity's heart—focusing on the moon and letters.

With inhalation, repeat the above.

Whispered repetition

Focusing on the three—the front deity, moon, and letters—repeat mantra in whisper, as if reading the letters, while exhaling.

While inhaling, switch to observing yourself as a deity without repetition.

Repeat the above.

Mental repetition

Holding your breath after inhalation and focusing on the three—the front deity, moon, and letters—repeat mantra mentally as if listening to your own recitation.

While exhaling, switch to observing yourself as a deity without repetition.

Repeat the above.

Resting

Stop repeating mantra.

Ceasing to visualize the forms of the mantra letters, observe the moon on which they stood at the heart in the deity in front (which is the moon branch).

Ceasing to visualize the moon, observe the deity in front (which is the branch called "other-base").

Ceasing to visualize the deity in front, observe your own divine body (which is the branch called "self-base" and, within it, the sixth deity, the sign deity, as well as the fourth deity, the form deity).

Ceasing to visualize your divine body, observe the letters on the moon disc in space (which is the second part of the third deity, the "letter deity").

Ceasing to visualize the letters on the moon, observe the moon disc in space (which is the first part of the letter deity).

Ceasing to visualize the moon disc, observe the sounds of the mantra reverberating in space (which is the second deity, the "sound deity").

Ceasing to observe the sounds of the mantra, observe the pride of the sameness of the nature of yourself and the deity (which is the last part of the first deity, the "ultimate deity").

Ceasing to observe the pride of the sameness of the nature of yourself and the deity, observe the suchness of self, your own emptiness of inherent existence (which is the first part of the "ultimate deity").

Remain in meditative equipoise on your own emptiness.

All at once rise in a divine body, which is the same as that visualized earlier.

Between sessions

Between sessions remain within deity yoga, albeit not as complete as before, going about daily activities.

(b) Repeat mantra within observing the form of the letters at your own heart

Whispered repetition

Inhale—into your own heart from the heart of the deity in front—the moon disc together with the mantra letters standing at its edge.

Perform whispered repetition, focusing on the moon and letters.

At the end of exhaling, emit the moon and letters back to the deity in front, focusing on moon and letters, without repetition.

Repeat the above.

Mental repetition

Inhale—into your own heart from the heart of the deity in front—the moon disc together with the mantra letters standing at its edge without repetition.

Stop your breath and recite mantra mentally, focusing on moon and letters, as if your mind is in the center of the moon disc and is reading the letters of the mantra standing on the edge of the moon disc facing inward.

When exhaling, stop repetition of mantra, and move the moon and letters with your breath to the deity's heart—focusing on the moon and letters.

With inhalation, repeat the above.

(2) Repeat mantra within observing the sound of the letters

Whispered repetition

Within retaining visualization of the deity in front and yourself as a deity with the moon and the mantra letters on the moon at your heart, repeat mantra in whisper, focusing on just the sounds.

Mental repetition

Within retaining visualization of the deity in front and yourself as a deity with the moon and the mantra letters on the moon at your heart, repeat mantra mentally while stopping breath and distraction, focusing on just the sounds.

c. Concluding the concentration of the four-branched repetition

With the vase seal (seal 36) offer the virtue of the session for the sake of feats:

> **I offer this virtuous root of mine to the Supramundane Victor as a cause of such and such feat. O Protector, please bestow such and such feat.**

Arrange whatever offerings have been newly acquired, and clear away obstructors in the flowers and so forth through repeating into scented water either the mantra of Kuṇḍali:

> ***Namo ratnatrayāya, namaṣcaṇḍa-vajrapāṇaye, mahāyakṣasena-pataye, namo vajra-krodhāya, tadyathā oṃ hulu hulu tiṣṭha tiṣṭha bandha bandha hana hana amṛte hūṃ phaṭ.***

or the mantra of all activities of the lotus lineage:

> ***Oṃ namo mahā-śrīyāyai, sau me siddhi siddha sādhaya, śivi śivaṃkari, abhaha, sarva-artha-sādhani svāhā.***

Putting scented water into the left hand, repeat into the water the lineage essence:

> ***Ārolik.***

and sprinkle the flowers and so forth. From the seal of dispelling obstructors (seal 10), construct the seal of generating magnificence (seal 14), and with it distribute magnificence on top of the perfume, flowers, and so forth and repeat the mantra of generating magnificence:

> ***Oṃ divya divya dhipaya, avesha mahāśrīye svāhā.***

thinking that thereby:

The offerings turn into perfect divine substances.

Then, bless them into magnificence with the mantra of Kuṇḍali:

Namo ratnatrayāya, namaṣcaṇḍa-vajrapāṇaye, mahāyakṣasena-pataye, namo vajra-krodhāya, tadyathā oṃ hulu hulu tiṣṭha tiṣṭha bandha bandha hana hana amṛte hūṃ phaṭ.

and repeat the essence mantra of the lotus lineage:

Ārolik.

With the oblation seal (seal 28), offer oblation, saying:

You have come blissfully, Supramundane Victor.
Come here and please be seated.
Receiving my oblation also,
Please take pleasure mentally from this.
I have respect for you.
Arghaṃ pratīccha svāhā.

With the foot-bath seal (seal 29), offer a foot-bath, saying:

You have come blissfully, Supramundane Victor.
Come here and please be seated.
Receiving my foot-bath also,
Please take pleasure mentally from this.
I have respect for you.
Oṃ pravarasatkaraṃ pratīccha svāhā.

With the seal of washing the body (seal 30), imagine washing the deity's body with great clouds of perfumed water which have risen from many precious gold vases and so forth filled with fragrant perfumes; say:

You have come blissfully, Supramundane Victor.
Come here and please be seated.
Receiving my bath also,
Please take pleasure mentally from this.
I have respect for you.
Oṃ sarva-devatā-acinta-amṛta svāhā.

Mentally offer clothing and adornments; offer music, and mentally raise up melodies of praise.

With the perfume seal (seal 31), offer perfume, saying:

With faith I offer these perfumes
Of wholesome divine substances
Arisen from the clean, most clean.
Receiving them, be pleased with me.
Āhara āhara sarva-vidyādhari pūjite svāhā.

With the flower seal (seal 32), offer flowers, saying:

With faith I offer these flowers
Of auspicious divine substance,
Grown from the clean, most clean.
Receiving them, be pleased with me.
Āhara āhara sarva-vidyādhari pūjite svāhā.

With the incense seal (seal 33), offer incense, saying:

With faith I offer divine substances
Made with perfume,
Pleasant essences of the forest.
Receiving them, be pleased with me.
Āhara āhara sarva-vidyādhari pūjite svāhā.

With the seal of divine food (seal 34), offer food, saying:

With faith I offer
These foods of mantra,
Pleasant medicinal essences.
Receiving them, be pleased with me.
Āhara āhara sarva-vidyādhari pūjite svāhā.

With the lamp seal (seal 35), offer lamps, saying:

With faith I offer these dispellers
Of darkness, conquering harmers,
Auspicious and virtuous.
I beg you to receive these lamps.
Ālokāya ālokāya vidhādhare pūjite svāhā.

Praise the Three Jewels—Buddha, his doctrine, and the spiritual community:

Homage to the One-Gone-Thus,
Protector with great compassion,
Omniscient teacher,
Oceanic field of merit and attainments.

Homage to the pacifying doctrine,
Through purity separating from desire,
Through virtue liberating from bad transmigrations,
In all ways the supreme ultimate.

Respectful homage to the spiritual community,
Liberated, teaching the path of liberation,
Completely dwelling in the precepts,
Excellent field of merit, endowed with attainments.

Praise the lords of the three lineages—Mañjushrī, who is the physical manifestation of the wisdom of all Buddhas; Avalokiteshvara, who is the physical manifestation of the compassion of all Buddhas; and Vajrapāṇi, who is the physical manifestation of the power of all Buddhas:

> **Homage also to Mañjushrī,**
> **Bearer of the appearance of a youth,**
> **Vividly adorned with the lamp of wisdom,**
> **Dispeller of the three worlds' darkness.**
>
> **Homage to the always merciful,**
> **Whose name is Avalokiteshvara,**
> **Composite of all excellent qualities,**
> **Strongly praised by all Buddhas.**
>
> **Homage to Vajrapāṇi,**
> **Powerful and fierce,**
> **Virtuous king of knowledge-mantra,**
> **Tamer of the hard to tame.**

Ask for forbearance for not having the circumstances to perform the rite exactly according to the tantra:

> **Whatever even slightly has been done wrongly**
> **Out of the obscuration in my mind,**
> **Please, O Protector, bear with it all**
> **Since you are the refuge of all the embodied.**
>
> **Whatever has been done here**
> **Due to non-acquisition, lack of thorough knowledge,**
> **Or not having the capacity,**
> **It is right for the Chief to bear with it all.**

Request Avalokiteshvara to depart together with his inestimable mansion, saying:

> ***Oṃ* may you bestow yogic feats**
> **Concordant with effecting the welfare of all sentient beings.**
> **Having gone to a Buddha Land,**
> **Please may you come again.**

From the seal of invitation (seal 20), make the seal of requesting departure (seal 37), and say:

> ***Ārolik gaccha.* Together with his inestimable mansion he has gone to his natural abode.**

Free the directions and intermediate directions that were bound earlier by making the seal of unequal limbs (seal 38), circling it from the left, and saying:

Oṃ hulu hulu caṇḍali-mataṃ givi svāhā.

Between sessions

Between sessions remain within deity yoga, albeit not as complete as before, going about daily activities.[a]

CONTINUATION OF MEDITATIVE STABILIZATION OF EXALTED SPEECH

B. Concentration Without Repetition

1. Concentration of Abiding in Fire

(Because mantra is heard as if recited by someone else, it is said to be without repetition.)

1. Contemplate the emptiness of inherent existence of yourself and the deity through the six deities.

2. While visualizing yourself in the form of Avalokiteshvara and conceiving of yourself to be Avalokiteshvara, imagine a tiny moon at your heart with a blazing tongue of fire, like the flame of a butter lamp.

3. Your mind of wisdom realizing emptiness appears as the mantra sounds in the flame at your heart, resounding continuously like bells. Within stopping breath and distraction, your mind is as if dwelling inside the tongue of flame and itself is appearing in that flame as the sounds, as if listening to recitation by someone else or resounding of their own accord. Observe mainly the flame and sounds. Because your mind of wisdom itself is appearing as the mantra sounds, the sounds of the mantra and your own final nature are completely mixed like water and milk.

4. Exhaling, observe your own larger divine body.

Repeat steps 3 and 4.

2. Concentration of Abiding in Sound

(Because mantra is heard as if recited by someone else, it is said to be without repetition.)

1. While visualizing yourself in the form of a deity and conceiving of yourself to be a deity with a flame at the heart, imagine a tiny deity within the flame.

---

[a] For more on this, see *Deity Yoga*, 152-153.

2. Imagine a moon disc at the heart of the tiny deity.

3. Imagine a flame on the moon disc at the heart of the tiny deity.

4. When this visualization becomes firm, your own mind appears as the mantra sounds within the flame at the heart of the tiny deity. Within stopping breath and distraction, your mind is as if dwelling inside the tongue of flame and itself is appearing in that flame as the sounds as if you were listening to recitation by someone else or the letters were sounding of their own accord. Observe mainly the sounds of the mantra. Because your mind of wisdom itself is appearing as the mantra sounds, the sounds of the mantra and your own final nature are completely mixed like water and milk.[a]

5. Exhaling, observe your own larger divine body.

Repeat steps 4 and 5.

Gradually, calm abiding, which is a state of meditative stabilization conjoined with the bliss of mental and physical pliancy, is achieved. The final stages of achieving calm abiding are:

> The "winds" (currents of energy) involved in unhealthy physical states are calmed and leave the body through the top of the head, where a tingly sensation is felt.
>
> Then, a *mental pliancy,* which is a pacification of unhealthy states making the mind heavy and preventing its usage in virtue according to will, is generated; this makes the mind serviceable.
>
> Through its force, a "wind" of serviceability moves throughout the body, inducing a *physical pliancy* that causes separation from physical states of roughness and heaviness, whereupon you are able to use the body at will in virtuous actions without any sense of hardship. Your body is light like cotton and as if filled with this serviceable wind.
>
> Experiencing this special internal sense of smoothness, you have a *bliss of physical pliancy.*

---

[a] A far simpler alternative version of the concentration of abiding in sound replaces the first four steps with first observing the written letters of the mantra around the edge of the moon disc at one's heart and then leaving the written letters and contemplating only the sounds.

Due to the mental consciousness paying attention to this bliss accompanying the body consciousness, a *bliss of mental pliancy* is generated. Your body seems to have dissolved, and nothing but the object of meditative observation appears.

Your mind is so buoyantly joyous that it now seems almost unable to remain on its object, but the excessive buoyancy is gradually removed, and you attain an *immovable pliancy,* remaining stably and joyously on the object of observation. This is calm abiding.

YOGA WITHOUT SIGNS

MEDITATIVE STABILIZATION OF EXALTED MIND

3. Concentration Bestowing Liberation at the End of Sound

1. Focus not on appearance in a divine body, whispered repetition, mental repetition, or the concentrations of abiding in fire and abiding in sound but on the emptiness of inherent existence. Although there are still divine appearances to the *appearance* factor of your consciousness, they no longer appear to the *ascertainment* factor, which is concerned only with the emptiness of inherent existence, which is now the focus. Because of the previous training, these other factors remain appearing without effort, and you simultaneously and explicitly realize their absence of being established from their own side.

2. Alternate analytical and stabilizing meditation on the emptiness of inherent existence in order to make them of equal strength.

3. Gradually the power of analysis itself is able to induce physical and mental pliancies similar to those of calm abiding, but to a greater degree. Thereby, special insight, which is a union of calm abiding and special insight, is attained.

II. Effecting the achievement of yogic feats

Feats are in three categories:

1. *pacification,* such as avoiding untimely death, illnesses, epidemics, harmful influences, and contagion
2. *increase,* such as enhancing life span, youthfulness, magnificence, power, qualities of realization, and resources
3. ferocity such as killing, expelling, or confusing harmful beings.

These feats—which also include clairvoyance, invisibility, the capacity to understand all treatises immediately upon reading them, swift footedness, and empowering pills for youthfulness and so forth—are sought in order to enhance the power of the very yoga that comprises prior approximation. Thus, although the triad of prior approximation, effecting achievement of feats, and engaging in altruistic activities suggests a movement from the first to the last, the yoga that constitutes the first phase is the most important. The feats that allow a practitioner to perform special activities for the benefit of others bring about merit further enhancing the capacity of this same yoga so that Buddhahood can be achieved.

A. Analyzing dreams

See *Deity Yoga,* 176-177.

B. Performing the above meditation in modified form and burnt offerings or repetitions of mantra and so forth

See *Deity Yoga,* 177-179.

III. Activities

Using the yogic feats of pacification, increase, and ferocity for your own and others' temporary and final aims.

Part Two:
The Difference Between Sūtra and Mantra

8. Bu-tön Rin-chen-drup's Stimulating Catalogue

The distinctiveness of the tantric practice of deity yoga and Tsong-kha-pa's choosing it as the sole central distinguishing feature of Mantra is put into perspective through considering his prime source, the encyclopedic presentation of the difference between Sūtra and Mantra by the "omniscient"[a] Bu-tön Rin-chen-drup[b] (1290-1364), who is reported to have been first a Nying-ma and then a Sa-kya[c] but is more appropriately identified by the sect named after him, Bu-luk (Bu System). All presentations of the distinctiveness of Mantra, except that by Tsong-kha-pa and his followers, employ multiple formats for demonstrating its greatness through its central features, and Bu-tön in his *Extensive Presentation of the General Tantra Sets: Ornament Beautifying the Precious Tantra Sets,*[d] drawing from Atisha's *Compilation of All Pledges,* cites nine Indian scholars' varying descriptions of the multiple ways in which the Mantra Vehicle surpasses the Perfection Vehicle:

1. Tripiṭakamāla as well as Vajrapāṇi's commentary, 4 ways
    1. being for the nonobscured
    2. having many skillful methods
    3. no difficulties

---

[a] "Omniscient" is a Tibetan epithet for an accomplished scholar versed in many topics, a polymath.

[b] *bu ston rin chen grub.*

[c] Reported orally by the Nying-ma lama and biographer, Khetsun Sangpo Rinpoche, who himself studied at a Ge-luk-pa monastic university, Dre-pung, before pursuing the Nying-ma path.

[d] *rgyud sde spyi'i rnam par gzhag pa: rgyud sde rin po che'i mdzes rgyan,* Collected Works vol. 15 (New Delhi: International Academy of Indian Culture, 1969), 6.1-32.5, hereafter referred to as "*Extensive* version." The very same presentation, with minor printing differences, is repeated in Bu-tön's middling version called the *Medium-Length Presentation of the General Tantra Sets: Illuminating the Secrets of All Tantra Sets* (*rgyud sde spyi'i rnam par gzhag pa rgyud sde thams cad kyi gsang ba gsal bar byed pa*), Collected Works vol. 15, 614.7-641.7, hereafter referred to as "*Medium-Length* version"; it has been used for text comparison. A considerably abbreviated version of the same is given in his *Condensed Presentation of the General Tantra Sets: Key Opening the Door to the Precious Treasury of Tantra Sets* (*rgyud sde spyi'i rnam par gzhag pa rgyud sde rin po che'i gter sgo 'byed pa'i lde mig*), Collected Works vol. 14, 845.1-859.1, hereafter referred to as "*Condensed* version."

4. being created for those with sharp faculties.

2. Jñānashrī, 11 ways
    1. observing an unsurpassed object of observation
    2. unsurpassed achieving
    3. unsurpassed pristine wisdom
    4. unsurpassed effort
    5. ability to take care of all trainees without exception
    6. blessing afflictive emotions into a magnificent state
    7. swifter blessings into magnificence
    8. quick emergence
    9. abandonment of afflictive emotions
    10. unsurpassed contemplation
    11. unsurpassed deeds.

3. Ratnākarashānti, 3 ways
    1. very pure objects of observation
    2. power of aids
    3. deeds

4. Nāgārjuna, 6 ways
    1. implanting of everything with the seal of the all-good
    2. blessing into a magnificent state
    3. faster achievement of feats
    4. separation from the frights of cyclic existence and bad transmigrations and becoming rested
    5. lack of interference
    6. nondeterioration of pledges, and natural restoration if deteriorated

5. Indrabhūti, 7 ways
    1. guru
    2. vessel
    3. rite
    4. activity
    5. pledge
    6. view
    7. behavior

6. Jñānapāda, 3 ways
    1. practitioner
    2. path
    3. fruit

7. Ḍombhīheruka, 5 ways
    1. vessels
    2. doctrine making vessels (initiation)
    3. texts
    4. paths
    5. fruits

8. Vajraghaṇṭapāda, 4 ways
    1. persons who are the bases
    2. paths that are the means of entry
    3. fruit which is the finality
    4. definite emergence

9. Samayavajra, 5 ways
    1. guru
    2. initiation
    3. pledges
    4. quintessential instructions
    5. and effort

Bu-tön begins with Tripiṭakamāla's *Lamp for the Three Modes,*[a] quoting his stanzas on each of the four features and paraphrasing Tripiṭakamāla's own prose explanations, after which he expansively describes Jñānashrī's eleven ways, and then quotes Atisha's brief accounts of the remaining seven. He occasionally explains and defends the positions of these nine scholars.

[a] *tshul gsum gyi sgron ma, nayatrayapradīpa;* P4530; Toh. 3707, Nying ma edition of *sde dge,* vol. 62.

Translation

[How Tripiṭakamāla Divides the Perfection and Mantra Vehicles]

With respect to how the scriptural collections[a] of Mantra surpass those of the Perfection Vehicle, Tripiṭakamāla's *Lamp for the Three Modes* says:

> Though the object is the same, Mantra treatises
> Are superior because of being for the nonobscured,
> Having many skillful methods, no difficulties,
> And being created for those with sharp faculties.

It is thus: the two—the Mantra and Perfection Great Vehicles—do not differ regarding the fruit, which is described [in both as non-dual omniscience]; however, through four distinctive features the Mantra Great Vehicle just surpasses the Perfection Great Vehicle.

About the first of the four distinctive features [that is, being for the nonobscured], Tripiṭakamāla's *Lamp for the Three Modes* says:

> The skillful having great compassion,
> Upon analysis,[b] assume the supreme of methods.
> Looking down on ordinary methods,
> They attain a state of nonfluctuation.

When Bodhisattvas practicing the Perfection [Vehicle] engage in giving and so forth, concerning those [deeds] they dwell in the perfection of wisdom by way of a purification of [misconceptions about] the object of giving,[c] the giver, and the fruit [accrued by] the giver, whereby they are not very obscured. Nevertheless, because they engage in external giving and so forth and are not of sharp faculties, they complete the collections [of merit and wisdom] over a long period. [However,] Bodhisattvas practicing Mantra analyze

---

[a] *sde gnod, piṭaka.*

[b] The Peking edition (P4530, vol. 81, 115.2.8), the *Extensive* version (6.4 and 6.6), and the *Medium-Length* version (615.3 and 615.6) read *dpyad,* whereas the *Condensed* version (par pa dpal ldan edition, 2a.5) reads *spyad.*

[c] In the *Condensed* version (845.6) read *sbyin bya* for *sbyin ba* to accord with the *Medium-Length* version (615.4), the *Extensive* version (6.5), and Tripiṭakamāla (P4530, vol. 81, 115.3.1).

what the method for completing the perfections of giving and so forth is, whereby they understand that since giving away [one's] head and so forth cannot fulfill simultaneously the wants of all, [such giving] does not go beyond [the mundane] and hence is not a perfection [or transcendence].[a] Looking down on that method, they seek the supreme of methods.

Since it, furthermore, is none other than meditative stabilization[b] endowed with an essence of method and wisdom, those skilled in means—upon generating compassion for limitless sentient beings—thoroughly realize the meditative stabilization of nondual method and wisdom having an essence of limitless objects. Through cultivating it uninterruptedly and without partiality in terms of the directions, they fully develop abandonment [of obstructions] and realization [of the selflessness of persons and phenomena], whereby they, like wish-granting jewels, completely fulfill the wants of all sentient beings.

Hence, since this is a method superior to the ordinary giving of [one's own] head and so forth, (1) the perfection of giving is completed. Just this completes the perfections [of (2) ethics, which comprises] the three forms of ethics—bringing about the welfare of sentient beings, and so forth,[c] (3) patience, helping living beings through hosts of emanations and forbearing harm done by others, (4) effort, the means of simultaneously attaining all aims and purposes, (5) concentration attaining the meditative stabilizations which are the source of all concentrations, and (6) wisdom through the completion of which [all of the other perfections] are completed. Thereby, one thoroughly completes the six perfections, and due to that completion, the four—method, power, aspirational wishes, and pristine wisdom[d]—are also completed. Thereby, [Mantra] is not obscured with respect to method.

About the second [of the four distinctive features of Mantra—having many skillful methods—Tripiṭakamāla's *Lamp for the Three Modes* says]:

---

[a] *pha rol tu phyin pa, pāramitā.*

[b] *ting nge 'dzin, samādhi.*

[c] "And so forth" indicates the other two forms of ethics—the ethics that is the composite of virtuous activities and the ethics of restraining ill deeds.

[d] These four are the seventh through tenth perfections when ten, instead of six, are enumerated.

In order to achieve well the aims of all sentient beings
The Teacher of Transmigrators taught to the intelligent
All methods, the supreme modes,
Dividing them into four types [as the four tantras].

In the other systems [that is, the Sūtra approaches], asceticism, vows of restraint, and so forth are described as methods for [achieving] high status [within cyclic existence] and liberation [from cyclic existence and the great liberation of Buddhahood], but all sentient beings cannot practice these. Since some course in very peaceful actions, [these practices] were set forth in terms of them, but these cannot accommodate all. However, Secret Mantra was set forth in order to join all sentient beings to virtue.

Concerning this, either oneself or a lama determines one's nature through analyzing dreams, dropping a flower [on a maṇḍala divided into quadrants indicating temperament], the descent of wisdom,[a] constructing seals,[b] and so forth, and by way of [noticing predominant styles of] behavior. Having recognized the afflictive emotion, such as desire, in which one predominantly courses, one also identifies [the deity who is] one's lord of lineage [in that each lineage is associated with a particular afflictive emotion]. If desire is predominant, one generates [the minds and mental factors of desire][c] as Amitābha and, having made offerings [to that deity], enters—by way of mindfulness of his mantra and seal [that is, hand-gesture]—into a meditative stabilization having the style of great desire. With a nature of joy pervaded by compassion, all conceptions are abandoned.

Similarly, [practitioners of Mantra who have predominant obscuration and so forth][d] generate the minds and mental factors of obscuration and so forth as Buddhas, such as Vairochana, and Bodhisattvas, Wrathful Males, and Wrathful Females and so forth, in accordance with the individual tantra set. This is the meditative stabilization of exalted vajra mind.

For those who cannot set the mind in this way on the subtle,

---

[a] This likely refers to a method of divination through the appearance of configurations on a mirror and so forth.

[b] The meaning of "constructing seals," which would seem to mean the construction of hand-gestures (*phyag rgya, mudrā*), is unclear.

[c] The bracketed material is added in accordance with Bu-tön's explanation in the next section on obscuration.

[d] Added from Tripiṭakamāla, vol. 81, 116.1.3.

that is, on minds and mental factors, a meditative stabilization of exalted vajra speech is taught so that they transmute desire into a vajra entity through the utterance of speech. *Oṃ āḥ hūṃ* are respectively the essence [mantras] of Vairochana, Amitābha, and Akṣhobhya. Similarly, all the various mantras indicated by other letters arise from the mantras of the five Ones-Gone-Thus. Thereby, abiding in one's respective suchness, one performs the respective activity through the yoga of the respective lord [of the lineage]. For example, the five short [vowels] *a, i, ṛ, u, ḷ* are the mantras [of the Ones-Gone-Thus][a] of the five lineages and the [corresponding] long [vowels] are the mantras of the five Mothers. When one does repetition within contemplating the appropriate mantra as the very entity of the respective deity and one's mind is set in suchness, ill deeds are consumed and the collections [of merit and wisdom] completed. This is the meditative stabilization of exalted vajra speech.

For those who are attached to gross objects and who initially cannot apply themselves to meditation on subtle [mental or verbal phenomena], a gross body maṇḍala is taught. Having generated a maṇḍala involving a residence and residents in accordance with what appears in the tantras, they repeat mantra, and having dissolved [everything] into suchness, they become separate from the defilements of conceptions such as hatred, whereby they gradually enter the element of attributes.[b]

Omniscience is attained through even all three meditative stabilizations; hence, although there is no difference in the fruit [of the Perfection and Mantra vehicles], there is a difference of direct and indirect generation [of omniscience]. Thus, it is suitable to teach desire and so forth themselves as doors of method by way of cultivating the three maṇḍalas, for it is said that all phenomena are naturally pure. Here, desire and so forth are not objects of abandonment, nor are states free from desire and so forth objects to be adopted since through realizing unerroneous suchness, the view of reality is generated, and through it one is released. It is said:[c]

---

[a] The bracketed addition is drawn from Tripiṭakamāla, vol. 81, 116.4.7.

[b] *chos kyi dbyings, dharmadhātu.*

[c] Tripiṭakamāla (vol. 81, 117.2.8) identifies the quote as from Nāgārjuna. In any case, it is found in Maitreya's *Ornament for Clear Realization,* V.21:

> *'di la bsal bya ci yang med/*
> *bzhag par bya ba cung zad med/*

Here there is nothing to be removed,
Nor anything at all to be established.
Just the real is to be viewed as real.
One who sees reality is released.

In this way, knowing the thoughts and latent predispositions of sentient beings, [Buddha] taught in the manner of laying out four tantra sets—whatever was suitable for whosoever. Therefore, [Mantra] has more methods.

About the third [of the four distinctive features, nondifficulty, Tripiṭakamāla's *Lamp for the Three Modes* says]:

The Subduer set forth the ultimate object,
The desired aim that is attained
Through making application in accordance
With just what one desires.

[In Mantra] enlightenment is attained by just a blissful method—a specific sentient being making application at whatever object at whatever time in accordance with that being's desires. It is said:

A being bound by whatsoever
Awful action is released through just this
From the bonds of cyclic existence,
If accompanied by method.

Therefore, difficult deeds are not taught in the Mantra Vehicle. Still, in the Perfection [Vehicle] enlightenment is by all means taught with the name of nondifficulty.

Objection: There the mere word ["difficult"] is eliminated.

Response: Is it not that through eliminating the name, difficulty [itself] is eliminated? That which, when done, is affixed with the name "difficult" is difficult; it is not the mere activity. When the word "blissful" is applied to a Bodhisattva's attaining joy from giving away [one's own] head and so forth for the sake of others [by

---

yang dag nyid la yang dag lta/
yang dag mthong nas rnam par grol//

nāpaneyataḥ kiṃcitprakṣeptatyaṃ na kiṃ cana/
draṣṭavyaṃ bhūtato bhūtaṃ bhūtadarśo vimucyate//

The Sanskrit is from Th. Stcherbatsky and E. Obermiller, ed., *Abhisamayālaṅkāra-Prajñāpāramitā-Upadeśa-Śāstra,* Bibliotheca Buddhica XXIII (Osnabrück: Biblio Verlag, 1970), 29. For Edward Conze's translation, see his *Abhisamayālaṅkāra,* Serie Orientale Roma VI (Rome, Is.M.E.O, 1954), 86.

way of having familiarized with nondual meditative stabilization],[a] how could such be difficult?

Objection: It is renowned to others to be difficult.

Answer: Then, since [a Māntrika's] simultaneous bringing about the aims sought by trainees is also renowned to others to be difficult, [the two vehicles] would be the same [in being renowned to others as difficult]. Therefore, since difficulty here is not used in connection even a little with others' meaning,[b] this is not fit to have the name of being difficult. Hence, since the name is eliminated, the meaning is also eliminated; [here] it indicates the consummate aim of a yogi of suchness.[c]

Therefore, difficulty and ease refer mainly not to activities but to desires, whereby acting in accordance with one's own desires is what is easy. Hence, because [in Mantra] bliss is attained through bliss, difficult deeds are not taught in Mantra.

Furthermore, it is as follows:

- The best among those with the best faculties—who have few afflictive emotions and little conceptuality but have great compassion and are making effort to seek suchness—are taught the Great Seal[d] of indivisible emptiness and compassion without reference to the proliferations of external and internal activities [such as actual or imagined consorts].
- The middling among those with the best faculties—who although they have turned away from enjoying ordinary objects, have not abandoned conceptions [produced by] latencies of afflictive emotions and who are not able to enter into ultimate wisdom—are taught a Wisdom Seal,[e] a Knowledge Woman [consort] emanated [in imagination] who serves as a method [for attaining] the Great Seal.
- The least among those with the best faculties—who, although they have faith in nondualistic wisdom, have not abandoned

[a] Tripiṭakamāla, vol. 81, 117.4.6.

[b] The Par pa dpal ldan edition (5a.2) reads *'dir don cung zad* whereas the Lokesh Chandra edition (10.2) reads *'dir gzhan don cung zad,* which is more likely since Tripiṭakamāla's text (Golden reprint, *rgyud 'grel nu,* 29b.2/ vol. 75, 58.2) reads *'dir rnam pa thams cad du gzhan gyi gzhan don gang cung zad;* the meaning is conjectured.

[c] *de kho na nyid kyi rnal 'byor pa nyid kyi don phun sum tshogs par bstan no; Extensive* version, 10.2.

[d] *phyag rgya chen po, mahāmudrā.*

[e] *ye shes kyi phyag rgya, jñānamudrā.*

the desires of the Desire [Realm] and are distracted when such an object is near, and do not [remain] in meditative stabilization—are taught pledge seals,[a] [actual consorts] who possess [the qualifications of] being of the same lineage as oneself, youth, and so forth.

- The least of the least among those with the best faculties—whose desire is very great but whose intelligence is little—are taught action seals[b] [actual consorts who do not have all the qualifications].[c]

Thus, because sentient beings are set in Buddhahood through making application at just what they desire, [Mantra] is not difficult.

About the fourth [distinctive feature, being created for those with sharp faculties,] since Hearers do not know the method [for realizing] suchness, they are of dull faculties. Those of the Perfection [Vehicle] are mistaken with respect to method and hence are of dull faculties. [However,] because Secret Māntrikas are not obscured with respect to anything, they are of sharp faculties. For, through skill in unerring means they are able to transform into a cause of Buddhahood just that which, if done by others, would cause them to go to a bad transmigration [as an animal, hungry ghost, or hell being]. Thus, in four [ways] the Mantra Vehicle is superior.

[Vajrapāṇi's commentary]

Moreover, in explaining the meaning of that stanza [in Tripiṭakamāla's *Lamp for the Three Modes:*

Though the object is the same, Mantra treatises
Are superior because of being for the nonobscured,
Having many skillful methods, no difficulties,
And being created for those with sharp faculties.]

the Indian Vajrapāṇi[d] says [in his *Quintessential Instructions on the Stages of Guru Transmission*]:[e]

---

[a] *dam tshig gi phyag rgya, samayamudrā.*

[b] *las gyi phyag rgya, karmamudrā.*

[c] Based on the above descriptions, I assume that this is the meaning.

[d] Born 1017, he was a disciple of Maitrīpāda; see George N. Roerich, *The Blue Annals* (Delhi: Motilal Banarsidass, 1976), 842.

[e] *bla ma brgyud pa'i rim pa'i man ngag, guruparaṃparakramopadeśa;* P4539, vol. 81,

> Although there is no division regarding the fact, that is, suchness, those of the Perfection Vehicle realize it upon settling it through scripture and reasoning and hence are obscured. Māntrikas realize it experientially through scripture, reasoning, and a guru's quintessential instructions; hence, they are not obscured. Those of the Perfection Vehicle do not have experience and take [states of] neutral [feeling] as the path, whereas Māntrikas take great bliss as the path; hence [Mantra] is not difficult. Those of the Perfection Vehicle take causes as the path, whereas Māntrikas take the effect as the path, and hence [Mantra] is superior.

Though Vajrapāṇi says such, just the former explanation [by Tripiṭakamāla of his own stanza] is understood to be better.

[How Jñānashrī Divides the Perfection and Mantra Vehicles]

Also, the master Jñānashrī [in his *Eradicating the Two Extremes with respect to the Vajra Vehicle*] says:[a]

> It is to be indicated how this Mantra Vehicle differs even from the Perfection Great Vehicle of the Middle Way School. It is superior by way of eleven aspects of skill in means—(1) skill in means in the sense of observing an unsurpassed object of observation, (2) unsurpassed achieving, (3) unsurpassed pristine wisdom, (4) unsurpassed effort, (5) ability to take care of all trainees without exception, (6) blessing afflictive emotions into a magnificent state, (7) swifter blessings into magnificence, (8) quick emergence, (9) abandonment of afflictive emotions, (10) unsurpassed contemplation, and (11) unsurpassed deeds.

The Meaning

Unsurpassed object of observation: On the path [of the Perfection Vehicle] one takes cognizance of the *Perfection of Wisdom*, the *Buddhāvataṃsaka*,[b] and so forth, but here [in Mantra] one takes

---

184.3.7-184.4.1.

[a] *rdo rje theg pa'i mtha' gnyis sel ba, vajrayānakoṭidvayāpoha;* P4537, vol. 81, 159.3.8-159.4.3

[b] *sangs rgyas phal po che zhes bya ba shin tu rgyas pa chen po'i mdo, buddhāvataṃsaka-nāmamahāvaipulyasūtra;* P761, vol. 25.

cognizance of the uncommon *Five Hundred Thousand Stanza Hevajra,*[a] the *One Hundred Twenty-five Thousand Stanza Kṛṣhṇayamāri,*[b] the *One Hundred Thousand Stanza Equality with Space*[c]—these not being renowned to that [Perfection Vehicle].

Unsurpassed achieving: On the path [of the Perfection Vehicle], having attained physical creations, one is able to perform hidden functions, but here one is able to perform hidden functions through attaining meditative stabilization without attaining those [physical creations].

Unsurpassed pristine wisdom: The causes of pristine wisdom are just swifter [in the Mantra Vehicle] by way of cause, entity, and activity in dependence on special meditative stabilization of firm mind.

Unsurpassed effort: This is due to the great powerless [that is, natural] commencement of great effort through the force of pledges.

Ability to accommodate all trainees: Those who have committed crimes of immediate retribution[d] and so forth, who are neglected by other vehicles, dwell here in achievement.

Blessing afflictive emotions into a magnificent state: This is through [Mantra's] nature of offering [that transforms objects of desire] as well as through the completion stage that relies on bliss.

Swifter blessings into magnificence: On the path [of the Perfection Vehicle] it is said that conferral of initiation by a One-Gone-Thus is attained upon entering a [Bodhisattva] ground, whereas here [in Mantra], in dependence on skillful means, a One-Gone-Thus confers initiations and blesses one into magnificence just now.

Quick emergence: There [in the Perfection Vehicle] it is said that [Bodhisattvas] become completely purified [as Buddhas] in three

---

[a] *dgyes rdor 'bum phrag lnga pa;* this is the longer version no longer extant. For the surviving version, see *kye'i rdo rje'i rgyud, hevajratantra;* P10, vol. 1.

[b] *gshin rje dgra nag 'bum phrag nyi khri lnga stong pa;* this is the longer version no longer extant. For the surviving version, see *gshin rje gshed nag po'i rgyud, kṛṣṇayamāritantra;* P103, vol. 4.

[c] *nam mkha' dang mnyam pa 'bum pa;* this is the longer version no longer extant. For the surviving version, see *nam mkha' dang mnyam pa'i rgyud kyi rgyal po, khasamatantrarāja;* P31, vol. 3 or *bde mchog nam mkha' dang mnyam pa'i rgyud kyi rgyal po, saṃbarakhasamatantrarāja;* P59, vol. 3.

[d] Killing one's father, killing one's mother, killing a Foe Destroyer, causing blood to flow from the body of a Buddha with evil intention, and causing dissension in the spiritual community.

periods of countless eons and so forth, whereas here [in Mantra] one is completely purified in a single lifetime, in seven births, or sixteen births.

Abandonment of afflictive emotions: Afflictive emotions are naturally abandoned through pledges of color and shape and through treating all [phenomena] as special objects.

Unsurpassed contemplation: This is applied to exalted body, speech, and mind. Through applying unsurpassed contemplation to exalted body, four qualities are generated: (1) quickly overcoming predispositions for the proliferation of the ordinary, (2) quickly overcoming the fruition of karma, (3) engendering great collections of merit, and (4) naturally entering into the selflessness of phenomena. [To describe those four:]

1. Through overcoming conceptions of being ordinary and thereupon abiding in an exalted Buddha body, one overcomes conceptions of an [ordinary] body of beginningless time as well as name,[a] lineage, and so forth.
2. A divine body is the supreme path for [achieving] a union of calm abiding and special insight; hence, when that meditative stabilization [which is a union of calm abiding and special insight] is attained, the effects of earlier actions are quickly overcome. The *Vairochanābhisambodhi Tantra* says:[b]

   [Through] the ripening here of fruitions
   The effects of karmas are attained.
   When adepthood is attained,
   Karmas are overcome.

   Because the mind is without its own thingness[c]
   And because the causes of effects have been abandoned,
   One is freed from karmic births.
   Births are like space.

3. Through mindfulness of Buddhas and having faith upon recognizing Buddhas and making offerings with resources,

---

[a] Read *ming rigs* for *mi rigs* (13.1) in accordance with the *Medium-Length* version, 622.1.

[b] *rnam par snang mdzad chen po mngon par rdzogs par byang chub pa rnam par sprul ba, mahāvairocanābhisaṃbodhivikurvatī;* P126, vol. 5.

[c] *rang dngos med* (13.3).

collections of merit are always produced. Also, when meditation of a divine body has become manifest, all phenomena are understood as just appearances of one's own mind, and moreover, understanding that even the mind is not established arises. Through this and since pristine wisdom is generated in the mental continuum of one with merit, such serves as a cause of pristine wisdom.

4. For this reason, meditation of a divine body involves natural entry into the meaning of the selflessness of phenomena.

Through applying unsurpassed contemplation to exalted speech, there are twelve qualities: (1) reciting the word of a Conqueror, (2) mindfulness of doctrine, (3) having faith upon knowing the doctrine, (4) achieving [the utterance of] true words of speech, (5) attaining method, pristine wisdom, and mindfulness due to possessing wisdom, (6) attaining one-pointed meditative stabilization, (7) offering to Superiors, (8) bringing about the welfare of transmigrators, (9) deities becoming close and one's speedily achieving them, (10) all phenomena coming under the control of the magic of letters, (11) generation of knowledge of all sounds as like echoes, and (12) naturally entering into the selflessness of phenomena. [To describe these:]

1. Through reciting one syllable of a secret essence [mantra] of a One-Gone-Thus, one attains qualities that cannot be rivaled even by reciting profound and vast sūtras.

2. and 3. Mindfulness of doctrine and having faith upon knowing the doctrine are due to again and again remembering the power of secret mantra and the arising of the faith of conviction and trust in the power of secret mantra.

4. Achieving [the utterance of] true words of speech is due to the mantra words of one who has achieved repetition, these not being surpassed by anyone.

5. Attaining method, pristine wisdom, and mindfulness due to possessing wisdom is due to the fact that through the power of secret-mantras, knowledge-mantras, and retention-mantras one attains [respectively] wisdom and method, wisdom and pristine wisdom, and wisdom and mindfulness.

6. In dependence upon vajra repetition and so forth, one-pointed meditative stabilization is attained.

7. and 8. Through emitting light rays, one makes offerings to

Superiors and brings about the welfare of transmigrators.

9. Through the power of emitting and withdrawing [hand-symbols such as vajras, and so forth], obstructions are purified, due to which deities become close, and one quickly attains feats.
10. When one attains [constant] observation of the forms of letters, all appearances are seen in the nature of letters, and one can demonstrate the magic of letters.
11. The pledge of repetition is to know sounds as like echoes; therefore, through the power of familiarity all sounds are naturally known as like echoes.
12. Having attained [constant] observation of what is repeated, one knows all phenomena as just appearances of one's mind, and knows the mind also as without inherent existence. Because of that and because it is said, "Even through reciting once this essence [mantra] all ill deeds are definitely burnt away," and so forth, obstructions are extinguished through repetition, and when they are extinguished, pristine wisdom is engendered, whereby one achieves the quality of naturally entering into the meaning of selflessness.

Through applying unsurpassed contemplation to exalted mind, all qualities are achieved. This is because at all times and on all occasions one is not separated from viewing all phenomena as like illusions, and due to this afflictive emotions are abandoned without difficulty and attitudes fancying that one is virtuous are discarded, whereby all supramundane marvels are attained.

Objection: This is also asserted by the Proponents of the Middle Way School of the Definition Vehicle. It is said, "Do not have a mind fancying, 'I am set in meditative equipoise and [then] rise,'" and "The Conqueror said that taking cognizance of wholesome practices[a] is like eating good food mixed with poison." Hence, it is said that all phenomena are to be viewed as like illusions.

Answer: That is true, but there [in the Definition Vehicle] since one is not bound by [Tantric] vows, one is very loose, whereas here [in the Mantra Vehicle] if one does not meditate such, this is posited as allowing the pledge of exalted mind to deteriorate, due to which, fearing this, one does not ever become separated from meditative stabilization, and even if one does, one restrains [such

---

[a] *chos, dharma.*

distraction] and confesses it. Therefore, just as the exalted mind of a One-Gone-Thus is devoid of conceiving inherent existence, so a Māntrika's consciousness is also released from conceiving inherent existence and is indivisible from realizing [all phenomena] as having the single nature of being like illusions; hence, it is called the "Vajra [or Diamond] Vehicle." Also, it is faster than other paths.

Unsurpassed deeds: Three [types of] unfavorable deeds are abandoned. With respect to deeds that diminish capacity, it is said:

> Through resorting to hard asceticism [and] vows of restraint
> Achievement does not come,
> But if one resorts to all desired resources,
> Achievement quickly comes.

Hence, through practicing virtue strongly upon having nurtured the body and made the mind joyful, achievement comes. How could yoga be achieved with a degenerated body and joyless mind! Qualities of purification, and so forth, are taught for those of little mental power who, through nurturing the body and thereupon practicing virtue, cannot eradicate the afflictive emotions. Here, in consideration of those with great mental power, it is permitted to make use of desire.

With respect to activities causing distraction, it is said:

> If you want the supreme enlightenment,
> You should not read books
> And should not circumambulate monuments.
> If you do, it is difficult to gain enlightenment.

Therefore, since the main cause for achieving enlightenment, the sought-after fruit, is the mind, initially the mind should be brought under control, and other activities should not be done. Having abandoned elaborative deeds, one should meditate just mentally with nonelaborative deeds. This is the supreme method.

With respect to deeds of conceiving inherent existence, it is said:

> Make use of the five fleshes and the five ambrosias
> In order to abandon conceptions.

Because cleanliness, uncleanliness, and so forth are bonds of conceptualization, one should, having abandoned conceptions of cleanliness and uncleanliness, use them upon blessing them into a magnificent state as ambrosia. When this is done, one comes to definitely know that the arising of conceptions of differences concerning phenomena is false. There are certain nonhumans who take joy in just this, coming to [give] protection according to the doctrine and to take up instructions on it.[a] The five fleshes and five ambrosias are illustrations; one should, without attachment, use just those objects conceived to be unclean—meat and so forth. This is swiftness through deeds.

Since [the Mantra Vehicle] is superior by way of these eleven modes of skill in means, it is called the "Method Vehicle" and the "Great of the Great Vehicles." That is the assertion [of the master Jñānashrī].

Also, this master's description of [Mantra as] "swifter, having easier and more [methods], and having greater skill in means" can mostly be understood through the earlier [description]; however, let us explain these a little. In the external Definition Vehicle it is said that [Bodhisattvas] become completely purified [as Buddhas] in thirty-three periods of countless eons or ten periods of countless eons, that Hearers and Solitary Realizers who reverse and enter the Great Vehicle path do so in four periods of countless eons, and others, in three periods of countless eons. However, here [in Mantra] the three—those of the best, middling, and lowest faculties—achieve it [respectively] in this lifetime, in seven births, and sixteen births and so forth.

Objection: Even in the Perfection Vehicle it is said that having thoroughly attained forbearance with respect to the doctrine of nonproduction, if one wishes, one can become manifestly and fully purified [as a Buddha] in even seven days. Also, it is explained that through praising the One-Gone-Thus [called] Tiṣhya[b] for seven days with a single stanza, the collections of [merit usually acquired over] nine eons are shortened, and so on. Therefore, if one has effort, there is no definiteness [that it will take] three periods of countless eons and so on, and if one does not have effort, even through Mantra [Buddhahood] is not attained quickly. Hence, there is no difference [of speed between the Perfection and Mantra vehicles].

Answer: There is no fallacy, because:

1. One who attains forbearance with respect to the doctrine of

---

[a] The meaning of this sentence is doubtful.

[b] *skar rgyal.*

nonproduction is an eighth grounder, and although upon its attainment one can become fully purified [as a Buddha] in seven days, it is explained that two periods of countless eons are needed to get to that point; nothing faster than this is described [in the Perfection Vehicle].

2. Also, although the collections [usually amassed in] nine eons and so forth can be completed in a short time, it is not said that the collections of a period of countless eons can be completed.
3. Also, there are pure scriptural [sources] for the achievement [of Buddhahood] in one lifetime and so forth here [in Mantra].

Objection: Although that is so in Highest Yoga Mantra, it is not suitable in the lower tantra sets.

Answer: It is not so because the *Mañjushrī Root Tantra*[a] [an Action Tantra] says:

> Working well at asceticism in this life,
> Those possessing goodness will achieve [fruits of] mantra
> Even in this life without striving.
> If the activities are illumined even in this [life],
> [Buddhahood] will be achieved in this birth.

and the Continuation of the *Vairochanābhisambodhi Tantra* [a Performance Tantra] says:

> Those Bodhisattvas who practice the Bodhisattva deeds through the approach of Secret Mantra will manifestly and thoroughly accomplish the purity of unsurpassed complete perfect enlightenment in this very life. Also, why is this? Caretaker of the Secret, this called "life" is only something discriminated [that is, designated] as birth by the One-Gone-Thus, for even Bodhisattvas cease this discrimination prior to attaining the meditative stabilization of penetrating the nature of phenomena.

and the *Vajrashekhara* [a Yoga Tantra] says:[b]

> [Through] having attained the high secrecy
> Of the supreme perfections of the grounds
> Arisen over countless eons

---

[a] *'jam dpal rtsa rgyud, mañjuśrīmūlatantra;* P162, vol. 6.

[b] *gsang ba rnal 'byor chen po'i rgyud rdo rje rtse mo, vajraśekharamahāguhyayogatantra;* P113, vol. 5; Toh. 480, vol. *nya.*

> The Very Joyful[a] will be achieved.
> If those yogis make effort, they will pass
> Beyond sorrow in this very life.

Furthermore, the meaning of those [passages] is that the Action and Performance systems assert that having attained the feat of the knowledge fund [of long life] in dependence on substances and mantra, one attains Buddhahood through cultivating the path while enjoying the desirous attributes of a god.[b] For, the *Mañjushrī Root Tantra* says:

> Having put up a painting [of the deity?], and sat on the peacock seat, they instantaneously have power over[c] the Brahmā world. They become universal emperors who are Knowledge Bearers having the manifold retinue of a hundred thousand ten thousand ten million Knowledge Bearers. They live for sixty intermediate eons. They go about as they wish and make use of what they wish. They are not obstructed in movement and possess the glorious wealth of the gods. They also manifestly meet the Superior Mañjushrī, and just he becomes their spiritual guide. Also, finally they attain Buddhahood.

and the *Imagination of the Courageous Achala* [a Performance Tantra] says:[d]

> These become eagles of universal emperors
> Of all the Knowledge Bearers
> In the Buddha lands.
> Having attained inconceivable qualities,
> They live for a hundred eons.
> With the glory of the light of sun and moon
> They tame those difficult to tame.
> Doing everything with a good mind,

---

[a] This is the first Bodhisattva ground.

[b] Read *lha'i* for *lho'i* at 18.3 in accordance with the *Medium-Length* version, 627.4.

[c] The *Medium-Length* version (627.4) reads *gnon* for *non*, both of which literally mean "suppress."

[d] *de bzhin gshegs pa thams cad kyi khro bo'i rgyal po 'phags pa mi g.yo ba de'i stobs dpag tu med pa brtul phod pa 'dul bar gsungs pa zhes bya ba'i rtog pa, acalamahākrodharājasya self-arisenvatathāgatasya balāparimitavīravinayasvākhyātonāmakalpa;* P127, vol. 5. The Nyingma catalog records Bu-tön's comment that this text is a Performance Tantra.

> They illuminate sources of worship
> In countless Buddha lands.
> They listen to the unthinkable excellent doctrine.[a]
> Through hearing[b] such with intelligence,
> The unthinkable qualities of a Buddha arise.

and the *Vairochanābhisambodhi* also says:

> Having practiced this, Māntrikas
> Themselves go about in space.
> Living for an eon with great magnificence,
> Those Conqueror Children die when they wish.
> They even go to other worldly realms.
> They assume various forms of principal beings.
> Through achieving mantras arisen from substance,
> They thoroughly make offerings to the glorious.
> This is described as the feat
> Of nondeteriorating substance.

and:

> Through this their minds become very joyous, and having also attained long life, they thoroughly enjoy play and joy with the five attributes of the Desire [Realm]. They make offering to the Buddhas, the Supramundane Victors, and achieve this path discordant with the world. The Ones-Gone-Thus and the Bodhisattvas, having perceived the import of this, happily set forth rites of the mode of Secret Mantra practice. Why? That which is not attained even upon endeavoring at difficult deeds with exertion and striving over many eons is attained in only this one life by Bodhisattvas practicing the Bodhisattva deeds by way of Secret Mantra.

Objection: This contradicts the statement in [Ratnākarashānti's] *Commentary on the "All Secret Tantra"*[c] [a Yoga Tantra text] that [Buddhahood] is not quickly attained through Action and

[a] Read *bsam med* for *bsa pa* at 18.7 in accordance with the *Medium-Length* version, 628.1.

[b] Read *nyan* for *nyang* in accordance with the *Extensive* version (18.7).

[c] *thams cad gsang ba'i bshad sbyar gsang ba'i sgron ma, sarvarahasyanibandharahasya-pradīpa;* P3450, vol. 76. This is a commentary on *thams cad gsang ba rgyud kyi rgyal po, sarvarahasyo nāma tantrarāja;* P114, vol. 5.

Performance:

> Full purification through causal yoga is described in the systems of the Perfection [Vehicle] as well as Action Tantra, and so forth; it arises over a very long time. [However,] because all of the Great Vehicle is included in Yoga Tantra through causal and resultant yogas and so forth, enlightenment is attained just very quickly.

Answer: There is no such fallacy because that [passage] is referring to attaining the fruit [of Buddhahood in Action and Performance] more slowly than in Yoga Tantra and above, whereas here the reference is to [attainment of Buddhahood in the Mantra Vehicle, which,] due to method, is speedier than in the external Definition [Vehicle]. Since there is no bestowal of feats[a] through the power of a deity in the external Definition [Vehicle] but there is here [in Mantra], there is a difference [between the two]. For, (1) a *Commentary on the Kṛṣhṇayamāri Tantra* says:[b]

> Even in the Action and Performance systems, the object of achievement and the means of achievement do not work but for a long time; those are just arisen from imagination because there feats are completed through the power of a god[c] included in a painting, and so forth. Yoga Tantra differs in this way: through the yoga of one's own deity, concordant feats are achieved upon observing the deity included in the painting, and so forth.

(2) In Yoga Tantra practiced persons[d] enter a maṇḍala, and through the mere descent of pristine wisdom the first ground is attained; then, they become fully purified [as Buddhas] very quickly. Non-practiced persons assume a vow henceforth to turn away from nonvirtue and gradually become completely purified; even

---

[a] *dngos grub, siddhi.*

[b] There are four commentaries on the *Kṛṣhṇayamāri Tantra*, P2782-2785, vols. 66-67, by Ratnākarashānti, Kṛṣhṇa chen po, Avadhūta Kumāracandra, and Padmapāṇi; for instance, the one by Kṛṣhṇa chen po is *gshin rje gshed nag po'i rgyud kyi rgyal po mngon par mthong ba lam gyi sgron ma zhes bya ba'i rgya cher bshad pa, kṛṣṇayamāri-tantrarājāprekṣaṇapathapradīpanāmaṭīkā.*

[c] Read *lha'i* for *lhas* at 20.2 in accordance with the *Medium-Length* version, 629.3.

[d] *chos ldan gyi gang zag.* Kensur Yeshi Thupten tentatively identified this as someone who is maintaining vows.

the lowest [among them] definitely become fully purified in sixteen births. After the passage [quoted] above from the *Vajrashekhara Tantra,* it says:

> The Very Joyful ground is attained,
> There is no doubt about Vajrahood.
> Or through only seeing [the maṇḍala] they pass
> Beyond sorrow in sixteen births.
> The Very Joyful is attained
> Or even Vajrahood itself.
> They make sun and moon fall to the earth
> And become of the nature of space.
> A common being achieves Buddhahood,
> It is not otherwise.

The master Ānandagarbha says on the occasion of indicating the benefits of seeing a maṇḍala:

> Through mere entry [into a maṇḍala] pristine wisdom descends. Then, those on whom wisdom has descended attain the Very Joyful ground and so forth. Therefore, it is said that if it is not difficult to gain even the full achievement of a One-Gone-Thus, what need is there to say anything about other feats! This indicates that due to abiding in the vows of a fully ordained monk, a fully ordained nun, and so forth feats are attained very quickly and that others [will attain feats] later upon taking vows of restraint.[a]

On the occasion of the benefits of having achieved the great seal, in commentary on the passage:

> If you become mindful [of yourself] as a Buddha,
> You will quickly become just a Buddha.

[Ānandagarbha] says:

> That [indicates that] when this [deity yoga] is thoroughly accomplished, one becomes just a Buddha. In this very life, one attains Buddhahood.

(3) In Great Yoga Tantra [that is, Highest Yoga Mantra] those of sharp faculties and great effort achieve [Buddhahood] in this very

[a] The meaning of "vows of restraint" (*ldog pa'i sdom pa,* 21.2) is unclear; according to Yeshi Thupten, it may mean to turn away from the unfavorable.

life; the middling achieve it as they are about to die or in the intermediate state, and the lowest, at the most in seven or sixteen births. The *Guhyasamāja Tantra*[a] says:

> The enlightenment that Bodhisattvas do not attain, though they strive and seek it for as many eons as there are grains of sands of the Ganges, [is attained] in this very life by Bodhisattvas who take joy in the union of the secret,[b] who come to be among the number whom the Ones-Gone-Thus call "Buddha."[c]

and the *Saṃpuṭa Tantra* says:[d]

> In brief, the Buddhahood
> Achieved over countless
> [Or] ten million eons
> You will attain in this birth
> Through the most excellent bliss.
> Or [the ground of] Vajradhara,
> Or Universal Emperorhood,
> Or the eight great feats here [in this life]
> As well as attaining what is desired in mind.

and the *Kālachakra Tantra*[e] says:

> Those yogis knowing all the magical devices and the gurus
> of the three realms [attain Buddhahood] in this birth.
> If, having thoroughly entered the path, they die, then it is
> in another birth through the assistance of this.

With respect to the meaning of this, the master Jñānākara [in his *Introduction to Mantra*] says:[f]

> For example, one who has achieved swift feet

---

[a] *de bzhin gshegs pa thams cad kyi sku gsung thugs kyi gsang chen gsang ba 'dus pa zhes bya ba brtag pa'i rgyal po chen po, sarvatathāgatakāyavākcittarahasya-guhyasamāja-nāmamahākalparāja;* P81, vol. 3.

[b] *gsang ba 'dus pa, guhyasamāja.*

[c] The *Medium-Length* (270.5) reads *de bzhin gshegs pa rnams* ***kyi*** rather than *de bzhin gshegs pa rnams* ***kyis*** (21.5).

[d] *rnal 'byor ma bzhi'i kha sbyor kyi rgyud, caturyoginīsaṃpuṭatantra;* P24, vol. 2. The first six lines are cited in *Tantra in Tibet*, 139.

[e] *rgyud kyi rgyal po dpal dus kyi 'khor lo, kālacakranāmatantrarāja;* P4, vol. 1.

[f] *gsang sngags la 'jug pa, mantrāvatāra;* P4541, vol. 81, 195.5.8-196.1.2.

Or the sun and moon goes just speedily
To a place arrived at over a long time
By a person of little power
Or by an animal cart.
Just so, Māntrikas enter in this life
Into that entered over a long time
In reliance upon
The Perfection [Vehicle] or other paths.
This depends upon unequaled power.

For this, marvelous causes and conditions are required. Concerning the causes, from the force of salutary actions in the past one's body and speech must be fully endowed, and one's mind must have fewer afflictive emotions. With respect to the conditions, there are the three deeds—the deed of entry which is to have initiation, the deed of application which is to meditatively cultivate the two stages [that is, the generation stage and completion stage] as well as their branches, and the deed of achievement which is to set [the mind] one-pointedly on its object of observation upon having abandoned whatever is unfavorable. That same text says:[a]

Moreover this is through marvelous causes and conditions.
The causes also are that by performing actions well
Of body, speech, and mind in former lives
One presently has attained a fully endowed body
As a continuum of fruition,
As well as speech melodious like a cuckoo,
And a mind of slight afflictive emotions—
The hosts of desires, hatreds, and obscurations.
The conditions also are just threefold—
The threefold behavior
Of entry, application, and practice.
Among them, the behavior of entry
Is for students who have previously acquainted for a long time
With a guru endowed with good qualities
To make a supplication and thereupon
To enter a maṇḍala and be conferred initiation
And to identify their own favored deity.

---

[a] P4541, vol. 81, 196.1.2-196.2.1.

That is called the "basic condition."[a]
Among those, the behavior of application
Is to make effort in a concordant place and so forth
Initially at emptiness, love, and so forth,
And through the rite of one's favored deity
To meditate, repeat [mantra], recite,
Give food-offerings, or make offerings and so forth
In three sessions or four.
Released from all great ill deeds,
One becomes the equivalent of a Bodhisattva
Who has practiced for many eons.
This is indicated as the second condition
[Making one] fit for transformation.
Among those, about the condition of achievement,
For example, when a well washed cloth
Is to be dyed another color,
It is done with little difficulty and care is to be taken,
So with the behavior of achievement one must tighten [the mind]
But not with great hardship.
When persons, whose continuums have been ripened
Through the behavior of application, engage in achievement,
They abandon unfavorable places,
Friends, resources, and thoughts
And set one-pointedly on the object of observation.
This is indicated as the third,
The condition of speedy elevation.

One attains the knowledge fund of feats, which is achieved through such causes and conditions and, having attained it, achieves the fulfillment of one's own and others' welfare—the behavior of adepthood.

Thereby, if the causes and conditions are fulfilled, [Buddhahood] is achieved in this very life. The same text says:[b]

What are the feats of adepthood?

---

[a] Read ***gzhi yi*** *rkyen* for ***g.yo*** *rkyen* at 22.6 in accordance with the *Medium-Length* version, 631.7; the Peking edition (196.1.6) reads ***gzhi'i*** *rkyen*.

[b] P4541, vol. 81, 196.2.5-196.3.2.

One's body, locality, and resources
Exceed those of humans.
One has power over one's life span
And is forever released from birth without leisure.
One meets and so forth with Buddhas who arise,
And consciously uses the five desirous attributes
Without becoming bound,
And can engender help for oneself and others.
What is the behavior of adepthood?
One enjoys the happiness of wealth
In this and that place and time
And likewise makes offerings to Superiors
According to one's capacity.
With various appropriate magical emanations
One tames sentient beings who are tamed
Through help [or] through eradication.
One gives coolness, heat, and so forth
Even for brief periods in the hells and so forth.
Likewise, one teaches various doctrines
To the varieties of sentient beings.
One helps all through being seen,
Heard, touched, or remembered.[a]
What is the time of adepthood?
The feat will be attained
Even in this very life by an ascetic
Who has accumulated all causes and conditions,
Continually repeats [mantra] and meditates,
And has faith in the Conqueror as well as his Children.

The thought of this master is that the attainment of a ground or the attainment [of the level] of a Knowledge Bearer is adepthood and that such is attained in a single life.

The second stage of Nāgārjuna's *Five Stages* says:[b]

> Initially through union with an action [seal, that is, consort]
> The eighth ground is attained.
> Those who perceive the three appearances

[a] Read *thos* **dang** for *thos* **skang** at 23.7 in accordance with the *Medium-Length* version, 633.1, and the Peking (196.2.1).

[b] *rim pa lnga pa, pañcakrama;* P2667, vol. 61.

Thoroughly abide on the tenth ground.
Having attained manifest enlightenment well,
They go to a state of purity.
Since they do not turn back from a Buddha land,
They become omniscient in this very life.

Thus, it is explained that through the generation stage one attains the eighth ground: through mental observation, the tenth ground; and through illusory body and clear light, the eleventh or twelfth, and thereupon through union one is fully purified [as a Buddha].

With respect to this, in (1) the *Clear Meaning Commentary on (Nāgārjuna's) "Five Stages"* which is said to be by Nāgabodhi,[a] (2) the commentary on the root text of the *Ornament for Clear Realization [of Guhyasamāja]* which is said to be by Chandrakīrti,[b] and (3) the *Commentary on (Āryadeva's) "Lamp Compendium for Practice"* by Shākyamitra,[c] it is asserted that through considering each of the four (heat, peak, forbearance, and supreme mundane qualities) to have three [subdivisions] each (great, middling, [and small]) there are twelve grounds and that the very joyful ground is the Buddha ground. For instance, Chandrakīrti's *Commentary on the "Ornament for Clear Realization [of Guhyasamāja]"* says:

Progressing over the particulars of the grounds—
The middling forbearance, and high supreme qualities,
And the first through tenth grounds—
One abandons conceptions of body, speech, and mind.

and Shākyamitra's *Commentary on (Āryadeva's) "Lamp Compendium for Practice"* explains [the process] together with citing scripture:

The generation stage is not the first. Why? Because the completion stage is.

Question: Then, what is [the meaning of] this "first"?

Answer: It is the vajra repetition together with its support and generation.

Question: Through this what ground is attained?

Answer: The eighth ground, the ground of middling for-

---

[a] *rim pa lnga pa'i bshad pa nor bu'i phreng ba, pañcakramaṭīkāmaṇimālā;* P2697, vol. 62.

[b] *gsang ba 'dus pa'i mngon par rtogs pa'i rgyan gyi 'grel pa, guhyasamājābhisamayālaṃkāravṛtti;* P2681, vol. 62.

[c] *spyod pa bsdus pa'i sgron ma shes bya ba rgya cher bshad pa, caryāmelāyanapradīpanāmaṭīkā;* P2703, vol. 62.

bearance. Moreover, from that called "vajra meaning," one abides on the ground of vajra repetition, whereupon the middling forbearance is attained.

Clear realization of exalted body, speech, and mind is to know exalted body, speech, and mind as the entity of the mind itself. Through this what grounds are attained? The ten grounds. The ground of observing mind is to arrive at[a] the lesser or middling level of supreme qualities. Through the illusion-like meditative stabilization, one abides on the great level of supreme qualities. Another [passage] says:

> [The levels] from great forbearance through supreme qualities
> Are attained through observation of mind
> And the illusion-like.
> Through being obscured with respect to the lower ground
> One does not achieve ascension
> To the Very Joyful and so forth, like an animal.

Then, what ground is attained through the clear light? The Very Joyful, the first of the ten grounds.

Question: Then, does this not contradict the statement:

> Through the yoga of clear light
> One thoroughly abides on the thirteenth [ground].

Answer: There is no contradiction; that [count of thirteen] is in terms of [considering the levels of the path of preparation,] heat and so forth [as among the first twelve grounds]:

> Having become the final heat,
> Through applying [small,] middling, and great
>
> In terms of [peak,] forbearance, and supreme qualities
> There are twelve; the Very Joyful is the thirteenth.

Through this called "union" how many particular grounds

---

[a] Read ***reg*** *pa* for ***rag*** *pa* at 25.1 in accordance with the *Medium-Length* version, 634.3.

are attained? It is as it is said:

> [The grounds] from the Very Joyful through the
> Cloud of Doctrine
> Attained from its imprint
> Are arrived at through union.
> They are objects of another.[a]

The other commentators on *Nāgārjuna's "Five Stages"* describe this as literal.

Also, it is explained in the commentary on the *Buddha Union*[b] that in dependence upon the practice of Secret Mantra, [the level of] a Knowledge Bearer is attained and that in this very life as a Knowledge Bearer Buddhahood is attained. The seventh chapter of the *Buddha Union* says:[c]

> In this life [the level of] a Knowledge Bearer is attained.
> Then, through the force of gradual familiarization,
> One achieves the definitive great Buddhahood,
> The three bodies of great bliss, nondual.

In the *Kālachakra Tantra* it is asserted that it is achieved in the birth [that is, lifetime] of a human who is endowed with the two collections and who is a great being endowed with the six constituents. Kalkī Puṇḍarīka's *Stainless Light* says:[d]

> The statement, "Thoroughly bestowing the fruit of Buddhahood in this birth," [means that this *Kālachakra Tantra*] is a king of tantras thoroughly bestowing the fruit of Buddhahood in this birth as a human, not in a birth as any of

---

[a] The meaning of the last line is unclear.

[b] There are four commentaries: (1) *rgyud kyi don rnam par bshad pa, tantrārthaṭīkā;* P2531, vol. 58; (2) *mnyam sbyor gyi rgyan, samayogālaṃkāra;* P2532, vol. 58; (3) *sangs rgyas thams cad dang mnyam par sbyor ba shes bya ba'i rgyud kyi dka' 'grel, sarvabuddhasamayoganāmatantrapañjikā;* P2533, vol. 58; (4) *sangs rgyas thams cad dang mnyam par sbyor ba'i dka' 'grel, sarvabuddhasamayogapañjikā;* P2535, vol. 58.

[c] *sangs rgyas thams cad dang mnyam par sbyor ba mkha' 'gro ma sgyu ma bde ba'i mchog, sarvabuddhasamayogaḍākinījālasaṃbara;* P8, vol. 1.

[d] *bsdus pa'i rgyud kyi rgyal po dus kyi 'khor lo'i 'grel bshad rtsa ba'i rgyud kyi rjes su 'jug pa stong phrag bcu gnyis pa dri ma med pa'i 'od ces bya ba / 'grel chen dri med 'od, vimālaprabhānāmamūlatantrānusāriṇīdvādaśasāhasrikālaghukālacakratantrarājaṭīkā;* P2064, vol. 46.

the five [other] transmigrations—gods, and so forth.

Vajragarbha's commentary [on the *Hevajra Tantra* in the manner of the *Kālachakra Tantra*] says:[a]

> The statement, "Thoroughly bestowing the fruit of Buddhahood in this birth," [means that this] is accomplished upon having taken human birth again and again, and not as a god, demigod, and so forth.

Objection: The explanation that such is accomplished in one life is in consideration of a person who, having amassed vast collections [of merit and wisdom], has entered a high ground and is not [in reference] to accomplishment by a common being.

Answer: It is not so. The root *Kālachakra Tantra* says:

> If low caste persons, bamboo weavers, and so forth
> Or those having done [any of] the five deeds of immediate retribution
> Practice the deeds of Mantra,
> They will become Buddhas in this very birth.

Therefore, it is explained that if persons who are doing actions of immediate retribution practice later with effort, they will become fully purified [as Buddhas], and it is not possible for a Superior to commit an action of immediate retribution; [hence, the reference must be to common beings]. Kalkī Puṇḍarīka's *Stainless Light* says:

> Having overcome with the meditative stabilization of immutable bliss of the great seal in this Mantra Vehicle the commission of the awful actions of the deeds of immediate retribution, in order not to allow the sudden occurrence of other nonvirtues, one bars—with the bars of love, compassion, joy, and equanimity and so forth, as well as the harmonies with enlightenment—the doors of entry of the four demonic sounds[b] and of obstructors to the house that is the source of vajra doctrine. Doing such, in just this [life] one gains achievement together with the Vajrasattva great seal. Even those who are agents of the deeds of immediate retribution attain the fruit of Buddhahood in this birth. This is what the One-Gone-Thus asserts. The One-Gone-Thus does

---

[a] *kye'i rdo rje bsdus pa'i don gyi rgya cher 'grel pa, hevajrapiṇḍārthaṭīkā;* P2310, vol. 53.

[b] Both texts (26.6 and 636.1) read *sgra* (sounds).

> not assert that even those who have committed the awful actions of the five deeds of immediate retribution *after* entering the Vajra Vehicle will attain the fruit of Buddhahood in this birth.

Also, the earlier passages from the *Vajrashekhara* (222 and 226) establish such.

Furthermore, there are cases of persons who see the truth of the clear light of the completion stage but, due to laziness or due to [lack of] wealth, do not perform the deeds [related with using a consort]. In dependence upon concentration combining quintessential instructions for dying and for the intermediate state they become fully purified in the intermediate state in a Complete Enjoyment Body of union [of pure body and mind], this being from the Body of Attributes of the clear light of death. Āryadeva's *Lamp Compendium for Practice* says:[a]

> The vajra student asks, "If though practitioners see the truth, they do not perform [any of] the three types of deeds due to being distracted by farming, commerce, goods and services, and so forth through the force of being accustomed to earlier predispositions and if other practitioners, because of lacking wealth, do not perform the deeds due to being unable to perform fully the rites as they are set forth in the Tantra, will they, upon dying, go to another rebirth or will they attain Vajradharahood?"
>
> In answer to this question, he, having first taught the mode of being and given an example, makes the actual answer: "Therefore, one who has knowledge of suchness but has not engaged in the deeds that were just explained, realizes thoroughly and manifestly—upon having forsaken all views—that dying is ultimate truth and birth is conventional truth[b] and thereupon generates a firm attitude: 'Upon eventually[c] abiding in the clear light, I will set aside the ordinary [mental and physical] aggregates and thereupon rise in the stage of blessing myself into a magnificent state.' When through taking this to mind they dwell [in such a

---

[a] *spyod bsdus sgron ma, caryāmelāpakapradīpa;* P2668, vol. 61.

[b] Read *kun rdzob* ***kyi*** for *kun rdzob* ***kyis*** at 27.6 in accordance with the *Medium-Length* version, 637.1.

[c] *brgya lam na.*

state], they will not lose this mental application in another birth, whereby they become omniscient."

and the *Guhyasamāja Tantra* also says:

Drink the fruit with desire
In accordance with the rite for restraining emission of semen.
If you kill the collection of Ones-Gone-Thus,
The very supreme feat will be attained.

and the *Great Sacred Word*[a] also says:

When your mind has entered the basal sphere,
You realize clarity and strong joy, like space.
Then when you achieve the form
Of a five-year-old child endowed
With the force of magical emanation,
Unexampled bliss is fully realized.
From that, when impelled to another birth,
You thoroughly realize the form of an emanation.

Moreover, persons who cannot gain achievement in that lifetime and see the signs of impending death will achieve the supreme [feat of Buddhahood] if they implement transference [of consciousness] prior to the onset of infectious disease, and so forth. The *Four Seats* says:[b]

Through certain approaches
They cross over cyclic existence.
Then, through certain avenues
When the time of death arises
For one on the good yogic path
Seeing the signs of death and transmigration,
Transference without allowing contagion and so forth
Is the supreme of yogas.

Also, with respect to the benefits of that [practice], it says:

---

[a] *zhal lung chen mo.* There are two texts by Buddhajñānapāda called *zhal gyi lung: rim pa gnyis pa'i de kho na nyid sgom pa zhes bya ba'i zhal gyi lung, dvikramatattvabhāvanā-nāma-mukhāgama,* P2716, vol. 65, and *zhal gyi lung, mukhāgama;* P2717, vol. 65.

[b] *gdan bzhi/ rnal 'byor ma'i rgyud kyi rgyal po chen po dpal gdan bzhi pa, caturpīṭhamahāyoginītantrarāja;* P67, vol. 3.

When it is sent above the ninth joint,[a]
There is that called "transference."
Through this path [the ill effects
Of] killing Brahmins daily,
Committing the five deeds of immediate retribution,
Theft, and using desirous attributes are stopped.
One will not be polluted with ill deeds,
And the phenomena of cyclic existence will become distant.
Just as the color of a lotus
Grown from mud is beautiful,
So a pristine wisdom body arises of its own accord
From the body of an excellent [yogi].
When the time comes, transference is to be done.
When through this the physical signs arise,
The intelligent initiate the yoga.[b]

It is said that if the supreme [feat of Buddhahood] is not achieved through transference, one achieves [the level of] a Knowledge Bearer, and then gradually achieves the supreme. For, the *Great Sacred Word* says:

If the three bodies are not achieved,
One will become a chief of Knowledge Bearers,
Gradually becoming the great seal.

and the *Condensed Kālachakra Tantra* also says:

When the winds of the two [channels] are stopped, an opening is made at the crown of the head, whereupon one goes to the cities of the supreme.
By thoroughly activating the vajra in the mind, everything together with the area becomes just [a land of deities] making use of space.

If one is not endowed with effort [but] is without infractions, one achieves [the supreme feat of Buddhahood] in three or seven births. Jñānākara's *Introduction to Secret Mantra* says:[c]

Those who are endowed with the cause but lack

---

[a] Translation doubtful; the text (28.5) reads *tshigs dgu las ni yar gtong na*.

[b] Whether *sbyor ba* (yoga) here refers to the main part of the yoga of transference or to the connection to the new life-situation, the meaning is similar.

[c] *gsang sngags la 'jug pa, mantrāvatāra;* P4541, vol. 81, 196.3.2.

> Certain conditions, like a great medicinal tree,
> Will in three lives see emptiness well
> And be released without [the passage of much] time.[a]

and the *Buddha Skull* says:[b]

> Though the [supreme] feat is not attained in this birth,
> In another birth the feat is attained.

and the *Secret Treasury* says:[c]

> If one is endowed with thorough bestowal of initiation,
> Initiation will be conferred in birth after birth.
> In the seventh birth of that [person]
> Feats will be attained even without meditation.
> If those who possess feats
> Abide in the pledges and vows,
> Even though due to karma they do not achieve [the supreme feat] in this birth,
> They will attain the [supreme] feat in another birth.
> For those who temporarily let their pledges deteriorate,
> Never mind the attainment of feats
> Even human birth is difficult to attain.

Also, Kalkī Puṇḍarīka's *Stainless Light* says:

> When those who have thoroughly entered the path die without having attained yoga, then through the force of predispositions they attain all in another human birth again. Over seven births at the most, even those who are not endowed with effort and do not meditatively cultivate pristine wisdom [do so].

In the *Kālachakra Tantra* there is no mention of more than seven births, but lamas say that the lowest achieve [the supreme feat of Buddhahood] in sixteen births. Moreover, the *Vajrashekhara* says:

---

[a] Peking (196.3.2) misreads: *stong nyid legs mthong* **du** *med grol,* whereas it should read *stong nyid legs mthong* **dus** *med grol* in accordance with 29.3.

[b] *sangs rgyas thod pa shes bya ba rnal 'byor ma'i rgyud kyi rgyal po, buddhakapālanāmayoginītantrarāja,* P63, vol. 3.

[c] *de bzhin gshegs pa thams cad kyi gsang ba gsang ba'i mdzod chen po mi zad pa gter gyi sgron ma brtul zhugs chen po bsgrub pa'i rgyud, sarvatathāgataguhyamahāguhyakośa-akṣayayanidhidīpamahāvratasādhanatantra;* P453, vol. 9.

[If] vajric [practitioners] make manifest effort
In all births—birth after birth—
At the most in sixteen births
They will attain peace, Buddhahood.

The main causes of accomplishing this path are purity of pledges and vows of restraint, predisposing latencies for a good path in this life, and the power of aspirational wishes such as:

May I in birth after birth
Be born in [a family of good] lineage,
Have a sane[a] Hevajra teacher endowed with the pledges,
Have respect for gurus, and possess the pledges.

May I in birth after birth
[Hold in] my hands vajra and resounding bell.
May I read the doctrine of the profound
And have the food of a consort's essential fluid.[b]

The Chapter on the Internal in the *Kālachakra Tantra* says:

If yogis—who due to a very fluctuating mind do not attain the king of yogas—die,
They will be born in a glorious human world possessing yoga in a [family of good] lineage able [to accomplish] the very supreme.
Due to prior familiarization, those who lack the yoga of pristine wisdom will again thoroughly encompass it.
When pristine wisdom has been attained, they will proceed to the inexhaustible supreme state without being reborn.

That is the feature of a swifter path. [The features of] having easier and more methods were explained earlier [in connection with Tripiṭakamāla's *Lamp for the Three Modes,* 209] and [the feature of] greater skill in means is similar to [Tripiṭakamāla's description of] nonobscuration [208].

---

[a] Read ***smyo*** *med* for ***snyo*** *med* at 29.2 in accordance with the *Medium-Length* version, 639.4.

[b] Read *mnyam* ***zas*** for *mnyam* ***za*** at 29.3 in accordance with the *Medium-Length* version, 639.5. The meaning of *mnyam* is unclear.

[How Ratnākarashānti Divides the Perfection and Mantra Vehicles]

Moreover, the master Ratnākarashānti [in his *Presentation of the Three Vehicles*][a] says that the Perfection and Mantra vehicles do not differ with respect to the ultimate truth but do differ with respect to the profundity and vastness of conventional truths. Because whatever objects of observation appear are meditated as deities, [Mantra] is more vast. Since [Māntrikas] hold in mind the pledges that the Buddhas of the three times have undergone, special blessings into a magnificent state are engendered, whereby [Mantra] has vaster assistance. Also, in accordance with how Buddhas and Bodhisattvas bring about the welfare of transmigrators and bless lands into purity, [Māntrikas] similarly engender [such marvelous deeds]; therefore, [Mantra] has vaster deeds. Because Proponents of the Middle Way School, Proponents of the Mind-Only School, Hearers, and Solitary Realizers do not have these three, they become fully purified over three or four periods of countless eons. However, since Mantra has these, full purification occurs in a short time; hence, there is a great difference. [As Ratnākarashānti says:][b]

> Because of very pure objects of observation,
> The power of aids, and also deeds,
> The vehicle of the intelligent
> Is renowned as the greatest of the great.

[How Nāgārjuna Divides the Perfection and Mantra Vehicles]

Furthermore, the Foremost Elder [Atisha's] *Compilation of All Pledges* says:[c]

> Bodhisattvas who have entered the door of Mantra are to understand as follows. This great of the Great Vehicles surpasses the lower [vehicles]. How? The Superior Nāgārjuna

---

[a] *theg pa gsum rnam par bzhag pa, triyānavyavasthāna;* P4535, vol. 81. The passage quoted below is cited in *Tantra in Tibet,* 134.

[b] Cited in *Tantra in Tibet,* 134.

[c] *dam tshig thams cad bsdus pa, sarvasamayasaṃgraha;* P4547, vol. 81, 209.4.8-209.5.5. The citations from Nāgārjuna through Samayavajra come from Atisha's *Compilation of All Pledges;* they are mostly consecutive with the exception that Atisha cites Tripiṭakamāla and Ratnākarashānti, while Bu-tön omits these passages at this point, since he has already given them earlier.

says, "Through realizing all as the Body of Attributes, [everything] is implanted with the seal of the all-good.[a] Through being treated as an object of service[b] by the great worldly gods who have pledges [to help tantric practitioners, and so forth] as well as by their retinues, one is blessed into a magnificent state. Through being mentally cared for and blessed by the Buddhas of the three times [past, present, and future] as well as their Children, feats are [achieved] more quickly. Through having the same sphere of activity as Ones-Gone-to-Bliss, one becomes separate from the frights of cyclic existence and bad transmigrations, and rests. Through possessing the vajra mind of enlightenment and the indivisibility of body, speech, and mind, there is no interference at all. Through believing that all external and internal [phenomena] are naturally pure, pledges do not deteriorate, and even if they do deteriorate, they are naturally restored. There are these distinctive features [of the Mantra Vehicle]."

[How Indrabhūti Divides the Perfection and Mantra Vehicles][c]

Also, the great master Indrabhūti says, "[Mantra] is superior by way of seven features: guru, vessel, rite, activity, pledge, view, and behavior."

[How Jñānapāda Divides the Perfection and Mantra Vehicles][d]

The great master Jñānapāda says, "The Mantra Vehicle is uncommon in three ways: practitioner, path, and fruit."

[How Ḍombhīheruka Divides the Perfection and Mantra Vehicles][e]

The master Ḍombhīheruka also says:

> About this, the Mantra Vehicle is superior

---

[a] *kun tu bzang po, samantabhadra.*

[b] Read *bkur **gnas*** for *bkur **ste nas*** at 31.4 in accordance with the *Medium-Length* version, 640.6.

[c] Atisha's *Compilation of All Pledges,* 209.5.5-209.5.6.

[d] Ibid., 209.5.6-209.5.7.

[e] Ibid., 209.5.8-210.1.1.

> By way of the feature of vessels,
> The doctrine making vessels,[a]
> The features of texts and paths, and the feature of fruits.

[How Vajraghaṇṭapāda Divides the Perfection and Mantra Vehicles][b]

Furthermore, Vajraghaṇṭapāda says:

> The Mantra Vehicle is the great of the Great Vehicles, for it has the feature of the persons who are the bases, the feature of the paths that are the means of entry, the feature of the fruit which is the finality, and the feature of definite emergence.

[How Samayavajra Divides the Perfection and Mantra Vehicles][c]

My lama, the foremost venerable Samayavajra, said:

> This Vehicle is higher than the Perfection Vehicle; it is superior by way of guru, initiation, pledges, quintessential instructions, and effort.

The meaning of these is to be understood through the reasonings explained earlier, as appropriate.

---

[a] Most likely this is initiation.
[b] Atisha's *Compilation of All Pledges,* 210.1.1-210.1.2.
[c] Ibid., 210.1.3-210.1.4.

9. Long-chen-rap-jam's Dramatic Evocation

The Nying-ma master Long-chen-rap-jam,[a] 1308-1363, whose writings are to much of Nying-ma as Tsong-kha-pa's are to Ge-luk (despite not being its founder), gives a presentation of the difference between the Perfection Vehicle, also called the Definition Vehicle, and the Mantra Vehicle in his *Precious Treasury of Tenets: Illuminating the Meaning of All Vehicles.*[b] Though he cites several of the same sources as Bu-tön, the appeal is different; his creative comments and psychologically evocative style show that the primary concern is not with providing a partially explained catalogue, like that of Bu-tön. The basic thread of discourse is the evocation of an experience of the tantric path and result through the usage of special, experientially oriented vocabulary.

Long-chen-pa begins by giving a highly interpretive rendition of Tripiṭakamāla's four features distinguishing the Mantra Vehicle from the Perfection Vehicle, an explanation by no means bound by Tripiṭakamāla's own commentary, as Bu-tön's was. Then, he lists five features:

1. objects of observation
2. accompaniers
3. view
4. behavior
5. achievement of the nature

and cites Ratnākarashānti's three features:

1. very pure object
2. the power of aids
3. deeds.

He also gives extensive commentary on the fifteen distinctive features found in the *Tantra of the Inconceivable Ra-li:*

---

[a] *klong chen rab 'byams.*

[b] *theg pa mtha' dag gi don gsal bar byed pa grub pa'i mtha' rin po che'i mdzod* (Gangtok: Dodrup Chen Rinpoche, 1969?), 258.1-275.2; for a translation of the entire text see Albion Moonlight Butters, "The Doxographical Genius of Kun mkhyen kLong chen rab 'byams pa," Ph.D. diss., Columbia University, 2006, 298-707. The corresponding section in Long-chen-pa's *Precious Treasury of the Supreme Vehicle (theg pa'i mchog rin po che'i mdzod)* (Gangtok, Dodrup Chen Rinpoche, 1969?) is much shorter (128.5-130.2).

1. view
2. behavior
3. mental stabilization
4. cause
5. path
6. fruit
7. grounds
8. time
9. enjoyment
10. yoga
11. welfare of self and others
12. scope
13. forsaking extremes of fatigue
14. little difficulty
15. way of amassing the collections.

He concludes with a threefold explanation of why Mantra is posited as the Effect Vehicle—by way of speed, superior method, and taking a similitude of the effect as the path.

Translation

The presentation of how the Secret Mantra Vajra Vehicle surpasses the Definition Vehicle[a] [that is to say, the Sūtra systems] has three parts: the divisions of the Great Vehicle in general, how [the Vajra Vehicle] surpasses the Definition Vehicle in particular, and identification of how [the Vajra Vehicle] is the effect.

Divisions of the Great Vehicle in general

Furthermore, the Great Vehicle is twofold, a Causal Definition [Vehicle] and an Effect Secret Mantra [Vehicle]. The *Tantra Thoroughly Establishing the Great Vehicle* says:[b]

> The Great Vehicle is of two aspects,
> The Perfection Vehicle
> And the unsurpassed Vajra Vehicle.

and the *Susiddhi Tantra* says:[c]

> Through the divisions of cause and effect
> There are a Perfection Vehicle
> And an unsurpassed Vajra Vehicle.

How the Vajra Vehicle surpasses the Definition Vehicle in particular

This section has two parts: a brief indication and an extensive explanation.

Brief indication of how the Vajra Vehicle surpasses the Definition Vehicle

The internal Secret Mantra Vehicle greatly surpasses the external Definition Vehicle.[d] Although both are similar in ascertaining the

---

[a] *mtshan nyid kyi theg pa, *lakṣaṇayāna.*

[b] *theg pa chen po yongs su grub pa'i rgyud.*

[c] *legs par grub pa'i rgyud, susiddhitantra;* P431, vol. 9.

[d] Here Long-chen-pa expands on the passage from Tripiṭakamāla's *Lamp for the Three Modes* listing the four features, which he cites at the end of this section:

> Though the object [or basis] is the same, the Mantra Vehicle

matrix of clear light—the basis—and the phenomena[a] that depend on it, they differ in terms of knowledge in that the Definition [Vehicle] is obscured but Mantra is not obscured with respect to delineating the bases, paths, and fruits just as they are. For, when they comprehend the profound[b] and the vast, the Definition [Vehicle] has no more than only a profundity concerned with:

1. a *basis* fabricated by the mind, an ultimate truth known through determinative inferential valid cognition[c] breaking down [objects] through reasoning
2. only the *paths* of calm abiding and special insight established through effort in terms of such [a fabricated basis]
3. a *fruit,* the attainment of which is approached over many eons

and, with respect to the vast, has no more than only a discarding [of nonvirtues] and adopting [of virtues] within delineating as conventional truths the aggregates,[d] constituents,[e] senses-spheres,[f] and so forth which depend on the basic constituent.[g]

Mantra, however, delineates—as the ground—nonconceptual pristine wisdom unfabricated by the mind, the essence of the Body of Attributes, merely through concentrative emphasis on focal points of body, speech, channels, winds, drops of essential fluid, and so forth without depending on reasoning. Thereupon, natural awareness[h] abides within it, whereby in one lifetime and so forth the expanse of reality,[i] the ultimate truth, is realized, enlightenment being actualized. Through this, the profound is just manifestly generated [and not merely viewed as an effect].

Also, with respect to the vast, having delineated the expanse as the *basic tantra* primordially established as the maṇḍala of clear

Is superior because of being nonobscured,
Having many skillful methods, no difficulties,
And being created for those with sharp faculties.

[a] *chos, dharma.*

[b] The "profound" (*zab mo*) mainly refers to the view of reality, and the vast (*rgya che ba*) mainly refers to practices related with conventionalities.

[c] *rjes dpag nges pa'i tshad ma.*

[d] *phung po, skandha.*

[e] *khams, dhātu.*

[f] *skye mched, ayatana.*

[g] *khams, dhātu.*

[h] *rang bzhin gyi blo.*

[i] *dbyings.*

light, [Mantra] teaches the practice of *path tantras* in which all conventional aspects—aggregates, constituents, and sense-spheres—which depend on that [expanse of reality] are delineated as gods, inestimable mansions, and creations of [pure] lands without adopting or discarding. Actualization thereby of the eight feats temporarily and supreme enlightenment and so forth finally and the teaching of whatsoever path doctrines are delineated [as] the *fruit tantras*. Therefore, [the Mantra Vehicle] is **not obscured** with respect to the meaning of the profound and the vast.

[The Mantra Vehicle] also surpasses [the Definition Vehicle] through **having more skillful methods.** Even with respect to abandoning a single object of abandonment such as desire, desire is purified in the expanse without [having to work at] abandoning it. This is done in the common way through transformation by [the stage of] generation or in the uncommon way through using in the path heightened desire as the great bliss of individual investigation [of reality]. The Definition Vehicle, on the other hand, relies on abandoning objects and subjects.

Also, with respect to common objects of achievement such as wealth, since [in the Definition Vehicle wealth is viewed as] following after charity, it is created in accordance with former actions and hence is achieved by the likes of ordinary causes. However, surpassing the hard work of the Definition Vehicle—which is [like] commerce, farming, and so forth—is Secret Mantra, in which wealth is manifestly increased through the use of the water initiation, the practice of Shumbha,[a] and so forth. Therefore, [such methods] surpass the former actions and ordinary systems of achievement [in the Definition Vehicle]. Since [the Mantra Vehicle] describes even for a single purpose many forms [of methods for] lengthening life, bringing [persons and resources under one's] control, and so forth, it surpasses [the Definition Vehicle.

Mantra] also surpasses [the Definition Vehicle] because of **not being difficult.** On the path of the Definition Vehicle one finally becomes tired and exhausted by the asceticism of abandoning [nonvirtues] and adopting [virtues]. However, in Mantra everything shines as a help-mate, due to which entities to be abandoned and adopted are naturally pure, whereby achievement comes through using the attributes of the Desire Realm and so forth.

[a] *gnod mdzes;* a god of wealth.

[Mantra] also surpasses [the Definition Vehicle] due to being a path **for those with sharp faculties.** For, it has a final nature of excellent quintessential instructions of great meaning but little difficulty.

Furthermore, with respect to its superiority in these four ways, Tripiṭakamāla's *Lamp for the Three Modes* says:

> Though the object [or basis] is the same, the Mantra Vehicle
> Is superior because of being nonobscured,
> Having many skillful methods, no difficulties,
> And being created for those with sharp faculties.

Also, concerning those, the Mantra Vehicle is posited as great because its objects of observation, accompaniers, view, behavior, and achievement of the nature are sublime.[a] Ratnākarashānti's *Presentation of the Three Vehicles* says:[b]

> Because of a very pure object,
> The power of aids, and also deeds,
> The vehicle of the intelligent
> Is renowned as the greatest of the great.

Extensive explanation of how Secret Mantra surpasses the Definition Vehicle

The *Tantra of the Inconceivable Ra-li* says:[c]

> The small vehicles such as that of the Hearers
> Do not have quintessential instructions.
> The vehicle of the Knowledge Bearers
> Is superior by fifteen distinctive features:
> View, behavior, mental stabilization,[d]
> Cause, path, fruit, grounds,
> Time, enjoyment, yoga,
> Welfare of self and others, scope,[e]

---

[a] *phun sum tshogs pa.*

[b] *theg pa gsum rnam par bzhag pa, triyānavyavasthāna;* P4535, vol. 81.

[c] *ra li bsam gyis mi khyab pa'i rgyud.*

[d] *sems bzung.*

[e] The text (262.1) reads *dgos pa,* but I have emended it to *dgongs pa* to accord with the commentary below.

Forsaking extremes of fatigue, little difficulty,
And way of amassing the collections.

The ***view*** of the Definition Vehicle is only an emptiness, free from [dualistic] proliferations; the two truths are not realized as undifferentiable, primordially abiding with a nature of gods and mantras. However, the Mantra Vehicle realizes [such a view]; conventionalities are nonexistent, and appearances are taken to be divinely pure as mere emanations. The ultimate expanse and wisdom are primordially nondual; the two [that is, the ultimate and the conventional] are realized as undifferentiable within an original naturelessness. [Buddhaguhya's] *Stages of the Path of Magical Emanation* says:[a]

In the great maṇḍala of equality
Where the ultimate and the conventional are undifferentiable...

Also, with respect to the divine purity of the five aggregates, the *Tantra of Pristine Wisdom [Already] Established* says:[b]

Forms are just Vairochana,
Feelings are Ratnasambhava,
Discriminations are Amitābha,
Compositional factors are Amoghasiddhi,
Consciousnesses are Akṣhobhya.

Also, with respect to the purity of the five elements as the five mothers, the same tantra says:

The five elements are actualities of the five mothers;
The aggregates, sense-spheres, and constituents
Are all pure Buddha lands.

Also, the *Miraculous Secret Essence* says,[c] "Only a One-Gone-Thus knows that all phenomena are primordially buddhafied."[d]

Also, with respect to ***practice***, the Definition Vehicle has no more than the two, adoption and discarding. In Mantra, within the state of gods and marvelous mansions of pure equality and illusory

---

[a] *sgyu 'phrul lam rim/ lam rnam par bkod pa, mārgavyūha;* P4736, vol. 83; rnying ma bka' ma rgyas pa, vol. 23.

[b] *ye shes grub pa'i rgyud.*

[c] *gsang ba'i snying po de kho na nyid rnam par nges pa, guhyagarbhatattvaviniścaya;* P455, vol. 9; THDL, Ng3.1.1.1.

[d] *ye nas sangs rgyas pa.*

nature there are offerings to deities, accordance with the noumenon, purification of afflictions, and so forth, as in the explanations of feast offerings,[a] protector-like conduct,[b] and so forth on the occasion of the individual maṇḍalas, and hence it is superior.

Also, with respect to ***mental stabilization,*** in the Definition Vehicle striving is just required over a long time with the great hardship of holding the mind in order to achieve calm abiding and special insight. In Mantra, having pacified the proliferations of conceptuality through the generation stage having signs, pristine wisdom dawns in the signless completion stage through merely focusing on the central points of the channels and winds. Therefore, it is superior.

Also, with respect to ***causation***, in the Definition Vehicle it is asserted that the ultimate is realized from prior [engagement in the] conventionalities of producer and produced. In Mantra the self-abiding pristine wisdom which is to be purified or separated [from stain] is dramatically identified and thereupon cultivated in meditation, whereby realization of the ultimate is entered right now. Therefore, it is superior.

Also, with respect to ***paths,*** since in the Definition Vehicle meditative equipoise and subsequent realization are alternated for the two collections [of wisdom and merit], the five paths are just not traveled even in an eon. Since in Mantra one enters on the path of pristine wisdom of undifferentiable [meditative equipoise and subsequent realization], progress is swift. Therefore, it is superior.

Also, in the Definition Vehicle the ***fruit*** is asserted to arise later after a long time. In Mantra [the fruit] is asserted to abide in itself now spontaneously. Therefore, it is superior.

Also, in the Definition Vehicle the ***grounds*** are asserted to be eleven in number due to the divisions of graduated objects of abandonment and their antidotes. In Mantra there are three: (1) the ground of undifferentiated nature, the spontaneously established thusness, (2) the ground of the wisdom of equal purity, the excellent clear light of the two stages, and (3) the ground of pure supreme spontaneous attributes, the great pure fruit. Or in another way, the Mantra Vehicle has, in addition to the causal grounds [of the Definition Vehicle], a twelfth ground of endowment with the

---

[a] *tshogs.*

[b] *mgon po kun tu spyod pa.*

lotus of nonattachment, a thirteenth ground of a vajra bearer, and so forth. Therefore, it is superior. The *Secret Essence* says, "The specifics of grounds are the ten and the three."

Also with respect to ***time***, in the Definition Vehicle [the fruit] is not achieved [except] over three periods of countless eons and so forth. In Mantra, one who makes effort and keeps pure pledges achieves it in this lifetime. The *Revelation of the Thought* says:[a]

> The perfect enlightenment realized
> By Buddhas over very many countless eons
> Is attained by practitioners of Mantra
> In one lifetime simultaneously.

Also, with respect to ***enjoyments***, the Definition Vehicle achieves [its goals] through abandoning attributes of the Desire Realm. In Mantra, the attributes of the Desire Realm are just used as aids. The *Vajra Array* says:[b]

> The five forms of enjoyable attributes of the Desire Realm,
> Abandoned and despised [in the Definition Vehicle],
> Are the best of aids in the Mantra of skillful means,
> To be thoroughly enjoyed by the fortunate.

Also, with respect to ***yoga***, in the Definition Vehicle an objectless emptiness like space is cultivated during meditative equipoise, and then during subsequent attainment a yoga of illusion is taken as the path. In Mantra an undifferentiated, inconceivable yoga is taken as the path. Therefore, it is superior.

Also, with respect to achieving ***one's own and others' welfare***, not much more than a little temporary help is achieved through the Definition Vehicle. Through Mantra others' welfare is achieved in the form of good fortune even for a region—starvation is extinguished through causing rain to shower; a rain of food, drink, jewels and so forth is made to fall by an adept in yoga; sickness and disturbance are pacified, and so forth. Also, one's own welfare is achieved through moment by moment increase, higher and higher,

---

[a] *dgongs pa lung ston / dgongs pa lung bstan pa'i rgyud, saṃdhivyākaraṇatantra;* P83, vol. 3; THDL, Ng3.2.2.2.9.

[b] *rdo rje bkod pa / de bzhin gshegs pa thams cad kyi thugs gsang ba'i ye shes don gyi snying po rdo rje bkod pa'i rgyud, sarvatathāgatacittajñānaguhyārthagarbhavyūhavajratantra;* P452, vol. 9; THDL, Ng2.1.2.

of internal realization and meditative stabilization by means of the inconceivable two stages [of generation and completion]. Therefore, it is superior.

Also, with respect to ***scope***, through the Definition Vehicle no more than the mere causal vehicle is known. Through Mantra the great secret fruit is ascertained. The *Vajra Points* says:[a]

> The character of all Mantras
> Is the mind of all Buddhas.
> Since these are the means of achieving the matrix of attributes,[b]
> These are thoroughly endowed with the element of attributes.

The Mantra Vehicle has ***forsaken the extremes*** of fatigue because it is not difficult. Also, because a great effect is achieved with ***little difficulty***, it is superior to the Definition Vehicle. As was quoted before from the *Lamp for the Three Modes*, "Having many skillful methods, no difficulties..."

Also, with respect to the ways of ***amassing the collections*** of merit, in the Definition Vehicle there are no more than common collections, that is, the six perfections such as mere giving, mere ethics, and so forth; hence, it takes a long time. However, in Mantra everything is known as a Buddha land whereby all enjoyments become [amassings of] the collections of merit; hence, it is vast. And since all articles are known as ambrosia, it is thoroughly good. And since the natures [of all objects] are cognized as equally pure, it is supreme. And since afflictive emotions are naturally purified without abandoning them, the two collections are brought together quickly and completed. Thereby, release is achieved in one lifetime.

Just as the methods of the Mantra Vehicle are surpassing, so the wisdom established through these methods is also to be known as even more surpassing when practicing the paths. In brief, one should know these three: the secrecy of Buddha body is taken as the path, the secrecy of Buddha speech is taken as the path, and the secrecy of Buddha mind is taken as the path. The *Tantra of Pristine*

---

[a] *rdo rje rtse mo.* The bka' 'gyur contains a *gsang ba rnal 'byor chen po'i rgyud rdo rje rtse mo, vajraśikharamahāguhyayogatantra;* P113, vol. 4. The rnying ma rgyud 'bum contains a *rdo rje rtse mo 'dus pa'i rgyud;* THDL, Ng1.3.2.6, and a *rdo rje rtse mo'i rgyud;* THDL, Ng3.3.76.

[b] *chos kyi snying po.*

Wisdom [Already] Established says:

> Supreme Secret Mantra is to be known
> As very elevated beyond the Causal Great Vehicle
> Through the great secrecy
> Of the paths of body, speech, and mind.

The Definition Vehicle has no more than the appearing but illusory nature of bodies and an engaging in virtues from the viewpoint of ordinary physical activities. In Mantra the physical secrecy—emitting and gathering back of mudrā, dance, and so forth in which all appearances are fulfilled as deities and inestimable mansions, and bodies are fulfilled as maṇḍalas—is taken as the path. Therefore, it is superior.

In the Definition Vehicle speech is empty like an echo, and virtue is performed either through recitations or through restraining from and ceasing speech. However, in Mantra the secrecy of speech is to know sounds and tones as the nature of the [Sanskrit] vowels and consonants and thereby cause them to shower as a rain of doctrine. Also, since speech primordially abides as speech maṇḍalas, sounds and words naturally appear as mantras, whereupon through unimpeded power of repetition one's aims are accomplished. Therefore, it is superior.

In the Definition Vehicle all memories and conceptions are impressed with the seal of the absence of inherent existence, and calm abiding and special insight—in which the spreading and withdrawal of ordinary thoughts are reversed and deliberately stopped—are achieved. However, in Mantra the secrecy of mind is that memories and conceptions dawn as the sport of the noumenon, whereby the mind dawns as self-illuminating self-arisen pristine wisdom, due to which meditative stabilization is established in the yoga of the flow of a river, through which the mind is spontaneously established as a maṇḍala of nonconceptual shine. Therefore, it is superior.

Moreover, Ḍombhīheruka says:

> Here through the features of vessel,
> Doctrine [of initiation] making the vessel,
> Texts, paths, and fruits,
> The Mantra Vehicle is superior.

Indrabhūti says, "It is superior by way of the features of guru, vessel, rite, activity, pledge, view meditated, and practice." The *Magical*

Net says:[a]

> Knowing these profound rites
> Of all their secret-mantras,
> The hero found immeasurable omniscience
> At the base of the tree of enlightenment.

Though an extensive [rendition of] the ways in which the Mantra Vehicle surpasses the Definition Vehicle were expressed for an eon, an end would not be known.

Identification of how Secret Mantra is the effect

This section has three parts: assigning Mantra as the effect based on temporal speed, assigning Mantra as the effect due to supreme method, and assigning Mantra as the effect due to taking a similitude of the effect as the path.

Assigning Mantra as the effect based on speed

Because it is the means by which enlightenment is quickly attained, the Mantra Vehicle is assigned as the effect. For instance, about a sharp instrument that cuts through a tree quickly it is said, "This cuts a tree," whereas although a dull instrument cuts a tree slowly over a long time, it is said, "This does not cut." Just so, the enlightenment attained over a long time through the Definition Vehicle is attained within one lifetime and so forth in Mantra. Therefore, from the viewpoint of temporal proximity, the Mantra Vehicle is called the Effect Vehicle.

Moreover, it is explained that with great effort enlightenment is attained in one lifetime. The *Saṃpuṭi Tantra* says:[b]

> Even the Buddhahood difficult to achieve
> Over many ten millions of eons
> It bestows in just this lifetime.
> Hence it is called the Effect Vehicle.

and the *Buddha Union* says:[c]

---

[a] *rgyud kyi rgyal po chen po sgyu 'phrul dra ba, māyājālamahātantrarāja;* P102, vol. 4; THDL, Ng3.3.5.

[b] *yang dag par sbyor ba shes bya ba'i rgyud chen po, saṃpuṭināmamahātantra;* P26, vol. 2.

[c] *sangs rgyas thams cad dang mnyam par sbyor ba mkha' 'gro ma sgyu ma bde ba'i*

The actuality of all Buddhas not attained
Over innumerable ten millions of eons
Is attained in just this lifetime
Through the rites of this great Secret Mantra.

With middling effort release is attained in the intermediate state. The *Four Vajra Sites* says:[a]

If suddenly the mind ejects
From the upper of the nine openings,[b]
By this path one is liberated
From having killed brahmins daily,
Committing the five acts of immediate retribution,
And partaking of acts of banditry.
One will not be contaminated by sins.

and the *Sacred Word of Mañjushrī* says:[c]

Though with this body of physical aggregates
One does not achieve [Buddhahood] in this very life,
Through the mind's achieving a vajra body,
It is completely achieved in the intermediate state.

and [Buddhaguhya's] *Stages of the Path of Magical Emanation* says:

A yogi of middling effort leaves this body,
The remainder of the arising of fruition,
And goes by means of intrinsic awareness[d] to the ground of a Vajradhara;
This is called "fructification."

and the *Wisdom Drop* says:[e]

Alternatively, even those without effort
Just after forsaking this body

---

mchog, sarvabuddhasamayogaḍākinījālasaṃbara; P8, vol. 1; THDL, Ng3.1.3.1.1.2.

[a] *rdo rje gdan bzhi;* this may be the *sangs rgyas thams cad dang mnyam par sbyor ba zhes bya ba'i rgyud kyi rgyal po,* THDL Ng3.1.3.1.1.1; see the colophon for that text, 250.2-250.3.

[b] These are the nine openings of the body—ears, eyes, nostrils, anus, genitals, and top of the head.

[c] *'jam dpal zhal lung.*

[d] *rig pa.*

[e] *ye shes thig le rnal 'byor ma'i rgyud kyi rgyal po chen po, jñānatilakayoginītantrarāja;* P14, vol. 2. Also, *ye shes thig le zang thal gyi rgyud,* THDL, Ng1.6.105.

Achieve the body of unsurpassed pristine wisdom.
What need to speak of those with effort?

The best of those with lowest faculties are released in the next birth. The *Expression of the Names* says,[a] "Lord of transmigrators just after birth...," and the *Buddha Skull Tantra* says:[b]

Therefore, intelligent yogis
With a mind of great yoga
Might not attain the feat in this birth,
But they will attain the feat in the next birth.

The middling of those with lowest faculties are released in seven births. The *Secret Treasury* says:[c]

If one has the gift of thorough initiation,
One will be conferred initiation in birth after birth.
Through that, even without meditation
Achievement is gained in seven births.

Even the lowest of those with lowest faculties achieve it in sixteen births. The *Vajrashekhara* says:

Through the Vehicle of the Perfections
It is not achieved in countless eons,
But if yogis make effort [in Mantra], they pass
Beyond sorrow in just this life.

Otherwise, merely through seeing
They pass beyond sorrow over sixteen births.
Common beings will attain Buddhahood,
It is not otherwise.

Assigning Mantra as the effect due to supreme method

For instance, when someone accomplishes in a moment a task at which another strives for seven days, the effort of the two tasks is

---

[a] *'jam dpal ye shes sems dpa'i don dam pa'i mtshan yang dag par brjod pa, mañjuśrījñāna-sattvasyaparamārthanāmasaṃgīti;* P2, vol. 1; THDL, Ng3.1.1.6.

[b] *sangs rgyas thod pa shes bya ba rnal 'byor ma'i rgyud kyi rgyal po, buddhakapālanāma-yoginītantrarāja;* P63, vol. 3.

[c] *de bzhin gshegs pa thams cad kyi gsang ba gsang ba'i mdzod chen po mi zad pa gter gyi sgron ma brtul zhugs chen po bsgrub pa'i rgyud, sarvathāgataguhyamahāguhyakośākṣaya-yanidhidīpamahāvratasādhanatantra;* P453, vol. 9; perhaps THDL, Ng2.1.3.

different but the entities [accomplished] are similar. Just so, in the Definition Vehicle the meditative equipoises of calm abiding and special insight are achieved with great mental effort, not over months and years but over a long time; however, in the Mantra path the dawning [of these meditative states] is manifestly actualized in only a day by way of essential factors in the body and channels. Therefore, Mantra is assigned as taking the effect as the path. The *Lotus Points* says:[a]

> Because what is not achieved with very great effort
> Is thoroughly engaged in a moment
> And because without depending on preceding causes
> The effect is drawn forth from essential factors,
> It is called the Effect Vehicle.

Assigning Mantra as the effect due to taking a similitude of the effect as the path

When one has become a Buddha, freed from all defilements, the features of a land appear adorned in thorough array within the context of body and wisdom [being so indivisible that they are] without conjunction or disjunction. Such is actualized [in Mantra] through the force of clearing away the defilements to [realizing] the existence of such in the expanse of reality by means of meditating on a similitude of such a land. Therefore, it is called the Effect Vehicle. The same [*Lotus Points*] says:

> When the nature of the stainless expanse
> Having the three bodies, wisdom, and land
> Is purified, it manifestly appears
> In self-illumination. This which takes
> A similitude of that as the path
> Is correctly called the Vehicle of Effect.

Therefore, [in Mantra] knowledge of the nature abiding primordially in the sacred inherent effect of the expanse is taken as the foundation and trained in, due to which it is called the Effect Vehicle.

Moreover, in terms of clearing away defilements, through training in suchness within meditatively cultivating [the stages of] generation and completion, adventitious defilements are purified.

[a] *padma rtse mo.*

Therefore, the gods, maṇḍalas, and so forth that are meditated mentally are projections of one's own mind, but this is not meditation taking actual gods and maṇḍalas—effects of the expanse—as the path; nevertheless, because it is close to the meaning of the expanse, it is to be viewed as a profound nondelusive path.

Though the Mantra Vehicle is similar to the Cause Vehicle in not being able to take the expanse as the actual path, there is a great difference in the closeness or distance of the paths [to the fruit] due to differing in having or not having a similarity of feature [with the fruit]. For example, a jewel and an oil lamp are next to each other at night; of two robbers, the dull one apprehends the light as a jewel and, taking it, gets the lamp, whereas the unobscured skillful one gets the jewel. In the same way, there is a great difference with respect to the vehicles causing quick attainment of the desired aim or not. This is as explained in Dharmakīrti's *Ascertainment of Valid Cognition:*[a]

> Those who run with the thought of jewels
> To the light of a jewel and the light of a lamp
> Are not different in terms of wrong idea[b]
> But different in terms of functionality.

Therefore, here the effect is the body, speech, and mind [of a Buddha], and also with regard to actualizing a similitude of them:

- Initially when initiation is bestowed, a qualified master—having performed the preliminary familiarization [with the deity], the rite for the area, and the preparation [of the student]—has the maṇḍala drawn, activates it, and makes offerings, after which he/she assumes self-entry [into the maṇḍala] and then causes the student to enter, and having given the pledges and vows, causes pristine wisdom manifestly to descend, this being actualization of exalted mind.
- Upon having scattered flowers, covering and uncovering the face [by having the student put on and take off a blindfold], the

[a] *tshad ma rnam par nges pa, pramāṇaviniścaya,* stanza II.5; P5710, vol. 130; Toh. 4211, *sde dge, tshad ma,* vol. *ce,* 168a.4. Long-chen-pa cites Dharmakīrti's *Ascertainment;* the same verse also appears in Dharmakīrti's *Commentary on (Dignāga's) "Compilation of Prime Cognition"* : *tshad ma rnam 'grel, pramāṇavārttika,* stanza III.57 (Miyasaka's II.57).

[b] Both are mistaken in that both the light of a jewel and the light of a lamp are not a jewel.

master reveals the maṇḍala, this being actualization of exalted body.

- After bestowing initiation, the master bestows the subsequent permissions of mantra and seal, this being actualization of exalted speech.
- Through bestowing the four initiations on the three—body, speech, and mind—their defilements are cleansed, and the three—exalted body, speech, and mind—are actualized. Thus, initially initiation is received, and then during the path of release its continuum is meditatively cultivated, and [all phenomena] are known as of the nature of the Three Bodies and the five pristine wisdoms.

Hence, this is called "taking the effect as the path." The *Secret Oceanic Tantra* says:[a]

> All without exception of the circle of objects of knowledge
> Are thoroughly established as the three bodies.
> This is Great Vehicle Secret Mantra, causing entry
> Into the three bodies, the Effect Vehicle,
> Without the coming together or separation of the Three
> Bodies, the Vajra Vehicle.

Question: How are the exalted body and pristine wisdom [of a Buddha] taken as the path?

Answer: From between the two—the generation stage and the completion stage—in initial meditation, meditation on emptiness is the Body of Attributes; meditating on the body of a deity within meditation on emptiness is the Enjoyment Body; emitting and withdrawing rays of light promoting the welfare of sentient beings is the Emanation Body; the five afflictive emotions purified through skillful means are the five aspects of pristine wisdom. The *Guhyasamāja* says:[b]

> Through this, the great nature of the doctrine,
> The thoroughly adorned ocean of wisdom
> Arisen from the indivisible Three Bodies,
> Is attained in just this lifetime.

---

[a] *gsang ba rgya mtsho'i rgyud;* THDL, Ng1.6.144.

[b] *gsang ba 'dus pa zhes bya ba brtag pa'i rgyal po chen po, guhyasamājanāmamahākalpa-rāja;* P81, vol. 3; THDL, Ng3.1.3.1.3.1.

and the *Cemetery Adornment* says:[a]

> In the Body of Attributes of manifest emptiness,
> The blissful Enjoyment Body with marks and beauties,
> And the sporting Emanation Bodies...

and the *Tantra of Oceanic Spontaneous Pristine Wisdom* says:[b]

> From the great pristine wisdom of the element of
> attributes
> Is the marvelous Body of Complete
> Enjoyment, entity of great bliss.
> Arisen from great compassion,
> The marvelous Emanation Bodies dawn as [its] sport.

Question: If even the Mantra Vehicle partakes of a path purifying defilements, what does it mean that it takes the effect as the path? Since the Cause Vehicle is generated as a means of purifying defilements, it would be similar.

Answer: Though the Definition Vehicle and the Mantra Vehicle are the same in achieving Buddhahood upon simultaneously cleansing the defilements of the basic constituent, there is a difference of temporal proximity and distance [in relation to accomplishing Buddhahood], and the mere warmth of the path for which the Definition Vehicle strives over a long time is taken as the path in one instant of Mantra, but due to cultivating in meditation a similitude of how it is to abide in the maṇḍala of the expanse of reality, even objects of abandonment shine as aids. Thereby, the effect is taken as the path; however, the exact final fruit is not actually taken as the path; hence, it is necessary to cultivate the profound and vast paths in meditation.

In general, [the vehicles] are posited in the aspects of cause and effect to make known conventions. Hence, a path that purifies obstructions by completing the collections of the effects through meditative stabilizations and so forth generated by the cause of very arduous work is designated "cause," this being the Definition Vehicle. That which purifies defilements by [completing] the collections through meditative stabilizations attained with little hardship, and is posited as the effect due to not being produced by

---

[a] *'khor sdom pa'i rgyud kyi rgyal po dur khrod kyi rgyan rmad du byung ba, cakrasaṃbaratantrarājādbhutaśmaśānālaṃkāra;* P57, vol. 3.

[b] *ye shes rgya mtsho lhun gyis grub pa'i rgyud.*

causes involving striving, is called the "Effect Vehicle."

Also with respect to their forms of doctrine, [the Definition Vehicle] initially teaches mainly the path of the presentations of causes and conditions and then teaches the final effect, whereas [the Mantra Vehicle] initially teaches mainly the presentation of the effect, the maṇḍala of the purified expanse, uncompounded, with adoption and discarding of equal taste, primordially buddhafied.

It is fitting that when [Mantra] is divided into the likes of cause and effect, the three bodies—as well as pristine wisdom—are taken as the path, whereby an effect similar to it is produced. Through the force of having purified the defilements of the basic constituent, propitious qualities newly appear, whereupon finally perfect Buddhahood adorned with bodies and pristine wisdom is most certainly attained. In the Definition Vehicle, aside from only the two collections, there is no meditation [of phenomena] as [Buddha] bodies and pristine wisdoms. Hence, the aspect of the cause and the aspect of the effect are mutually exclusive; therefore, nonattainment for a long time also is due to the internal contradiction in their own tenets about cause and effect. For that reason, Secret Mantra is established as superior.

10. Tsong-kha-pa's Reasoned Analysis of Path-Structure

Having highlighted the plurality of approaches to explaining the difference between Sūtra and Mantra by Bu-tön and Long-chen-pa, let us now turn to contrast these with Tsong-kha-pa's emphasis on a single feature, deity yoga. His system has thereby been put into historical context; the radical nature of his distilling the distinctive essence of Mantra down to the single central feature of deity yoga stands out in juxtaposition to the earlier multifaceted approaches of Bu-tön and Long-chen-pa.

In the first of fourteen sections in his *Great Exposition of Secret Mantra,*[a] Tsong-kha-pa, 1357-1419, founder of the Ge-luk-pa (Virtuous Way or Joyous Way)[b] sect of Tibetan Buddhism, presents his view on the difference between Sūtra and Mantra in his highly rationalistic style. The section is a long, involved argument in which, although Indian sources are cited, the central appeal is to reasoning. Typical of much of Tsong-kha-pa's writing, the argument is so involved and the principles behind the steps so taken for granted that an introduction presenting the same material in a more straightforward manner is needed. Through translating and editing

---

[a] *sngags rim chen mo.* The longer title of Tsong-kha-pa's text is *Stages of the Path to a Conqueror and Pervasive Master, a Great Vajradhara: Revealing All Secret Topics* (*rgyal ba khyab bdag rdo rje 'chang chen po'i lam gyi rim pa gsang ba kun gyi gnad rnam par phye ba*). In the Peking edition it is P6210, vol. 161 (Toh. 5281), but I mainly used the Dharmsala (Shes rig par khang) edition of 1969, despite flaws, because of its legibility, checking questionable passages against the Ngawang Gelek edition (New Delhi, 1978), which is a retouched version of the 1897 Hla-sa old Zhol blocks.

The first part of this chapter is adapted, in part, from my article "Reason as the Prime Principle in Dzong-ka-ba's Delineating Deity Yoga as the Demarcation Between Sūtra and Mantra," *Journal of the International Association of Buddhist Studies* 7, no. 2 (1984): 95-115, and has appeared in my introduction to His Holiness Tenzin Gyatso and Jeffrey Hopkins, *The Kālachakra Tantra: Rite of Initiation for the Stage of Generation* (London: Wisdom Publications, 1985; second revd. edition, Boston, 1989), 23-30. For a detailed discussion of the distinction between Sūtra and Mantra, see H.H. the Dalai Lama, Tsong-kha-pa, and Hopkins, *Tantra in Tibet,* and Jeffrey Hopkins, *The Tantric Distinction* (London: Wisdom Publications, 1984). Since the presentation closely follows Tsong-kha-pa's argument in and the Dalai Lama's introduction to *Tantra in Tibet,* detailed page references are given in the notes.

[b] *dge lugs pa.* Several Tibetan scholars have reported that *dge* (virtuous) was originally *dga'* (joyous).

an oral commentary by His Holiness the Dalai Lama XIV,[a] I have provided this in *Tantra in Tibet,* which is centered around translation of Tsong-kha-pa's first section.

The extreme rules of redundancy that often make Tibetan writing laconic to the point of obfuscation do not apply to oral commentary, and thus the Dalai Lama's explanation provides a more free-flowing introduction to this complex argument, which he gave me privately in his office for eventual publication. It is the type of exposition that a well-versed Tibetan scholar will give to a student before launching into a topic and while reading the text line by line; it smoothes the way and thus is invaluable for a beginner. This more accessible version, however, is not meant to replace the twists and turns of Tsong-kha-pa's argument; rather, one is encouraged to become acquainted with the system to the point where the implicit principles are explicit to the mind of the reader of Tsong-kha-pa's text. This is likely the Dalai Lama's point when, during public lectures, he has encouraged Ge-luk-pas not to forsake Tsong-kha-pa's writings for later simplified presentations.

In the same spirit of providing an accessible reformulation of Tsong-kha-pa's exposition, the First Paṇchen Lama Lo-sang-chö-kyi-gyel-tsen[b] wrote an extremely readable version of his argument (see Donald S. Lopez's translation in Appendix 1). Here, I will encapsulate Tsong-kha-pa's and the Dalai Lama's arguments for the sake of getting a firm grip on the broad structure of the myriad points being made. I read the argument as follows.

Outlining the Tantric difference

Because people are of different capacities, dispositions, and interests, Shākyamuni Buddha taught many different paths. He set forth Sūtra and Mantra, and within Sūtra he taught four different schools of tenets (Great Exposition School, Sūtra School, Mind-Only School, and Middle Way School)[c] and within Mantra, he set out four different tantra sets—Action, Performance, Yoga, and Highest Yoga (literally "Unsurpassed Yoga").[d]

---

[a] The Dalai Lama's introduction in *Tantra in Tibet,* 13-79.

[b] *blo bzang chos kyi rgyal mtshan,* 1567[?]-1662.

[c] *bye brag smra ba, vaibhāṣika; mdo sde pa, sautrāntika; sems tsam pa, cittamātra; dbu ma pa, mādhyamika.*

[d] *bya ba, kriyā; spyod pa, caryā; rnal 'byor, yoga; rnal 'byor bla med, anuttarayoga.*

In each of the four schools of the Sūtra system he described three varieties of paths—for Hearers, Solitary Realizers, and Bodhisattvas. Each of the four schools also has internal subdivisions, and the four divisions of Mantra also contain many different types of processes and procedures of meditation. The result is that there are many different levels of commitment—ranging from the assumption of tantric vows down to the assumption of only the refuge vow—many different paths and many different styles.[a]

To appreciate the special distinctiveness of Mantra, it is necessary to determine the difference between the Sūtra and Mantra vehicles, and to do that, first it is necessary to settle the difference between the vehicles in Sūtra—the Hearer Vehicle, Solitary Realizer Vehicle, and Bodhisattva Vehicle or Great Vehicle—and then consider the further division of the latter into its Sūtra and Mantra forms.

Difference between the Sūtra vehicles

"Vehicle" (*theg pa, yāna*) has two meanings:

1. Since *yā* means "to go," and *na* indicates the "means" of going, a vehicle comprises those practices carrying one to a higher state—those practices that when actualized in the mental continuum cause manifestation of a higher type of mind.
2. Somewhat unusually, "vehicle" can also refer to the destination—the place or state at which one is aiming. This is because just as a vehicle can bear or carry a certain load, so the state of Buddhahood, which is the goal of the Bodhisattva Vehicle, can bear or carry the welfare of all sentient beings, whereas the state of a Lesser Vehicle Foe Destroyer can bear much less.[b]

Since "vehicle" has these two meanings, the distinction between the two Buddhist Vehicles—Hearer and Solitary Realizer (being Lesser Vehicle) and Bodhisattva (or Great Vehicle)—must occur

[a] The Dalai Lama's introduction in *Tantra in Tibet*, 20-21.

[b] The Dalai Lama's introduction in *Tantra in Tibet*, 43. Tsong-kha-pa's exposition of these two meanings of "vehicle" was unintentionally deleted from the first edition of *Tantra in Tibet* at the beginning of the last paragraph on p. 106. It should read: "About 'vehicle,' there is an Effect Vehicle which is that to which one is proceeding and a cause vehicle which is that by which one proceeds. Due to proceeding [it is called] a vehicle. With respect to..." This change has been incorporated into the reprint by Snow Lion Publications, 1987 and later.

either within the sense of vehicle as the means by which one progresses or within the sense of vehicle as the destination, or state, to which one is progressing, or in both meanings.

In the exposition of the Lesser Vehicle and the Great Vehicle according to the Middle Way Consequence School, considered to be the acme of philosophical systems by most Tibetan schools, there is a tremendous difference between the two in the sense of vehicle as that to which one is progressing. In the Lesser Vehicle, practice culminates as a Foe Destroyer, one who has overcome the foe of ignorance but is not omniscient and thus is not a Buddha. Unlike a Buddha, a Foe Destroyer does not have the ability spontaneously to manifest in myriad forms in order to help beings. Since the states of being a Buddha and a Foe Destroyer are very different, there is a significant difference between the Lesser and Great vehicles in the sense of vehicle as that to which one is progressing—the respective goals of Buddhahood and Foe Destroyerhood.

With this difference in goal, there must also be a difference in the two vehicles in the sense of the practices by which one progresses to these goals. The difference between the Lesser and Great vehicles in terms of the means of progress can occur in only two places—method and wisdom, these two comprising the entire path, in that method mainly produces the form body of a Buddha and wisdom mainly produces the Body of Attributes.[a] In the Consequence School's explanation, the Lesser and Great vehicles do not differ with respect to wisdom in that both require realization of the subtle emptiness of inherent existence of *all* phenomena such as body, mind, head, eye, wall, consciousness, and so forth.[b] The Lesser and Great vehicles differ in terms of *how* wisdom is cultivated—Bodhisattvas using myriad reasonings for getting at the subtle emptiness and Hearers and Solitary Realizers using only a few to realize the same emptiness; however, in terms of the object of the mind of wisdom, the emptiness of inherent existence, there is no difference between the emptiness a Lesser Vehicle practitioner realizes and the emptiness a Great Vehicle practitioner realizes. In this sense there is no difference in wisdom. Tsong-kha-pa discusses this point in some detail in his commentary on

---

[a] The Dalai Lama's introduction in *Tantra in Tibet,* 57.

[b] The Dalai Lama's introduction in *Tantra in Tibet,* 38-41, and Tsong-kha-pa's exposition, 98-99.

Chandrakīrti's *Supplement to (Nāgārjuna's) "Treatise on the Middle"*[a] and also indicates a nuanced way that there is a difference in approach:

> To establish that even a single phenomenon does not truly exist, Great Vehicle practitioners use limitless different reasonings as set forth in Nāgārjuna's *Treatise on the Middle,* due to which their minds become greatly broadened with respect to suchness. Lesser Vehicle practitioners use only brief reasoning to establish suchness by valid cognition, and since they do not establish emptiness the way Great Vehicle practitioners do, they do not have a mind broadened with respect to suchness....This difference arises because Hearers and Solitary Realizers strive to abandon only the afflictive emotions [the obstructions to liberation], and realization of a mere abbreviation of the meaning of suchness is sufficient for that. Great Vehicle practitioners are intent on abandoning the obstructions to omniscience, and for this it is necessary to have a very broadened mind of wisdom opened to suchness.

Bodhisattvas' more extensive use of reasoning helps in achieving their greater aim of overcoming the obstructions to omniscience, though how this is accomplished is left for the reader to ponder.

Since wisdom in the Lesser and Great vehicles does not differ in terms of the type of emptiness being realized, the difference between the two vehicles must lie in method.[b] "Method" here specifically means motivation and the deeds that it impels. No matter how much compassion Lesser Vehicle practitioners have, their primary motivation is to release themselves from cyclic existence. However, in the Great Vehicle the primary motivation is the *altruistic* aspiration to highest enlightenment[c] induced by great love and compassion in which one takes on the burden of the welfare of all beings.

---

[a] *madhyamakāvatāra, dbu ma la 'jug pa.* The first five chapters of Tsong-kha-pa's commentary (*dgongs pa rab gsal*) are translated in Jeffrey Hopkins, *Compassion in Tibetan Buddhism* (London: Rider and Co., 1980; rpt. Ithaca, N.Y.: Snow Lion Publications), 174-175. (For discussion of the translation of the title *Madhyamakāvatāra* as "*Supplement to the 'Treatise on the Middle,'*" see Hopkins, *Meditation on Emptiness,* 462-469 and 866-869.)

[b] The Dalai Lama's introduction in *Tantra in Tibet,* 55.

[c] *byang chub kyi sems, bodhicitta.*

Thus, there is a significant difference between the Lesser and Great vehicles in terms of method, even though not in wisdom.[a]

Hence, the Lesser and Great vehicles differ in both senses of vehicle, as the means by which one progresses as well as that to which one progresses.

Difference between the Perfection Vehicle and the Mantra Vehicle

In the Great Vehicle itself, there are two vehicles—the Perfection Vehicle[b] and the Mantra (or Tantra) Vehicle.[c] The Perfection Vehicle is Sūtra Great Vehicle, and the Mantra Vehicle is Mantra (or Tantra) Great Vehicle.

Do the Sūtra Great Vehicle and the Mantra Great Vehicle differ in the sense of vehicle as that to which one is progressing? The goal of the Sūtra Great Vehicle is Buddhahood, but the Mantra Great Vehicle cannot have another goal separate from Buddhahood as there is no attainment higher than the Buddhahood described in Sūtra as attainment of the Body of Attributes and form bodies. Sūtra describes a Buddha as having removed all obstructions and attained all auspicious attributes, having no movement of coarse winds, or inner energies;[d] thus such Buddhahood has to include the attainments of even Highest Yoga Mantra, the primary aim of which is to stop the movement of all coarse winds and manifest the most subtle consciousness—the mind of clear light—while simultaneously appearing in totally pure form.[e] Hence, the Vajradharahood often mentioned as the goal of Mantra and the Buddhahood

---

[a] *Tantra in Tibet,* 98-99.

[b] *phar phyin kyi theg pa, pāramitāyāna.*

[c] *sngags kyi theg pa, mantrayāna.* The term "Tantrayāna" has great favor in much of current non-Tibetan scholarship but does not appear to have been popular in the Tibetan cultural region. There the favored term is Mantrayāna or Guhyamantrayāna (*gsang sngags kyi theg pa*).

[d] *rlung, prāṇa.* This is one among many points that Jam-yang-shay-pa (*'jam dbyangs bzhad pa,* 1648-1721) makes in defending the position that the Buddhahoods of Sūtra and Mantra are the same in his *Great Exposition of Tenets;* see Hopkins, *Maps of the Profound,* 637-645.

[e] See Lati Rinbochay and Jeffrey Hopkins, *Death, Intermediate State and Rebirth in Tibetan Buddhism* (London: Rider and Co., 1979; rpt. Ithaca, N.Y.: Snow Lion Publications, 1980), 69-73.

described in Sūtra are the same.[a]

There being no difference between the Perfection Vehicle and the Mantra Vehicle in terms of the goal—the destination—they must differ in the sense of vehicle as the means by which one progresses. Therefore, they must differ either in terms of method or wisdom or both. If the difference lay in wisdom, there would be many problems because the Perfection Vehicle contains Nāgārjuna's Middle Way teachings on emptiness, and there would have to be some other more subtle emptiness than that which Nāgārjuna establishes with many different reasonings in the twenty-seven chapters of his *Treatise on the Middle,* whereas there is none. Thus there is no difference between Sūtra and Mantra in the view, which here refers to the objective view, that is, the object that is viewed[b]—emptiness or ultimate truth—and does not refer to the realizing consciousness, since Sūtra Great Vehicle and Highest Yoga Mantra do differ with respect to the subtlety of the consciousness realizing emptiness. Specifically, in Highest Yoga Tantras such as the *Guhyasamāja Tantra* or the *Kālachakra Tantra,* more subtle, enhanced consciousnesses are generated to realize the same emptiness of inherent existence. Still, because the object realized is the same whether the consciousness is more subtle or not, the "objective view" is the same.[c]

In this way, between the Sūtra and Mantra Great Vehicles there cannot be any difference in the factor of wisdom in terms of the object understood by a mind of wisdom. Hence, the difference again has to lie in method. Nevertheless, in both the Sūtra and the Mantra Great Vehicles, the foundation of method is the altruistic intention to become enlightened for the sake of all sentient beings, and thus the motivational basis of the deeds of the path is the same. The other main factor of method has to do with the deeds induced by that motivation. In the Sūtra Great Vehicle these are the practices induced by that altruistic aspiration—the perfections of giving, ethics, and patience, and since these are also practiced in Mantra, the difference cannot be found there either. Furthermore, Mantra has an even greater emphasis than Sūtra on the deeds of

---

[a] The Dalai Lama's introduction in *Tantra in Tibet,* 55, and Tsong-kha-pa's own exposition, 139-142.

[b] *yul gyi lta ba.*

[c] The Dalai Lama's introduction in *Tantra in Tibet,* 55-57, and Tsong-kha-pa's own exposition, 110.

the perfections in that a tantric practitioner is committed to engage in them at least six times during each day.[a]

Moreover, the distinction could not be made on the basis of speed of progress on the path because within the four tantra sets—Action, Performance, Yoga, and Highest Yoga Mantra—there are great differences in speed, such as the possibility of achieving Buddhahood in one lifetime in Highest Yoga Mantra but taking at least two periods of countless eons in the other three, according to Tsong-kha-pa. Also, in the Sūtra Great Vehicle there are five different modes of progress, slow to fast, which are compared to an ox chariot, elephant chariot, sun and moon, magical creation of a Hearer, and magical creation of a One-Gone-Thus.[b] In addition, the difference must not lie in some small or insignificant feature, but in an important one.[c]

Tsong-kha-pa's intricate comparison of the Perfection and the Mantra vehicles has shown how similar these two vehicles are in their basic structure in terms of goal, wisdom of emptiness, and altruistic motivation, thereby literally setting the stage for appreciating the central difference. He finds the profound distinction in the fact that in Mantra there is meditation in which one meditates on one's body as similar in aspect to a Buddha's form body, whereas in the Sūtra Great Vehicle there is no such meditation. This is deity yoga,[d] which all four tantra sets have but Sūtra systems do not. Deity yoga means to imagine oneself as now having the form body of a Buddha; one meditates on oneself in the aspect of a Buddha's form body,[e] imagining oneself as presently an ideal, altruistically active being. This is the central distinctive feature of Tantra in that it occurs in all four sets, even though it does not occur in all tantras, due to which it is not a definition of tantra.

In the Perfection Vehicle there is meditation similar in aspect to a Buddha's Body of Attributes—a Buddha's mind of wisdom. A Bodhisattva enters into meditative equipoise directly realizing emptiness with nothing appearing to the mind except the final

---

[a] The Dalai Lama's introduction in *Tantra in Tibet,* 57-58.

[b] See *Tantra in Tibet,* 238-239 n. 20.

[c] The Dalai Lama's introduction in *Tantra in Tibet,* 58, and Tsong-kha-pa's own exposition, 100-101.

[d] *lha'i rnal 'byor, *devatāyoga.*

[e] The Dalai Lama's introduction in *Tantra in Tibet,* 61-65, and Tsong-kha-pa's own exposition, 115-116.

nature of phenomena, the emptiness of inherent existence; the mind of wisdom and emptiness are like water poured into water, undifferentiable. Even though, unlike their tantric counterparts, Sūtra Bodhisattvas do not specifically imagine that the state of meditative equipoise *is* a Buddha's Body of Attributes,[a] meditation similar in aspect to a Buddha's Body of Attributes does occur in the Sūtra system in the sense that the state of meditative equipoise on emptiness mimics a Buddha's pristine mind of wisdom in its aspect of perceiving the ultimate. However, the Sūtra Perfection Vehicle does not involve meditation similar in aspect to a Buddha's *form* body. There is meditation on Buddhas and so forth as objects of offering and so forth, but there is no meditation on oneself in the physical body of a Buddha.[b]

Such meditative cultivation of a divine body is included within the factor of method because it is mainly aimed at achieving a Buddha's form body. In the Sūtra system the sole means for achieving a Buddha's form body is, on the basis of the altruistic intention to become enlightened, to engage in the first three perfections—giving, ethics, and patience—in "limitless" ways over a "limitless" period of time, specifically three periods of "countless" great eons ("countless" being said to be a figure with fifty-nine zeros). Though the Mantra Vehicle also involves practice of the perfections of giving, ethics, and patience, it is not in "limitless" ways over "limitless" periods of time. Despite emphasis on the perfections in the Mantra Vehicle, practice in "limitless" ways over "limitless" time is unnecessary because one is engaging in the additional technique of meditation on oneself in a body similar in aspect to a Buddha's form body.[c] In other words, in the tantric systems, in order to become a Buddha more quickly, one meditates on oneself as similar in aspect to a Buddha in terms of both body and mind. This practice is significantly distinctive and thus those systems that involve it constitute a separate vehicle, the Mantra Great Vehicle.

In deity yoga one first meditates on emptiness and then uses

---

[a] The source here is the late Jam-pel-shen-pen, abbot of the Tantric College of Lower Hla-sa during the time of its relocation in South India and later the Throne-Holder of Gan-den, head of the Ge-luk-pa order.

[b] The Dalai Lama's introduction in *Tantra in Tibet,* 60 and 62, and Tsong-kha-pa's own exposition, 115.

[c] See the Mongolian scholar Nga-wang-pel-den's (*ngag dbang dpal ldan*) statement of this in H.H. the Dalai Lama, Tsong-kha-pa, and Hopkins, *Deity Yoga,* 211-212.

this consciousness realizing emptiness—or at least an imitation of it—as the basis of emanation of a Buddha. The mind of wisdom itself appears as the physical form of a Buddha. This one consciousness thus has two parts—a factor of wisdom and a factor of method, or factors of (1) ascertainment of emptiness and (2) appearance as an ideal being—and hence, through the practice of deity yoga, one *simultaneously* accumulates the collections of merit and wisdom, making their amassing much faster.[a]

The systems that have this practice are called the *Vajra* Vehicle because the appearance of a deity is the display of a consciousness which is a *fusion* of wisdom understanding emptiness and compassion seeking the welfare of others—an inseparable union symbolized by a vajra, a diamond, the foremost of stones as it is "unbreakable."[b] Since the two elements of the fusion, compassionate method and penetrating wisdom, are the very core of the Perfection Vehicle, one can understand that Sūtra and Mantra, despite being different, are integrated systems. One can understand that compassion is not superseded in Mantra but is essential to Mantra and that the wisdom of the Perfection Vehicle is not forsaken for a deeper understanding of reality in the Mantra Vehicle.

Summary

To encapsulate the points made in Tsong-kha-pa's argument up to here: The difference between the vehicles as explained in the Consequence School must lie in the sense of vehicle as that by which one progresses or that to which one progresses. The Lesser Vehicle differs from the Great Vehicle in both. The destination of the lower one is the state of a Hearer or Solitary Realizer Foe Destroyer and of the higher one, Buddhahood. Concerning "vehicle" in the sense of means by which one progresses, although there is no difference in the wisdom realizing the subtlest nature of phenomena, there is a difference in method—Lesser Vehicle not having and Great Vehicle having the altruistic intention to become enlightened and its attendant deeds.

Sūtra Great Vehicle and Mantra Great Vehicle do not differ in terms of the goal, the state being sought, since both seek the

[a] The Dalai Lama's introduction in *Tantra in Tibet,* 62-63.

[b] The Dalai Lama's introduction in *Tantra in Tibet,* 22-23, and Tsong-kha-pa's own exposition, 107-108.

highest enlightenment of a Buddha, but there is a difference in the means of progress, again not in wisdom but in method. Within method they differ not in the basis, or motivation, of the deeds, this being the altruistic intention to become enlightened, nor in having the perfections as deeds, but in the additional technique of deity yoga. A deity is a supramundane being who is a manifestation of compassion and wisdom. Thus, in the special practice of deity yoga one joins one's own body, speech, mind, and activities with the exalted body, speech, mind, and activities of a supramundane being, manifesting on the path a similitude of the state of the effect.

Reason as the arbiter

The basic appeal throughout Tsong-kha-pa's presentation of the difference between the vehicles is to a rational investigation of path structure, but it is not that he does not cite supportive Indian sources. For instance, in establishing that according to the Middle Way Consequence School even those who are of the Lesser Vehicle by path[a] must realize the most subtle emptiness, he presents an abridged version of his own extensive argument on this in his commentary to Chandrakīrti's *Supplement to (Nāgārjuna's) "Treatise on the Middle,"*[b] citing Chandrakīrti's *Supplement,*[c] and Nāgārjuna's *Precious Garland,*[d] *Treatise on the Middle,*[e] and *Praise of the Nonconceptual*[f] as well as two Perfection of Wisdom Sūtras,[g] and a Lesser Vehicle Sūtra.[h] (That the Middle Way Consequence School's view on the emptiness of inherent existence is needed in order to become a Foe Destroyer is controversial, as it means that no follower of the Great Exposition School, the Sūtra School, the Mind-Only School, or even the Autonomy School can complete the Lesser Vehicle path

[a] The reference here is to Hearers and Solitary Realizers, as opposed to those who are of the Lesser Vehicle by tenet, the Proponents of the Great Exposition and the Proponents of Sūtra. For a discussion of this point, see the first appendix in *Tantra in Tibet,* 173-177.

[b] Tsong-kha-pa's argument can be found in Hopkins, *Compassion in Tibetan Buddhism,* 150-181.

[c] *Tantra in Tibet,* 94.

[d] Ibid., 94.

[e] Ibid., 95 and 96.

[f] *rnam par mi rtog pa la bstod pa, nirvikalpastava*[?]; ibid., 95.

[g] Ibid., 95-96.

[h] Ibid., 96.

and become a Foe Destroyer by means of any of those paths alone.)

Considering counterarguments, Tsong-kha-pa makes reference[a] to presentations in both Lesser Vehicle and Great Vehicle texts that propound the opposite, that is, that to get out of cyclic existence it is sufficient to have the fully developed wisdom understanding that the person is not substantially existent, which is a coarser type of selflessness.[b] Again, the conflict is settled by reasoning through differentiating what is definitive[c] and what requires interpretation.[d] This not being a main subject of the *Great Exposition of Secret Mantra,* he leaves the matter with a brief admonition to learn how to make such distinctions—implicitly indicating the benefit of studying his *The Essence of Eloquence*[e] where the dominant argument is that scriptural reference is not sufficient since a supporting scripture would require another which, in turn, would require another *ad infinitum,* and thus reasoning is necessary. The working principles revolve around showing that the conception of inherent existence is the root of cyclic existence and that some trainees are temporarily incapable of receiving teaching on such a subtle topic. Adjudication of the opposing scriptures is made:

1. on the basis of the ontological fact, determined by reasoning, that the emptiness of inherent existence is the final mode of subsistence of phenomena
2. in the context of the existential situation of the epistemological needs of the trainees to whom the doctrines were taught
3. in the face of reasoned refutation of opposing scriptures.

---

[a] Ibid., 96-97.

[b] Ibid., 179-181.

[c] *nges don, nītārtha.*

[d] *drang don, neyārtha.*

[e] *drang ba dang nges pa'i don rnam par phye ba'i bstan bcos legs bshad snying po;* Peking 6142, vol. 153. My annotated translation of the General Explanation and the section on the Mind-Only School is in *Emptiness in the Mind-Only School of Buddhism* (Berkeley: University of California Press, 1999); for the point made here, see 69-71; see also Jeffrey Hopkins, *Reflections on Reality* (Berkeley: University of California Press, 2002), 96-99. For a translation of the complete text, see Robert A. F. Thurman, *Tsong Khapa's Speech of Gold in the Essence of True Eloquence* (Princeton, N.J.: Princeton University Press, 1984). A Chinese translation was completed in Hla-sa on the day commemorating Buddha's enlightenment in 1916 by Venerable Fa Zun, "Bian Liao Yi Bu Liao Yi Shuo Cang Lun," in *Xi Zang Fo Jiao Jiao Yi Lun Ji* (Taipei: Da Sheng Wen Hua Chu Ban She, 1979), vol. 2, 159-276.

Tsong-kha-pa resolves other seeming contradictions by taking into account the frame of reference of a remark. For instance, Kalkī Puṇḍarīka's[a] commentary on the *Kālachakra Tantra,* called the *Stainless Light,*[b] explains the term "vajra" in "Vajra Vehicle" in the context of the *Kālachakra Tantra,* a Highest Yoga Tantra, in such a way that the meaning applies only to that class of tantra and not to all four classes. Tsong-kha-pa comments:[c]

> The meaning of "Vajra Vehicle" is given through taking "Vajra" as an indivisibility of the effect—the Mantra mode—and the cause, the Perfection mode. Here, "cause and effect" refer to totally supreme emptiness and supreme immutable bliss. The *Brief Explication of Initiations* [included in the Kālachakra cycle] says:[d]
>
> > That bearing the form of emptiness is the cause,
> > That bearing immutable compassion is the effect.
> > Emptiness and compassion indivisible
> > Are called the mind of enlightenment.
>
> The indivisibility of these two is a Cause Vehicle in the sense of being the means by which one progresses, and it is an Effect Vehicle in the sense of being that to which one is progressing. Such a Vajra Vehicle has reference to Highest Yoga Mantra and cannot occur in the lower tantras. For the supreme immutable bliss can arise only when one has attained the branch of meditative stabilization [in the Kālachakra system] and thus the branches of mindfulness and those below must be the means of achieving it. The three lower tantras do not have all the factors included in these causal branches.
>
> Therefore, [this description] is too narrow here in the context of identifying the general meaning of the Vajra Vehicle, and positing the meaning of the Vehicles of Cause and Effect through that mode [of explanation] is also too narrow in a general presentation. Here the meaning of "Vajra Vehicle" should be taken in accordance with what is

---

[a] *rigs ldan pad ma dkar po.*

[b] *dri med 'od, vimalaprabhā;* P2064, vol. 46.

[c] *Tantra in Tibet,* 107-108.

[d] *dbang mdor bstan pa, śekhoddeśa;* P3, vol. 1.

said in Ratnākarashānti's *Handful of Flowers, Explanation of the Guhyasamāja Tantra:*[a]

> With regard to its being called the Vajra Vehicle, those which include all the Great Vehicle are the six perfections. Those that include them are method and wisdom; that which includes them as one taste is the mind of enlightenment. That is the Vajrasattva meditative stabilization; just this is a vajra. Because it is both a vajra and a vehicle, it is the Vajra Vehicle, the Mantra Vehicle.

Thus, the Vajrasattva yoga indivisibly uniting method and wisdom is the Vajra Vehicle. It occurs at the time of both the path and the fruit.

Tsong-kha-pa explains that since the three lower tantra sets do not have the paths necessary for the generation of a fusion of totally supreme emptiness (here referring to a form empty, or devoid, of material particles) and supreme immutable bliss ("immutable" here referring to nonemission), this explanation—in the Kālachakra mode—of "Vajra Vehicle" is too narrow. He adds that explaining "Vehicles of Cause and Effect" in this way is also too narrow for a general presentation. Rather, the general meaning of "Vajra Vehicle" must apply to all four classes of tantra, not just Highest Yoga. Tsong-kha-pa is making the point that the type of union of method and wisdom described in those texts applies only to Highest Yoga Mantra and that a meaning of "Vajrayāna" applicable to all four tantra sets must be found elsewhere. As explained above, he indicates that this is deity yoga, an indivisible union of method and wisdom.

Regarding scriptural authority for the distinction between the Sūtra and Mantra Great Vehicles, Tsong-kha-pa quotes a passage from the *Lady Sky-Traveler Vajra Tent Tantra,*[b] rejects the commentaries of Kṛṣhṇapāda and Indrabodhi,[c] and critically uses the

[a] *gsang ba 'dus pa'i bshad sbyar snyim pa'i me tog, kusumāñjaliguhyasamājanibandha;* P2714, vol. 64.

[b] *mkha' 'gro ma rdo rje gur shes bya ba'i rgyud kyi rgyal po chen po'i brtag pa, ḍākinīvajrapañjara-mahātantrarāja-kalpa;* P11, vol. 1. See *Tantra in Tibet,* 117.

[c] Ibid., 120. Kṛṣhṇapāda's commentary is *mkha' 'gro ma rdo rje gur zhes bya ba'i rgyud kyi rgyal po chen po'i brtag pa'i rgyal po'i bshad sbyar, ḍākinīvajrapañjaranāma-mahātantrarājakalpamukhabandha;* P2325, vol. 54. Indrabodhi's commentary is *mkha' 'gro ma*

commentary of Devakulamahāmati,[a] accepting some parts and rejecting others. Having established that deity yoga is the dividing line between the two Great Vehicles, he reinforces this with citations from or references to works on Highest Yoga Mantra by Jñānapāda,[b] Ratnākarashānti,[c] Abhayākara,[d] Durjayachandra,[e] Shrīdhara,[f] Samayavajra,[g] Jinadatta,[h] and Vinayadatta.[i] The general drift is illustrated by a passage[j] from Ratnākarashānti's *Commentary on (Dīpaṅkarabhadra's) "Four Hundred and Fifty"*[k] as Tsong-kha-pa cites the title, or *Commentary on (Dīpaṅkarabhadra's) "Rite of the Guhyasamāja Maṇḍala"* as it is listed in the *Tibetan Tripitaka:*[l]

> If one cultivates only [a path] having the nature of a deity, one cannot become fully enlightened through that because the fulfillment of [yogic] activities is not complete. Or, if one meditates on the suchness of a deity and not on that deity, one will attain Buddhahood in many countless eons but not quickly. Through meditating on both, one will attain the highest perfect complete enlightenment very quickly because to do so is very appropriate and has special empowering blessings.

Since a Buddha has both a Body of Attributes and a form body it is *very appropriate* that on the path one cultivate both emptiness yoga and deity yoga, the former having as its main result the Body of Attributes and the latter, the form body. In short, the path to speedy attainment of enlightenment must involve both deity yoga and emptiness yoga; one without the other is not sufficient.

---

rdo rje gur gyi dka' 'grel shal nas brgyud pa, ḍākinīvajrapañjaramahātantrarājasya-pañjikāprathamapaṭalamukhabandha; P2324, vol. 54.

[a] *Tantra in Tibet,* 120-121.

[b] Ibid., 122-128.

[c] Ibid., 129, 134.

[d] Ibid., 129-130.

[e] Ibid., 130.

[f] Ibid., 130.

[g] Ibid., 131.

[h] Ibid., 131.

[i] Ibid., 131-132.

[j] Ibid., 129.

[k] *bzhi rgya lnga cu pa'i 'grel pa.*

[l] *dpal gsang ba 'dus pa'i dkyil 'khor gyi cho ga'i 'grel pa, guhyasamājamaṇḍalavidhiṭīkā;* P2734, vol. 65.

Furthermore, as Tsong-kha-pa points out, these two exist in one consciousness; thus, his assertion of the difference between the Sūtra and Mantra Great Vehicles is made on the basis of the simultaneous union in one consciousness of the factors of method and wisdom, specifically the appearance of the divine form and ascertainment of its emptiness.

Having cited such passages in Highest Yoga Tantras and commentaries to show the distinctive presence of deity yoga, he makes brief citations for Yoga, Performance, and Action Tantras by referring to Shākyamitra,[a] Ānandagarbha,[b] and Buddhaguhya,[c] skirting for the time being the considerable controversy over whether Action Tantra and Performance Tantra have deity yoga, since he tackles that problem at the beginning of the section on Action Tantra.[d]

Despite Tsong-kha-pa's many citations of tantras and Indian commentaries, it is clear that they are used only as evidence for his argument. Tradition is only supportive, not the final authority. The arbiter is reason, specifically in the sense of determining coherence and consistency within a path structure. Tsong-kha-pa refutes Ratnarakṣhita and Tripiṭakamāla,[e] for instance, not because they differ from the aforementioned sources but because their presentations fail in terms of consistency with the path structure. By doing so, he moves the basis of the argument from scriptural citation to reasoned analysis of a meditative structure.

Refutation of Ratnarakṣhita

Tsong-kha-pa analyzes and refutes Ratnarakṣhita's[f] and Tripiṭakamāla's[g] presentations on the difference between the Perfection and Mantra vehicles (the first is not included in Bu-tön's presentation and the second is). In his *Commentary on the Difficult Points of the Saṃvarodaya Tantra*,[h] Ratnarakṣhita explains that the generation

---

[a] *Tantra in Tibet*, 132.

[b] Ibid., 133.

[c] Ibid., 133.

[d] See chapter 11 and also *Deity Yoga*, 47-62.

[e] *Tantra in Tibet*, 143-150.

[f] Ibid., 143-144.

[g] Ibid., 145-150.

[h] *sdom pa 'byung ba'i rgyud kyi rgyal po chen po'i dka' 'grel padma can, saṃvarodayama-*

stage, which he takes to be deity yoga, is the distinctive feature of Mantra. He rejects meditation on emptiness as a distinctive feature because it occurs also in the Perfection Vehicle, and he rejects bliss because Bodhisattvas of the Perfection Vehicle are able to maintain a feeling of pleasure or bliss even in the midst of extreme torture.

In a typically laconic way, Tsong-kha-pa leaves many points unsaid or only hints at them. He merely says:[a]

> [Ratnarakṣhita] says this, thinking that all cultivations of deity yoga are included in the generation stage, that the yogas of channels, winds, and drops are for generating bliss, and that bliss is similar [in the Sūtra and Mantra Great Vehicles].

Tsong-kha-pa is making several points important to his own system:

1. Although all four tantra sets involve deity yoga, only Highest Yoga Mantra has a generation stage; Action, Performance, and Yoga Tantra do not. The reason is that the deity yoga of the generation stage in Highest Yoga Mantra must be modeled after the processes of death, intermediate state, and rebirth, whereas the three lower tantras, while using deity yoga, do not present this way. Specifically, the meditation on emptiness that is at the beginning of deity yoga must, in Highest Yoga Mantra, include a mimicking of the eight signs of death:

   four appearances
   (1) like a mirage
   (2) like smoke
   (3) like fireflies within smoke, and
   (4) like the flame of a butter lamp

   the dawning of three subtler consciousnesses
   (5) the mind of vivid white appearance
   (6) the mind of vivid red or orange increase, and
   (7) the mind of vivid black near attainment

   and the dawning of the most subtle consciousness
   (8) the mind of clear light.

---

hātantrarājasya padminīnāmapañjikā; P2137, vol. 51.

[a] *Tantra in Tibet,* 144.

This is called "bringing death to the path as the Body of Attributes." The yoga must also mimic the process of assuming an intermediate state through appearance as a seed syllable and then the process of rebirth through appearance in divine physical form. These latter two are called "bringing the intermediate state and birth to the path as the Complete Enjoyment Body and Emanation Body" respectively. Since the deity yogas of the three lower tantras—Action, Performance, and Yoga—do not involve such a patterning on the stages of being born in cyclic existence, they cannot fulfill the characteristics of a generation stage. Since the generation stage does not occur in three out of the four tantra sets, it cannot differentiate the Sūtra and Mantra Great Vehicles, and thus Ratnarakṣhita is wrong to hold that the generation stage is the distinctive feature of Mantra.

2. Just as meditation on emptiness occurs in Highest Yoga Mantra in both the generation stage and the completion stage, deity yoga also occurs in both stages. (The distinctive feature of the completion stage is that the three subtler minds and the fourth subtlest one are *actually* manifested through causing the winds to enter, dissolve, and remain in the central channel.) Therefore, Ratnarakṣhita is wrong in holding that all cultivations of deity yoga are included in the generation stage.
3. The blissful minds generated in the completion stage in Highest Yoga Mantra are more subtle consciousnesses than any generated through Sūtra practice, and once generated, they are used to realize the emptiness of inherent existence. Hence, Ratnarakṣhita is wrong in holding that bliss is similar in the Sūtra and Mantra Great Vehicles.

According to Tsong-kha-pa, when these points are not differentiated, the distinctive features of Highest Yoga Mantra are blurred. It can be seen that one of his aims in finely and critically delineating the difference between the Sūtra and Mantra Great Vehicles is so that the uncommon techniques of Highest Yoga Mantra can be appreciated. The doctrine of the most esoteric system affects the presentation of the less esoteric.

Refutation of Tripiṭakamāla

The second position that Tsong-kha-pa examines is that of

Tripiṭakamāla as found in his *Lamp for the Three Modes*.[a] Though Tsong-kha-pa earlier[b] cited the *Lamp for the Three Modes* as a source for the division of vehicles into three types—Lesser Vehicle, Sūtra Great Vehicle, and Mantra Great Vehicle—from the viewpoint of trainees' interests (and abilities) and although he cites it later[c] as a source for etymologies of the names of the four tantra sets, here he presents and refutes the *Lamp for the Three Modes* at length. Since, as we have seen, Tripiṭakamāla's presentation is central to the expositions not only of Bu-tön and Long-chen-pa (as well as other major scholars in Tibetan orders), Tsong-kha-pa's refutation of it is a radical and dramatic attempt to change the focus of tantric exposition. Let us consider the refutation in detail.

Tripiṭakamāla holds that the Mantra Vehicle is superior by way of four features: being for the nonobscured, having many methods, not being difficult, and being contrived for those of sharp faculties. Bu-tön paraphrases Tripiṭakamāla's own explanation of these, and Tsong-kha-pa condenses it (both without, to my sight, any warpage), and I shall condense it even further.

1. ***Being for the nonobscured.*** Tripiṭakamāla explains that those following the Perfection Vehicle try to complete the perfection of giving, for instance, by physical acts of charity that include, in dire instances, even giving away one's own body. He says that followers of the Mantra Vehicle see that since "a perfection is the ability to fulfill a want of all sentient beings simultaneously"[d] and since this cannot possibly be done by giving away one's body, head, or the like, Māntrikas engage in the superior technique of meditatively satisfying the wishes of all beings. This lack of obscuration, according to Tripiṭakamāla, characterizes the trainees of the Mantra Vehicle as superior.

Tsong-kha-pa disagrees with Tripiṭakamāla's basic notion of how the Perfection Vehicle describes fulfillment of a perfection. He cites Shāntideva's description of the perfection of giving in his *Engaging in the Bodhisattva Deeds*,[e] an unchallengeable treatise of Sūtra Great Vehicle:

---

[a] Ibid., 145-150.

[b] Ibid., 91.

[c] Ibid., 163-164.

[d] Ibid., 145.

[e] V.9-10.

If through eliminating the poverty of beings
A perfection of giving occurred,
Then since there are still poor beings, how did
The former Protectors achieve perfection?

Through an attitude of giving to all beings
All one's possessions with their fruits
A perfection of giving is said to occur,
Thus it is just in attitude.

According to Shāntideva, the perfection of giving is a matter of bringing the *attitude* of generosity to full development, not of satisfying the wants of all sentient beings. Otherwise, a perfection of giving never could have previously occurred, since obviously there are still beggars in the world. In that case, Shākyamuni Buddha could not have become enlightened, since he would not have attained the perfection of giving. Tripiṭakamāla's description of this first feature of Mantra's being for the nonobscured is, as Tsong-kha-pa says, "in trouble."[a]

2. ***Having many methods.*** Tripiṭakamāla explains that the techniques of the Sūtra system are all peaceful and thus "cannot take care of all sentient beings."[b] It might seem that he is suggesting that the achievement of activities of pacification, increase, control, and ferocity in Mantra is unique to Mantra, but he does not even mention this line of argument and, instead, speaks of the mental, verbal, and physical aspects of maṇḍala meditation for the sake of undermining a single afflictive emotion, such as desire. Tsong-kha-pa does not address this explanation, only mentioning[c] that Tibetan explanations of this feature as referring to the four types of activities are not based on Tripiṭakamāla's own words.

3. and 4. ***Not being difficult and being contrived for those of sharp faculties.*** Under these headings Tripiṭakamāla discusses four levels of capacity of Mantra trainees:

1. The supreme of the supreme meditate on the Great Seal—an indivisibility of wisdom and method—without using either a meditated consort or actual one.
2. The next beneath them use a meditated consort, called a

[a] Ibid., 149.
[b] Ibid., 146.
[c] Ibid., 150.

Wisdom Seal.

3. The next use a fully qualified actual consort, called a pledge seal.
4. The next use an actual consort not necessarily endowed with all attributes.

If we add Jñānakīrti's explanation,[a] there is a fifth level, that of trainees of Yoga Tantra and below who meditate on the body of a deity that is given the name "Great Seal"—in other words, deity yoga without a consort.

The first four represent levels within Highest Yoga Mantra. Thus, according to Tripiṭakamāla,[b] the supreme of the supreme trainees of Highest Yoga Mantra do not use desire for attractive visible forms, sounds, odors, tastes, and touches in the path; they do not make use of even a meditated consort, never mind an actual one. Tripiṭakamāla holds that those just below the very top rank meditate on an imaginary consort, and he posits the usage of an actual consort only for the third and fourth levels of practitioners. It is clear that he does not hold Tsong-kha-pa's view that an actual consort is needed even by the very best of trainees in order to bring about a withdrawal of the grosser levels of consciousness as in the process of dying. It seems that he views the usage of a meditated or actual consort only as a technique for those distracted by desire. His thought is likely that by meditating on emptiness and so forth in the midst of ritualized sex, a practitioner could overcome the sense that sex is separate from the scope of emptiness and thereby could undermine sexual desire.

The psychological value of exposing oneself to one's own inner desires, fears, and so forth in the midst of a different, intentional background in meditating on emptiness is unquestionable (if one can succeed). However, it seems that Tripiṭakamāla was not cognizant of the doctrine of the levels of consciousness manifested in orgasmic bliss and thus did not even conceive of utilizing them in the path. He had a completely different notion of the purpose of using desire in the path; for him desire is brought to the path only by those whose meditation is disturbed by lustful thoughts.

---

[a] In his *de kho na nyid la 'jug pa shes bya ba bde bar gshegs pa'i bka' ma lus pa mdor bsdus te bshad pa'i rab tu byed pa, tattvāvatārākhyasakalasugatavacastātparyavyākhyāprakaraṇa;* P4532, vol. 81.

[b] *Tantra in Tibet,* 146-148.

According to Tsong-kha-pa,[a] just the opposite is the case. Through using an actual consort a person proficient in the meditations of Highest Yoga Mantra manifests the three subtler and the final, subtlest consciousness, thereby enabling completion of the path—from the path of accumulation[b] to the path of no-more-learning[c]—in one lifetime. Later in the *Great Exposition of Secret Mantra* Tsong-kha-pa explains this to be the system of the *Guhyasamāja Tantra,* and thus, from his point of view, it is totally mistaken to claim that the supreme of the supreme trainees of Highest Yoga Mantra do not use desire in the path; it misses what, for Tsong-kha-pa, is the most powerful feature of the Highest Yoga Mantra path. Also, it is self-contradictory (1) to claim that the Mantra Great Vehicle is superior to the Sūtra Great Vehicle due to not being difficult in the sense of using desire in the path and (2) then to hold that the supreme of the supreme trainees do not use desire in the path.

Again, Tsong-kha-pa is emphasizing the special features of Highest Yoga Mantra. As with his refutation of Ratnarakṣhita, this refutation of Tripiṭakamāla is primarily based on a difference of views on Highest Yoga Mantra; Tripiṭakamāla is indicted for being misinformed about the most profound form of the path. For Tsong-kha-pa, sense, coherence, and consistency are of utmost importance; thus, divergent views *must* be refuted; they cannot just be repeated.

The Nying-ma master Long-chen-pa's exposition of Tripiṭakamāla's stanza is different in both style and content. He takes the "object" of the first line ("Though the object is the same")—which Bu-tön explains as referring to the fact that nondual omniscience is similarly the goal of both the Sūtra and Mantra systems—as indicating not that the goal of Buddhahood is the same, but that the basis, the essence of clear light, is similarly described in both systems. He takes the line as meaning that the Sūtra and Mantra Great Vehicles similarly delineate this basis as well as the phenomena that depend upon it; thus, he incurs no self-contradiction when later he says that the goal of Mantra is higher than that of Sūtra. Long-chen-pa creatively comments on Tripiṭakamāla's stanza in a way that fits his own system, without even hinting that Tripiṭakamāla himself

[a] Ibid., 150.

[b] *tshogs lam, saṃbhāramārga.*

[c] *mi slob lam, aśaikṣamārga.*

explains this stanza differently.[a]

From Long-chen-pa's explanation of the four distinctive features of Mantra, let us consider how Tsong-kha-pa and his followers might object to two of them—being for the nonobscured and not being difficult. Long-chen-pa says that those of the Perfection, or Definition, Vehicle are obscured with respect to the basis, paths, and fruits. He identifies the basis as the profound and the vast—the first being ultimate reality and the paths to it and the second being (1) the mode of procedure of the path of compassion and (2) the conventional phenomena in terms of which that procedure is carried out. He says (246):

> The Definition [Vehicle] has no more than only a profundity that is concerned with a basis fabricated by the mind, an ultimate truth known by determinative inferential valid cognition breaking down [objects] through reasoning.

His assertion that in the Perfection Vehicle the ultimate truth is known only inferentially would not sit well with Tsong-kha-pa who holds that in the Perfection Vehicle inferential realization is a necessary prerequisite to direct realization of the ultimate. Indeed, if there were no direct realization of emptiness in the Perfection Vehicle, it would contradict the assertion of ten Bodhisattva grounds, which are levels centering around direct realization of emptiness in meditative equipoise. Long-chen-pa's view that the ultimate truth described in the Perfection Vehicle is a mere mental fabrication is diametrically opposite to Tsong-kha-pa's who holds that inference incontrovertibly knows the actual ultimate truth, albeit by the route of a generic image[b] and not directly. For Tsong-kha-pa, inferential realization leads to direct perception of the same emptiness. The change is epistemological, not ontological.

For Long-chen-pa, however, the ultimate truth as presented in Mantra or, more specifically, in Highest Yoga Mantra is actualized in the completion stage of the path of method in Highest Yoga Mantra through concentrating on special points in the body to induce the winds to enter the central channel so that the inner heat[c] can be generated, melting the drops at the top of the head and

---

[a] For Döl-po-pa Shay-rap-gyel-tsen's explanation of this stanza, see Hopkins, *Mountain Doctrine*, 207, 447, and 456.

[b] *don spyi, arthasāmānya.*

[c] *gtum mo.*

causing their descent within the channel structure and the subsequent generation of the four empties, or four subtle consciousnesses.[a] He says (246):

> Mantra, however, delineates—as the ground—nonconceptual pristine wisdom unfabricated by the mind, the essence of the Body of Attributes, merely through concentrative emphasis on focal points of body, speech, channels, winds, drops of essential fluid, and so forth without depending on reasoning.

Here the procedure for getting at the ultimate truth is not reasoning but special techniques for inducing manifestation of pristine wisdom; a more profound means of perception realizes a more profound reality.

When the mind of clear light is actualized and objects are seen as manifestations of it, one is beyond the need for discarding nonvirtues and adopting virtues as everything has become an appearance of this fundamental mind; everyone and everything of its own nature appears as divine. The style of the narrative itself is meant to yield glimpses of this hierophany in which everything, of its own accord, shines in self-established purity, divinity.

One can see how difficult it might be for those trained in Long-chen-pa's and Tsong-kha-pa's traditions to appreciate the other's approach. Neither could find in the other's teaching the particularly attractive taste that they find in their own—it would appear to be devoid of the most intriguing essence of their own path. Yet, for me, once this distinction of approach and of content is made, the two styles are more like two sides of a coin, without appreciation of which the whole picture might not be gained. I would suggest that to appreciate both styles, it is helpful to recognize the seeming contradictions and inconsistencies in each presentation when viewed from the other perspective.

With respect to Mantra's feature of not being for the difficult, Long-chen-pa concludes that "achievement arises through using the attributes of the Desire Realm and so forth." This specifically refers to making use of the pleasant visible forms, sounds, odors, tastes, and touches of a consort in the path. As we have seen, desire

---

[a] In Nying-ma this is the general procedure of the path of method (*thabs lam*); the Great Completeness utilizes a more direct procedure in the path of release (*grol lam*). See, for instance, the second of Mi-pam-gya-tso's *Trilogy on Fundamental Mind*.

for these is used in or as the path[a] in the sense that desire leads to a bliss consciousness realizing emptiness. Specifically, in Highest Yoga Mantra sexual union is used to manifest (in orgasm but without emission) the subtler levels of consciousness mentioned above.[b] However, their mere actualization is not sufficient; those bliss consciousnesses, according to Tsong-kha-pa, must take the emptiness of inherent existence as their object, thereby eradicating desire. Long-chen-pa does not explicitly say such, but he would seem to hold that, far from merely arising from being fed up with the rigors of a wearying path, the practice of using desire in the path serves as a technique for highly qualified persons to proceed on the path more quickly.

As will be discussed later (340), in the three lower tantras—Action, Performance, and Yoga—desire is also used in the path, though not to generate subtler consciousnesses. However, Tsong-kha-pa is unwilling to hold that the usage of desire in the path is a distinguishing feature of Mantra because Sūtra Bodhisattvas are well known for using the afflictive emotions of desire and so forth to aid sentient beings, thereby accumulating merit[c] which contributes to their eventual full enlightenment. As a source he cites the *Kāshyapa Chapter Sūtra:*[d]

> Just as the filth of city-dwellers
> Helps the field of a sugarcane grower,
> So the manure of a Bodhisattva's afflictive emotions
> Assists in growing the qualities of a Buddha.

In his commentary, the Dalai Lama[e] gives as an example a Sūtra Bodhisattva king's using desire in the path in order to father children so that they can be of service to the kingdom. The implication is that desire is necessary for erection and orgasm; thus, even though

---

[a] *chags pa lam du byed pa.*

[b] In the Great Completeness manifestation of these subtle minds is not sufficient; a permanent fundamental mind must be realized. See, for instance, Mi-pam-gya-tso, *Fundamental Mind: The Nyingma View of the Great Completeness* with practical commentary by Khetsun Sangbo Rinbochay, trans. and ed. by Jeffrey Hopkins (Ithaca, N.Y.: Snow Lion Publications, 2006).

[c] *bsod nams, puṇya.*

[d] *'od srung gi le'u, kāśyapaparivarta;* P760.43, vol. 24. Cited in *Tantra in Tibet* by the Dalai Lama, 71, and by Tsong-kha-pa in laying out Ratnarakṣhita's position, 144.

[e] *Tantra in Tibet,* 58-59.

the causal motivation[a] for such copulation is compassion and thus is nonafflicted, the motivation at the time of the act[b] is mixed with the afflictive emotion of desire.

As an amusing aside, let me cite the comment by the late seventeenth- and early eighteenth-century Ge-luk scholar Jam-yang-shay-pa[c] that Bodhisattva Superiors,[d] those who have reached the path of seeing[e] and above, can have a "serviceable organ"[f] without an afflictive emotion being involved:[g]

> If [Bodhisattva Superiors] are able to display endless emanations in actuality [and not just in imagination], what need is there to mention that they could emanate an actual serviceable organ!

Since Bodhisattvas on the first ground and above could magically display an erection, they would have no need to use such an afflictive emotion to father a child. More seriously, this calls into question the assertion that the scope of Sūtra Bodhisattvas' usage of desire in the path would be limited to those on the paths of accumulation.

Hatred also is said to be used in the Sūtra Great Vehicle path, as in killing a highly injurious person who cannot be tamed in any other way. Again, the causal motivation is compassion (both for the evil person and for others oppressed by him/her), but does the act itself have to involve hatred or does it just *look* like a hateful act? Among my Tibetan teachers, one lama said that hatred might be necessary to bring the act of stopping the other person's life to completion, whereas another said it would not.[h]

In any case, the Sūtra ways of using the afflictive emotions in the path in which negative emotions impel virtuous acts are not

---

[a] *rgyu'i kun slong.*

[b] *dus kyi kun slong.*

[c] *'jam dbyangs bzhad pa ngag dbang brtson grus,* 1648-1722.

[d] *'phags pa, ārya.*

[e] *mthong lam, darśanamārga.*

[f] *dbang po las rung.*

[g] Jam-yang-shay-pa's *Great Exposition of the Concentrations and Formless Absorptions,* 149b.2.

[h] This issue is crucial to determining how the afflictive emotion of hatred itself actually is used in the path in the Sūtra Great Vehicle and if it is, on what levels it is used, but a definitive answer is elusive.

comparable to the tantric use of a bliss consciousness arising from desire *to realize emptiness*. Hence, there remains the question of whether the usage of desire in this particularly tantric way could be indeed a differentiator of the Sūtra and Mantra Great Vehicles. Tsong-kha-pa briefly addresses this more refined position:[a]

> We must assert that the trainees of the four tantras each use pleasure in the path in dependence on the four types of desire for the attributes of the desire realm [gazing, smiling, holding hands, and union. The presence or absence of such an ability to use pleasure in the path] is suitable as a difference between persons who are initially entering the Mantra or Perfection Vehicles; however, such cannot distinguish the vehicles.

Is Tsong-kha-pa making the point that differences between practitioners of vehicles cannot determine differences in vehicles? This seems unlikely, since the difference in persons comes by way of an ability to practice a certain path, or vehicle. Or, is he saying that such a difference occurs with respect to trainees "initially" entering these vehicles but does not hold true throughout the practice of the vehicle and thus cannot distinguish the vehicles? If this is the case, then in Tsong-kha-pa's system deity yoga would absurdly have to be practiced at *every single* point in the Mantra Vehicle, something that he himself does not assert.[b] Rather, he seems to be admitting that the difference in the trainees of the respective vehicles indeed indicates a difference in the paths but is not *sufficient* to distinguish the vehicles since it is not central. The Dalai Lama speaks directly to this point:[c]

> Although it indicates an inequality in the capacities of the two types of persons, it is not the profound and complete

---

[a] *Tantra in Tibet*, 112.

[b] As the *Presentation of the Grounds and Paths of the Four Great Secret Tantra Sets: Illumination of the Texts of Tantra* (*gsang chen rgyud sde bzhi'i sa lam gyi rnam bzhag rgyud gzhung gsal byed*) (rgyud smad par khang edition, no other data), 5b.4, by Nga-wang-pel-den (*ngag dbang dpal ldan;* born 1797) says:

> In general, whatever is either of the two, a yoga with signs or a yoga without signs, does not necessarily perceive the body of a deity who has the aspects of a face and arms because on this occasion there exist the four—deity and emptiness yogas and wind and repetition yogas.

[c] Ibid., 59.

distinction between the Perfection and Mantra vehicles.

This statement reinforces a focal point in Tsong-kha-pa's basic argument, namely, that the difference between the vehicles must be *significant* in terms of the general structure of the path, this being in terms of method and wisdom, which are the chief progenitors respectively of the two aspects of the goal of the path—a Buddha's Body of Attributes and form bodies. Deity yoga does indeed fulfill this criterion.

The special tantric way of using desire in the path can perhaps be subsumed under deity yoga, the special union of method and wisdom found only in Mantra, since it is performed within imagination of oneself and the consort as deities, whether the consort is an actual one or not. However, because the technique of using desire in the path is for the sake of enhancing the *mind of wisdom* realizing emptiness—not necessarily in the sense of generating a subtler consciousness realizing emptiness as is done in Highest Yoga Mantra but at least in the sense of generating a bliss consciousness realizing emptiness—it should be included within the factor of wisdom, in which case there would be a difference between the Sūtra and Mantra Great Vehicles in terms of how wisdom is enhanced, a difference not limited to Highest Yoga Mantra but also present in the three lower tantras. Still, for Tsong-kha-pa, this would not make the factor of wisdom the differentiator between the two vehicles since just as he recognizes the difference between the Lesser Vehicle and Great Vehicle modes of cultivating wisdom—the former by just a brief form of reasoning and the later by "endless" reasonings—and yet does not posit it as a sufficiently significant difference to be the central distinction between those vehicles, so here the difference in the usage of desire in the path in the two Great Vehicles is clearly for him not sufficiently significant. Rather, in Tsong-kha-pa's system, the centrally significant distinguishing feature of Mantra is deity yoga—meditation on oneself as having a body similar in aspect to a Buddha's form body.

Deity yoga involves an enactment in meditation of the pure condition of Buddhahood while still on the path. The abode, body, resources, and deeds of a Buddha are an Effect Vehicle[a] in the sense of being that to which one is progressing. Because in Mantra the cause vehicle—the means by which one progresses to that state—

---

[a] *'bras bu'i theg pa, phalayāna.*

involves using an imitation of the state of the effect in the path, it is also called an Effect Vehicle. Thus, the term "Effect Vehicle" has two meanings: (1) the actual state of the effect that is the goal of the path and (2) the means of progress (cause vehicle) that is called an Effect Vehicle since it involves a meditative assumption of the state of the effect. Tsong-kha-pa says:

> About "Vehicle," there is an Effect Vehicle which is that to which one is proceeding and a cause vehicle which is that by which one progresses. Due to proceeding [it is called] a vehicle. With respect to the "Effect Vehicle," the word "Effect" refers to the four thorough purities—abode, body, resources, and deeds, which are a Buddha's palace, body, fortune, and activities. In accordance with them one meditates on oneself as one presently having an inconceivable mansion, divine companions, sacred articles, and deeds such as purification of environments and beings. Thus, it is called the "Effect Vehicle" because one is progressing through meditation in accordance with the aspects of the effect [or fruit, Buddhahood].

"Vehicle" as the goal of the path—Buddhahood—"proceeds" most likely in the sense of being able to carry or bear the welfare of limitless sentient beings.

The imagination of oneself in the body of a Buddha in an inestimable mansion with divine companions and articles and emanating radiance that purifies lands and the persons therein is *mantra,* which is understood as "mind-protection." With *man* meaning "mind" and *tra* (taken to be *trā*[a] with the final long vowel *ā* being dropped in the compound) meaning "protection," *mantra* means to protect the mind from ordinary appearances and apprehension of oneself and one's surroundings as ordinary. Clear appearance of the divine figure and so forth protects the mind from ordinary appearances of a usual body, house, resources, and activities, for the mental consciousness is involved in divine appearances to the point where the factors necessary to generate an eye consciousness, for instance, deteriorate for the time being and the sense consciousnesses do not operate. With clear appearance of pure mind and body there is a sense of being the divine "I" designated in

[a] Or also as *trāya.*

dependence upon them; this counters the conception of ordinariness,[a] that is to say, being an ordinary person with an ordinary impure body of flesh, blood, and bone and with an ordinary impure mind.

This practice is found in all four tantra sets and occupies a significant place in the path as an enhancement of method. Since it is not found in Sūtra systems, it can serve as the central differentiator between the two Great Vehicles, Sūtra and Mantra, or Perfection Vehicle and Mantra Vehicle.

Comments

Tsong-kha-pa's style of exposition is as an appeal to the intellect, a carefully constructed argument based on scriptural sources and reasoning, with the emphasis on the latter. Consistency, coherence, and elegance of system are the cornerstones. His procedure is that of a thorough-going scholar, analyzing sources and counter-opinions with careful scrutiny and determining the place of the pillars of his analysis in the general structure of a system. By extending the scope of analysis beyond that seen in Bu-tön, his adjudication of conflicting systems of exposition establishes a radically new one.

Still, this new mode of exposition of Mantra did not carry the day with the other orders of Tibetan Buddhism. For instance, with respect to whether Action Tantra actually does involve deity yoga, the sixteenth-century Druk-pa Ka-gyu[b] master Padma-kar-po[c] in his *Presentation of the General Tantra Sets, Captivating the Wise*[d] first cites the explanation in an authoritative Highest Yoga Tantra, the *Wisdom Vajra Compendium* (see below, page 303), that there is no self-generation in Action Tantra and then after citing Buddhaguhya's and Varabodhi's opinions (see 304) disposes of them:[e]

> One need not take this to be very important, for if it is treated that way, one must deny the tantras as well as texts by many adepts, whereby it would be very sinful.

---

[a] *tha mal pa'i zhen pa.*

[b] *'brug pa bka' rgyud.*

[c] *padma dkar po,* 1527-1592.

[d] *rgyud sde spyi'i rnam gzhag mkhas pa'i yid 'phrog,* 18b.6.

[e] Ibid., 20a.5.

The implicit characterization of Tsong-kha-pa's approach to this topic as sinful highlights the innovation of his exposition, a radical departure from the approach of the other Tibetan orders on such topics, a turn from maintenance of tradition to critical analysis.

We more than glimpse here a different picture from that painted by Herbert Guenther who declares that Tsong-kha-pa "was not an independent thinker."[a] Far from being an uneventful repeater of Indian Buddhism, Tsong-kha-pa's *Great Exposition of Secret Mantra* is a dramatic development through subjecting sources to wide-ranging critical examination. The change indicates the liveliness and development of Buddhist thought in Tibet, as does Long-chen-pa's highly creative presentation, dispelling any notion that Tibetans merely blindly repeated the conclusions of their Indian predecessors.

Some have suggested that Long-chen-pa has less concern with Indian sources; however, the claim of authenticity in terms of lineage of source-teachings from India is as strong in Long-chen-pa as in Tsong-kha-pa. Rather, a salient difference between the two approaches may rest in a difference of style that stems from a difference in the mode of procedure of the path (though I make this suggestion with considerable trepidation as it is likely overblown). Tsong-kha-pa's presentations are often more intellectually evocative, the place of the intellect in the long process of finally generating the subtler levels of consciousness being emphasized. For Long-chen-pa, the chief technique for uncovering fundamental mind is to identify it in the midst of any sort of consciousness; thus, the texts, though certainly as long as others, tend to use psychologically evocative terminology, a special language that even immediately evokes glimpses of deeper states. For instance, Long-chen-pa's *Precious Treasury of Tenets* on the difference between the Sūtra and Mantra Great Vehicles (above on page 253) says:

> In Mantra the secrecy of mind is that memories and conceptions dawn as the sport of the noumenon, whereby the mind dawns as self-illuminating self-arisen pristine wisdom, due to which meditative stabilization is established in the yoga of the flow of a river, through which the mind is spontaneously established as a maṇḍala of nonconceptual

[a] Herbert Guenther, "Buddhism in Tibet," in M. Eliade, ed., *Encyclopedia of Religion* (New York: Macmillan, 1986), vol. 2, 411.

shine.

The song of the text itself contributes to the immediately evocative terminology, whereas in Tsong-kha-pa's presentation—as well as those by his followers—the style is that of methodical conceptual construction. Though Tsong-kha-pa's texts also can eventually become highly evocative, one would have to cite a lengthy passage, if not a complete book or several books, and ask the reader to study it over months if not years to experience it, for it is often only through extensive conceptual familiarity with his overall system that glimpses of profound experience begin to dawn.

In terms of immediately evocative style, the intellectual intricacy of Tsong-kha-pa's presentation is no match for Long-chen-pa's; however, when the principles of his position have been so internalized that the reader can supply the unspoken interstices, the experience of re-reading the text can evoke palpable glimpses into the experience of deity yoga. The argument itself becomes an exercise moving the mind toward developing the ability to combine profound realization of emptiness and manifestation as an ideal being such that one senses the possibility of consciousness itself appearing as form—the union of method and wisdom that, for Tsong-kha-pa, is at the heart of Mantra.

Tsong-kha-pa is often criticized, both in Tibet and beyond, for being overly verbal, overly abstract, but I would suggest that this criticism often is due to not having put sufficient time into first ascertaining the positions of Ge-luk scholars and then allowing the metaphysical imagination to be stimulated. The danger of over-abstraction in some areas of Tsong-kha-pa's thought is great, but the intricately woven arguments, when probed over time, lead to an internalization of knowledge and palpable experience of principles that are then the basis for verbalization. In the beginning, the words seem to use the reader, but later a changed person uses the words.

We need both patience to go through this process as well as willingness to become absorbed in these complex systems. The dilemma posed by such openness and the need for discrimination is certainly not solved by refusing to spend the time needed to probe the material or by an affectation of either closeness or distance from a tradition that prevents actual involvement. Tsong-kha-pa seems to have conquered this dilemma within his own culture through startlingly refreshing reasoned analysis of traditional accounts that functions as an expository method, bringing all the more focus to a pivotal practice in Mantra, deity yoga which itself is founded on the reasoned analysis performed in emptiness yoga.[a] The lesson may be that the type of mind needed to follow his argument is also needed in this central practice of deity yoga founded on the necessarily analytical approach of emptiness yoga. Seen in this light, there is a harmony between the form of Tsong-kha-pa's elaborately reasoned argument on the difference between Sūtra and Mantra and the content, the identification of deity yoga—the first step of which is reasoned meditation on emptiness—as the central tantric feature. The style itself makes the point that this type of reason is not cast aside in Mantra.

Utilization of many perspectives

The tantric tradition that Bu-tön cataloged was far more complex in terms of its strains and directions than the one that emerged after Tsong-kha-pa's reasoned reformulation of it. If we valued only early forms of religious and cultural traditions, the latter's system would not be of much interest, but in terms of the development of an idea, form, or paradigm much as in music or art where the first expression may be crude, his systematic formulation is enticingly rich in complex coherence, providing a world-view in the architecture of which conceptual thought can thrive, producing insights and creatively ordering and transforming experience. In order to open ourselves to the magnificently creative coherence of his vision, we need to discount the claims of his followers that this is *only* Indian Buddhism.

Also, the critical reasonableness of Tsong-kha-pa's system should not blind us to the value of Bu-tön's contribution—the historical richness, the variety of approaches that he sought to preserve. *This* richness is lost in Tsong-kha-pa's reduction of these diverse traditions to a single view, but his perspective has its own richness—a grand design—that invites creatively interpretive thought to juxtapose facets and to attempt to resolve remaining contradictions. One might expect that the reduction to a single

[a] See chapter two; other examples of the reasonings required in emptiness yoga are presented in my *Meditation on Emptiness* (London: Wisdom Publications, 1983), especially in Parts One and Two (47-196) as well as the last chapter of Part Five (549-560).

central distinguishing feature of Tantra would stifle dynamism, but it does not. For centuries, his view has beckoned many of the best minds of the vast Tibetan cultural region to apply its principles both to resolve inconsistencies and to gain insights and psychological development.

The world-view becomes a dynamically interactive structure that does far more than just serve as an interpretive grid for ordering an inherited tradition and for ordering experience. It is also a future-directed schema that leads a practitioner to make connections vital to a process of psychological and spiritual transformation. Through this route, the world-view exerts a constructive, transformative effect on the mind.

Long-chen-pa's perspective provides opportunities for his more evocative discourse that, while systematic, beckons one to an experience beyond systems, an epiphany in which all is resolved by the very nature of the experience. The overriding perspective is not one of conceptual architecture, but a call to experience in which objects shine in their own self-nature, unencumbered and unimpeded by overlays of misperception. Long-chen-pa's conceptual system even provides interstices in thought, liminals which through the stimulation of his evocative prose can be noticed. Resolution will principally be found there, not in making new conceptual connections.

Long-chen-pa's discourse is aimed mainly at providing such avenues, windows, or gaps in which the conceptual mind is stilled and the richness of the perceptual situation is directly experienced in a dramatic unveiling of its ever-present but hidden completeness. These insights become what influence, organize, and provide directionality, uncovering the primordial enlightenment in which everything subsists. This is not to suggest that the conceptual system implicit in Long-chen-pa's presentation is not defined and defended, for it certainly has been by Nying-ma scholar-yogis such as Ju Mi-pam-gya-tso. Rather, as the contemporary Nying-ma lama Khetsun Sangpo said, a true lama speaks the doctrine from within the one great expanse of the noumenon.[a] I would suggest that the dominant message is just this.

Whereas Tsong-kha-pa is speaking mainly to communicate the means to reach reality, Long-chen-pa is seeking to communicate

---

[a] *chos nyid kyi klong chen po gcig.*

mainly the perspective of that reality itself. Because of the different nature of these systems, it would be difficult for a person wedded to either of them to appreciate both, given the incompatibility of their perspectives. However, the mind is capable of pragmatic compartmentalization, utilizing various perspectives, roles, and world-views at different times which, if attempted to be forced together into one coherent system, would be cacophonously impossible. Through compartmentalization, different world-views can be alternated, not in psychotic dissociation but in a manner in which the two perspectives feed on and interact with each other in a creative way outside the realm of superficial consistency. Perhaps this was a force that attracted several Ge-luk-pa scholar-practitioners such as Ten-dar-hla-ram-pa[a] to embrace Nying-ma without forsaking their Ge-luk background, and perhaps it is this that is behind the educative procedure of the Nying-ma master Do-drup-chen[b] in which the Ge-luk curriculum is used for Sūtra study and Nying-ma is used for Mantra.

The rich context of the Tsong-kha-pa world-view, derived more from ordinary epistemology, provides a stimulatingly creative basis for practice, whereas the evocative Long-chen-pa expositions from the viewpoint of the final state make sure that the architecture of a spiritual system does not become a trap preventing the emergence of the very insights that it is seeking to promote. In this way, the two systems are a dynamically interactive whole.

Long-chen-pa's presentation can be seen both as quickly moving the discourse on to his explanation of Highest Yoga Mantra (especially the Great Completeness) and as providing opportunities for discourse evoking insights into that system. The absence of involved explanation of the lower tantras, as in his reduction of Action Tantra to external bathing rites and so forth, is not so much a lack as a technique for moving the discourse to the more important topic, the Great Completeness, the suggestion being that if one is capable of the highest system, then excessive involvement with the intricacies of Action Tantra is a distraction. A value of utilizing both Tsong-kha-pa and Long-chen-pa presentations is that for those not ready to appreciate the visionary heights of the Great Completeness, the former provides for the construction of a

---

[a] *bstan dar lha ram pa*, born 1759.

[b] *rdo grub chen 'jigs med bstan pa'i nyi ma*, 1865-1926.

context in which the latter can eventually work its marvels.

Later Ge-luk literature on the topic

As can be seen in the next chapter, Ke-drup's *Extensive Explanation of the Format of the General Tantra Sets* treats the question of the presence or absence of deity yoga in Action Tantra at length; however, except for a very brief mention, it does not treat the question of the difference between the two Great Vehicles. Given Ke-drup's selective mode of presentation—sometimes expanding on topics barely mentioned in Tsong-kha-pa's *Great Exposition of Secret Mantra* and sometimes simplifying—his absence of explanation on this topic suggests that he found his teacher's argument sufficiently extensive, clear, and straightforward. However, Paṇ-chen Sö-nam-drak-pa[a] (1478-1554) gives a brilliant distillation of Tsong-kha-pa's presentation of the difference between the four tantras in his *Presentation of the General Tantra Sets: Captivating the Minds of the Fortunate.*[b] Also, Lo-sang-chö-kyi-gyel-tsen (1570-1662), retroactively called the First Paṇ-chen Lama,[c] turns many of Tsong-kha-pa's points into syllogistic statements with great clarity in his *Presentation of the General Teaching and the Four Tantra Sets, Based on Notes* (see the Appendix for a translation of the relevant portion by Donald S. Lopez).[d] The aim of both of these texts is to provide exegesis of Tsong-kha-pa's thought that enhances its accessibility by providing helpful background, such as in detailing opponents' positions, and by summarizing the argument in a more straightforward manner.

Long-döl Nga-wang-lo-sang (1719-1794), on the other hand, puts forward a synthesis of (1) Tsong-kha-pa's delineation of only

---

[a] *paṇ chen bsod nams grags pa.*

[b] *rgyud sde spyi'i rnam par bzhag pa skal bzang gi yid 'phrog* (Dharmsala, India: Library of Tibetan Works and Archives, 1975), 18.6-32.1.

[c] In the seventeenth century the Fifth Dalai Lama gave Tashi Lhunpo Monastery to his teacher, Lo-sang-chö-kyi-gyel-tsen, the fifteenth abbot of the monastery. As abbot of the monastery, he was called "Paṇ-chen" (*mahāpaṇḍita,* "Great Scholar"). When Lo-sang-chö-kyi-gyel-tsen died, the Fifth Dalai Lama announced that his teacher would reappear as a recognizable child-successor, so his line of incarnations retained the title "Paṇ-chen Lama" and became the abbots of Tashi Lhunpo Monastery. The title "Paṇ-chen Lama" switched from being an elected one for a specific term of office to a line of reincarnations.

[d] *bstan pa spyi dang rgyud sde'i bzhi'i rnam gzhag zin bris su byas pa,* Collected Works, vol. 4 (New Delhi: Gurudeva, 1973).

deity yoga as the chief distinguishing feature of the two vehicles and (2) presentations by many other scholars of several unique features. In his verse summary of Tsong-kha-pa's *Great Exposition of Secret Mantra,* called *Terminology Arising in Secret Mantra, the Scriptural Collections of the Knowledge Bearers,*[a] he combines rather than contrasts these two presentations, thereby suggesting that his text was written at a point when sufficient time had passed since Tsong-kha-pa's radically new paradigm of critical analysis such that the new critical paradigm came to absorb the old paradigm of recounting a tradition of a multitude of differences. Of particular interest is that the four features mentioned by Tripiṭakamāla are resurrected within being attributed to the great Mongolian scholar Jang-kya Röl-pay-dor-jay. Unfortunately, the author does no more than list the four as if their consistency with Tsong-kha-pa's views is obvious! Otherwise, this section of Long-döl Nga-wang-lo-sang's poem is self-explanatory and provides a succinct summary of the Ge-luk perspective:[b]

> If, having passed beyond the nature
> Of the elders of the world who wish
> To achieve happiness and avoid suffering
> As long as alive and until dying,
> One thinks to achieve the final aim
> Of happiness in all future lives,
> There is definitely no way to achieve it
> Without entering into the Conqueror's doctrine.
> The doors of entry are twofold:
> Posited by way of tenet, there are four—
> Great Exposition, Sūtra, Mind-Only, and Consequence schools.
> Posited by way of vehicle there are three—
> Hearer, Solitary Realizer, and Great vehicles.
> These in brief are two—the Lesser Vehicle and the Great Vehicle.
> How are the two differentiated?
> Between view and behavior, they are differentiated by

---

[a] *gsang sngags rig pa 'dzin pa'i sde snod las byung ba'i ming gi grang,* The Collected Works of Longdol Lama, Part 1 (New Delhi: International Academy of Indian Culture, 1973), 87-170.

[b] Ibid., 87.4-91.4.

behavior.
The behavior is of three types, since Lesser Vehicle and Great Vehicle
Are differentiated by the presence and absence
Of (1) the mind of the seven cause and effect instructions
And of equalizing and switching self and other,
(2) The deeds of the six perfections and the four means of gathering [students],[a]
And (3) the aspirational mind, vow of practice, and their precepts.
The Great Vehicle also is of two types,
The Perfection Vehicle acting on causes
And the Secret Mantra Vajra Vehicle acting in the manner of effects.
How are the two differentiated?
About this the Mañjunātha Lama [Tsong-kha-pa] said:
Sūtra and Mantra are differentiated
By the presence and absence of meditation
Taking the fruit as the path [through divine] pride,
Clear appearance, and so forth by taking as objects of mind,
Even as a beginner, the four—a Buddha's abode,
Body, resources, and exalted activities.
Though not factors differentiating Sūtra and Mantra,
There are seven features not occurring in Sūtra
But in all four tantra sets elevating them:
(1) Blessing of one's continuum by Conquerors and their Children,
(2) Being taken care of by one's favored deity,
(3) Mindfulness of Buddha in all lives,
(4) Completing the collections through obeisance, offering,

---

[a] As Nāgārjuna's *Precious Garland of Advice* (stanza 133) says, the four means of gathering students are by way of giving gifts, giving doctrine, teaching others to fulfill their aims, and oneself acting according to that teaching:

> You should cause the assembling
> Of the religious and the worldly
> Through giving, speaking pleasantly,
> Purposeful behavior, and concordant behavior.

"Speaking pleasantly" is conversation based on high status and definite goodness. "Purposeful behavior" is to cause others to practice what is beneficial. "Concordant behavior" is for one to practice what one teaches others.

and praise,
(5) Overcoming obstructors through meditating a wheel of protection,
(6) Achieving common feats in this life,
(7) Gathering great waves of collections [of merit and wisdom] through movements of body and speech.
These were mentioned by those supreme lamas again and again.
The Lord of Adepts [Jang-kya] Röl-pay-dor-jay spoke
Of four features—nonobscuration,
Having many methods, not being difficult, and [being contrived for those with] sharp faculties.

11. Controversy over Deity Yoga in Action Tantra

Is meditation on oneself as deity actually to be found in Action Tantras themselves, or is it brought over from other tantra sets? Bu-tön[a] catalogues conflicting opinions on the topic, but does not come to a conclusion. His presentation of the argument against there being deity yoga in Action Tantra is strong, and thus he seems to side with the position that there is no deity yoga in Action Tantra; however, in explaining the path procedure of Action Tantra,[b] he presents the system of those who say there is. The apparent self-contradiction is perhaps explained by the encyclopedic nature of his work, built on an intention to include a wide range of systems and viewpoints.

Bu-tön introduces the topic by citing a passage in the *Wisdom Vajra Compendium,*[c] an explanatory Tantra in the Guhyasamāja cycle and thus a Highest Yoga Tantra, that indicates that there is no imagination of oneself as a deity in Action Tantra:[d]

> Those who are terrified and are very cleanly, who lack the excellent bliss of a wisdom-being and lack pride in themselves as a deity, who are not an object of the unusual practice, and who practice with thoughts on the features of defects abide in Action Tantra.

Bu-tön elaborates on the meaning:[e]

> "Those who are terrified and are very cleanly" are terrified of the profound meaning [of reality].[f] The meaning of "who lack the excellent bliss of a wisdom-being and pride in themselves as a deity" is that they do not generate [that is,

---

[a] *Extensive Presentation of the General Tantra Sets,* 86.6-88.7.

[b] Ibid., 54.5-61.7.

[c] *ye shes rdo rje kun las btus pa zhes bya ba'i rgyud, vajrajñānasamuccaya-nāma-tantra;* P84, vol. 3.

[d] *Extensive Presentation of the General Tantra Sets,* 84.4; cited by Tsong-kha-pa, *Deity Yoga,* 47.

[e] *Extensive Presentation of the General Tantra Sets,* 86.5.

[f] Tsong-kha-pa (*Deity Yoga,* 58) identifies "One who is terrified" differently as referring to "several types of trainees of Action Tantras who are frightened and terrified by the activity of single-pointed cultivation of deity yoga."

imagine] themselves as deities and do not [perform the practice of] the wisdom-being [that is, the actual deity] entering into themselves. This is clear in fact and also is what earlier lamas have said. Also, such is explained in Shrīdhara's *Commentary on the Difficult Points of the "Yamāri Tantra": Innate Illumination*[a] as well as a commentary on the *Vajrapañjara Tantra*,[b] and so forth. However:

1. Buddhaguhya in his *Commentary on the "Concentration Continuation"* says:[c]

> The *Glorious Condensed [Tantra of] Imaginations*[d] teaches familiarization with the selflessness of phenomena and deity yoga in a great many passages; therefore, I will not cite them here. In such tantras the bodies of deities and the repetition that is performed prior[e] to the secret mantra concentrations on sound [that is, before the concentrations of abiding in fire and in sound] are described. Those [rites of deity yoga] that were not described in whatsoever [tantras] due to [the mental outlook of] trainees were set forth in the *Questions of Subāhu*[f] which is a tantra containing the rites of all tantras,[g] the *Glorious Condensed [Tantra of] Imaginations*, and so forth.

[Buddhaguhya] uses as his sources the *Condensed [Tantra of]*

---

[a] *gshin rje gshed kyi rgyud kyi dka' 'grel lhan cig skyes pa'i snang ba, yamāritantrapañjikāsahajāloka*; P2781, vol. 66. Tsong-kha-pa cites the passage; see *Deity Yoga*, 48.

[b] As mentioned in an earlier note, there are three commentaries—by Devakulamahāmati (P2326), by Kṛṣhṇapāda (P2325), and by Indrabodhi (P2324), the last being Indrabhūti according to the Tohoku catalogue.

[c] *bsam gtan phyi ma rim par phye ba rgya cher bshad pa, dhyānottarapaṭalaṭīkā*; P3495, vol. 78. Tsong-kha-pa cites the first two sentences of this passage; see *Deity Yoga*, 51.

[d] *rdo rje khro bo'i rgyal po'i rtog pa bsdus pa'i rgyud, vajrakrodharājakalpalaghutantra*; P319, vol. 7.

[e] *bsam gtan du byas* (87.2) should read *bsam gtan* **sngon** *du byas* in accordance with Buddhaguhya's text (P3495, vol. 78, 71.1.5).

[f] *dpung bzang gis zhus pa'i rgyud, subāhuparipṛcchātantra*; P428, vol. 9.

[g] The *Questions of Subāhu* is a *general* Action Tantra, applicable to all lineages of trainees, as opposed to Tantras spoken only for a specific lineage, and thus contains "the rites of *all* tantras."

Imaginations, the *Vairochanābhisambodhi Tantra,*[a] the *Vajrapāṇi Initiation Tantra,*[b] and so forth. Also, he describes deity yoga as being generation of oneself as a deity by way of the six deities. Moreover, his description is similar in his *Commentary on the "Vajraviḍāraṇa Tantra."*[c]

2. The master Varabodhi, in his *Condensed Means of Achievement of Susiddhi* describes generation of oneself as a deity:[d]

> Do not think that the stages of the yoga of achieving a deity are not taught in Action Tantras. Though the Supramundane Victor did not teach these in most [Action Tantras], they are taught as main subjects in the *Vajrapāṇi Initiation* and the *Entry to the Ten Principles.*[e] In brief, all feats depend on a secret mantra deity and on suchness; if these are deficient, activities of pacification and so forth will not be achieved. Hence, these should be understood through a guru's explanations and through a little analysis of the features of tantras. Thus, a divine body is to be generated through these stages.

These two masters do not speak of the entry of a wisdom-being [that is, an actual deity entering into the imagined deity].

The master Nāgārjuna speaks of self-generation and entry of a wisdom-being as well as initiation in his *Means of Achievement of the Retention of the Thousand-Armed Avalokiteshvara.*[f] Also, self-generation, entry of a wisdom-

---

[a] *rnam par snang mdzad chen po mngon par rdzogs par byang chub pa rnam par sprul ba, mahāvairocanābhisaṃbodhivikurvatī;* P126, vol. 5. Tsong-kha-pa holds that this is a Performance Tantra.

[b] *lag na rdo rje dbang bskur ba'i rgyud chen po, vajrapāṇi-abhiṣekamahātantra;* P130, vol. 6. Tsong-kha-pa considers this a Performance Tantra.

[c] *rdo rje rnam par 'joms pa zhes bya ba'i bzungs kyi rgya cher 'grel pa rin po che gsal ba, vajravidāraṇi* [or *vidāraṇa*] *nāmadhāraṇīṭīkāratnābhāsvarā;* P3504, vol. 78. The tantra itself is not extant in Tibetan, nor has the Sanskrit been located to date.

[d] Tsong-kha-pa cites the same passage, except for the last sentence; see *Deity Yoga,* 52. Varabodhi's text is *legs par grub par byed pa'i sgrub pa'i thabs bsdus pa, susiddhikarasādhanasaṃgraha;* P3890, vol. 79.

[e] *de kho na nyid bcu la 'jug pa, *daśatattvātara.*

[f] *spyan ras gzigs dbang phyug phyag stong sgrub thabs, sahasrabhujāvalokiteśvarasādha-*

being, and so forth are described in other Means of Achievement which are based on Action Tantras such as the *Means of Achievement of Mahākāruṇika*[a] by the master Padmasambhava, the *Means of Achievement of the Eleven-Faced Avalokiteshvara*[b] by Bhikṣhuṇī Lakṣhmi,[c] the *Means of Achievement of Sitātapatrāparājitā*[d] which is said to be by Chandragomin, the *Means of Achievement of the Five Guards*[e] by Ratnākarashānti and Jetāri,[f] and the *Means of Achievement of Vimaloṣhṇīṣha*[g] by the Foremost Elder [Atisha], as well as the *Ocean of Means of Achievement,*[h] the *One Hundred and Fifty Means of Achievement,*[i] the *Hundred Means of Achievement,*[j] and so forth.[k]

Buddhaguhya and so forth assert that even the *Vairochanābhisambodhi* and so forth are Action Tantras;

---

na; P3555, vol. 79. This text is *based* on an Action Tantra, but it is doubtful that it can serve as a source of Action Tantra itself.

Tsong-kha-pa cites the remainder of this passage, in toto, up to but not including the last sentence, attributing it to "latter-day scholars" (*phyis kyis mkhas pa dag na re*). See *Deity Yoga*, 53-55.

[a] *sems ngal so ba'i thugs rje chen po'i sgrub thabs, cittaviśrāmaṇamahākāruṇikasādhana;* P3569, vol. 79.

[b] *rje btsun 'phags pa spyan ras gzigs dbang phyug zhal bcu gcig pa'i sgrub thabs, bhaṭṭārakāryaikādaśamukhāvalokiteśvarasādhana*; P3557, vol. 97.

[c] *dge slong ma dpal mo.*

[d] *gdugs dkar mo can gzhan gyis mi thub ma shes bya ba'i sgrub thabs, sitātapatrāparājitāsādhana;* P3903, vol. 80.

[e] *bsrung ba lnga'i cho ga, pañcarakṣāvidhi;* Ratnākarashānti's text is P3947, vol. 80; Jetāri's are listed under five separate titles: *so sor 'brang ma'i sgrub thabs, pratisarāsādhana; rma bya chen mo'i sgrub thabs, mahāmāyūrīsādhana; stong chen mo rab tu 'joms ma'i sgrub thabs, mahāsahasrapramardanīsādhana; gsang sngags chen mo rjes su 'dzin ma'i sgrub thabs, mahāmantrānudhāraṇīsādhana; bsil ba'i tshal chen mo'i sgrub thabs, mahāsītavatīsādhana;* P3940-3944, vol. 80.

[f] These are separate texts with the same title.

[g] *gtsug tor dri ma med pa'i gzungs kyi cho ga, vimaloṣṇīṣadhāraṇīvidhi;* P3901, vol. 79.

[h] *sgrub thabs rgya mtsho, sādhanasāgara;* P4221-4466, vols. 80-81, where the collection is also identified as *sgrub thabs kun las btus pa, sādhanasamuccaya* (Toh. 3400-3644).

[i] *phyed dang nyis brgya pa;* P3964-4126, vol. 80 (Toh. 3143-3304).

[j] *sgrub thabs brgya rtsa*; P4127-4220, vol. 80 (Toh. 3306-3309).

[k] Bu-tön's point is likely that it should be analyzed whether Buddhaguhya and Varabodhi mistook Means of Achievement *based* on Actions for presentations of Action Tantra.

therefore, it should be analyzed whether [their position that there is self-generation in Action Tantra] is founded on a mixing of Action and Performance Tantras. Or, perhaps [their position] is founded on explanations by other masters that it is suitable to apply the format of Yoga Tantra even to Action and Performance rites, as is taught in the *Compendium of Principles* [the root Yoga Tantra]:[a]

The essence, seal, mantra, and knowledge
Explained in the four sections [of this Tantra]
Are all achieved through whatever mode one wishes,
[The rites of Yoga Tantra] itself or [the others].

Or, just as deities similar to [Highest Yoga ones] such as Pratisarā, Mārīchi, and Parṇashavarī as well as their mantras, appear in Action Tantras, so Saṃpuṭa,[b] and so forth, [usually associated with Action Tantra] also appear in Highest Yoga Tantras. Hence, it should be analyzed whether the thought of Highest Yoga is being carried over to Action Tantra or whether the latter has self-generation in its own right.

With respect to the phrase "who is not an object of the unusual practice" in the *Wisdom Vajra Compendium*, Shraddhākaravarman[c] explains this as meaning that they are not objects of the activity of teaching the profound meaning explained in an intentional manner or as meaning that they practice with the activity of thoughts of faults with respect to the unusual sphere.[d]

After presenting this detailed case of possible unfounded reasons

---

[a] *de kho na nyid bsdus pa, tattvasaṃgraha;* P112, vol. 4; Toh. 479, vol. *nya.*

[b] The text (88.5) reads *sambhuṭa.*

[c] *ye shes rdo rje kun las btus pa'i rgyud las 'byung ba'i rgyan bdun rnam par dgrol ba, jñānavajrasamuccayatantrodbhavasaptālaṃkāravimocana;* P2654, vol. 60.

[d] In his second explanation, Shraddhākaravarman combines "who is not an object of the unusual practice" and "who practices with thoughts on the features of defects." Tsong-kha-pa (*Deity Yoga,* 58) keeps the two separate, explaining them as meaning "who are not receptacles for using in the path deeds of desire—this being unusual or contrary to the world—and who achieve the path through practices involving thoughts on features of faults such as birth, aging, and so forth, in conjunction with the conception of true existence."

behind Buddhaguhya's and Varabodhi's assertion that Action Tantras involve imagination of oneself as a deity, Bu-tön leaves the issue with advice to analyze which side is right. He was content to be somewhat noncommittal, although the weight of his argument is on the side that Action Tantras do not themselves call for self-generation, when he says, "This both is clear in fact and is what earlier lamas have said."

Reacting to Bu-tön's presentation, Tsong-kha-pa, at the beginning of the section on Action Tantra in his *Great Exposition of Secret Mantra,* argues the case that indeed deity yoga is required for the main but not the majority of trainees of Action Tantra and refutes in detail the opposite position as presented by Bu-tön. His argument is conducted with such intense examination of the Indian sources that the broad movements of his case are often implicit and unclear, except when juxtaposed to Bu-tön's text. This is perhaps the reason why Tsong-kha-pa's disciple Ke-drup made a clear summary of the argument in his *Extensive Explanation of the Format of the General Tantra Sets.*[a]

Ke-drup's summation

Ke-drup begins by citing the opposing opinion:

> Earlier Tibetan lamas made a [mistaken] presentation in which they posit the four tantra sets by way of four different rites of deity generation and so forth:
>
>> In Action Tantra there is no meditation on oneself as a deity and feats are received from a deity meditated in front [of oneself]; therefore [the mode of procedure for gaining feats in Action Tantra] is called "receiving feats from a deity who is like a master [giving a boon to a subject]."
>>
>> In Performance Tantra, although there is cultivation of self-generation [that is, imagination of oneself as a deity], there is no bestowal of initiation upon having caused the wisdom-being [the actual deity] to enter this [deity as whom one is imagining

[a] Though this has been translated by Ferdinand Lessing and Alex Wayman in their *Mkhas Grub Rje's Fundamentals of the Buddhist Tantras* (The Hague: Mouton, 1968), 163-171, the rendering contains so many errors that the argument is obscured.

> oneself] and no implanting of the seal of lineage lord [that is, imagination of the deity who is lord of the particular lineage on the top of one's head]. Also, without generating a pledge-being[a] in front [of oneself], one invites a wisdom-being, who upon [arriving and] residing there is worshipped and from whom feats are taken. Therefore, [the mode of procedure of gaining feats in Performance Tantra] is called "receiving feats from a deity who is like a friend [in that both giver and recipient—the deity and oneself—are equally meditated as deities]."
>
> In Yoga Tantra one generates oneself as a deity, into whom the wisdom-being is caused to enter; initiation is conferred; the seal of the lineage lord is implanted, and in the end the deity is asked to leave. Moreover, in Highest Yoga Mantra one generates oneself as a deity into whom the wisdom-being is caused to enter; initiation is conferred; and the seal of the lineage lord is implanted; at the end the wisdom-being is not asked to leave.

As a source [these earlier Tibetan lamas cite] the *Wisdom Vajra Compendium* (see 303 above), an explanatory tantra of the Guhyasamāja [cycle which, in paraphrase, says], "One who practices without the excellent bliss of a wisdom-being and without pride in oneself as a deity abides in Action Tantra."

Bu-tön Rin-po-che says, "The master Buddhaguhya says that Action Tantra has self-generation, [but] it should be examined whether [he says this] thinking that Action and Performance Tantras are not mutually exclusive..." However, he does not come to a decision.

The view of these "earlier Tibetan lamas" that the four tantra sets represent four different modes of deity generation is in brief:

1. In Action Tantra meditators do not imagine themselves as a deity and only meditate on a deity in front.
2. In Performance Tantra there is generation in front of oneself of

[a] That is, an imagined deity which, like a pledge, does not deviate from serving as a basis for the entry into it of an actual deity or wisdom-being.

an invited actual deity, and there is self-generation but without imagining a small representation of the lineage lord on the top of the head.

3. In Yoga Tantra both generation in front and self-generation occur, and in addition the deity in front enters oneself after which the representation of the lineage lord is meditated on top of one's head and initiation is conferred.
4. The difference between the generation rites in Yoga Tantra and Highest Yoga Tantra is that in the former the deity that has entered oneself is eventually asked to leave, this being at the end of the session (with an invitation to return at the next session), whereas in the latter the deity remains in oneself.

(The fourteenth-century Nying-ma master Long-chen-pa puts forth a similar demarcation of the four tantras in his *Treasury of the Supreme Vehicles.*)

Ke-drup's source, Tsong-kha-pa,[a] cites a tantra (the *Wisdom Vajra Compendium*) and quotes or refers to three Indian scholars—Shrīdhara, Jinadatta, and "Indrabhūti"—as Indian commentarial sources for this presentation. Then, Tsong-kha-pa presents the favored, opposite opinion of two Indian Action Tantra commentators, Buddhaguhya and Varabodhi, who hold that deity yoga (self-generation) is essential to the mode of procedure in Action Tantra.

As mentioned above, Bu-tön questions but does not resolve whether Buddhaguhya's view that Action Tantras have deity yoga comes from conflating Action Tantra and Performance Tantra, when he lists the *Vairochanābhisambodhi Tantra* and the *Vajrapāṇi Initiation Tantra* as Action Tantras that have deity yoga. Ke-drup indirectly praises his own teacher, Tsong-kha-pa, for his decisiveness when he reports that Bu-tön says only that this matter should be examined and does not come to a decision. Whereas one of Bu-tön's great contributions is a catalogue of traditions, one of Tsong-kha-pa's is critical decisiveness, and Ke-drup, like his teacher, tackles the issue with analytical directness:

> In our own system, it is asserted that Action Tantra has all of these—generation of oneself as a deity, granting of initiation upon causing the wisdom-being to enter oneself, and impression with the seal of the lineage lord. Therefore,

[a] *Deity Yoga*, 48-49.

> aside from the master Buddhaguhya's quoting the *Vairochanābhisambodhi* and the *Vajrapāṇi Initiation Tantra* in the context of these being commonly established as Action Tantras, he did not quote them due to not having found explanations of self-generation that could be quoted. For, in his commentary on the *Concentration Continuation Tantra* he quotes statements on the mode of cultivating the six deities in the *Vajroṣhṇīṣha Tantra* and the *Vajraviḍāraṇa Tantra* and explains them well. There is no one who does not assert that those two are Action Tantras, and, furthermore, [Āryadeva's] *Lamp Compendium for Practice*[a] says, "The *Vairochanābhisambodhi*, a Performance Tantra, says..."

The evidence that at least some Action Tantras have self-generation is cogent, but each part of Ke-drup's statement needs to be examined to appreciate the argument.

First, it is Tsong-kha-pa's opinion that for Buddhaguhya certain tantras can be either Action or Performance depending on the trainee:[b]

> The master Buddhaguhya asserts that the deity yoga of the four-branched repetition and so forth is similar in both Action and Performance Tantras. He says that the *Vairochanābhisambodhi,* for instance, can be an Action Tantra depending on the trainee; therefore, except for dividing Action and Performance Tantras by way of their trainees, he does not divide them from the viewpoint of the tantras themselves.

Therefore, Ke-drup's explanation would more accurately reflect Tsong-kha-pa's opinion if he indicated that for Buddhaguhya it was commonly established, that is, an opinion shared with many, that the *Vairochanābhisambodhi* and the *Vajrapāṇi Initiation* **could** be considered either an Action or a Performance Tantra.

This is how Tsong-kha-pa presents Buddhaguhya's view, even though he disagrees with Buddhaguhya on this point, for just a little later, he says:[c]

---

[a] *spyod bsdus sgron ma, caryāmelāpakapradīpa;* P2668, vol. 61. Ke-drup is suggesting that Buddhaguhya would have known of Āryadeva's remark.

[b] *Deity Yoga,* 51-52.

[c] *Deity Yoga,* 52.

> If the *Vairochanābhisambodhi* and the *Vajrapāṇi Initiation* are not considered to be Performance Tantras, it would be impossible to find one.

Thus, for Tsong-kha-pa, from the viewpoint of the tantras themselves these are Performance Tantras, not Action Tantras, whereas for Buddhaguhya the *Vairochanābhisambodhi* and the *Vajrapāṇi Initiation* could be Action Tantras depending on the practitioner.

We need to notice that:

- Since neither the *Vajroṣhṇīṣha Tantra* nor the *Vajravidāraṇa Tantra* were translated into Tibetan, that these have passages detailing self-generation is known only from Buddhaguhya's commentary on the *Concentration Continuation Tantra* and commentary on the *Vajravidāraṇa Tantra.*[a] Specifically, since the *Concentration Continuation* (Tsong-kha-pa's source for the mode of meditation in Action Tantra) itself does not clearly explain deity yoga, only saying, "Flow to the bases, mind, and sound," Buddhaguhya,[b] relying on the *Vajroṣhṇīṣha Tantra,* explains "bases" as twofold—the deity generated in front and oneself generated as a deity, these being the bases of mantra letters that are set on a moon disc at the heart. Then, when the *Concentration Continuation* says, "Meditate with the mantra minds," Buddhaguhya explains "mantra minds" as the six deities—the six steps involved in self-generation—based on the *Vajravidāraṇa Tantra.*
- Hence, the two references to self-generation in the *Concentration Continuation,* Buddhaguhya's and Tsong-kha-pa's prime source for the meditative procedure of Action Tantra, are so unclear that outside explanations must be sought. Buddhaguhya's justification for this is that the *Concentration Continuation* is "related" with the *Vajroṣhṇīṣha Tantra,* this being taken as meaning that it is a continuation of the *Vajroṣhṇīṣha Tantra* itself or an explanation of its further practice.
- Since it appears that no one challenges that the *Vajroṣhṇīṣha*

---

[a] For the citations, see *Deity Yoga,* 55 and 109. The Translation of the Treatises (*bstan 'gyur*) contains Buddhaguhya's commentary to the *Vidāraṇādhāraṇī,* titled *Extensive Commentary on the Vajravidāraṇī Retention: Precious Illumination* (*rdo rje rnam par 'joms pa shes bya ba'i gzungs kyi rgya cher 'grel pa rin po che gsal ba, vajravidāraṇānāmadhāraṇīṭīkāratnābhāsvarā;* P3504, vol. 78).

[b] Cited in ibid., 55.

Tantra and the *Vajraviḍāraṇa Tantra* existed in India, Tsong-kha-pa and Ke-drup emphasize merely that these are accepted as Action Tantras.

- That the reference to "bases" in the *Concentration Continuation* includes a reference to self-generation is also linguistically supported through a comparison with a similar usage of terminology in the *Vairochanābhisambodhi*, a Performance Tantra:[a]

 "Base" is to imagine one's own body
 As that of one's deity.
 That called the second base
 Is a perfect Buddha [imagined
 In front], the best of the two-legged.

 As Tsong-kha-pa suggests, one would have to come up with a difference between the usages of the "base" in the two passages to say that the one does and the other does not include a reference to self-generation.

The rest of Ke-drup's re-formulation of Tsong-kha-pa's argument can be summarized as nine contradictions in the assertion that Action Tantra and Performance Tantra do not involve self-generation:

1. Contradiction with scripture: To assert that Performance Tantras have no self-generation manifestly contradicts the presentation of such in the *Vairochanābhisambodhi*, given just above.
2. Contradiction with scripture and authoritative exegesis: To assert that Action Tantra has no self-generation contradicts the clear explanation of meditation by way of six deities in the *Vajraviḍāraṇa Tantra* and the mode of cultivating concentration by way of the four branches of approximation and achievement—one of the branches being the self-base—in *Vajroṣhṇīṣha Tantra* and the explanations by both Buddhaguhya and Varabodhi that these are set forth in most Action Tantras in an unclear way.
3. Contradiction with a linguistic parallel: If the "base" mentioned in the *Concentration Continuation* cannot be taken as meditating on oneself as a deity, then the same would have to be said about the passage from the Performance Tantra, the *Vairochanābhisambodhi*, quoted above. Since the opposing scholars would

[a] *Deity Yoga*, 56.

then be forced into the position of asserting that Performance Tantra does not have deity yoga, this would contradict their assertion that it does.

4. Contradiction with an authoritative, scripturally based explanation of the procedure of the path: The master Varabodhi explains in his *Clear Realization of Susiddhi*[a] that if the pride of ordinariness is not reversed through meditating on oneself as a deity and if one does not meditate on the emptiness which is the final status of all phenomena, one will not achieve any of the feats of pacification and so forth. Also, the *Vajrapāṇi Initiation* (a Performance Tantra) makes exactly this point. Hence, if there is no self-generation in Action Tantra, there would absurdly be no achievement of feats in dependence on it.
5. Contradiction with a wide tradition: Most descriptions of Means of Achievement for Action Tantra such as those composed by Nāgārjuna, Asaṅga, Lakṣhmi, Ratnākarashānti, and Jetāri as well as those in collections of Means of Achievement speak of self-generation and so forth. To say that Action Tantra does not have self-generation would contradict all of these.[b]
6. Contradiction with one's own practice when giving initiation: In the process of initiation both master and student must imagine themselves as deities, and also the wisdom-being (the actual deity) must enter the student imagined as a deity. Thus, even initiation would be impossible in Action Tantra if there were no self-generation. This would manifestly contradict the opposing scholars' own presentation of the master's and student's self-generation, the placing of deities at important places in the body and so forth, in the initiation rites of the five guards and the like.
7. Contradiction with critical analysis of the difference between the Perfection and Mantra vehicles: If Action Tantra had no

---

[a] Also called *Means of Achievement of Susiddhi.*

[b] Tsong-kha-pa (*Deity Yoga,* 58) admits that "the *Ocean of Means of Achievement* and so forth frequently treat rites of generation and so on for deities explained in Action and Performance Tantras like Highest Yoga," but says that this is merely "in consideration of the similarity of the deities, such as Mārīchi, and their mantras, that are described in both Action and Highest Yoga Tantras." Ke-drup, however, is speaking here about instances in those texts where actual Action Tantra rites are set forth, and since they speak of self-generation and so on, anyone who held that Action Tantra does not involve such would contradict these texts.

self-generation, it would not have the full complement of the means for positing the Secret Mantra Great Vehicle as superior to the Perfection Great Vehicle, this being that it has a cause of similar type for a Buddha's form body—deity yoga.

8. Contradiction with the universally accepted description of Mantra as taking the effect as the path: Action Tantra would not have the full complement of making the effect (Buddhahood) into the path because it would not involve meditation at present (while still on the path) in an aspect similar to the four marvels of the effect state—abode, body, resources, and deeds.
9. Contradiction with accepted statements in Highest Yoga Mantra about the difference between the tantra sets: Action Tantra would not have the full complement of using desire in the path because whereas the *Hevajra Tantra* and the *Saṃpuṭa*—in the context of associating four types of desire with the four tantra sets—speak of Action Tantras as using the mutual gazing of the male and female *deities* in the path, Action Tantra would not do so, since meditation on oneself as a deity would be unsuitable.

The evidence presented in this carefully framed argument requires that the statement in the *Wisdom Vajra Compendium Tantra* that in Action Tantra there is no pride of being a deity must be explained away. Ke-drup says:

> With respect to the meaning of the passage in the *Wisdom Vajra Compendium,* it is not teaching that "In Action Tantra there is no meditation on oneself as a deity and no entry of a wisdom-being into that [deity]." Rather, it is indicating that in Action Tantra there is a mode of worshipping a deity in front [of oneself] and receiving a feat [from that deity] without meditating on oneself as a deity and without making the wisdom-being enter oneself. For the *secondary* trainees of Action Tantra—those of dull faculties, a type whose minds cannot accommodate meditation of oneself as a deity—a system of receiving feats upon meditating on a deity in front, without meditating on oneself as a deity, is described. [However,] whoever is a *specially intended* trainee of Action Tantra is necessarily someone for whom cultivation of self-generation was taught. It is as the master Buddhaguhya explains it.

This explanation implies that since the *majority* of trainees of

Action Tantra are not able to practice deity yoga, they are not its *chief* trainees[a] or its *specially intended* trainees[b] but its *secondary* trainees.[c] As Tsong-kha-pa explicitly says:[d]

> Because such trainees are predominant in both Action and Performance, deity yoga is not manifest in them, and even those tantras that have it are not extensive. Nevertheless, the *chief* trainees of Action and Performance Tantras are not those who either do not like or are not able to cultivate one-pointedly a deity yoga by way of restraining vitality and exertion [breath and distraction], and so forth.

That the chief trainees are in the minority is the reason why so few Action Tantras clearly speak of self-generation. (That the chief trainees of a tantra set could be in the minority of trainees of that same tantra set is the bitter pill that has to be swallowed to maintain the point that Action Tantra, as a set, does indeed call for self-generation.)

Having shown that Action Tantra involves self-generation, Ke-drup considers briefly the remaining question of whether (1) entry of the wisdom-being (the actual deity) into oneself imagined as a deity and (2) visualizing the lineage lord at the top of one's head, called impression with the seal of the lineage lord, are suitable in Action and Performance Tantras. The qualm revolves around the undisputed fact that Buddhaguhya and Varabodhi do not mention these, but Ke-drup explains that the mere absence of description by those two masters does not mean that these are not to be done and thus cannot serve as a proof that it is not suitable to do them. He says that since entry of a wisdom-being and seal-impression are branches making the yoga more wonderful (that is, powerful), they do not have to be done but could be done.

Tsong-kha-pa's treatment of this last issue comes at the end of his critical inquiry into the arguments into whether Action Tantra has self-generation and is much more dramatic than Ke-drup's distillation. Tsong-kha-pa uses the issue as a means to make his main point—that deity yoga is at the very heart of tantric practice:[e]

---

[a] *'dul bya'i gtso bo.*

[b] *ched du bya ba'i 'dul bya.*

[c] *'dul bya phal pa.*

[d] *Deity Yoga*, 59.

[e] Ibid., 60-62.

Although the two masters Buddhaguhya and Varabodhi do not describe entry of a wisdom-being into oneself [in their commentaries on Action Tantra and Performance Tantra], such entry is suitable, for it is described by many Indian scholars and adepts. Were it unsuitable, it would have to be because [trainees of these tantras] hold themselves and the deity—the wisdom-being—as separate and do not believe in holding them as one. However, this is not the case, for it is said that through the power of believing one's own body, speech, and mind to be undifferentiable from the deity's exalted body, speech, and mind, all one's physical actions and movements are seals[a] and all one's speech is mantra. In this way the *Vajrapāṇi Initiation Tantra* says:

> ...If mantra practitioners believe in this way that these are undifferentiable, they attain purity of mind. At those times when they have a pure mind, they always view in all ways their own body to be the same as the deity's body, their own speech to be the same as the deity's speech, and their own mind to be the same as the deity's mind; then, they are in meditative equipoise....

This is also similar in Action Tantra because, when generation of oneself as a deity occurs, one must apply the pride that is the thought that one is the actual deity being generated, whether it is Vairochana or any other.

Therefore, to view one's body as a deity, one's speech as mantra, and one's mind as absorbed in suchness is not a distinguishing feature of Highest Yoga. It is definitely required also in the lower tantra sets.

Tsong-kha-pa emphasizes the importance and centrality of imagining oneself as a deity for all four tantra sets, refuting claims about Highest Yoga Mantra that denigrate central features of the other tantra sets. By doing so, he brings to the fore what he considers the actual special features of Highest Yoga Mantra.

His cogent analysis created a new approach to a complex received tradition by absorbing it in a coherent and consistent fashion into a high tradition of training in compassion and wisdom,

---

[a] *phyag rgya, mudrā.*

showing how these remain the foundation of tantric practice. Tsong-kha-pa did this largely through noticing and emphasizing certain of the tradition's own features, and thus he could view his own work as *exposing* a system integral to it rather than *creating* a new one.

Part Three: The Difference Between the Four Tantras

12. Bu-tön and Tsong-kha-pa: The Four Tantra Sets

Within the Mantra Vehicle, there are many presentations of varying numbers of tantra sets, but the dominant tradition is of a division into four.[a] Bu-tön's three *Presentations of the General Tantra Sets*—called *Condensed, Medium-Length,* and *Extensive*[b]—give a total of nine different ways of dividing the tantras into four groups. Tsong-kha-pa in his *Great Exposition of Secret Mantra* critically examines most of these and accepts only two with modification. While the brief explanations in Bu-tön's catalogue provide glimpses of the rich culture of Tantra, Tsong-kha-pa's critical appraisal fits Tantra into a coherent, high world-view. Let us consider these nine approaches to ordering the tantras.

Four tantras and four castes

Bu-tön reports that some hold that the four tantra sets are for the different castes. For instance, Alaṃkakalasha says in his *Commentary on the "Vajra Garland Tantra":*[c]

> Action Tantras were taught in order to accommodate Brahmins since they like bathing and cleanliness, hold the view that one is liberated through asceticism, consider their caste to be important, and hold that one is liberated through repetition and burnt offerings....Performance Tantras, teaching both internal yoga of wisdom and method and external activities, were set forth in order to accommodate the merchant caste since they cannot engage in severe asceticism, will not become involved in low actions, and look down on external cleanliness and so forth....Yoga Tantras [in which the gods and goddesses of the maṇḍalas

[a] This is so even in Nying-ma in which the fourth division is further divided into Mahāyoga, Anuyoga, and Atiyoga.

[b] *Condensed* version, 27a.1ff.; *Medium-Length* version, 641.7-650.5; *Extensive* version, 32.6-41.3.

[c] *rnal 'byor chen po'i rgyud dpal rdo rje phreng ba'i rgya cher 'grel pa zab mo'i don gyi 'grel pa, vajramālāmahāyogatantraṭīkāgambhīrārthadīpikā;* P2660, vol. 61 (Toh. 1795); this passage is Cone *rgyud gi,* 3a.2-4a.3. Cited in my supplement in *Tantra in Tibet,* 202. For Tsong-kha-pa's rebuttal see *Tantra in Tibet,* 155-156.

> correspond to a king and his retinue] were taught in order to accommodate those of the royal caste since they cannot engage in asceticism but enjoy the pleasures of the five attributes of the desire realm....Highest Yoga Tantras, which teach the nonconceptual usage of the five fleshes and so forth, as well as low actions, were taught for those of the servant class who—without any regard for cleanliness—eat everything, engage in all actions, and have little conceptuality.

Bu-tön attributes this tradition both to Alaṃkakalasha and also to "the speech of lamas," giving it additional authority. Also, he gives the impression that this one has his approval when immediately thereafter he cites a passage on the four tantras and declares that it should be analyzed as to whether it is fake or not.

That Alaṃkakalasha, certain lamas, and, most likely, Bu-tön himself approved this tradition highlights how radical Tsong-kha-pa's criticism, scathing in its devastating reasonableness, is. Tsong-kha-pa says:[a]

> If Alaṃkakalasha propounds this thinking that there is a similarity between the trainees of the four tantras and the four castes, such does not encompass the different features of those who engage in Mantra through the four tantra sets. If it is asserted that members of the four castes are needed for the trainees of the four tantras sets, this is not seen to be correct because such is never definite and is not even predominantly so. Though the deities of, for instance, the vajra element (*rdo rje'i dbyings, vajradhātu*) [taught in the *Compendium of Principles*] are described as having features that accord with kings and their retinue, this does not prove that trainees [of Yoga Tantra] are members of the royal caste.

The First Paṇ-chen Lama, Lo-sang-chö-kyi-gyel-tsen, clarifies Tsong-kha-pa's points:[b]

> It is wrong to posit the four tantra sets from the viewpoint of the four castes. If this means that those of the four castes

---

[a] Ibid., 156.

[b] *Notes Presenting the General Teaching and the Four Tantra Sets,* Collected Works, vol. 4 (New Delhi: Gurudeva, 1973), 17a.2-17a.4; cited in *Tantra in Tibet,* 202-203.

> are the special trainees of the four tantras, then this entails the fault of being too broad [since not all members of the castes practice tantra]. If this means that members of the four castes are needed for the main trainees of the four tantras, then this entails the fault of being too narrow [because the main trainees of the four tantras come from any part of society, not from a specific caste]. If this means that there are cases of the four tantras taming members of the four castes, then this entails the fault of indefiniteness [since there are cases of each of the four taming members of each of the four; therefore, this could not serve to distinguish the tantras].

The criticism is unrelenting, not leaving a shred of a possible reasonable explanation.

In favor of sense, Tsong-kha-pa and his followers unceremoniously drop this tradition, despite its being found in the work of an Indian scholar and repeated in Tibet. Simply put, the trainees of all four tantra sets are drawn from all levels of society, and, furthermore, not all persons of any level of society are suitable as practitioners of Tantra. In the light of reasoned examination, this tradition looks ridiculous; one can appreciate how abrasive such analysis would appear to those who opted, instead, to maintain their traditions (and most did!). Hard to ignore but impossible to absorb, Tsong-kha-pa's reasoned paradigm would remain a thorn in the side.

Despite the old tradition's unreasonableness, I find some sense in it, albeit through a different perspective. It strikes me that the connection of the four tantra sets with the four castes might have arisen from masters' using the four castes as examples in order to illustrate certain practices, such as ritual bathing. For instance, a master might exhort initiates that, in order to meditate on themselves as the main figure in a Yoga Tantra maṇḍala, they would have to consider themselves as kings; or in order to practice the strict cleanliness that is found in the preliminary rituals of Action Tantra, they would have to be like Brahmins, who are renowned for bathing three times a day; or, in order to practice the nondifferentiation of conceptions of cleanliness and uncleanliness in Highest Yoga Mantra, they would have to be like members of the lowest class. The energy that is involved in the imagination of kingly behavior or low-class behavior is drawn to the path by associating the path with it; this indeed is a fundamental procedure of Tantra, mimicking ordinary activities and affairs in a different context, both so that these are understood differently and so that the energy associated with them is made available for and associated with deeper practice. Still, such are only metaphors and cannot reasonably be put forward as the means of differentiating the four tantra sets by way of their trainees.

Four tantras and four schools of tenets

Others say that the mode of procedure in the deity yogas of the four tantra sets are for persons holding the views of the four schools of Buddhist tenets. Bu-tön disapproves of this tradition, as does his predecessor Sö-nam-tzay-mo[a] of the Sa-kya sect, whose exposition appears to have been the basis for Bu-tön's elaboration. Sö-nam-tzay-mo shows his disapproval merely by reporting that this tradition *claimed* to be following Nāgārjuna, but Bu-tön makes his disapproval clearer, "Tibetan lamas have said this, but I have not seen a source for it." The Druk-pa Ka-gyu master Padma-kar-po is even more explicit:[b]

> Some Tibetan teachers have explained that [the tantras] are differentiated into four types based on accommodations to [four types of non-Buddhist] Forders[c] or based on four schools of Buddhist tenets. Since the sources that they cite do not appear in any texts, these explanations are only their own thoughts.

Let us state the assertion as reported in Sö-nam-tzay-mo's[d] and Bu-tön's[e] expositions together with Tsong-kha-pa's reasoned refutation of it; the latter's usage of explicitly delineated reasoning again shifts the emphasis from the presence or absence of sources to whether or not the presentation reasonably fits into a larger

---

[a] *bsod nams rtse mo*, 1142-1182.

[b] *Presentation of the General Tantra Sets: Captivating the Wise* (*rgyud sde spyi'i rnam gzhag mkhas pa'i yid 'phrog*), Collected Works, vol. 11 (Darjeeling: Kargyud Sungrab Nyamso Khang, 1974), 16a.5.

[c] *mu stegs pa, tīrthika.*

[d] *Presentation of the General Tantra Sets* (*rgyud sde spyi'i rnam par gzhag pa*) (Gangtok, 'Bras-ljongs-sa-ngor-chos-tshogs, 1969), 30b.4-31b.5.

[e] *Condensed* version, 89b.6ff. Bu-tön does not give this particular presentation in his *Extensive* version.

schematization of the path. About Action Tantra trainees, this tradition says:

> Just as Vātsīputrīyas and Aparantaka-Vaibhāṣhikas assert truly existent external objects and an inexpressible self, so the rites of deity generation in Action Tantras involve laying out a painting of a deity in front of oneself, arranging offerings, bathing, observing cleanliness, inviting a wisdom being [an actual deity] in front of oneself—corresponding to an external object—placing the mantra in the deity's heart, and engaging in repetition within the context of viewing the deity as like a master and oneself as a servant. Just as these schools assert an inexpressible self, so the wisdom-being is neither the painting nor oneself.

As Tsong-kha-pa points out, the assumption that Action Tantras do not involve imagination of oneself as a deity but call only for meditation on a deity in front indeed has what appears to be a most reliable source, for it is based on the *Wisdom Vajra Compendium,* an explanatory Tantra of the Guhyasamāja cycle which, in paraphrase, says,[a] "One who practices without the excellent bliss of a wisdom-being and without pride in oneself as a deity abides in Action Tantra." Tsong-kha-pa has a problem because although he can criticize scholars who present this same opinion, he cannot disagree with a statement in a bona fide tantra; thus, he must explain it away. Also, since Tsong-kha-pa holds that imagination of oneself as a deity is the central distinguishing feature of Tantra, he *must* find it somewhere in Action Tantra, and, indeed, as we saw above in chapter eleven, he presents an elaborate and cogent argument that such does occur in Action Tantra. Attempting to resolve the problem, Tsong-kha-pa holds that the statement in the *Wisdom Vajra Compendium* refers only to the lowest trainees of Action Tantras, who are frightened by meditating on themselves as a deity, and hence does not refer to the *main* trainees of Action Tantra who, despite being a minority within Action Tantra trainees, are fully capable of practicing self-generation. He has no source from the *Wisdom Vajra Compendium* for this apologetic; reasoned analysis alone is the arbiter that allows a re-reading of the tantra.

Tsong-kha-pa does not bother to mention what, in the face of

---

[a] Cited also on 303 and 309 above.

the fact that he and all other Tibetan scholars consider the tantric systems to be Great Vehicle in terms of the view of emptiness, is the most absurd aspect of this tradition—that is, that there could be a harmony of view on the nature of phenomena between a Tantric system and Lesser Vehicle tenet system such as Vātsīputrīya or Aparantaka-Vaibhāṣhika.[a]

About Performance Tantra trainees, this tradition similarly posits a correspondence with a Lesser Vehicle school:

> Performance Tantras involving generation of oneself as a pledge-being and generation of a deity in front as a wisdom-being were taught for Kashmiri Vaibhāṣhikas and Sautrāntikas. Repetition is performed within the context of viewing the deity (the wisdom-being in front) and oneself (the pledge-being) as companions. This is similar to these schools' assertion of ultimately existent subject and object.

As before, in the perspective of the developed tradition, the Mantra Vehicle is part of the Great Vehicle from the viewpoints both of tenet and of path, and since emptiness yoga is an integral part of deity generation, adherents of Lesser Vehicle tenets, who assert ultimately established subject and object that are different entities, are not the intended trainees of any tantra.

About Yoga Tantra, this tradition makes what perhaps is its most untutored comparison:

> Yoga Tantras involving generation of oneself as a pledge-being and then causing the wisdom-being to enter oneself were taught for Solitary Realizers. This rite of deity generation is similar to Solitary Realizers' assertion of conventionally existent object and subject.

Since all four schools of tenets—Great Exposition, Sūtra, Mind-Only, and Middle Way schools—present the path of Solitary Realizers, "Solitary Realizer" itself is not a school of tenets. As Tsong-kha-pa says:[b]

> Even [if one mistakenly imagined] a relation between

---

[a] This tradition is likely just a fanciful creation by gurus or lamas untrained in philosophical systems but intent on pretending erudition by drawing parallels. Though it may stem from a time in the history of Tantra when trainees also came from Lesser Vehicle schools, the detail is crafted to make a pretense of scholarship.

[b] *Tantra in Tibet*, 155.

> Solitary Realizers and the rites of generation in Yoga Tantra, Solitary Realizers are not a division of the four schools of tenets.

Tsong-kha-pa's straightforward, understated refutation masks a huge guffaw.

About Highest Yoga Tantra the tradition says:

> Highest Yoga Tantras were taught for the Great Vehicle Proponents of Mind-Only and Proponents of the Middle Way School who assert that neither subject nor object ultimately exists but exists only conventionally. These tantras involve generation of oneself as a pledge-being and the entry of a wisdom-being, corresponding to their assertion of subject and object conventionally, but do not involve requesting the deity to leave, corresponding to not asserting either subject or object ultimately.

The correspondence is so superficially facile that it suggests that the main purpose of the tradition is to subsume the four Indian schools of tenets under tantra. Most likely, the tradition stems from teachers who knew little of the four schools of tenets but wanted to affect knowledge of them.

Four tantras and four faces of Kālachakra

Bu-tön,[a] most likely merely to fulfill an intention to thoroughly catalogue all the varieties of means for dividing the tantras, reports a tradition that the four tantra sets were spoken by the four faces of Kālachakra, the principal deity of one of the main Highest Yoga Tantras. Obviously an attempt to subsume all tantras under the tantra of a single deity, this tradition aligns the four faces, four groups of tantras, and four appearances arisen from four types of predispositions, the latter being a topic central to the *Kālachakra Tantra*.[b] Namely, Action and Performance Tantras were set forth by the left face of Kālachakra for the sake of purifying adherence to gross external objects that appear due to predispositions for the waking state. Yoga Tantras were set forth by the right face for the sake of purifying adherence to mere mental appearances that occur due to predispositions for the dream state. Yoginī Tantras were set forth

---

[a] *Extensive* version 40.4-40.7.

[b] *rgyud kyi rgyal po dpal dus kyi 'khor lo, kālacakranāmatantrarāja;* P4, vol. 1.

by the front face for the sake of purifying adherence to a nonconceptual state in which all external conceptuality has disappeared and which occurs due to predispositions for the deep sleep state. Yoga Noble Class Tantras[a] are set forth by the back face for the sake of purifying adherence to bliss that occurs due to predispositions for the state of sexual absorption called the fourth state.

In this system, the four tantra sets become grist for creative reformulation around topics central to the *Kālachakra Tantra.* Tsong-kha-pa does not even mention this means of classification, most likely because of its obvious inadequacy to the task, whereas Bu-tön includes it without comment.

Four tantras and four periods of the day

Bu-tön[b] also reports a statement in Kalkī Puṇḍarīka's commentary on the *Kālachakra Tantra,* the *Stainless Light,*[c] that four tantra sets were spoken in order to purify four periods of the day—tantras of smiling in order to purify the first period, tantras of gazing in order to purify the third period, tantras of touching the breast in order to purify the fifth period, and tantras of holding hands in order to purify the seventh period. Bu-tön says no more; Tsong-kha-pa does not mention the tradition; and the First Paṇ-chen Lama, Lo-sang-chö-kyi-gyel-tsen (see 382),[d] explains it away as merely aligning techniques of purification—groups of tantras—with objects to be purified, which here are periods during the day. This tradition again evinces a wish to absorb a highly diverse corpus of tantric literature under a rubric that leaves one's own system at the top as the most inclusive.

Four tantras and four eras

Another tradition reported by Bu-tön[e] divides the four tantras by way of four eras in the history of this world-system. Citing

---

[a] *rnal 'byor rje'u rigs kyi rgyud: Extensive* version, 40.7.

[b] Ibid., 40.7-41.2.

[c] *dus kyi 'khor lo'i 'grel bshad rtsa ba'i rgyud kyi rjes su 'jug pa stong phrag bcu gnyis pa dri ma med pa'i 'od, vimālaprabhānāmamūlatantrānusāriṇīdvādaśasāhasrikālaghukālacakratantrarājaṭīkā;* P2064, vol. 46.

[d] *Presentation of the General Teaching and the Four Tantra Sets,* Collected Works, vol. 4, 40.1.

[e] *Extensive* version, 41.2-41.3.

Kṛṣhṇachārin's *Illumination of the Secret Principles,*[a] he explains that Action, Performance, Yoga, and Highest Yoga tantras were set forth in relation to eras during which the afflictive emotions of beings became progressively more coarse, presumably requiring more powerful means to conquer them. Tsong-kha-pa, again, does not mention this tradition, most likely because it reflects a familiar theme that he has handled in his earlier criticisms.

Four tantras and followers of four deities

Bu-tön[b] reports a tradition that says that the four tantra sets are for persons following particular non-Buddhist deities. He attributes the tradition to his predecessor Sö-nam-tzay-mo, who actually only reports it without endorsing it.[c] In this tradition, the desirous who are followers of Īshvara are taught Highest Yoga Tantra; the hateful who are followers of Viṣhṇu are taught Performance Tantra; the ignorant who are followers of Brahmā are taught Action Tantra; and those who are indefinite in the sense that they take up the tenets of any deity they encounter are taught Yoga Tantra.

Tsong-kha-pa criticizes this view with devastating reason. Simply put, his view is that it is not necessary before entering into the Mantra Vehicle to take up a non-Buddhist system that has what, for Buddhism, is a wrong view on the status of persons and other phenomena. Also, absurdly, someone who initially assumed Nāgārjuna's view of the emptiness of inherent existence could not be a main trainee of any tantra set if it were necessary first to assume a wrong view. He says:[d]

> Even if this is taken as meaning that there are instances of these types being trained by these tantras, such cannot identify the different features of those who engage in Mantra through the four tantra sets. This is because some persons of all four types are tamed by each of these tantras.
>
> It would be most unreasonable to assert that such persons are needed as the chief trainees of these tantra sets. Since the main trainees of the Mantra Vehicle are the superior among trainees engaging in the Conqueror's teaching,

---

[a] *gsang ba'i de kho na nyid gsal ba, guhyatattvaprakāśa;* P2167, vol. 51.

[b] *Condensed* version, 895.2-895.7.

[c] *Presentation of the General Tantra Sets,* 27a.4-30b.4.

[d] *Tantra in Tibet,* 153-154.

> they do not have to assume a wrong view before engaging in Mantra. Also, there would be the fault that those who initially engaged in correct instead of wrong tenets would not be chief trainees of these tantras.

Tsong-kha-pa's refutation is so devastating that it provokes laughter at such a simple-minded assertion. His open dismissal of these traditions is a conscious attempt to assimilate tantric traditions into a highly evolved style of critical examination.

Four tantras and four afflictive emotions to be abandoned

Others, seeing that Mantra involves the usage of desire, hatred, and ignorance in the path in order to overcome them and seeing that practices are geared for persons having a particular predominant afflictive emotion, say that the four tantra sets are for persons dominated by specific types of afflictive emotions. Without comment, Bu-tön[a] reports this tradition, citing the *Very Brilliant Lamp:*[b]

> Concerning this, in consideration of those having the lineage of great and middling obscuration, Action Tantras were taught. For those having the lineage of low obscuration, Performance Tantras were taught. For those having the lineage of low and of medium desire, hatred, and obscuration, Yoga Tantras were taught. For those having the lineage of great desire, hatred, and obscuration, Highest Yoga Tantras were taught. For those having the lineage of the great of the great desire, hatred, and obscuration, the Yoginī Tantras were taught.

In this tradition, the higher tantra sets are superior because they offer a path that can tame even lower types of trainees; the power of their techniques is so great that beings severely afflicted with desire, hatred, and obscuration can attain Buddhahood through their path. This mirrors Tripiṭakamāla's view that Tantra, in general, is superior to Sūtra because it has more methods. As Bu-tön summarizes Tripiṭakamāla's position (cited earlier, 210):

> In the other systems [that is, the Sūtra approaches], asceticism, vows of restraint, and so forth are described as

---

[a] *Extensive* version, 39.4-39.6.

[b] *rab tu sgron gsal.*

> methods for [achieving] high status [within cyclic existence] and liberation [from cyclic existence], but all sentient beings cannot practice these. Since some course in very peaceful actions, [these practices] were set forth in terms of them, but these cannot take care of all.
>
> However, Secret Mantra was set forth in order to join all sentient beings to virtue. Concerning this, either oneself or a lama determines one's nature; this is done through analyzing dreams, dropping a flower [on a maṇḍala divided into quadrants that indicate temperament], the descent of wisdom,[a] constructing seals and so forth, and by way of [noticing predominant styles of] behavior. Having recognized the afflictive emotion, such as desire, in which one predominantly courses, one also identifies [the deity who is] one's lord of lineage [in that each lineage is associated with a particular afflictive emotion]. If desire is predominant, one generates [the minds and mental factors of desire][b] as Amitābha and, having made offerings [to that deity], enters—by way of mindfulness of his mantra and seal [that is, hand-gesture]—into the meditative stabilization that has the mode of great desire. With a nature of joy pervaded by compassion, all conceptions are abandoned.

If Mantra, in general, is superior due to having more techniques that are capable of taming a wider scope of trainees, it is consistent to hold that the higher tantra sets are superior to the lower due to being able to tame ever grosser afflictive emotions.

Tsong-kha-pa's criticism is, again, scathing. In refuting Alaṃkakalasha's similar position that the *Guhyasamāja Tantra* is taught to those in the merchant caste whose desire and hatred are great but whose ignorance is slight, he says:[c]

> In general, the chief trainees of the Great Vehicle must have strong compassion. In particular, the chief trainees of

---

[a] This probably refers to a method of divination through the appearance of configurations on a mirror, and so forth. The meaning of "constructing seals," which would seem to mean the construction of hand-gestures (*phyag rgya*, *mudrā*), is obscure.

[b] The bracketed material is added in accordance with Bu-tön's own explanation in the next section on obscuration.

[c] *Tantra in Tibet*, 156-157.

> Highest Yoga wish to attain Buddhahood extremely quickly in order to accomplish the welfare of others due to their being highly moved by great compassion. Therefore, it is nonsense to propound that they must have very great hatred.

His point is that although a certain afflictive emotion in a tantric practitioner may be predominant in the sense of being stronger than the other afflictive emotions, tantrists are simply not dominated by afflictive emotions. Rather, they are especially motivated by compassion, intent on the quickest means of attaining highest enlightenment in order to be of service to others.

In this vein, with regard to trainees of Highest Yoga Mantra, the Seventh Dalai Lama Kel-sang-gya-tso[a] in his *Explanation of the Maṇḍala Rite of the Glorious Guhyasamāja Akṣhobhyavajra: Illumination Brilliantly Clarifying the Principles of the Meaning of Initiation: Sacred Word of Vajrasattva* says that practitioners of Mantra are especially motivated by compassion, intent on the quickest means of attaining highest enlightenment in order to be of service to others:[b]

> Some see that if they rely on the Perfection Vehicle and so forth, they must amass the collections [of merit and wisdom] for three periods of countless great eons, and thus it would take a long time and involve great difficulty. They cannot bear such hardship and seek to attain Buddhahood in a short time and by a path with little difficulty. These people who claim that they, therefore, are engaging in the short path of the Secret Mantra Vehicle are outside the realm of Mantra trainees. For, to be a person of the Great Vehicle in general one cannot seek peace for oneself alone but from the viewpoint of holding others more dear than oneself must be able, for the sake of the welfare of others, to bear whatever type of hardship or suffering might arise. Secret Māntrikas are those of extremely sharp faculties within followers of the Great Vehicle, and, therefore, persons who have turned their backs on others' welfare and want little difficulty for themselves are not even close to the quarter of Highest Secret Mantra....One should engage

---

[a] *bskal bzang rgya mtsho*, 1708-1757.

[b] *gsang 'dus dkyil 'khor cho ga'i rnam bshad* (New Delhi: Tanzin Kunga, 1972), 17.2-18.2.

> in Highest Yoga Mantra, the secret short path, with the motivation of an altruistic intention to become enlightened, unable to bear that sentient beings will be troubled for a long time by cyclic existence in general and by strong sufferings in particular, thinking, "How nice it would be if I could achieve right now a means to free them!"

Similarly, the Mongolian scholar-yogi Jang-kya Röl-pay-dor-jay,[a] lama to the Ch'ien-lung Emperor during the Manchu domination of China in the eighteenth century, emphasizes that the practitioners for whom Tantra was specifically taught are even more compassionate and of a higher type than the practitioners of the Sūtra version of the Great Vehicle. In his *Clear Exposition of the Presentations of Tenets: Beautiful Ornament for the Meru of the Subduer's Teaching*, he says:[b]

> In the precious tantras and in many commentaries it is said that even those trainees of the Mantra Vehicle who have low faculties must have far greater compassion, sharper faculties, and a more superior lot than the trainees of sharpest faculties in the Perfection Vehicle. Therefore, those who think and propound that the Mantra Vehicle was taught for persons discouraged about achieving enlightenment over a long time and with great difficulty make clear that they have no penetration of the meaning of Tantra. Furthermore, the statement that the Mantra Vehicle is quicker than the Perfection Vehicle is in relation to trainees who are suitable vessels, not in terms of just anyone. Therefore, it is not sufficient that the doctrine be the Mantra Vehicle; the person must be properly engaged in the Mantra Vehicle.

Even though the path of the Mantra Vehicle is quicker and easier, a practitioner cannot seek it out of fearing the difficulties of the longer Sūtra path. Rather, the quicker path is sought from being particularly moved by compassion; a Mantra practitioner wants to achieve enlightenment sooner in order more quickly to be of service to others.

---

[a] *lcang skya rol pa'i rdo rje*, 1717-1786.

[b] *grub pa'i mtha'i rnam par bzhag pa gsal bar bshad pa thub bstan lhun po'i mdzes rgyan* (Sarnath: Pleasure of Elegant Sayings Press, 1970), 529.18-530.8.

In a similar vein, the present Dalai Lama has said[a] that proper contemplation of the difficulties and length of the Sūtra path generates greater determination and courage. I surmise that this is because contemplating one's own altruistic activity over great periods of time undermines the thresholds of impatience, anger, and discouragement. We can extrapolate from this that those who are frightened by the length of the Sūtra Vehicle path or are incapable of being tamed by it are outside of the province of the Great Vehicle in general, let alone the Mantra Vehicle in particular.

From this perspective, far from being taught for those who are unable to proceed on the Perfection Vehicle, the four tantras were expounded for persons of particularly great compassion, and Jang-kya emphasizes that, in addition, the person must be *capable* of its practice. The position that the four tantra sets are for persons dominated by different types of afflictive emotions such as desire or hatred is thereby rendered impossible. That the trainees of Mantra, who are supposed to be the sharpest of all Bodhisattvas, would be discouraged in the face of a long path and—from that depression—seek a short path is raucously ridiculous, for the altruism of Māntrikas, in this view, is even more intense than that of practitioners of the Perfection Vehicle.

One can perceive the ever-widening gulf between those in Tibet who accepted traditional views of Mantra (or who repeated them without much attention) and those who sought to incorporate Mantra in a consistent way into a high Great Vehicle tradition. I detect a reserve of criticism in Bu-tön's catalogue of traditional views—in this case, his citing it in quotation without the slightest comment—but Tsong-kha-pa takes it much further, launching a critical attack that, despite its negative style, communicates confidence in an overall view of Tantra as consistent within a grand tradition; this vision is what gradually comes to the fore with patient reading and re-reading.

Tsong-kha-pa's stark critique stands in bold contrast to many tradition-oriented perspectives of his time that also have come to constitute much of the knowledge of Tantra outside Tibet. For instance, Mircea Eliade, who contributed greatly to our understanding of many fields of intellectual endeavor and had much to do with creating an atmosphere of appreciation for the multifaceted a

[a] In public lecture.

ppearance of world and local religions, describes Tantrism as suited for persons of lower sensibilities than those practicing Great Vehicle Buddhism. He says:[a]

> For Buddhists...the Vajrayāna represents a new revelation of Buddha's doctrine, adapted to the much diminished capacities of modern man.

Though Eliade's view contrasts even with that of Tripiṭakamāla, who held that the top rank among the highest tantric practitioners did not need to use sexual union in the spiritual path, it is somewhat similar in that Tripiṭakamāla viewed the use of consorts merely as a technique suited for those of limited capacity distracted by desire, and so forth.

Numerous contemporary scholars describe Tantrism as a frustrated attempt to turn away from monastic celibacy and prolonged practice of the path to immediate gratification in sexual ritual. Though echoing some trends within traditional views of Tantrism, these opinions obviously do not take into account the exactly opposite view of Tsong-kha-pa and his Ge-luk followers, whose school of exposition, important throughout a vast region of Central Asia, offers a diametrically opposite view of Tantra. A more rounded view needs to present both of these perspectives.

Four tantras and four levels of desire to be purified

Bu-tön[b] reports at length a tradition that divides the four tantras by the type of desire that is utilized and purified in the path. The tradition stems from presentations in Highest Yoga Mantra, a principal source being the one that Bu-tön cites first, the *Saṃpuṭa Tantra:*[c]

> The four aspects of smiling, gazing,
> Holding hands, and the two embracing
> Reside as the four tantras
> In the manner of insects.

Based on such descriptions of the four tantra sets found in Highest Yoga Tantras and their commentaries, it is said that in Action

[a] Mircea Eliade, *Patañjali and Yoga,* translated by C.L. Markmann (New York: Funk and Wagnalls, 1969), 179.

[b] *Extensive* version, 32.7-35.7.

[c] *rnal 'byor ma bzhi'i kha sbyor kyi rgyud, catur-yoginī-saṃpuṭatantra;* P24, vol. 2.

Tantra the desire involved in male and female gazing, or looking, at each other is used in the path; in Performance Tantra the desire involved in male and female smiling at each other is used in the path; in Yoga Tantra the desire involved in male and female embracing and touching each other is used in the path, and in Highest Yoga Mantra the desire involved in sexual union is used in the path.

When desire arising from gazing, smiling, holding hands or embracing, and sexual union is used in the path in conjunction with emptiness and deity yogas, desire itself is extinguished. Specifically, in Highest Yoga Mantra, desire for sexual union leads to sexual union and generation of a blissful consciousness withdrawn from the usual myriad objects; a practitioner uses this consciousness to realize emptiness. The realization of the emptiness of inherent existence, in turn, destroys the possibility of desire since it is built on the misperception that phenomena inherently exist.

The process is compared to a bug being born from moist wood and then eating the wood. In this ancient example (formed at a time when it was assumed that this type of bug, or worm, was generated only from wood and heat), the wood is desire; the bug is the blissful consciousness; the consumption of the wood is the blissful consciousness's destruction of desire through realizing emptiness. The reason why a blissful consciousness is used for this process is that it is more intense, and thus realization of emptiness by such a consciousness is more powerful. As the First Paṇ-chen Lama, Losang-chö-kyi-gyel-tsen, says (see also 382):[a]

> A wood-engendered insect is born from wood but consumes it completely. In the same way, great bliss is generated in dependence upon a causal motivation that is the desire of gazing, smiling, holding hands or embracing, or union of the two organs. The wisdom of undifferentiable bliss and emptiness, which is this great bliss generated undifferentiably with a mind realizing emptiness at the same time, consumes completely the afflictive emotions—desire, ignorance, and so forth.

The process is clearly explained in Ge-luk commentarial literature on Highest Yoga Mantra, where consciousnesses are divided into

[a] *Presentation of the General Teaching and the Four Tantra Sets,* Collected Works, vol. 4, 17b.5-18a.1.

the gross, the subtle, and the very subtle.[a] According to the system of *Guhyasamāja Tantra,* the very subtle level of consciousness is the mind of clear light, called the fundamental innate mind of clear light; the subtle are three levels of consciousness called the minds of vivid white, red (or orange), and black appearance; and the gross are the five sense consciousnesses and the mental consciousness, when the latter is not manifesting one of the above subtler levels. When the grosser levels of consciousness cease as is said to occur in the process of orgasm, going to sleep, fainting, sneezing, and dying, the more subtle become manifest. The first to manifest is the mind of vivid white appearance that is described as like a clear night sky filled with moonlight, not the moon shining in empty space but space filled with white light. All conceptuality has ceased, and nothing appears except this slightly dualistic vivid white appearance, which is one's consciousness itself.

When that mind ceases, a more subtle mind of vivid red or orange increase dawns; this is compared to a clear sky filled with sunlight, again not the sun shining in the sky but space filled with red or orange light. When this mind ceases, a still more subtle mind of vivid black near-attainment dawns; it is called "near-attainment" because one is close to manifesting the mind of clear light. The mind of black near-attainment is compared to a moonless, very black sky just after dusk when no stars shine; during the first part of this phase one remains aware but then becomes unconscious in thick blackness. Then, with the three "pollutants"—the white, red, and black appearances—cleared away, the mind of clear light, the most subtle level of consciousness, dawns.

Because the subtler levels of consciousness are considered to be more powerful and thus more effective in realizing the truth of the emptiness of inherent existence and in overcoming obstructions, the systems of Highest Yoga Mantra seek to manifest the mind of clear light by way of various techniques. One of these techniques is blissful orgasm because, according to the psychology of Highest Yoga Mantra, orgasm, like dying, going to sleep, and fainting—involves the ceasing of the grosser levels of consciousness and

---

[a] The material on the levels of consciousness is drawn from a text by Yang-jen-ga-way-lo-drö (*dbyangs can dga' ba'i blo gros, a kya yongs 'dzin,* c. 1750), which is translated in Lati Rinbochay and Jeffrey Hopkins, *Death, Intermediate State, and Rebirth in Tibetan Buddhism* (London: Rider, 1980; reprint, Ithaca, N.Y.: Snow Lion Publications, 1985).

manifestation of the more subtle. The intent in using a blissful, orgasmic mind in the path is to manifest the most subtle mind, the fundamental innate mind of clear light, and use it to realize the emptiness of inherent existence. In this way, the power of the path-consciousness realizing emptiness is enhanced such that it is more effective in overcoming the obstructions to liberation from cyclic existence and obstructions to the altruistic omniscience of Buddhahood.

A consciousness of orgasmic bliss is put to use in the spiritual path because when the sense of pleasure is powerful, one's consciousness is totally involved with that pleasure and thus completely withdrawn; this is the reason why the subtler levels of consciousness manifest during the intense bliss of orgasm, even if they are not noticed, never mind utilized, in common copulation. Without desire, involvement in bliss would be minimal, and thus Highest Yoga Mantra employs the arts of love-making, and so forth, to enhance the process. This is ordinary desire used in an extraordinary way.

The usage of desire in the path is, therefore, explicitly for the sake of making the mind of wisdom more powerful by way of accessing a subtler level of consciousness. The difficulty of using an orgasmic consciousness to realize anything indicates that it would take a person of great psychological development to be able to utilize such a subtle state in the path. Since other, not so intense, levels of bliss are used in a similar way in the other tantra sets, actual practitioners of Tantra in general and Highest Yoga Mantra in particular must, in this presentation by Tsong-kha-pa and his followers, be more highly developed than the practitioners of the Sūtra version of the Great Vehicle. Through this, it can be seen that there are good reasons why they say that the tantric systems are for persons of a high level of development, quite a contrast to traditions holding that Tantra is superior because it has more powerful techniques for grosser personality types.

Tsong-kha-pa relates the usage of desire in the path to the general Great Vehicle process of heightening—through altruism and altruistic deeds (called "method" in the basic path-structure of wisdom and method)—the power of the wisdom-consciousness realizing emptiness so that it can overcome the obstructions to omniscience. Such relation of tantric practices to broader principles of spiritual development is an organizing feature of his exposition; it is what creates a sense of a unified system, replete with purpose and consistent in aim. He says:[a]

> As was explained before, the special cause of a form body is deity yoga, which is the main method [in Mantra]. That methods act as heighteners of the wisdom realizing emptiness is the system of both Great Vehicles. Shāntideva's *Engaging in the Bodhisattva Deeds* [IX.1] says:
>
>> The Subduer said that all these branches [of giving,
>> Ethics, and so forth] are for the sake of wisdom.

In the system of both the Perfection and the Mantra Vehicles, factors of method (altruistic motivation and the deeds that it induces) enhance the mind of wisdom realizing emptiness in order to strengthen it to the point where it can abandon the obstructions to omniscience. The early nineteenth-century Mongolian scholar Nga-wang-pel-den[b] explains that in the Perfection Vehicle, this is done through training in "limitless varieties of giving and so forth for a limitless time"—"limitless" referring to at least three periods of countless (that is, a very high number) great eons. In Mantra also, there is intense training in the perfections of giving and so forth but not in limitless varieties for a limitless time, since deity yoga speeds up the process. Tsong-kha-pa continues:

> The way that the path of wisdom is heightened through deity yoga is this: The special method and wisdom is deity yoga, that is, the appearance of one's chosen deity in the aspect of a father and mother union. Though Highest Yoga has many distinctive features in its path, it is called "tantra of union of the two" from this point of view, and in these tantras themselves there are a great many descriptions of deities in the aspect of union. From this approach one uses desire in the path and develops the essential of the meeting and staying together of the two minds of enlightenment [that is, drops of essential fluid of male and female that induce powerful bliss and subtler levels of mind]. In dependence on this, realization of emptiness is heightened.

---

[a] *Tantra in Tibet*, 157.

[b] *ngag dbang dpal ldan*, born 1797; *gsang chen rgyud sde bzhi'i sa lam gyi rnam bzhag rgyud gzhung gsal byed* (rgyud smad par khang edition, no other data), 13.3.

Tsong-kha-pa goes on to speak of all four tantra sets as using desire in the path:[a]

> Because the lower tantras lack this special method of using desire in the path, among the seven branches [complete enjoyment, union, great bliss, absence of inherent existence, compassion, uninterrupted continuity, and noncessation] the one of union is not taught in the three lower tantras. Still, because the lower tantras do use joy arising from smiling, gazing, and holding hands or embracing in the path, in general they do use desire for the attributes of the Desire Realm in the path.

By relating the practice of using desire in the path to the larger schema of method and wisdom, Tsong-kha-pa's exposition establishes coherence with the overall path structure.

However, it is not that all parts of his presentation are fused together in a totally coherent picture, although one is certainly beckoned to such a perception. For instance, in this case it is clear how desire for sexual union is used in the path in Highest Yoga Mantra through the route of creating a blissful state in which grosser levels of consciousness cease and subtler ones are manifested, but it is not clear *how* or *when* desire is used in the path in the three lower tantras. Tsong-kha-pa himself says that subtler levels of consciousness are not generated from the desire involved in gazing, smiling, and touching/embracing, and even though he affirms that desire is used in the path in Action, Performance, and Yoga Tantras, he does not say how this practice serves to heighten wisdom.

Nga-wang-pel-den reports a tradition among Tsong-kha-pa's followers that holds the blissful consciousnesses that are generated through the desirous activities of gazing, smiling, and embracing are used in realizing emptiness, even though they are not subtler levels of mind. In his *Presentation of the Grounds and Paths of the Four Great Secret Tantra Sets: Illumination of the Texts of Tantra* he says:[b]

> The three lower tantras involve using in the path the bliss

---

[a] *Tantra in Tibet*, 158.

[b] 7b.4ff. This passage is cited in my brief explication of this point in *Deity Yoga*, 211; I have taken the passage out of the debate format in order to present the material more directly.

> that arises upon looking at, smiling at, and holding hands or embracing a meditated Knowledge Woman [consort]; however, this is not done for the sake of generating a special subject [a subtle consciousness] realizing emptiness, for such is a distinguishing feature only of Highest Yoga Mantra. Nonetheless, most of [Tsong-kha-pa's] followers explain that this does not mean that the bliss [consciousness] that arises upon gazing, smiling, and so forth does not realize emptiness. Still, it must be examined whether or not there is a source clearly stating such in the eloquent elucidations of the great Foremost One [Tsong-kha-pa] himself.

It makes a great deal of sense that Action, Performance, and Yoga Tantras would call for using desire in the path in generating a blissful consciousness that realizes emptiness, since such a mind would be powerful even if not more subtle. However, it does not appear that any of these tantras or any of the Indian scholars who commented on the actual procedure of the path (as distinct from those who commented on Highest Yoga Tantras' depictions of the other tantra sets) or even Tsong-kha-pa in his *Great Exposition of Secret Mantra* ever details the procedure for doing this. In his expositions of the yogas of Action, Performance, and Yoga tantras, Tsong-kha-pa does not even hint at when such would be done; indeed, it is much to his credit that, despite having accepted this explanation from Highest Yoga Mantra that four types of desire are used in the path, when it comes actually to presenting their paths, he does not interpolate such practices into their expositions.

Nevertheless, the lack of such a practice in the source texts casts doubt on the usefulness of this system of ordering the four tantras by way of how desire is used in the path. Though there are many references to embrace in Yoga Tantras such as the *Compendium of Principles,* there seems to be little emphasis on gazing and smiling in Action and Performance Tantras, and the presentations of the paths of all three of these tantra sets by competent Indian scholars, as well as Tibetans, do not speak of a level of the path when such practice is enacted. Since this technique is the very means used in Ge-luk and other Tibetan traditions for ordering the four tantras sets, its absence in their path-structures is an unavoidable statement of the inadequacy of the schema, revealed thereby to be only an attempt by Highest Yoga Tantras—which do indeed employ such a technique—to create a hierarchy assigning the top rung to themselves.

This schema is indeed useful in drawing attention to the Highest Yoga Mantra claim to greatness through utilizing a more subtle and more powerful level of consciousness in the path, but I am suggesting that to understand and appreciate the paths of the other three tantras there is little evidence to warrant adoption of this interpretive grid from Highest Yoga Tantra, for it obscures their features by suggesting that they have as a principal feature a practice that they actually lack.

To return to explaining this fourfold schema: The four forms of desire correspond to four types of satisfaction of desire found in the various levels of the Desire Realm in Buddhist cosmology. Bu-tön[a] cites Vasubandhu's *Treasury of Manifest Knowledge*[b] and explains that:

- the gods of the Land of the Thirty-three[c] and all beings below them, including humans, gain desirous satisfaction through sexual union
- the gods of the Land Without Combat,[d] through embracing
- the gods of Joyous Land,[e] through holding hands
- the gods of the Land of Liking Emanation,[f] through smiling
- the gods of the Land of Controlling Others' Emanations,[g] through gazing.

Bu-tön goes on to explain that gods in the Form and Formless Realms dwell without desire for Desire Realm attributes, that is to say, attractive objects of the five senses:[h]

> The Perfection Vehicle was taught for the sake of taming persons free from desire, whereas Secret Mantra was

---

[a] *Extensive* version, 33.1.

[b] *chos mngon pa'i mdzod, abhidharmakośa,* stanza III.69cd; Leo M. Pruden, *Abhidharmakośabhāṣyam,* vol. 2 (Berkeley, Calif.: Asian Humanities Press, 1988), 465; Toh. 4089, 9b.2-9b.3; Sanskrit in *Bonpon Zō-Kan-Ei-Wayaku gappeki Abidatsuma kusharon honshō no kenkyū* (Kyoto: Nagata Bunshōdō, 1977), 454: *dvandvāliṅganapāṇyāptihasitekṣitamaithunāḥ //.*

[c] *sum cu rtsa gsum, trayastriṃśa.*

[d] *'thab bral, yāma.*

[e] *dga' ldan, tuṣita.*

[f] *'phrul dga', nirmāṇarati.*

[g] *gzhan 'phrul dbang byed, paranirmitavaśavartin.*

[h] *Extensive* version, 33.3.

taught for those desirous persons who could not be tamed by a path devoid of desire. As an antidote to desire that is satisfied through gazing—of those of the Land of Controlling Others' Emanations and so forth—Action Tantras that use in the path the bliss of joy that is satisfied through the god and goddess gazing at each other were set forth. The *Detailed Rite of Amoghapāsha*[a] [an Action Tantra] says, "The Supramundane Victor faces Bhṛkuṭī," and:

> He aims his eye to the right at the goddess Tārā, bashful and with bent body, [displaying] the seal of bestowing the supreme. On the left, Sundarī of the lotus lineage—bashful, according with the ways of Secret Mantra—aims her eye at Amoghapāsha.

Notice that Bu-tön cites only one tantra in the Action class that speaks of gazing, thereby begging the question of whether such occurs in a significant number of tantras classified as Action Tantras. Tsong-kha-pa,[b] obviously relying on Bu-tön, repeats his citations, as he does for the other three tantra sets, saying:[c]

> Furthermore, not only does Highest Yoga speak of smiling and so forth [as a way of identifying the four tantras], but so are individual instances [of these] in the lower tantra sets.

Tsong-kha-pa cites two Action Tantra passages from a single tantra, two Performance passages, and two Yoga (all taken from Bu-tön), and adds as a final comment, "These are only illustrations [of instances in these tantra sets that mention looking, and so forth]," thereby suggesting that there are a great many more. However, he neither cites them nor mentions such a practice in any way whatsoever during his presentation of the paths of Action, Performance, and Yoga Tantras.

Though Tsong-kha-pa repeats the longer passage from the *Detailed Rite of Amoghapāsha,* given just above, that Bu-tön cited, he does not repeat Bu-tön's explanation of it, presumably because he sees it to be faulty. (On the difference between Sūtra and Mantra

---

[a] *don yod pa'i zhags pa'i cho ga zhib mo'i rgyal po, amoghapāśakalparāja*; P365, vol. 8 (Toh. 13).

[b] *Tantra in Tibet,* 159.

[c] Ibid., 159.

and the difference between the four tantra sets Bu-tön is both his chief source and his chief object of criticism.) One problem is that Bu-tön apparently considers the gods of the Land of Controlling Others' Emanations, and so on, *themselves* to be the chief trainees of the four tantra sets. Tsong-kha-pa,[a] on the other hand, in commenting on Abhayākara's statement, "A tantra of smiling is, for instance, the bliss of those of the [realm of gods called] Liking Emanation," says:

> Such statements merely cite gods as examples; they do not teach that these gods are the chief trainees of the tantra sets.

For Tsong-kha-pa, persons who are able to use desire in the path in this way are the chief trainees of Action Tantra and so forth, whereas it seems that, for Bu-tön, the inhabitants of these godly realms themselves are the chief trainees.

Another problem is that Bu-tön associates the usage of the four joys—joy, supreme joy, special joy, and innate joy—with the four tantras, whereas, for Tsong-kha-pa, the four joys are associated with subtler levels of consciousness and thus are found only with the practice of Highest Yoga Mantra. As he says in his *Lamp Thoroughly Illuminating the Five Stages:*[b]

> Using desire for the attributes of the Desire Realm in the path for the purpose of generating a special subject [that is, a subtler consciousness] meditating on emptiness does not exist elsewhere than in Highest Yoga Mantra.

For Tsong-kha-pa, the four joys are a topic limited to Highest Yoga Mantra, and he finds nothing equivalent to them in the three lower tantras. Again, Bu-tön,[c] based on an explanation by Abhayākara, approvingly reports a tradition that cannot bear much analysis.

About Performance Tantra and so forth Bu-tön continues:

> As an antidote to desire that is satisfied through smiling—of those of the Land of Liking Emanation—Performance Tantras that use in the path the bliss of supreme joy satisfied

[a] Ibid., 161.

[b] As cited in Nga-wang-pel-den's *Presentation of the Grounds and Paths of the Four Great Secret Tantra Sets: Illumination of the Texts of Tantra,* 14.5.

[c] *Extensive* version, 35.4.

through god and goddess smiling at each other were set forth. The *Vairochanābhisambodhi* [a Performance Tantra] says:

> On the right the goddess called
> Buddhalochanā, one with
> A slightly smiling face.
> With a circle of light a full fathom,
> Her Unequalled body is most clear.
> She is the consort of Shākyamuni.

Or:

> Draw an Avalokiteshvara,
> Like a conch, a jasmine, and a moon,
> Hero, sitting on a white lotus seat.
> On his head sits Amitābha,
> His face is wonderfully smiling.
> On his right is the goddess Tārā
> Of wide renown, virtuous,
> And removing fright.

These citations do indeed speak of smiling, but I would expect to find as many instances of smiling in Action Tantras as can be found in Performance Tantras, and, indeed, some traditions of Highest Yoga Mantra reverse the order and associate smiling with Action Tantras and gazing with Performance Tantras. Even Bu-tön's first source, the *Saṃpuṭa Tantra*, cited above, has the order reversed, as do four of the five other sources that Tsong-kha-pa cites for the general framework,[a] indeed without comment. Given Tsong-kha-pa's critical acumen, I take his lack of comment, in the face of obvious counterevidence, to be an admission of the weakness of a tradition that he cannot explain away and yet must accept, because of the great psychological and spiritual profundity of Highest Yoga Mantra.

For Yoga Tantra, Bu-tön cites two passages:

> As an antidote to desire satisfied through holding hands—of those of the Joyous Land—Yoga Tantras that use in the path the bliss of special joy satisfied through god and goddess holding hands with each other were set forth. The

[a] *Tantra in Tibet,* 157-161.

Vajrashekhara says:[a]

> One's own goddess embraced in the center,[b]
> The goddess Vajrakilikilā,
> Turns her head toward the side.
> Smiling and gazing everywhere,
> She holds the hand of the Supramundane Victor.

and the *Tantra of the Supreme Original Buddha* says:[c]

> To his side is Mahāvajra
> Holding an arrow upright.
> His proud embracing hand raises
> A banner of victory [adorned] with monsters of the sea.

Whereas the Action Tantra citations speak of gazing ("The Supramundane Victor faces Bhṛkuṭī," "aims his eye," and "aims her eye") and the Performance Tantra passages speak of smiling ("A slightly smiling face" and "His face is wonderfully smiling"), Bu-tön supplies a Yoga Tantra passage that has all three—embrace ("goddess embraced in the center") as well as gazing and smiling ("Smiling and gazing everywhere"). The citation appropriately indicates the intensity of the usage of desire between male and female in the path in Yoga Tantra, as is confirmed by even a cursory reading of the chief root Tantra, the *Compendium of Principles*.

Bu-tön continues:

> As an antidote to desire satisfied through the union of the

---

[a] *gsang ba rnal 'byor chen po'i rgyud rdo rje rtse mo, vajraśekharamahāguhyayogatantra*; P113, vol. 5, 16.2.8 (Toh. 480).

[b] 34.3: *dbus 'khyud*. The word *dbus* most likely refers to the center, since the text, just prior to this citation, speaks of two goddesses to the right and two to the left of the main figure. The problematic nature of the word is reflected in three variant readings: Long-chen-pa's *Treasury of Tenets* (293.6) has *dpung khyud* which would be "shoulder embrace"; Bu-tön's *Brief Exposition* (vol. 14, 860.6) has *pus khyud* which would be "knee embrace"; Paṇ-chen Sö-nam-drak-pa (*General Presentation*, 31.6) has *mgos khyud* which would be "head embrace." The last is clearly trying to clear up the ambiguity of *dbus* which could mean "center" or could mean head (*dbu*) with an instrumental ending; Paṇ-chen Sö-nam-drak-pa obviously prefers the latter reading. However, it seems to me that the context of the tantra suggests "center."

[c] *dpal mchog dang po zhes bya ba theg pa chen po'i rtog pa'i rgyal po, śrīparamādyanāmamahāyānakalparājā*; P119, vol. 5 (Toh. 487).

two organs—of those of the Land of the Thirty-three and below—Great Yoga Tantras that use in the path bliss of innate joy satisfied through the god and goddess becoming absorbed with each other were set forth. The *Glorious Guhyasamāja Tantra* says:

> Meditate on Lochanā and so forth,
> Supreme consorts of the One-Gone-Thus.
> Through union of the two organs,
> The feat of Buddhahood will be attained.

and the *Saṃpuṭa Tantra* says:

> In union together with lady selfless,
> Through joyous absorption of the two with each other,
> There is what has the nature of wavelessness.

Tsong-kha-pa does not cite these last two passages, most likely because of his earlier explanation of how desire is used in the path in Highest Yoga Mantra, obviating the need for source-quotes here. As he says, the depiction of sexual union is replete throughout Highest Yoga Mantra,[a] and I do not question either this or the emphasis on embrace in Yoga Tantras; however, I wonder whether gazing and smiling are significant features of Action and Performance Tantras, and thus it seems difficult to confirm the value of this tradition toward providing a suitable grid for distinguishing the four tantra sets.

Four tantras and four levels of faculties

Bu-tön[b] cites a passage from the *Lady Sky-Traveler Vajra Tent Tantra* that aligns the four tantra sets with four increasingly high levels of trainees' capacities:

> Action Tantra is for the inferior.
> Yoga without activities [that is, Performance Tantra] is for those above them.
> The supreme Yoga is for supreme beings
> The Highest Yoga is for those above them.

---

[a] As cited earlier (339), "...in these tantras themselves there are a great many descriptions of deities in the aspect of union"; *Tantra in Tibet,* 158.

[b] *Extensive* version, 39.6-40.4.

Bu-tön cites a commentary on the *Vajrapañjara Tantra*[a] and then gives his own rendition of this tradition, obviously approving of it:

> A commentary says:
>
> > "Action Tantras" are for those intent on apprehending external deities such as Dung-ma[b] and who are intent on cleanliness, restraint, and so forth. "Yoga with activities" [as opposed to Performance Tantra, which is yoga without activities,] is to apprehend [a deity] external to oneself, whereas "Yoga [without activities, that is, Performance Tantra]" is to apprehend the Wisdom Being, who is one's own sovereign,[c] and oneself to be of one taste. "Supreme Yoga" is to partake of the great secrecy of the supreme bliss arisen from embracing one's Knowledge Woman. "Highest Yoga" is to apprehend the supreme bliss generated from the union of the vajra [phallus] of one's own divine self and the lotus [vagina].[d]
>
> Hence, persons of the bottom level of faculties, who are of low intelligence, take delight in external activities, such as bathing; for their sake, Action Tantras that teach activities of cleanliness upon apprehending an external painted figure and so forth to be a deity were set forth. Performance Tantras were set forth for persons superior to them, who partake of apprehending themselves as a deity and, in addition, a deity externally. Yoga Tantras were set forth for

---

[a] There are three commentaries—by Devakulamahāmati (P2326), by Kṛṣhṇapāda (P2325), and by Indrabodhi (P2324), the last being Indrabhūti according to the Tohoku catalogue.

[b] *brdungs ma.*

[c] *rang gi 'khor los bsgyur ba'i ye shes.*

[d] Bu-tön's own commentary, which follows, suggests that he reads this commentary differently than I do. He seems to take *bya ba'i rnal 'byor* (39.7) as referring to Performance Tantra, in which case it would have to be a corrupt reading for *bya min rnal 'byor,* and the next clause as referring to Yoga Tantra, since he speaks of Yoga Tantra as involving apprehension of oneself and the wisdom being as being of one taste. He then seems to take the next two clauses as referring to Highest Yoga Mantra. This is improbable, since "embrace" usually refers to Yoga Tantra. It also could be that he was not concerned with carefully making his exposition fit the quoted commentary.

> persons of intelligence sharper even than them, who mainly partake of just meditative stabilization in which oneself and the deity that is the Wisdom Being [the actual deity] are apprehended as of one taste. For the sake of persons of even sharper intelligence who partake of a special type of meditative stabilization of which there is none higher, Highest Yoga Tantras were set forth.

Bu-tön indicates that Action Tantras do not involve imagination of oneself as a deity, whereas Performance Tantras do, and Yoga Tantras take the further step of conceiving of oneself and the actual deity as being of one taste.

For Tsong-kha-pa these are fit to occur in Action Tantra, and thus these features cannot serve to distinguish the three lower tantras. Tsong-kha-pa cites the stanza from the *Vajrapañjara Tantra,* but despite not explicitly considering the validity either of its commentary or of Bu-tön's re-rendering of it, his opinion is clear both from the material that he has already considered and from a statement he makes at the end of his exposition of self-generation in Action Tantra:[a]

> [In connection with self-generation] it is suitable to perform the entry of the wisdom-being [that is, the dissolving of the actual deity into oneself imagined as that deity], conferring of initiation [on oneself by an invited initiation deity], seal implanting [the affixing of the seal or sign of the lineage through imagining the lineage lord at the crown of the head after initiation], and so forth as explained by other masters.

Also, the stanza closing the section in his presentation of Action Tantra indicates that reducing Action Tantra to external rites of bathing and so forth is a severe deprecation:

> If one claims to know the meaning of Action and Performance tantras
> By knowing a portion of their meditations and repetitions
> Such as fasting, bathing rites, and so forth, it is a source of laughter.
> Therefore, cherish arrangement of the tantra meanings into paths.

---

[a] *Deity Yoga,* 114.

Tsong-kha-pa's concern is with laying out Action Tantra in accordance with the expositions of its path by Buddhaguhya and Varabodhi, whereas Bu-tön, in self-contradiction, says that these tantras do not involve self-generation and yet gives Buddhaguhya's rendition of the Action Tantra path of meditation of oneself as a deity, and so forth.[a] Bu-tön obviously wanted to maintain the full richness of the tradition that he inherited, even by taking both sides of an issue. Tsong-kha-pa, living within the richness of tradition provided by Bu-tön, had the opportunity to sift through these traditions to creatively find an elegant, internally consistent system; Bu-tön's catalogue made this possible. Tsong-kha-pa passed this coherent world-view on to his followers, who for the most part grew, over the centuries, distant from the rich tradition of variant explanation that was their founder's context.

Tsong-kha-pa undoubtedly found the presentation put forth in this commentary on the *Vajrapañjara Tantra* inappropriate for describing the four levels of capacity and, instead, relates the four with levels of capacity for generating the emptiness and deity yogas that use desire in the path. Here is how I read the impact of his presentation:

> The tantric path centers around emptiness yoga and deity yoga, and practitioners have different needs or mind-sets in relation to successfully implementing these yogas. Those who make use of a great many external activities in actualizing emptiness and deity yogas are trainees of Action Tantra. Still, this does not mean that Action Tantra lacks yoga, for (as we have seen) it has a complex and powerful yoga for developing a meditative stabilization that is a union of calm abiding and special insight; rather, it means that the *main* trainees of Action Tantra *also* engage in many ritual activities such as bathing, for they find that these activities enhance their meditation.
>
> Those who equally perform external activities and internal meditative stabilization are trainees of Performance Tantra. Those who mainly rely on meditative stabilization and use only a few external activities are trainees of Yoga Tantra. Those who do not make use of external activities and yet have the capacity to generate the yoga of which

[a] *Extensive* version, 54.5-61.7.

> there is none higher are trainees of Highest Yoga Mantra.[a]

This division of the four tantra sets by way of the capacity of their main trainees refers to their *ability* to generate the main yogas—the emptiness and deity yogas—of their respective systems within, in Action Tantra, an emphasis on external activities; in Performance Tantra, balanced emphasis on external activities and internal meditative stabilization; in Yoga Tantra, emphasis on meditative stabilization; and in Highest Yoga Mantra, with no such external activities. Tsong-kha-pa says that the division is not made merely by way of persons who are *interested* in such paths, for some persons become interested in paths that they do not presently have a capacity to practice:[b]

> Also, though trainees in general are more, or less, interested in external activities and in cultivation of yoga, there are instances of interest in a path that does not fit a person's faculties; thus, the main trainees of the four tantra sets cannot be identified through interest.

Rather, it refers to their respective abilities. Giving his stamp of approval to this tradition, Tsong-kha-pa concludes by citing a passage in Tripiṭakamāla's *Lamp for the Three Modes* that Bu-tön cites for the same purpose:[c]

> Therefore, it should be realized that explanations of their main trainees as relying or not relying on many or few external activities and so forth are correct. Tripiṭakamāla's *Lamp for the Three Modes* says:
>
>> By the force of potencies from conditioning in another birth, some cannot attain mental equipoise without a home in the forest away from people, or without activities such as bathing, drawing maṇḍala, offering, burnt offerings, asceticism, and repetition [of mantra]. Thus, Action Tantras were taught for them. Also, there are those whose minds

---

[a] Since Highest Yoga Mantra does indeed involve a great deal of ritual, the point is perhaps that Highest Yoga Mantra does not emphasize ritual bathing and so forth in the way that Action Tantra and so forth do.

[b] *Tantra in Tibet,* 163.

[c] Ibid., 163-164. The citation from Tripiṭakamāla is P4530, vol. 81, 117.3.3-117.3.5. For Bu-tön's citation, see his *Extensive* version, 41.5-42.4.

> adhere to suchness and who through the power of faith achieve wisdom by means of activities set forth by the One-Gone-to-Bliss [Buddha]. They rely on activities, and for them Fundamental Tantras that do not have too many branches of activities were set forth.
>
> "Fundamental Tantras" are the same as Performance Tantras. Tantras are assigned as Action if they predominantly teach external activities even though they contain internal meditative stabilization.

Tsong-kha-pa interrupts the citation to explain that a tantra is assigned as an Action Tantra if it *predominantly* teaches external activities even though it contains internal meditative stabilization. He makes this point to counter a possible impression gained from Tripiṭakamāla's not explicitly mentioning the practice of meditative stabilization by Action Tantra trainees, although it is implicit to his explanation that they engage in external activities in order to gain mental equipoise. Tsong-kha-pa's explanation takes this distinction into account:[a]

> I will now explain the designation of the names of the four tantra sets in accordance with how these names are commonly known in the higher and lower tantra sets [as Action, Performance, Yoga, and Highest Yoga] and will thereby explain the difference of their trainees. The means of using such attributes of the desire realm in the path are the emptiness and deity yogas. Those who resort to a great many external activities in order to actualize these two yogas are trainees of Action Tantras. Those who balance their external activities and internal meditative stabilization without using very many activities are trainees of Performance Tantras. Those who mainly rely on meditative stabilization and resort to only a few external activities are trainees of Yoga Tantras. Those who do not rely on external activities and are able to generate the yoga of which there is none higher are trainees of Highest Yoga Tantras.

Tsong-kha-pa, speaking from the viewpoint of the pillars of what he has determined to be the general structure of the tantric

---

[a] *Tantra in Tibet*, 162.

systems, their emptiness and deity yogas, reshapes Tripiṭakamāla's and others' descriptions so that the *purposes* for which external activities are used—actualization of emptiness and deity yogas—are emphasized. Notice that even while approving this way of distinguishing the four tantras, he redefines it so that it fits more elegantly into a grand schematization of the path.

I would add that although *many* Action Tantras involve a plethora of external activities, not just Action Tantras but also the other three types of tantras involve withdrawal into solitude for meditation as well as many "activities such as bathing, drawing maṇḍala, offering, burnt offerings, asceticism, and repetition [of mantra]." Also, and more significantly, an Action Tantra such as the *Concentration Continuation* (which even though a continuation of the *Vajraviḍāraṇa*, is a separate tantra) is mainly, and even *solely* concerned with meditative stabilization—yoga—as we have seen in elaborate detail. Furthermore, Tsong-kha-pa's own exposition of Action Tantra is mainly concerned with the stages of meditative stabilization.

It seems to me that these classificatory systems are employed in Highest Yoga Tantras to put themselves at the top of the list and to draw attention to what are indeed special features of their yoga. It may be helpful not to accept these schemes without considerable reservation, since they blind us to the richness of the yogas found, for instance, in the *Concentration Continuation*. For, it appears that except for Highest Yoga Tantras, the tantras of what came to be assigned as Action, Performance, and Yoga do not identify themselves as such.

Tsong-kha-pa goes on to quote Tripiṭakamāla's *Lamp for the Three Modes* which, in his citation, refers to Yoga Tantras as "Performance Tantras":[a]

> For the sake of others who are interested solely in meditation on nondual suchness and consider groups of many activities to be distracting, Performance Tantras[b] that mainly

---

[a] My translation here improves on that in *Tantra in Tibet*, 163-164.

[b] The Ngawang Gelek edition of Tsong-kha-pa's text (79.3) reads *ston par mdzad pa'i* ***spyod pa'i*** *rgyud*, and Bu-tön's *Extensive* version (42.2) has the same reading, but the Peking edition of Tripiṭakamāla's text (P4530, vol. 81, 117.3.5) reads *ston par mdzad pa'i rgyud*, omitting the term "Performance," thus merely saying, "Tantras that mainly employ yoga and secondarily teach only a few branches of activities were set forth." The Peking version obviates the need for Tsong-kha-pa's subse-

> employ yoga and secondarily teach only a few branches of activities were set forth.

Tsong-kha-pa adds, "Here, 'Performance Tantras' means Yoga Tantras."

The claim is that Yoga Tantras involve fewer external activities than Performance Tantras, and perhaps analysis will show that the *Vairochanābhisambodhi Tantra,* widely recognized as the chief Performance Tantra, does call for more external activities than the *Compendium of Principles,* the chief Yoga Tantra. Whatever the case, it is clear that Tsong-kha-pa's own expositions of Performance and Yoga Tantra in his *Great Exposition of Secret Mantra* do not reflect any such orientation, and it is a tribute to his scholarship that he does not allow this ordering of the four tantras to become an interpretive grid that distorts his presentations of their paths. Much like Bu-tön on many other occasions, he mentions the tradition and then does not let it interfere with his exposition. Consistency and coherence—the hallmarks of his own approach—were, it seems, sacrificed here.

With regard to Highest Yoga Mantra, Tsong-kha-pa does not cite Tripiṭakamāla's *Lamp for the Three Modes,* an omission suggesting disagreement, given that he cited that text as a source for his explanation of the other three tantras. Let us cite what Tripiṭakamāla says:[a]

> Also, for those great beings who are included in that lineage and who, through the force of conditioning in other births, do not partake of dualistic discriminations with respect to any activities and any things, the Supramundane Victor set forth the tantras of the Great Yoga, the foremost of all tantras, without prescribing specific activities and also not prohibiting doing anything or acting in any way.

As was seen above, for Tsong-kha-pa Highest Yoga Mantra has a specific way of utilizing afflictive emotions in the path; thus, the suggestion here that nothing is prohibited was perhaps objectionable since it does not take into account the specific context of the usage of desire and so forth in the path. About Highest Yoga

---

quent remark (which I mention just after the quote) that "Performance Tantras" means Yoga Tantras.

[a] P4530, vol. 81, 117.3.7.

Mantra, Tsong-kha-pa himself says:[a]

> Those who do not rely on external activities and are able to generate the yoga of which there is none higher are trainees of Highest Yoga Tantras.

His version is more symmetrical in that it extends the movement from "a great many external activities" in Action Tantra, to "without using very many activities" in Performance Tantra, to "only a few branches of activities" in Yoga Tantra, and now to nonreliance on external activities in Highest Yoga Tantra.

Since the rituals of initiation and the conduct of meditation retreats in Highest Yoga Tantra contain many external activities, this explanation that associates it solely with internal yoga seems aimed merely at pointing out that Highest Yoga Tantra has a distinctive yoga for manifesting the fundamental innate mind of clear light through using desire for sexual union in the path.

Summarizing Tsong-kha-pa's position

Utilizing two of Bu-tön's nine ways of distinguishing the four tantra sets, Tsong-kha-pa differentiates them by way of their main trainees as four very different types, since these trainees have (1) four different ways of using desire for the attributes of the Desire Realm in the path and (2) four different levels of capacity for generating emptiness and deity yogas that use desire in the path. As Long-döl Nga-wang-lo-sang says in his verse summary of Tsong-kha-pa's *Great Exposition of Secret Mantra:*[b]

> The effect Secret Mantra Vehicle is of four types—
> Action Tantra, Performance Tantra,
> Yoga Tantra, and Highest Yoga Tantra.
> Hence how are they differentiated?
> Though there are many assertions by scholars such as Bu-tön,
> Our own system is that they are posited by way of using the attributes of the Desire Realm in the path.
> That using in the path the bliss of gazing at the beautiful face

[a] *Tantra in Tibet,* 162.

[b] *Terminology Arising in Secret Mantra, the Scriptural Collections of the Knowledge Bearers,* 95.4ff.

Of one's own meditated goddess is Action Tantra.
That using in the path the bliss of smiling is Performance Tantra.
That using in the path the bliss of holding hands is Yoga Tantra.
That using in the path the bliss of union of the two is Highest Yoga.
According to the etymologies of the four tantra sets,
That mainly performing external activities is called Action Tantra.
That equally performing external and internal activities is called Performance Tantra.
That mainly practicing internal yoga is called Yoga Tantra.
That whose yoga has none higher is called Highest Yoga.

According to Tsong-kha-pa and his followers, the four tantras are not differentiated (1) by way of their *object of intent* since all four are aimed at bringing about others' welfare, or (2) by way of the *object of attainment* they are seeking since all four seek the full enlightenment of Buddhahood, or (3) by way of merely having different types of *deity yoga* since all four tantra sets have many different types of deity yoga but are each only one tantra set. Rather, the distinctive tantric practice of deity yoga, motivated by great compassion and beginning with emptiness yoga, is carried out in different ways in the four tantra sets. Various levels of desire—involved in gazing, smiling, touching, and sexual union—are utilized by the respective main trainees in accordance with their predispositions toward styles of practice—emphasizing external activities, balancing external activities and meditative stabilization, emphasizing meditative stabilization, or exclusively focusing on meditative stabilization.

The techniques are geared to the levels of capacity of trainees not only in terms of the degree of desire used in the path but also in terms of whether an actual consort is used. Tsong-kha-pa holds that in Action, Performance, and Yoga Tantras consorts are only imagined, whereas in Highest Yoga Mantra actual consorts are used. Speaking about the three lower tantras, he says:[a]

In the lower tantra sets this is not done while observing an

[a] *Tantra in Tibet*, 161.

> external Seal [an actual consort], and even in the higher tantra set [Highest Yoga] it is not indicated that such is done [in the lower tantras], due to which these should be understood as meditated goddesses, such as Lochanā.
>
> Based on the thought that trainees of little power cannot use great desire in the path, desire is taught for use in the path in stages beginning with the small. As will be explained, it is clear that when deity yoga has become firm and meditative stabilization on emptiness has been attained, one takes cognizance of a goddess, such as Lochanā, who is of one's own lineage, and then uses [desire in the path by way of gazing and so forth].

He clearly says that the use of a consort, either in imagination or in fact, is begun only when a practitioner has achieved proficiency in emptiness yoga and deity yoga.

This is a far cry from many traditions that depict Mantra as being for persons of crude emotions. Still, since initiations into Highest Yoga Mantra are sometimes given publicly, the attendees (including many who have achieved little, if any, success in meditating on emptiness) are required to perform daily meditation rituals that involve imagination of a consort. Such unqualified practice of Mantra is apologetically explained as being for the sake of establishing predispositions for actual practice in future lifetimes, but it may also be explained as a social, economic, and political technique for drawing persons by means of a mysterious ritual into a group that owes allegiance to a particular lama.

Though Tsong-kha-pa's reasoned presentation is effective in creating a world-view of gradual spiritual transformation that itself exerts an influence on those who comprehend its structure, his followers have also accommodated the system to more common aims. A dual system of high systemization with practical implementation by a limited few and of low accommodation to social, economic, and political spheres is as much a part of this sect as it is of others in Tibet.

Appendix: The First Paṇ-chen Lama's Reformulation of Tsong-kha-pa's Presentation of the Vehicles translated by Donald S. Lopez

Presentation of the General Teaching and the Four Sets of Tantras, Based on Notes[a]

Paṇ-chen Lama I
Lo-sang-chö-kyi-gyel-tsen (*Blo bzang chos kyi rgyal mtshan*, 1570-1662)

Namo Gurumañjughoṣāyā

May the supreme captains prevail in releasing
The collections of transmigrators into the jeweled land of liberation
Through the pleasing manifestation in saffron
Of the wisdom, compassion, and knowledge of all the buddhas.

May I be sustained by the pervasive master,
Lord of the maṇḍala, base of all that is pure—stable and moving—
Through the play of the magical emanations of union,
Like a rainbow in the vast sky of clear light.

I bow down to the glorious king of the mighty;
Hearing and remembering just his name grants the supreme fearlessness
That eradicates the pangs of saṃsāra and solitary peace.
Armies of inner and outer demons, take heed.

I will carefully set forth discourses related with that good explanation,

---

[a] The edition of the text translated here is *Bstan pa spyi dang rgyud sde bzhi'i rnam gzhag zin bris su byas pa* in Blo bzang chos kyi rgyal mtshan, *Collected Works*, vol. 4 (*nga*) (New Delhi: Mongolian Lama Gurudeva, 1973). The portion translated here ends at 20a3; the text ends at 37a6. Students of the First Paṇ chen Lama took notes on his lectures on Tsong kha pa's *Great Exposition of Secret Mantra*. The students then presented the notes to him with a request that he correct and complete them. In response, he produced this work.

Supreme key unlocking the treasury
Of all the countless scriptures of the Conqueror.
It is right that fortunate seekers listen.

The place of entry for those wishing for liberation is only the Conqueror's teaching

Mātṛceta and Dignāga's *Interwoven Praise* (*Miśrakastotra*) says:

> I abide in the ocean of saṃsāra of limitless depth.
> The powerful sea serpents of desire devour my body.
> Where will I go for refuge now?
>
> If one is intelligent, one will go for refuge
> To someone utterly without fault,
> Who abides in all good qualities in every way.
> It is proper to praise him, honor him, and abide in his teaching.[a]

The different doors that are stages of entry into the teaching

This section has two parts: a general presentation of the vehicles and the divisions of the Mahāyāna.

General presentation of the vehicles

The Hearer Vehicle, the Solitary Realizer Vehicle, and the Mahāyāna are divided in this way because there are two types of disciples: [1] those who bear the lineage of seeking pacification of just the suffering of saṃsāra—a low object of attainment—for themselves alone, their object of intention, and [2] those who bear the lineage of seeking the state of a perfect buddha—the supreme object of attainment—for the sake of all beings, their object of intention. There are also two path vehicles causing them to proceed to those states when the two types of disciples aim for their [fruitional] vehicle in accordance with their thought. Due to [there being two types of disciples and two types of paths,] two vehicles are posited: Hīnayāna and Mahāyāna. The doctrine spoken for these two disciples is also twofold: the Hīnayāna and Mahāyāna scriptural collections (*piṭaka*). Maitreya's *Ornament for the Mahāyāna Sūtras* (*Mahāyānasūtrālaṃkāra* XI.1) says:

---

[a] P2041, vol. 46, 87.5.2-6.

> The collections of the scriptures are either three or two.
> For nine reasons [three] are asserted.
> Due to inclusion [they are called collections].[a]

There is no contradiction in dividing the vehicles into two [Hīnayāna and Mahāyāna] or three. The vehicles are divided into three—Hearer Vehicle, Solitary Realizer Vehicle, and Mahāyāna—because among Hīnayāna disciples, those of superior faculties [Solitary Realizers] are able and those of inferior faculties [Hearers] are unable to extend their cultivation of the path [for one hundred eons]. Also, there is a difference in the superiority and inferiority of their fruition. Although Hearers and Solitary Realizers differ in faculty and fruition, it is said in Asaṅga's *Actuality of the Levels* (*Bhūmivastu*) that the presentation of their paths is for the most part similar. Still, there is no difference with respect to Hearer and Solitary Realizer learners' meditation: realization of the selflessness of persons, the antidote to the conception of self that is the root of saṃsāra. The Vaibhāṣikas, Sautrāntikas, Cittamātrins, and some Madhyamakas assert that realizing the person as empty of substantial existence and self-sufficiency is the meaning of fully realizing the selflessness of the person. The three former schools assert that Hearers and Solitary Realizers do not have an object of meditation of selflessness which exceeds that. The two Hearer [Hīnayāna] schools assert that even for Mahāyānists [as described by those schools] there is no object of meditation exceeding that selflessness.

Some Svātantrika-Madhyamakas assert three modes of realizing selflessness: [1] Hearers realize the selflessness of the person, [2] Solitary Realizers realize the emptiness of duality with respect to forms and their apprehenders, which is a negation of external objects, [3] Mahāyānists realize the emptiness of true existence of all phenomena.

The [Prāsaṅgika] masters Buddhapālita, Śāntideva, and Candrakīrti assert that as long as one does not understand all phenomena to be empty of intrinsic nature, then a realization of the full character of the selflessness of the person has not occurred. Through realizing that the person is empty of self-sufficiency or substantial existence and empty of being a permanent, single, independent self, one is not able to abandon, even in the least, the

[a] P5521, vol. 108, 8.1.6.

seeds of the conception of self that is the root of saṃsāra. This is true no matter how much one cultivates what has been realized. Therefore, they assert that all three superior beings (*āryan*) necessarily either are directly realizing or have directly experienced the subtle selflessness of phenomena. Just this is the flawless thought of the protector Nāgārjuna. Since this is established by hundreds of reasonings, our own system is presented in this way.

[Maitreya's *Ornament for the Realizations* (*Abhisamayālaṃkāra*)] says:

> Production of the aspiration to enlightenment is the wish for
> Complete enlightenment for others' welfare.

Just the training in the practices—the six perfections—after having produced the aspiration—the wish for the supreme of enlightenments for the sake of the objects of intention, all sentient beings—is the basic structure of the path of Mahāyānists in general. For it is said many times in the tantra sets that those training in the Vajrayāna must also engage in these. The body of the general path for the followers of the Perfection Vehicle is just this.

With respect to the Perfection Vehicle, there are two types from the perspective of view: Madhyamaka and Cittamātra, but separate vehicles are not posited. The chief disciples who are the intended objects of the Perfection Vehicle have the Madhyamaka lineage, whereas those with the Cittamātra lineage are the ordinary disciples.

Although the Mahāyāna thus has two views—Madhyamaka and Cittamātra—whoever holds the Madhyamaka view is not necessarily a Mahāyānist, because the view of Hearer and Solitary Realizer superiors is that of Madhyamaka. Therefore, the Hearers among the four schools of tenets and the Hearers in the division [of followers of the Hīnayāna] into two—Hearers and Solitary Realizers—are similar in name but completely different in meaning. The eighteen [Hīnayāna] schools are designated Hearers because they do not accept the Mahāyāna as the word of the Buddha and, within accepting only the scriptural collections of Hearers as the word of the Buddha, propound tenets following those texts. This is so even though they might not enter the Hearer path and make effort to attain the Hearer enlightenment.

When the Mahāyāna is divided by way of the speed or slowness of traversing the path, there are five types: two traveling as if by ox chariot and elephant chariot, one traveling as if by the sun and moon, and two traveling as if by the magical emanations of Hearers and Solitary Realizers or of buddhas. For, the *Introduction to the Forms of Definite and Indefinite Progress Sūtra* (*Niyatāniyatagatimudrāvatāra*) says that there are these five.

Although those having the Hearer and Solitary Realizer lineages do not make effort on their own path for the purpose of attaining buddhahood, their paths should not be held as hindrances to becoming fully enlightened, because their paths were taught as a means of establishing these persons in buddhahood. The *Saṃpuṭa Tantra* says:

> Through many doctrines
> There is one liberation,
> Just as by the flow of rivers, there is the sea.
> Therefore, many [forms of liberation] are not observed.

Also, the *Expression of the Ultimate Names of the Wisdom Being Mañjuśrī* (*Mañjuśrījñānasattvasyaparamārthanāmasaṃgīti*) says:

> The deliverance of the three vehicles
> Abides in the fruition of one vehicle.[a]

Divisions of the Mahāyāna

This section has two parts: the division of the Mahāyāna into two and a detailed explanation of the divisions of entry into the Vajra Vehicle.

Division of the Mahāyāna into two

This section has three parts: number of divisions, meaning of the individual divisions, and the reason for the division.

Number of divisions

Śraddhākaravarma's *Introduction to the Meaning of Highest Yoga Tantra* (*Yogānuttaratantrārthāvatāra*) says, "There are also two bodhisattva vehicles, a vehicle of the stages and perfections and a Secret Mantra Effect Vajra Vehicle."[b] Mantra Vehicle (*mantrayāna*),

[a] Textual note at 4b2: the Peking edition reads *theg pa gsum gyi nges 'byung ni.*

[b] P4536, vol. 81, 154.5.7.

Secret Mantra Vehicle (*guhyamantrayāna*), Effect Vehicle (*phala-yāna*), Vajra Vehicle (*vajrayāna*), Method Vehicle (*upāyayāna*), and vehicle of becoming purified through a path involving desire are synonyms. Similarly, the Perfection Vehicle is also called the vehicle of becoming fully purified by a path free from desire and the Cause Vehicle (*hetuyāna*). The *Sūtra Revealing the Secret*, as quoted in Jñānaśrī's *Eradication of the Two Extremes in the Vajra Vehicle* (*Vajrayā-nakoṭidvayāpoha*), says:

> When the wheel of the causal doctrine,
> Connected to causes, has been completely turned,
> The Effect Vehicle, the short path,
> Will arise at a future time.[a]

Similarly, in mantra texts it is also called the scriptural collections of the knowledge bearers (*vidyādhārapiṭaka*) and sets of tantras (*tantrānta*).

Meaning of the individual divisions

Secret Mantra Vehicle
There is a reason for calling the spontaneous Cause-Effect Vehicle or Mantra Vehicle, "Secret Mantra," because it is secret to those who are not vessels of it and is achieved in a hidden manner. Also, it is called mantra, meaning "mind protector," because *man* in the Sanskrit word *mantra* means "mind," and *trāya* means "protection." The continuation of the *Guhyasamāja Tantra* says:

> Minds arise through the cause
> Of a sense and an object.
> That mind is said to be *man*.
> The meaning of *trā* is protector.[b]

The Mantra Vehicle is called a vehicle because of meaning progression. When divided, there are two: cause vehicle or that by which one progresses, and Effect Vehicle or that to which one progresses.

Effect Vehicle
The Mantra Vehicle is also called the Effect Vehicle because it is a vehicle, or means of progressing, that involves cultivating a path

---

[a] P4537, vol. 81, 159.3.4

[b] 69c-70b; P81, vol. 3, 200.4.2.

according in aspect with the four complete purities of buddhahood, the effect. Śraddhākaravarma's *Introduction to the Meaning of Highest Yoga Tantra* says, "It is called 'effect' because of having the mode of completely pure body, resources, abode, and deeds."

Vajra Vehicle

The Mantra Vehicle is called the Vajra Vehicle because of being a vehicle that is a means of progress depending on the Vajrasattva yoga of inseparable method and wisdom. Ratnākaraśānti's *Handful of Flowers, Explanation of the Guhyasamāja Tantra* (*Kusumāñjaliguhyasamājanibandha*) says, "With regard to being called the Vajra Vehicle, that which includes all the Mahāyāna is the six perfections. That which includes them is method and wisdom. That which includes them as one taste is the mind of enlightenment. That is the Vajrasattva samādhi; just this is a vajra. Because it is both a vajra and a vehicle, it is the Vajra Vehicle, the Mantra Vehicle." From the point of view of its internal divisions, there are two [Vajra] vehicles, cause and effect.

Others [wrongly] assert that the meaning of Vajra Vehicle is indicated by a passage in the *Stainless Light* (*Vimalaprabhā*), which says, "Vajra is the unchangeable and the great unbreakable. Just that Mahāyāna is the Vajra Vehicle. It is the union in one taste of the mantra mode and the perfection mode, having the nature of effect and cause [respectively]." Their assertion is not correct because the names and meanings used in that passage refer to an undifferentiability of the two, a form body that is empty [of matter] and the supreme immutable bliss, and such does not apply to the lower sets of tantras. The *Brief Explication of Initiations* (*Śekhoddeśa*), says:

> The cause is that which holds the form of emptiness.
> The fruition holds unchangeable compassion.
> Emptiness and compassion inseparable
> Are described as the mind of enlightenment.

Method Vehicle

The Mantra Vehicle is called the Method Vehicle because of being a vehicle that surpasses the Perfection Vehicle by way of many skillful methods.

Sets of Tantras

There is a reason for calling the scriptural collections of the knowledge bearers "tantra sets" [literally, "continuum sets"]. For, the objects of discussion, the meaning tantras, are called tantras in the sense of being continuous, and the scriptural collections of the knowledge bearers take these as their main objects of discussion. In this way, the name of the object of discussion [tantra] is designated to the means of discussion [the scripture]. Also, because the scriptural collections of the knowledge bearers are collections of tantras, they are called "sets." The continuation of the *Guhyasamāja Tantra* says, "Tantra is known as 'continuum.'"[a]

Scriptural Collections of the Knowledge Bearers

There is a reason for calling the sets of tantras the scriptural collections of the knowledge bearers, because Buddhaguhya's *Condensation of the Questions of Subāhu Tantra* (*Subhāhuparipṛcchānāmatantrapiṇḍārtha*) says that they are so called due to teaching points of training and tenets of the bearers of the knowledge mantras.

In which scriptural collection are the tantra sets included? Śraddhākaravarma's *Introduction to the Meaning of Highest Yoga Tantra* explains one way of including them in the three scriptural collections, as well as a second way of making them a fourth scriptural collection.[b] However, Ratnākaraśānti's explanation of them as the scriptural collection of the sets of discourses (*sūtrānta*) due to teaching condensed profound meanings is good, because [the *Questions of Subāhu Tantra* says], "Listen and I will expound in the mode of the Secret Mantra sets of discourses." Furthermore, [the term] "sets of discourses" is mentioned many times in the tantras. The master Abhayākara's assertion of a way to include them in all scriptural collections is also good because, although from the viewpoint of entity they are assigned to the sets of discourses, when divided from the viewpoint of internal divisions, there are also portions of the other two scriptural collections.

Cause Vehicle

There is a reason for calling the Perfection Vehicle the Cause Vehicle, because it is a vehicle distinguished by not having a path of

---

[a] P81, vol. 3, 200.1.2-4.

[b] P4536, vol. 81, 155.2.3-7.

meditation according in aspect with the four complete purities of buddhahood, the fruition, and by having the creation of the aspiration to enlightenment as the basis of its deeds and only training in the six perfections as its deeds.

The reason for dividing the Mahāyāna into the Perfection and Mantra vehicles

They are not posited as separate vehicles based on the sharpness and dullness of faculties or the superiority or inferiority of the disciples for whose sake the two vehicles were set forth, because if they were, there would be the fallacy of having to posit the four sets of tantras as four vehicles.

Perfection and Mantra are not posited as separate vehicles from the point of view of quick or slow progress on the path. Since it was said that even in the Perfection Vehicle there are five [types of disciples] when divided by way of speed on the path, there would be the fallacy of having to present the Perfection Vehicle alone as five vehicles.

They are not posited as separate vehicles from having or not having the training in the aspiration to enlightenment as the intention and the six perfections as the deeds, because both Mahāyānists [of Perfection and Mantra] similarly train in those.

They are not posited as separate vehicles from the standpoint of the view, because even the Vajra Vehicle does not have a view superior to that determined in the protector Nāgārjuna's *Treatise on the Middle Way* (*Madhyamakaśāstra*). If they were, one would also have to present Madhyamaka and Cittamātra as two vehicles since they have different views.

Perfection and Mantra are not posited as separate vehicles from the standpoint of superior and inferior fruition because both Mahāyānists are similar in asserting the final fruition as a buddha who has extinguished all faults and fulfilled all attainments.

From which viewpoint are Perfection and Mantra posited as separate vehicles? Regarding this, the early and recent vajra masters of Tibet commonly [but mistakenly] follow Tripiṭakamāla's *Lamp for the Three Modes* (*Nayatrayapradīpa*), where it says:

> Even if the aim is the same, the Mantra Vehicle
> Is superior due to nonobscuration,
> Many skillful methods, nondifficulty, and

Being designed for those of sharp faculties.[a]

[According to their misunderstanding,] even though the three—the object of realization which is the *dharmadhātu,* the final fruition, and the mind of enlightenment which achieves that fruition—are the same, the Vajra Vehicle is superior to the Perfection Vehicles in four skillful methods because of having the features of: [1] nonobscuration regarding the view, or the object of realization, [2] many skillful methods, [3] achieving the mind of enlightenment quickly without difficulty, and [4] sharp faculties in terms of speed.

It possesses the first feature because the followers of the Perfection Vehicle realize the nature of phenomena through examples, proofs, and so forth, whereas here in the Vajra Vehicle there is superiority by way of nonobscuration in view through directly realizing emptiness—actually generating wisdom at the time of the descent of wisdom and the third initiation.

The Vajra Vehicle is superior by way of many skillful methods because of having many superior skillful methods for achieving temporary fruitions and for achieving the final fruition. For, those of the Perfection Vehicle achieve the temporary fruitions of great resources, long life, the increase of wisdom, and so forth by the methods of giving and so forth, whereas here in the Vajra Vehicle there are many means of achievement, such as Jambhala [a god of wealth] and Vasudhārā [a goddess of wealth], and so forth, and these are achieved without difficulty and quickly. Achievement of these temporary fruitions becomes an aid in quickly achieving enlightenment; thereby, the Vajra Vehicle is superior through having many skillful methods for achieving temporary fruitions.

The Vajra Vehicle is superior through having many skillful methods for achieving the final fruition because of being superior from the viewpoint of ultimate truths—the profound—and conventional truths—the vast. Regarding ultimate truths, the profound, although the followers of the Perfection Vehicle believe that "All phenomena are free of conceptual elaborations," they do not realize them in that way. However, here in the Vajra Vehicle, when *māntrikas* cultivate even the stage of generation, they meditate on the sixteen arms [of the deity] as sixteen emptinesses. Likewise, during the stage of completion, they meditate in the context of realizing emptiness directly through many methods, such as *caṇḍalī*

---

[a] P4530, vol. 81, 115.2.5-6; commentary through 118.2.6

[inner heat meditation] and so forth.

The Vajra Vehicle is superior in terms of conventional truths, the vast, through realization of vast conventionalities, such as the creation of worldly realms, and vast deeds—the performance of the three deeds [in the practice of sexual union]. The Vajra Vehicle is superior in terms of not being difficult, because those of the Perfection Vehicle progress on the path through severe asceticism and hardship, whereas here in the Vajra Vehicle progress on the path is made through blissful deeds. It is superior in terms of faculties, because the disciples who are the intended objects of the Perfection Vehicle actualize the fruition—even at the fastest—in three countless eons, but here in the Vajra Vehicle it is asserted that the best actualize the fruition in this lifetime, the middling in the intermediate state, and the low within sixteen lifetimes. Therefore, they assert that Perfection and Mantra are posited as separate vehicles from the viewpoint of having or not having four features.

The first feature is not correct, because the two do not differ from the standpoint of having or not having the view in terms of the object of realization [emptiness], for it is as Sa skya Paṇḍita's *Differentiation of the Three Vows* (*Sdom gsum rab dbye*) says:

> In Secret Mantra and Perfection
> A difference of view is not set forth.

The second feature is not correct, because the acquisition of resources by followers of the Perfection Vehicle through giving gifts and so forth and the acquisition of resources here in the Mantra Vehicle from the viewpoint of achieving Jambhala [in meditation] are similar in equally being aids for achieving enlightenment if the two practices are conjoined with extraordinary method and wisdom. They are also similar in equally not becoming aids if they are not so conjoined. The fourth feature is not correct because of not applying to the three lower tantric sets.[a] Furthermore, [regarding the third feature,] it is not correct that the mantra Vehicle is superior from the viewpoint of having or not having difficulty because the *Pile of Jewels Sūtra* (*Ratnakūṭa*) says that the revered protector Maitreya actualized the fruition by way of blissful paths and blissful engagement on the Perfection Vehicle's own path.

It is not correct to assert that one is following this passage in

[a] Textual note 8b.5: the text reads, "The third feature is not correct" but means that the fourth feature is not correct.

Tripiṭakamāla's *Lamp for the Three Modes* but then assert its meaning in this way, because of entailing the fault of contradicting the assertions in the *Lamp for the Three Modes* as well as its commentary by Paṇḍita Smṛti [also known as Jñānakīrti and Smṛtijñānakīrti].

Then what is the master Tripiṭakamāla's own explanation? According to Tripiṭakamāla, even though the goal [buddhahood] which is the object of attainment of Secret Mantra and Perfection is the same, the Mantra Vehicle is superior to the Perfection Vehicle by way of four features: [1] nonobscuration, [2] many methods, [3] ease, [4] sharp faculties. It is superior by way of nonobscuration because those of the Perfection Vehicle do not have very obscured faculties due to engaging in giving and so forth in which the three spheres [of agent, action, and object] are thoroughly purified, but do not have sharp faculties because of engaging in giving away one's own head and so forth. Giving away one's own head and so forth is not a perfection of giving and does not fulfill the intention of the creation of the aspiration to enlightenment. Here, in the Mantra Vehicle, *māntrikas,* due to having sharp faculties, look down on that method and fulfill all six perfections completely through the samādhi of nondual method and wisdom.

[According to Tripiṭakamāla,] the Mantra Vehicle is superior by way of having more methods, for the Perfection Vehicle is not able to accommodate all sentient beings, since its followers one-sidedly perform peaceful [practices] such as asceticism, vows, and disciplines, whereas here in the Mantra Vehicle, the four sets of tantras were set forth as means of accommodating all sentient beings. Also, [*māntrikas*] abandon the five poisons by skillful methods, transmuting the five poisons and so forth into the five tathāgata lineages. It is superior from the viewpoint of difficulty or ease because difficulty and ease are posited from the viewpoint of one's own mind, and here in the Mantra Vehicle, one achieves a blissful fruition by means of a blissful path in accordance with one's own desire. Also, from among the two types of special disciples of Highest Yoga Tantra who have the best faculties—those desiring and not desiring the Desire Realm attributes of a knowledge woman—the latter were taught the Great Seal (*mahāmudrā*), the wisdom of nonduality. With respect to the first [those desiring a knowledge woman], there are two types, those desiring and not desiring an external knowledge woman; a wisdom seal (*jñānamudrā*) was taught for the latter whereas as pledge seal (*samayamudrā*) or action seal (*karmamudrā*) was taught for the former. A Tibetan lama's assertion of this [description by Tripiṭakamāla] and his assertion that the special disciples of Highest Yoga Tantra who have the best faculties must greatly desire the Desire Realm attributes of an external knowledge woman are contradictory.

[According to Tripiṭakamāla,] Mantra's feature of [its disciples having] sharp faculties is correct because the yogins of the four noble truths have very dull faculties due to being obscured with regard to suchness, whereas the followers of the Perfection Vehicle have middling faculties due to being mistaken with regard to method. The followers of the Vajra Vehicle, however, have very sharp faculties due to not being obscured with regard to anything and thoroughly transform through skillful methods even that which, if used by others, would cause them to go to a bad rebirth. That is the assertion of this master [Tripiṭakamāla] and the master Jñānakīrti.

These [positions] appear to require analysis because the followers of the Perfection Vehicle do not assert that the mere fulfillment of the wishes of sentient beings through giving away one's head is a perfection of giving. For, they assert that a perfection of giving is fulfilled through becoming completely accustomed to the thought of giving. Also, nondual wisdom is the life of the path of the Perfection Vehicle.

The explanation that yogins of the four noble truths do not know suchness is not correct because of involving either an inconclusive or nonestablished reason. If the feature of sharpness of faculties is taken as meaning nonobscuration with respect to method, it would be a repetition of the first [feature of nonobscuration]. Nevertheless, if the feature of sharpness of faculties is taken to mean the use of Desire Realm attributes in the path, this would contradict the explanation of the difference between the disciples of Mantra of highest faculties. It is not correct to assert that the three, great seal, wisdom seal, and pledge or action seal, were taught respectively for the three types of disciples of Mantra—those having the best, middling, and lowest faculties—because there would be the fault of contradicting the teaching that a disciple of Mantra of highest faculties, a jewel-like person, attains buddhahood in one lifetime through training in any of the three deeds of enhancement [each of which entail sexual union] during the two stages.

Ratnarakṣita's Position on the Difference between the Perfection and Mantra vehicles

Ratnarakṣita's *Commentary on the Difficult Points of the Saṃvarodaya Tantra* (*Saṃvarodayapañjikā*) quotes Maitreya's *Ornament for Realizations*, which says, "[Bodhisattvas] have skillful methods for using desire." He also cites the *Kāśyapa Chapter Sūtra* (*Kāśyapaparivarta*), which says:

> Just as the unclean dung of the people of a city
> Benefits a sugarcane farmer,
> So the dung of a bodhisattva's afflictions
> Benefits the creation of buddha qualities.

Citing these sources, he asserts that [bodhisattvas] partake of the attributes of the Desire Realm and that great bliss as well as the means to achieve it are common to both Sūtra and Mantra.

Then from what point of view is the difference between Sūtra and Mantra made? They are differentiated by way of having or not having the stage of generation. As Ratnarakṣita says in his commentary to the thirteenth chapter of the *Saṃvarodaya Tantra*, "Therefore, without cultivating the stage of generation, there is just no feature of the mode of Mantra." This explanation also requires analysis because there would be the fault of being overly broad and lacking pervasion.

The master Jñānaśrī asserts that the Mantra Vehicle is superior to the Perfection Vehicle by way of eleven skillful methods or, if condensed, four.[a] The great elder Atiśa's *Collection of All Pledges* (*Sarvasamayasaṃgraha*) says that the master Indrabhūti asserts that the Mantra Vehicle is superior to the Perfection Vehicle by way of seven features[b]; the master Buddhajñānapāda by three features, and Vajraghaṇḍa by four features. The great adept Ḍombhīheruka says:

> Here, by way of the feature of vessels
> And the doctrine that makes [disciples] vessels,
> By the feature of texts, paths, and fruitions,
> The Mantra Vehicle is higher.

---

[a] For an explanation, see Bu ston, *rgyud sde spyi'i rnam par gzhag pa rgyud sde rin po che'i mdzes rgyan*, Collected Works, Part 15 (*ba*) (New Delhi: International Academy of Indian Culture, 1969), 11.5 ff.

[b] P4547, vol. 81, 209.5.5 to 210.1.2.

Samayavajra asserts that the Mantra Vehicle is superior to the Perfection Vehicle by five features.[a] These statements [reported by Atiśa] are suitable to explain [the difference in the vehicles] if applied only to Highest Yoga Tantra. Otherwise, they do not apply to the three lower tantras; therefore, those possessing discrimination should analyze them.

It is not correct to assert that the two Mahāyānas differ by way of having or not having cultivation of the path without abandoning desire, because both vehicles teach the cultivation of paths free from desire. For it is said in Sūtra that there are times of allowing impure deeds and so forth as a branch [of the path] related to the special purposes of others, as in the case of the Brahmin Khyi'u skar ma.

Our Own System

That which abides in the class of being distinguished by [1] being Mahāyāna and [2] having cultivation of a path according in aspect with the form body (*rūpakāya*) of a buddha is the definition of the Vajra Vehicle. This is established by texts of Highest Mantra as well as the lower tantras. The *Vajrapañjara Tantra* says:

> If emptiness were the method
> Then buddhahood could not be.
> Since other than this cause, no effect exists,
> The method is not emptiness.
>
> The conquerors teach emptiness
> For the sake of reversing adherence to self
> In those who seek the view of self
> And in those who have turned away from all [right] views.
>
> Therefore, it is called "the circle of the maṇḍala."
> It is a binding of the method of bliss.
> Through the yoga of buddha pride,
> Buddhahood is not distant.
>
> A Teacher possesses thirty-two major marks
> As well as eighty secondary marks.
> Therefore, by that method it will be attained.
> The method is to bear the Teacher's form.[b]

---

[a] See Bu ston, p. 31.6-32.5.

[b] P11, vol. 1, 223.4.4-7.

In his *Engaging in the Means of Self-Achievement* (*Ātmasādhanāvatāra*), the master Buddhajñānapāda cites passages in the *Ornament for the Mahāyāna Sūtras* (*Mahāyānasūtrālaṃkāra*) and the *Condensed Perfection of Wisdom Sūtra* (*Sañcayagāthāprajñāpāramitāsūtra*) setting forth the explanation that the methods of giving and so forth conjoined with the wisdom realizing selflessness are the highest method of achieving a form body.[a] Then he says, "However, this is not so because other than accustoming to a dissimilar cause, there is no cultivation of a path that accords with the manifestation of full enlightenment."[b] The meaning is that the method of achieving a form body explained in the Perfection Vehicle to be the highest is not the highest method of achieving a form body, because the Perfection Vehicle does not have cultivation of a path that accords in aspect with a form body, the fruition.

What is the highest method of achieving a form body? In order to indicate that deity yoga which is a nonduality of the profound and the manifest is the method, [Buddhajñānapāda's] *Self-Achievement* says, "As with selflessness, meditate on the entity of the vast in the mode of nondifference."[c] The master Ratnākaraśānti gives a similar explanation in his *Commentary on Dīpaṅkarabhadra's "Four Hundred and Fifty"* (*Guhyasamājamaṇḍalavidhiṭīkā*).[d] The master Abhayākara also explains the mode [of cultivating a form body] in this way in his *Clusters of Quintessential Instructions* (*Āmnāyāmañjari*).[e] Śrīdhara says in his *Innate Illumination, Commentary on the Difficult Points of the Yamāri Tantra* (*Yamāritantrapañjikāsahajāloka*):

> It should not be said that [form bodies] will arise by way of methods of giving and so forth and through the power of prayers. When one is doubtful concerning the nature of enjoyment (*saṃbhogakāya*) and emanation bodies (*nirmāṇakāya*) that are not meditated upon, how could one become certain? If someone says, "Still, they will arise by the power of prayer," then, since one could manifest [a truth body] without meditating on selflessness, what is accomplished by the fatigue of meditating upon it? If

---

[a] P2723, vol. 65, 28.2.6 through 28.3.5.

[b] P2723, vol. 65, 28.3.5.

[c] P2723, vol. 65, 28.4.8.

[d] P2734, vol. 65, 173.5.2-4.

[e] P2710, vol. 55, 180.2.8 through 180.3.1.

> someone says, "[A truth body] arises through meditation," then what fault is there with the two bodies of enjoyment and emanation? Why are these not meditated upon? Therefore, even those abiding in the Perfection Vehicle accept a buddhahood having a nature of the three bodies. They are manifested through meditation upon them.[a]

He finds this similarity: to achieve the two, the truth and form bodies that are the fruitions, if one is to be achieved by a path according in aspect with it, then the other must equally be so achieved, and if not, the other also is not. Then, regarding their achievement, the great adept Śrīdhara, to prove his point, quotes:

> The cause of achieving buddhahood
> Is buddha yoga.
> Is it not seen that in every way
> The fruition is similar to the cause?[b]

Also, Vinayadatta says in *Rite of the Great Illusion Maṇḍala* (*Mahāmayāmaṇḍalopāyika*):

> Meditating that one is a form body and a truth body,
> O, enlightenment is definitely attained.
> If a truth body is attained through the concentration of a Conqueror
> Should one not meditate on a body of form?[c]

It is also established [that the definition of the Vajra Vehicle above is consistent with the lower tantras] because it is clearly said in the first section of the *Compendium of Principles* (*Tattvasaṃgraha*):

> If one cultivates a buddha body
> With one's own subtle atoms
> Of body, speech, and mind as vajras,
> One becomes a complete buddha.[d]

[This method] is also clearly described in the commentary on this, Śākyamitra's *Ornament of Kosala* (*Kosalālaṃkāratattvasaṃgrahaṭīkā*), as well as in Ānandagarbha's *Illumination of Principles* (*Tattvāloka*) and

---

[a] P2781, vol. 66, 219.4.4-8.

[b] P2781, vol. 66, 219.4.8.

[c] P2517, vol. 57, 316.5.5-6.

[d] P84, vol. 3, 237.5.7.

Buddhaguhya's *Condensation of the Vairocanābhisaṃbodhi* (*Vairocanābhisaṃbodhitantrapiṇḍārtha*).

In summary, the two individual Mahāyānas are posited from the viewpoint of having or not having cultivation of a path having the four complete purities of the fruition [the body, abodes, resources, and activities of a buddha] or having three features [a very pure object, the power of aids, and deeds]. Ratnākaraśānti's *Presentation of the Three Vehicles* (*Triyānavyavasthāna*) says:

> Due to a very pure object,
> The power of aids, and deeds,
> The vehicle of the intelligent
> Is known as the great of the great.[a]

Regarding this someone objects: "It follows that it is not correct to define the Vajra Vehicle as that which abides in the class of being Mahāyāna and having cultivation of a path according in aspect with a form body that is the fruition, for it is established that achievement by a cause similar to the effect is extremely indefinite. If you say that it is not the case, then it follows that a body adorned with the major and secondary marks of a universal monarch (*cakravartin*), for example, or the physical base of a happy or bad transmigration must be achieved by a cause similar in aspect with it."

Answer: It is true that there would be a fault if one propounded that a path according in aspect with that [form body] is necessary for a maturation cause to take birth as a form body adorned with the major and secondary marks of a buddha, the fruition. However, we do not assert this. There is a reason for distinguishing the two Mahāyānas by whether or not, within the context of the Mahāyāna, they have cultivation of a path that accords in aspect with a form body, the fruition. For there is a very great difference in the way a follower of the Perfection Vehicle and a follower of the Vajra Vehicle achieve a form body adorned with the major and secondary marks of a buddha, the fruition.[b]

Those of the Perfection Vehicle assert that the cause of the entity of a form body is the collection of merit, whereas the particular causes of the instances of the major and secondary marks and so forth are to escort one's guru and so forth. Through accustoming to these [causes] over many lives, a [high] stage (*bhūmi*) is attained;

---

[a] Cone: rgyud *tsu*, 100b2.

[b] Textual note at 13a6: mistakenly reads *gsang sngags* instead of *sangs rgyas*.

the mode of assuming a birth of maturation improves, and finally, during the last lifetime, one attains the major and secondary marks of a learner and actualizes a truth body. A continuation of similar type of the major and secondary marks of a learner turns into a body adorned with the major and minor marks of a nonlearner.

Beginners in the Vajra Vehicle system who achieve buddhahood in one lifetime do not have marks naturally with them from birth, as is the case with those in their last lifetime in the Perfection Vehicle. Because that maturation body [an ordinary body] also does not turn into an enjoyment body, they must newly achieve a form body adorned with major and secondary marks of buddhahood, the fruition, and there is no means to achieve it other than deity yoga. Since this definitely is the cultivation of a path similar in aspect with a form body, the difference [between the vehicles] is very great.

Objection: The fruitions of the two Mahāyānas differ in superiority and inferiority because the paths for achieving those fruitions differ. It so follows because the difference in the paths is meaningful and because the thirteenth stage of a Vajradhara is superior to the eleventh stage of Complete Light in the Perfection Vehicle. The *Saṃpuṭa Tantra* says:

> In short, in this birth you will achieve,
> By the most excellent bliss
> The buddhahood achieved over
> Countless eons or ten million eons
> Or the state of Vajradhara.

Also, the same text says, "In this birth you will attain either buddhahood or [the state of] Vajradhara. Those who do not attain the state beyond thought are *sugatas*, buddhas."

Response: This is not correct because there is the fallacy of internal contradiction in asserting these passages of the *Saṃpuṭa Tantra* to be literal and asserting the passage from the *Lamp for the Three Modes* [which says that the goal is the same] to be literal. This assertion is also not correct because in that passage [just cited] the teaching is not of having a choice between attaining the buddhahood explained in the Perfection Vehicle or attaining the state of Vajradhara explained in the Vajra Vehicle. Further, the "buddha" literally indicated in that passage and the buddhahood of abiding in the eleventh stage, Complete Light, of the Perfection Vehicle's own path are not synonymous. For the "buddha" literally indicated in that passage and that in the following passage from the *Ornament for the Realizations* are the same:

> Passing the ninth stage, the wisdom
> By which one abides on the stage of a buddha
> Is known as the tenth
> Stage of a bodhisattva.

Therefore, another thirteenth stage of a Vajradhara that is superior to the eleventh stage of Complete Light does not exist. However, the description in the Vajra Vehicle of the modes of the twelve, thirteen, fourteen, or fifteen stages, etc. is a positing [of stages] by way of either further division or consolidation. Though the two, the Perfection Vehicle and the Vajra Vehicle, do not differ in superiority and inferiority regarding the fruition, a difference of superiority and inferiority in the causes is however not meaningless. For, by reason of there being a difference in superiority and inferiority of causes, there is a great difference in the speed of progressing on the path in the two vehicles.

Detailed explanation of the divisions of entry into the Vajra Vehicle

This section has three parts: the different doors of entry into Mantra, identification of the features that posit the different doors of entry, and the mode of proceeding on paths possessing those features. [The first two parts are translated here.]

The different doors of entry into Mantra

The *Vajrapañjara* says:

> Action Tantra is for the low.
> The yoga without actions is for those above that.
> The superior yoga is for superior beings.
> Highest yoga is for those above that.[a]

Because Action Tantras were set forth for low disciples, Performance Tantras for middling disciples—those above them—Yoga Tantras for superior disciples, and Highest Yoga Tantras for the superior of the superior, four sets of tantras are posited from the viewpoint of four different doors of entry. Śraddhākaravarma's

---

[a] P11, vol. 1, 234.1.5-6.

Introduction to the Meaning of Highest Yoga Tantra says, "These are known in general as Action, Performance, Yoga, and Highest Yoga Tantras."[a]

Identification of the features that posit the different doors of entry

Why are the four doors of entry of the different sets of tantras explained from the standpoint of superiority and inferiority of disciples?

They cannot be posited by way of only the inferiority and superiority of disciples, because if they were, one would have to posit five doors that are different sets of tantras for *Guhyasamāja* [alone]. This is because it says in the *Compendium of Wisdom Vajras* (*Vajrajñānasamuccaya*) that regarding the disciples of the *Guhyasamāja*, there are five: persons who are like the white lotus, utpala, lotus, sandalwood, and a jewel.

The four sets of tantras cannot be posited from the standpoint of superiority and inferiority of view or object of attainment, the fruition, because neither of those has any difference in the four sets of tantras.[b] Four sets of tantras cannot be posited from the standpoint of a difference in the general body of the path for achieving a truth body and a form body, because there is no difference among the four with respect to traveling a path whose life is constituted by the yoga of nonduality of the profound and the manifest, which is a union of two: the wisdom realizing emptiness—the profound—and deity yoga—the vast—and because all these are of one type, the Vajra Vehicle. The four sets of tantras are not posited from the viewpoint of different rites of deity generation, because if they were, even in the individual sets of tantra, there would be the fault of it being the case that many doors of entry which are different sets of tantras would have to be posited.

With respect to this, many early and recent Tibetan vajra masters agree in asserting that the reason for positing four sets of tantras is that it is said that since the outsider Forders [*tīrthikas*, that is, Hindus] have four lineages, the four sets of tantras are for the purpose of accommodating them. That is so because it is said that Highest Yoga, Yoga, Performance, and Action Tantra were spoken in order to accommodate the four lineages of the proponents of

a P4536, vol. 81, 155.1.6.

b Textual note at 15a4: mistakenly reads *yod* instead of *med*.

tenets respectively: the desirous following Īśvara, the hateful following Viṣṇu, the ignorant following Brahmā, and those of indefinite lineage who become followers of whichever of those three they encounter. Furthermore, the masters Ānandagarbha and Subhūtipālita say this following the *Compendium of Principles.*

Why do they assert this? Is it [1] that the desirous whose lineage follows Īśvara are the intended disciples of Highest Yoga Tantra and thus Highest Yoga Tantras are posited from the viewpoint of having been set forth for them? Or is it [2] that Highest Yoga Tantras are posited considering that, through being taught to such disciples, there are cases of any of those four types of disciples being tamed by them? The first is not correct because there is no possibility that the outsider Forders who are desirous followers of Īśvara and whose views and deeds are mistaken could be the intended disciples of Highest Mantra. The second possibility is also incorrect because the reasoning is definite. Even if it means that persons of such four lineages are needed for the main of the intended disciples of the four tantras, it is not acceptable. For, it is not feasible to posit the Forders who have mistaken views and deeds as the main disciples of the Vajra Vehicle, the essence of the Buddha's teaching.

Others hold this position: There is a reason for positing four sets of tantras because such is done from the viewpoint of four different rites of deity generation that are paired with the four proponents of Buddhist tenets. They are posited this way because Action Tantras, in accordance with the Hearer schools of Vātsīputrīya and Eastern Vaibhāṣika, involve the appropriation of feats through mainly performing ablution, purification, and so forth without generating oneself as a pledge being (*samayasattva*), but inviting the wisdom deity (*jñānasattva*) in front, and performing offering, praise, repetition, and so forth within viewing oneself and the wisdom deity as servant and master. Performance Tantras, in accordance with the tenets of Sautrāntikas and Kāshmīri Vaibhāṣikas, involve the appropriation of feats through generating oneself as a pledge being, then drawing the wisdom being into oneself or causing the wisdom being to enter oneself, inviting the wisdom deity in front, performing offering, praise, repetition, and so forth, within viewing oneself and the wisdom being as friends. Yoga Tantras, in accordance with the school of tenets of Solitary Realizer superiors, involve generating oneself as a pledge being, drawing the wisdom being to oneself and causing the wisdom deity to enter oneself, performing offering, praise, repetition, and so forth, and finally requesting the wisdom deity to depart. Highest Yoga Tantras involve generating oneself as a pledge being, drawing the wisdom deity to oneself and causing the wisdom deity to enter oneself, performing offering, praise, repetition, and so forth, and finally not requesting the wisdom deity to depart. This is because such is explained in the *Wisdom Vajra Compendium* and also is asserted by the protector Nāgārjuna, the master Jñānapāda, and so forth.

Response: Asserting this is not correct because the statement in the *Wisdom Vajra Compendium* that [in Action Tantra] there is no divine pride[a] of oneself and no excellent bliss of a wisdom being does not indicate that self-generation is lacking in Action Tantra in general. For, that was said in consideration of some types of the lowest disciples who, if they meditated on themselves as a deity, would be frightened. It is not correct that such is asserted by the protector Nāgārjuna and the master Jñānapāda, because these two do not explain such a system in any of their works. Further, such an assertion is not correct because Solitary Realizer is not one of the four schools of tenets.

Furthermore, the master Alaṃkakalaśa, in his *Commentary on the Vajra Garland Tantra* (*Vajramālaṭīkā*), asserts that the four sets of tantras are posited from the viewpoint of the four castes of humans, in that Action Tantras were spoken for Brahmins, Performance Tantras for the merchant caste (*vaiśya*), Yoga Tantras for the royal caste (*kṣatriya*), and Highest Yoga Tantra for the servant caste (*śūdra*) and outcastes (*cāṇḍāla*).

However, this is not correct because: [1] if the four castes are taken as the intended disciples of the four sets of tantras, there is the fault of being overly broad, [2] if it is asserted that the four castes are needed for the main disciples of the four sets of tantras, there is the fault of being overly narrow, and [3] if one thinks that it occurs that members of the four human castes are trained by this or that of the four sets of tantras, there is the fault of indefiniteness.

The condensed *Kālacakra Tantra* explains that the four sets of tantras were spoken from the four mouths of Kālacakra when it says, "From the east, wisdom tantras, then again from the western

[a] Textual note at 16b4: mistakenly reads *bsnyen* instead of *snyems*.

mouth, those of yogic realization.[a] From the right mouth, the Lord of Conquerors taught the Yoga Tantras, and from the left mouth, Action and so forth."[b] There is also the statement in the *Stainless Light* applying four periods [of the day] to the four sets of tantras.[c] Also,[d] the great adept Kṛṣṇacārin says in *Illumination of the Secret Principles* (*Guhyatattvaprakāśa*):

> From the divisions of the four eras
> The tantra sets are of four aspects.[e]

Some explain that these statements from the condensed *Kālacakra Tantra, Stainless Light,* and *Illumination of the Secret Principles* indicate the means of positing the four sets of tantras. However, this is incorrect because these are just correlations of objects purified with means of purification.

Our Own System

There is a reason for positing four different doors of entry by way of the four sets of tantras, because the main of its intended disciples who are engaging in the Vajra Vehicle are placed in four lineages. This, in turn, is because there are four different modes of using the desire for Desire Realm attributes in the path, and there are four different types of superior and inferior capacities for developing a yoga that is a union of the wisdom realizing emptiness and deity yoga—the path using such desire in the path. If these are explained according to the meaning of the names of the four tantra sets as explained in Highest Yoga Tantra, the *Saṃpuṭa Tantra* says:

> Laughing, looking, holding hands.
> The embrace of the two are four,
> The four tantras abide in the mode of worms.

The last line indicates the final essence of how to use the desire for Desire Realm attributes in the path. For example, even though wood-engendered worms are born from wood, they consume the

---

[a] Textual note at 17a4: mistakenly reads *rnal 'byor rjes su rigs pa nyid ni rgyud kyi zhal nas so* instead of *rnal 'byor rjes su rig pa nyid ni nub kyi zhal nas so.* See Bu ston 40.5.

[b] See Bu ston 40.5-7.

[c] See Bu ston 41.1-2.

[d] Textual note at 17a6: mistakenly reads *des* instead of *dang.*

[e] P2167, vol. 51, 225.1.4. See also Bu ston 41.2-3.

wood completely. Similarly, in dependence on a causal motivation that is the desire involved in laughing, looking, holding hands or mere embrace, or joining the two organs, a great bliss is generated. The wisdom of inseparable bliss and emptiness, which is the great bliss generated inseparably with a mind realizing emptiness at that same time, consumes the ignorance and afflictive nature of desire and so forth from the root. Therefore, in accordance with the names of the four tantras explained in Highest Yoga Tantra, they are also called tantras of Looking, Laughing, Holding Hands, and Meeting of the Two. The *Ornament of the Vajra Essence Tantra* (*Vajrahṛdayālaṃkāra*) says:

> This sets forth the tantra division
> Of the union of the two.
> In the same way, holding hands,
> Looking, and laughing are to be known.

The Meaning of the Names of the Four Sets of Tantras as Understood in the Four Sets of Tantras

The definition of an Action Tantra is either an actual tantra or one included in that group that, between external activities and internal yoga, mainly sets forth external activities and that was spoken mainly for its intended disciples who are either actual persons, or of that type, taking an interest in using in the path the bliss arising from the mutual gazing of the meditated goddess [and oneself]. The *Detailed Rite of Amoghapāśa* (*Amoghapāśakalparāja*) says, "The Blessed One looks at Bhṛkuṭī."

The definition of a Performance Tantra is either an actual tantra or one included in that group that [mainly sets forth] performance of external activities and internal deity yoga equally and was spoken mainly for its intended disciples who are actual persons, or of that type, who take an interest in using in the path not only the bliss arising from just the mutual gazing of the meditated goddess [and oneself] but also smiling at each other. The *Vairocanābhisaṃbodhi* says:

> On the right, the goddess
> Buddhalocanā,
> A goddess of slightly smiling face
> And an arm's span circle of light.
> Her peerless body is pure white,

She is Śākyamuni's consort.

The definition of a Yoga Tantra is an actual tantra or one included in that group that between external activities and internal deity yoga, sets forth mainly internal deity yoga and was set forth for disciples who are its actual intended disciples, or that type, who mainly take an interest in using in the path not just the bliss arising in dependence on gazing and smiling at the meditated goddess but also that arising from mutual embrace or holding hands. The *Vajraśekara* says:

> The vajra goddess sighs.
> Embraced at the waist, one's goddess
> Turns her head to the side
> And smiling, looks all around.
> She holds the hand of the Blessed One.

The definition of a Highest Yoga Tantra is an actual tantra or one included in that group that between the two, external activities and internal deity yoga, mainly sets forth only internal deity yoga, with respect to which tantras having a higher or superior yoga do not exist, and that are set forth for its intended disciples who are actual disciples, or of that type, who take an interest mainly in using in the path the desire for the Desire Realm attributes of the joining of the two organs. The *Guhyasamāja Root Tantra* (*Mūlaguhyasamājatantra*) says:

> Meditate on the supreme of the Tathāgata's
> Consorts, Locanā and so forth.
> Through uniting the two organs
> The feat of buddhahood will be attained.

Objection: It follows that the division into four sets of tantras is not correct because the master Buddhaguhya made a division into three, for he said:

> From the division of Yoga, Performance, and Action
> The sets of tantras are asserted as three.

Answer: This is incorrect because it is doubtful whether the passage is authentic. Even if it is assumed to be authentic, there is still no contradiction, since Action and Performance could be taken as two and Yoga and Highest Yoga taken as a single Yoga Tantra. Or, in another way, Action and Performance could have been condensed into one.

Objection: The sets of tantras are divided into five because the *Wisdom Vajra Compendium* makes a division of five consisting of Realization, Action, Performance, Yoga, and Highest Yoga Tantras.

Answer: There is no fault. There, Realization Tantra refers to Action Tantras that set forth external activities.

Objection: The sets of tantras are divided into six because such is described by the master Kampala and also set forth in the *Little Saṃvara Tantra* (*Laghusaṃvara*), which says:

> With the divisions of Sūtra, Action,
> Performance, Yoga, Secret, and Limit,
> Sentient beings engage from interest
> In accordance with what they like.

Thus, they are divided into six: Sūtrānta Realization, Action, Performance, Yoga, Secret—the father tantras such as *Guhyasamāja*—and Limit—the mother tantras such as the *Saṃvara Root Tantra* (*Mūlasaṃvaratantra*).

Answer: That is not correct. There is no clear explanation of this by the master Kampala, and this is also not the meaning of the passage from the *Saṃvara Root Tantra.* The meaning of the *Little Saṃvara Tantra* is that there is sūtra from the division [of the Buddha's word] into two—sūtra and tantra—and the four sets of tantras: Action, Performance, Yoga, and Secret Limit—or Secret Highest—and the teacher spoke them respectively for disciples who could be tamed by them.

If this is so, how many of each of the four tantras are there? Their measure can be posited, because the *Wisdom Vajra Compendium* says:

> Four thousand Realization Tantras,
> Four thousand Action Tantras
> Eight thousand Performance Tantras
> Six thousand Both Tantras
> Twelve thousand names of Yoga Tantras,
> Thus, there are thirty-four thousand tantras.
> If divided extensively, they are without measure.

Also, concerning Highest Yoga Tantra, the *Saṃvarodaya Tantra* says:

> The number of Yoga Tantras
> Is definite as sixty million.

> Likewise, the number of Yoginī Tantras
> Is known to be one hundred sixty million.

This is the number of titles, not stanzas, because, whereas it is said that there are four thousand Action Tantras, there are eight thousand stanzas in the *Amoghapāśa Tantra* alone.

List of Abbreviations

"*Condensed* version" refers to Bu-tön Rin-chen-drup, *Condensed Presentation of the General Tantra Sets: Key Opening the Door to the Precious Treasury of Tantra Sets* (*rgyud sde spyi'i rnam par gzhag pa rgyud sde rin po che'i gter sgo 'byed pa'i lde mig*), Collected Works, vol. 14 (New Delhi: International Academy of Indian Culture, 1969).

"Dharma" refers to the *sde dge* edition of the Tibetan canon published by Dharma Press: the *Nying-ma Edition of the sDe-dge bKa'-'gyur and bsTan-'gyur* (Oakland, Calif.: Dharma Press, 1980).

"*Extensive* version" refers to Bu-tön Rin-chen-drup, *Extensive Presentation of the General Tantra Sets: Ornament Beautifying the Precious Tantra Sets* (*rgyud sde spyi'i rnam par gzhag pa: rgyud sde rin po che'i mdzes rgyan*), Collected Works, vol. 15 (New Delhi: International Academy of Indian Culture, 1969).

"Golden Reprint" refers to the *gser bris bstan 'gyur* (Sichuan, China: krung go'i mtho rim nang bstan slob gling gi bod brgyud nang bstan zhib 'jug khang, 1989).

"Karmapa *sde dge*" refers to the *sde dge mtshal par bka' 'gyur: A Facsimile Edition of the 18th Century Redaction of Si tu chos kyi 'byung gnas Prepared under the Direction of H.H. the 16th rgyal dbang karma pa* (Delhi: Delhi Karmapae Chodhey Gyalwae Sungrab Partun Khang, 1977).

"*Medium-Length* version" refers to Bu-tön Rin-chen-drup, *Medium-Length Presentation of the General Tantra Sets: Illuminating the Secrets of All Tantra Sets* (*rgyud sde spyi'i rnam par gzhag pa rgyud sde thams cad kyi gsang ba gsal bar byed pa*), Collected Works, vol. 15 (New Delhi: International Academy of Indian Culture, 1969).

"P," standing for "Peking edition," refers to the *Tibetan Tripitaka* (Tokyo-Kyoto: Tibetan Tripitaka Research Foundation, 1955-1962).

"*stog* Palace" refers to the *Tog Palace Manuscript of the Tibetan Kanjur* (Leh, Ladakh: Smanrtsis Shesrig Dpemdzod, 1979).

"THDL" refers to The Tibetan and Himalayan Digital Library of the University of Virginia at www.thdl.org.

"Toh." refers to *A Complete Catalogue of the Tibetan Buddhist Canons,* edited by Hakuju Ui et al. (Sendai, Japan: Tohoku University, 1934), and *A Catalogue of the Tohoku University Collection of Tibetan Works on Buddhism,* edited by Yensho Kanakura et al. (Sendai,

Japan: Tohoku University, 1953).
"Tokyo *sde dge*" refers to the *sDe dge Tibetan Tripiṭaka—bsTan ḥgyur preserved at the Faculty of Letters, University of Tokyo,* edited by Z. Yamaguchi et al. (Tokyo: Tokyo University Press, 1977-1984).

Bibliography

1. *Sūtras and Tantras*

Amoghapāsha Tantra
amoghapāśahṛdayanāmamahāyānasūtra
'phags pa don yod zhags pa'i snying po zhes bya ba theg pa chen po'i mdo
P366, vol. 8

Brief Explication of Initiations
sekoddeśa
dbang mdor bstan
P3, vol. 1
Sanskrit and Tibetan: Giacomella Orofino. *Sekoddeśa: A Critical Edition of the Tibetan Translations.* Rome: Istituto Italiano per il Medio ed Estremo Oriente, 1994. The Sanskrit is found in the appendix, edited by Raniero Gnoli.

Buddha Skull
buddhakapālanāmayoginītantrarāja
sangs rgyas thod pa shes bya ba rnal 'byor ma'i rgyud kyi rgyal po
P63, vol. 3

Buddha Union Tantra
sarvabuddhasamayogaḍākinījālasaṃbara
sangs rgyas thams cad dang mnyam par sbyor ba mkha' 'gro ma sgyu ma bde ba'i mchog
P8, vol. 1

Buddhāvataṃsaka Sūtra
buddhāvataṃsakanāma-mahāvaipulyasūtra
sangs rgyas phal po che zhes bya ba shin tu rgyas pa chen po'i mdo
P761, vols. 25-26

Cemetery Adornment
cakrasaṃbaratantrarājādbhutaśmaśānālaṃkāra
'khor sdom pa'i rgyud kyi rgyal po dur khrod kyi rgyan rmad du byung ba
P57, vol. 3

Compendium of Principles Tantra (the root Yoga Tantra)
sarvatathāgatatattvasaṃgraha
de bzhin gshegs pa thams cad kyi de kho na nyid bsdus pa
P112, vol. 4; D479, vol. *nya*
Sanskrit: *Sarva-tathāgata-tattva-saṃgraha,* reproduced by Lokesh Chandra and David L. Snellgrove. Śata-piṭaka Series, vol. 269. New Delhi: International Academy of Indian Culture, 1981. Also: Isshi Yamada. *Sarva-tathāgata-tattva-saṅgraha.* Śata-piṭaka Series, vol. 262. New Delhi: International Academy of Indian Culture, 1981.

Compendium of Wisdom Vajras
vajrajñānasamuccaya
ye shes rdo rje kun las btus pa
P84, vol. 3; Toh. 447

Concentration Continuation Tantra (one of the four general Action Tantras)
dhyānottarapaṭalakramatantra
bsam gtan gyi phyi ma rim par phye ba
P430, vol. 9

Condensed Perfection of Wisdom Sūtra
prajñāpāramitāsañcayagāthā
shes rab kyi pha rol tu phyin pa sdud pa tshigs su bcad pa

P735, vol. 21; Toh. 13, vol. *ka* (*shes rab sna tshogs*)

Sanskrit and Tibetan: Akira Yuyama. *Prajñā-pāramitā-ratna-guṇa-saṃcaya-gāthā (Sanskrit Recension A): Edited with an Introduction, Bibliographical Notes and a Tibetan Version from Tunhuang*. London: Cambridge University Press, 1976.

Sanskrit: E. E. Obermiller. *Prajñāpāramitā-ratnaguṇa-sañcayagāthā*. Osnabrück, Germany: Biblio Verlag, 1970. Also: P. L. Vaidya. *Mahāyāna-sūtra-saṃgraha*. Part I. Buddhist Sanskrit Texts, 17. Darbhanga, India: Mithila Institute, 1961.

English translation: Edward Conze. *The Perfection of Wisdom in Eight Thousand Lines & Its Verse Summary*. Bolinas, Calif.: Four Seasons Foundation, 1973.

Detailed Rite of Amoghapāsha

amoghapāśakalparāja

don yod pa'i zhags pa'i cho ga zhib mo'i rgyal po

P365, vol. 8; Toh. 13

Eight Thousand Stanza Perfection of Wisdom Sūtra

aṣṭasāhasrikāprajñāpāramitā

shes rab kyi pha rol tu phyin pa brgyad stong pa

P734, vol. 21

Sanskrit: P. L. Vaidya. *Aṣṭasāhasrika Prajñāpāramitā, with Haribhadra's Commentary called Ālokā*. Buddhist Sanskrit Texts 4. Darbhanga, India: Mithila Institute, 1960.

English translation: Edward Conze. *The Perfection of Wisdom in Eight Thousand Lines & Its Verse Summary*. Bolinas, Calif.: Four Seasons Foundation, 1973.

Equality with Space Tantra

khasamatantrarāja

nam mkha' dang mnyam pa'i rgyud kyi rgyal po

P31, vol. 3

Expression of the Names / Expression of the Ultimate Names of the Wisdom Being Mañjushrī

mañjuśrījñānasattvasyaparamārthanāmasaṃgīti

'jam dpal ye shes sems dpa'i don dam pa'i mtshan yang dag par brjod pa

P2, vol. 1

English translation and Sanskrit edition: Ronald M. Davidson. "The Litany of Names of Mañjuśrī." In *Tantric and Taoist Studies in Honour of R.A. Stein*, edited by Michel Strickmann, vol. 1, 1-69. Mélanges Chinois et Bouddhiques, vol. 20. Brussels: Institut Belge des Hautes Études Chinoises, 1981. Translation reprinted, with minor changes, in: Ronald M. Davidson. "The Litany of Names of Mañjuśrī." In *Religions of India in Practice*, edited by Donald S. Lopez, Jr., 104-125. Princeton, N.J.: Princeton University Press, 1995.

Extensive Vidāraṇa Tantra

*vajravidāraṇāvaipūlya

rdo rje rnam 'joms kyi rgyud rgyas pa

[not extant and not translated into Tibetan]

Four Seats

caturpīṭhamahāyoginītantrarāja

gdan bzhi/ rnal 'byor ma'i rgyud kyi rgyal po chen po dpal gdan bzhi pa

P67, vol. 3

Four Vajra Sites

rdo rje gdan bzhi / [perhaps] sangs rgyas thams cad dang mnyam par sbyor ba zhes bya ba'i rgyud kyi rgyal po

THDL Ng3.1.3.1.1.1

General Secret Tantra (one of four general Action Tantras)

sarvamaṇḍalasāmānyavidhiguhyatantra

dkyil 'khor thams cad kyi spyi'i cho ga gsang ba'i rgyud

P429, vol. 9

Glorious Condensed [Tantra of] Imaginations
vajrakrodharājakalpalaghutantra
rdo rje khro bo'i rgyal po'i rtog pa bsdus pa'i rgyud
P319, vol. 7
Guhyasamāja Tantra
sarvatathāgatakāyavākcittarahasyaguhyasamājanāmamahākalparāja
de bzhin gshegs pa thams cad kyi sku gsung thugs kyi gsang chen gsang ba 'dus pa zhes bya ba brtag pa'i rgyal po chen po
P81, vol. 3; Toh. 442, vol. *ca*
Sanskrit text edited by S. Bagchi. *The Guhyasamāja Tantra*. Darbhanga, India: The Mithila Institute, 1965.
Hevajra Tantra
hevajratantrarāja
kye'i rdo rje zhes bya ba rgyud kyi rgyal po
P10, vol. 1
English translation: D. L. Snellgrove. *Hevajra Tantra,* Parts 1 and 2. London: Oxford University Press, 1959.
English translation together with Kṛṣṇāchārya's commentary: G. W. Farrow and I. Menon. *The Concealed Essence of the Hevajra Tantra with the Commentary of Yogaratnamālā*. Delhi: Motilal Banarsidass, 1992.
Imagination of the Courageous Achala Tantra
acalamahākrodharājasya-sarvatathāgatasyabalāparimitavīravinayasvākhyātonāmakalpa
de bzhin gshegs pa thams cad kyi khro bo'i rgyal po 'phags pa mi g.yo ba de'i stobs dpag tu med pa brtul phod pa 'dul bar gsungs pa zhes bya ba'i rtog pa
P127, vol. 5
Introduction to the Forms of Definite and Indefinite Progress Sūtra
niyatāniyatagatimudrāvatāra
nges pa dang mi nges par 'gro ba'i phyag rgya la 'jug pa
P868, vol. 34; Toh. 202
Kālachakra Tantra / Condensed Kālachakra Tantra
kālacakranāmatantrarāja
rgyud kyi rgyal po dpal dus kyi 'khor lo
P4, vol. 1
English translation (chapter 1): John Newman. *The Outer Wheel of Time: Vajrayāna Buddhist Cosmology in the Kālacakra Tantra.* Ann Arbor, MI: University Microfilms International, 1987.
English translation and Mongolian text (chapter 2): Vesna Acimovic Wallace. *The Inner* Kālacakratantra: *A Buddhist Tantric View of the Individual.* 2 vols. PhD diss., University of California at Berkeley, 1995; and *Kālacakratantra: The Chapter on the Individual together with the Vimalaprabhā.* New York: American Institute of Buddhist Studies, 2004.
Kāshyapa Chapter Sūtra / Questions of Kāshyapa Sūtra
kāśyapaparivartasūtra
'od srung gi le'u'i mdo
P760.43, vol. 24; Toh. 87, vol. *cha*
Sanskrit: Alexander von Staël-Holstein. *Kāçyapaparivarta: A Mahāyanasūtra of the Ratnakūṭa Class.* Shanghai: Commercial Press, 1926; reprint, Tokyo: Meicho-fukyū-kai, 1977.
English translation: Garma C. C. Chang, ed. *A Treasury of Mahāyāna Sūtras.* University Park: Pennsylvania State University Press, 1983.
King of Meditative Stabilizations Sūtra
samādhirājasūtra / sarvadharmasvabhāvasamatāvipañcatasamādhirājasūtra
ting nge 'dzin rgyal po'i mdo / chos thams cad kyi rang bzhin mnyam pa nyid rnam par spros pa ting nge 'dzin gyi rgyal po'i mdo

P795, vols. 31-32; Toh. 127, vol. *da*

Sanskrit: P. L. Vaidya. *Samādhirājasūtram*. Buddhist Sanskrit Texts, 2. Darbhanga, India: Mithila Institute, 1961.

Sanskrit, Tibetan, Chinese and English translation (of chap. 9): Cristoph Cüppers. *The IXth Chapter of the Samādhirājasūtra: A Text-critical Contribution to the Study of Mahāyāna Sūtras*. Alt-und Neu-Indische Studien, 41. Stuttgart: Franz Steiner Verlag, 1990.

Partial English translation (of chaps. 8, 19, and 22): K. Regamey. *Three Chapters from the Samādhirājasūtra*. Warsaw: Publications of the Oriental Commission, 1938.

Partial English translation (of chaps. 1-4): Translation Committee of the University of Michigan's Collegiate Institute for the Study of Buddhist Literature. "The Sūtra of the *King of Samādhis*: Chapters I-IV" in *Studies in the Literature of the Great Vehicle*. Michigan Studies in Buddhist Literature No. 1, edited by Luis O. Gómez and Jonathan A. Silk, 1-88. Ann Arbor: Collegiate Institute for the Study of Buddhist Literature and Center for South and Southeast Asian Studies, University of Michigan, 1989.

Kṛshṇayamāri Tantra

kṛṣṇayamāritantra

gshin rje gshed nag po'i rgyud

P103, vol. 4

Lady Sky-Traveler Vajra Tent Tantra

ḍākinīvajrapañjaramahātantrarājakalpa

mkha' 'gro ma rdo rje gur shes bya ba'i rgyud kyi rgyal po chen po'i brtag pa

P11, vol. 1

Little Saṃvara Tantra

tantrarājaśrīlaghusaṃvara

rgyud kyi rgyal po dpal bde mchog snyung ngu'i rgyud

P16, vol. 2; Toh. 368

Lotus Points

padma rtse mo

[?]

Magical Net

māyājālamahātantrarāja

rgyud kyi rgyal po chen po sgyu 'phrul dra ba

P102, vol. 4; THDL, Ng3.3.5

Mañjushrī Root Tantra

mañjuśrīmūlakalpa

'jam dpal rtsa ba'i rtog pa

P162, vol. 6

Miraculous Secret Essence

sgyu 'phrul gsang ba snying po

THDL Ng3.1.1.8

Ornament of the Vajra Essence Tantra

vajrahṛdayālaṃkāra

rdo rje snying po rgyan gyi rgyud

P86, vol. 3; Toh. 451

Pile of Jewels Sūtra

ratnakūṭa / mahāratnakūṭadharmaparyāyaśatasāhasrikagrantha

dkon brtsegs / dkon mchog brtsegs pa chen po'i chos kyi rnam grangs le'u stong phrag brgya pa

P760, vols. 22-24

Questions of Subāhu Tantra (one of the four general Action Tantras)

subāhuparipṛcchānāmatantra

dpung bzang gis zhus pa zhes bya ba'i rgyud

P428, vol. 9
Revelation of the Thought
saṃdhivyākaraṇatantra
dgongs pa lung ston / dgongs pa lung bstan pa'i rgyud
P83, vol. 3; THDL, Ng3.2.2.2.9
Saṃpuṭa Tantra
caturyoginīsaṃpuṭatantra
rnal 'byor ma bzhi'i kha sbyor kyi rgyud
P24, vol. 2
Saṃpuṭi Tantra
saṃpuṭināmamahātantra
yang dag par sbyor ba shes bya ba'i rgyud chen po
P26, vol. 2
Secret Treasury
sarvatathāgataguhyamahāguhyakośa-akṣayayanidhidīpa-mahāvratasādhanatantra
de bzhin gshegs pa thams cad kyi gsang ba gsang ba'i mdzod chen po mi zad pa gter gyi sgron ma brtul zhugs chen po bsgrub pa'i rgyud
P453, vol. 9
Susiddhi Tantra (one of the four general Action Tantras)
susiddhikaramahātantrasādhanopāyikapaṭala
legs par grub par byed pa'i rgyud chen po las sgrub pa'i thabs rim par phye ba
P431, vol. 9
Tantra of Oceanic Spontaneous Pristine Wisdom
ye shes rgya mtsho lhun gyis grub pa'i rgyud
[?]
Tantra of Pristine Wisdom [Already] Established
ye shes grub pa'i rgyud
[?]
Tantra of the Inconceivable Ra-li
ra li bsam gyis mi khyab pa'i rgyud
[?]
Tantra of the Supreme Original Buddha
śrīparamādya / śrīparamādyanāmamahāyānakalparājā
dpal dang po'i sangs rgyas / dpal mchog dang po zhes bya ba theg pa chen po'i rtog pa'i rgyal po
P119, vol. 5; Toh. 488, vol. *ta*
Tantra Thoroughly Establishing the Great Vehicle
theg pa chen po yongs su grub pa'i rgyud
[?]
Vairochanābhisambodhi (a Performance Tantra)
mahāvairocanābhisaṃbodhivikurvatī-adhiṣṭhānavaipūlyasūtra-indrarājanāmadharmaparyāya
rnam par snang mdzad chen po mngon par rdzogs par byang chub pa rnam par sprul ba byin gyis rlob pa shin tu rgyas pa mdo sde'i dbang po rgyal po zhes bya ba'i chos kyi rnam grangs
P126, vol. 5; Toh. 494, Dharma vol. 31
Vajra Array
sarvatathāgatacittajñānaguhyārthagarbhavyūhavajratantra
rdo rje bkod pa / de bzhin gshegs pa thams cad kyi thugs gsang ba'i ye shes don gyi snying po rdo rje bkod pa'i rgyud
P452, vol. 9; THDL, Ng2.1.2

Vajrapāṇi Initiation Tantra (a Performance Tantra)
vajrapāṇyabhiṣekamahātantra
lag na rdo rje dbang bskur ba'i rgyud chen mo
P130, vol. 6
Vajrapañjara Tantra (a Highest Yoga Tantra)
ḍākiṇīvajrapañjaramahātantrarājakalpa
mkha' 'gro ma rdo rje gur zhes bya ba'i rgyud kyi rgyal po chen po'i brtag pa
P11, vol. 6
Vajrashekhara Tantra (a Yoga Tantra)
vajraśekharamahāguhyayogatantra
gsang ba rnal 'byor chen po'i rgyud rdo rje rtse mo
P113, vol. 5; Toh. 480
Vajroṣhṇīṣha Tantra (an Action Tantra of which the *Concentration Continuation Tantra* is said to be a continuation)
rdo rje gtsug tor gyi rgyud
[not extant]
Wisdom Drop
jñānatilakayoginītantrarāja
ye shes thig le rnal 'byor ma'i rgyud kyi rgyal po chen po
P14, vol. 2
Also: ye shes thig le zang thal gyi rgyud
THDL, Ng1.6.105
Wisdom Vajra Compendium (an explanatory Highest Yoga Tantra, in the *Guhyasamāja* cycle)
jñānavajrasamuccayanāmasūtra
ye shes rdo rje kun las btus pa
P84, vol. 3

2. Other Sanskrit and Tibetan Works

Abhayākara (*'jigs med 'byung gnas sbas pa*)
Clusters of Quintessential Instructions: Commentary on the Saṃpuṭa Tantra
saṃpuṭatantrarājaṭīkā-āmnāyāmañjari
yang dag par sbyor ba'i rgyud kyi rgyal po'i rgya cher 'grel pa man ngag gi snye ma
P2328, vo. 55; Toh. 1198
Alaṃkakalasha
Commentary on the Vajra Garland Tantra
vajramālāmahāyogatantraṭīkāgambhīrārthadīpikā
rnal 'byor chen po'i rgyud dpal rdo rje phreng ba'i rgya cher 'grel pa zab mo'i don gyi 'grel pa
P2660, vol. 61; Toh. 1795
Āryadeva (*'phags pa lha*, second to third century C.E.)
Lamp Compendium for Practice
caryāmelāpakapradīpa
spyod bsdus sgron ma
P2668, vol. 61
Sanskrit, Tibetan, and English translation: Christian K. Wedemeyer. *Āryadeva's Lamp that Integrates the Practices.* New York: The American Institute of Buddhist Studies at Columbia University, 2007.
Asaṅga (*thogs med*, fourth century)
Explanation of (Maitreya's) "Sublime Continuum of the Great Vehicle"
mahāynottaratantraśāstravyākhya

theg pa chen po'i rgyud bla ma'i bstan bcos kyi rnam par bshad pa
P5526, vol. 108
Sanskrit: E. H. Johnston (and T. Chowdhury). *The Ratnagotravibhāga Mahāyānottaratantra-śāstra*. Patna, India: Bihar Research Society, 1950.
English translation: E. Obermiller. "Sublime Science of the Great Vehicle to Salvation." *Acta Orientalia* 9 (1931): 81-306. Also: J. Takasaki. *A Study on the Ratnagotravibhāga*. Serie Orientale Roma 33. Rome: Istituto Italiano per il Medio ed Estremo Oriente, 1966.

Five Treatises on the Grounds

1. *Grounds of Yogic Practice / Actuality of the Grounds*
   yogācārabhūmi / bhūmivastu
   rnal 'byor spyod pa'i sa / sa'i dngos gzhi
   P5536-5538, vols. 109-110
   Grounds of Bodhisattvas
   bodhisattvabhūmi
   byang chub sems pa'i sa
   P5538, vol. 110
   Sanskrit: Unrai Wogihara. *Bodhisattvabhūmi: A Statement of the Whole Course of the Bodhisattva (Being the Fifteenth Section of Yogācārabhūmi)*. Leipzig: 1908; Tokyo: Seigo Kenyūkai, 1930-1936. Also: Nalinaksha Dutt. *Bodhisattvabhumi (Being the XVth Section of Asangapada's Yogacarabhumi)*. Tibetan Sanskrit Works Series 7. Patna, India: K. P. Jayaswal Research Institute, 1966.
   English translation of the Chapter on Suchness, the fourth chapter of Part I, which is the fifteenth volume of the *Grounds of Yogic Practice:* Janice D. Willis. *On Knowing Reality*. New York: Columbia University Press, 1979; reprint, Delhi: Motilal Banarsidass, 1979.
2. *Compendium of Ascertainments*
   nirṇayasaṃgraha / viniścayasaṃgrahaṇī
   rnam par gtan la dbab pa bsdu ba
   P5539, vols. 110-111
3. *Compendium of Bases*
   vastusaṃgraha
   gzhi bsdu ba
   P5540, vol. 111
4. *Compendium of Enumerations*
   paryāyasaṃgraha
   rnam grang bsdu ba
   P5543, vol. 111
5. *Compendium of Explanations*
   vivaraṇasaṃgraha
   rnam par bshad pa bsdu ba
   P5543, vol. 111

Grounds of Hearers
nyan sa
śrāvakabhūmi
P5537, vol. 110
Sanskrit: Karunesha Shukla. *Śrāvakabhūmi*. Tibetan Sanskrit Works Series 14. Patna, India: K. P. Jayaswal Research Institute, 1973.

Two Summaries

1. *Summary of Manifest Knowledge*
   abhidharmasamuccaya
   chos mngon pa kun btus
   P5550, vol. 112

Sanskrit: Pralhad Pradhan. *Abhidharma Samuccaya of Asaṅga*. Visva-Bharati Series 12. Santiniketan, India: Visva-Bharati (Santiniketan Press), 1950.

French translation: Walpola Rahula. *La compendium de la super-doctrine (philosophie) (Abhidharmasamuccaya) d'Asaṅga.* Paris: École Française d'Extrème-Orient, 1971.

English translation from the French: Walpola Rahula. *Abhidharmasamuccaya: The Compendium of the Higher Teaching (Philosophy) by Asaṅga*. Trans. Sara Boin-Webb. Fremont, Calif.: Asian Humanities Press, 2001.

2. *Summary of the Great Vehicle*
mahāyānasaṃgraha
theg pa chen po bsdus pa
P5549, vol. 112
French translation and Chinese and Tibetan texts: Étienne Lamotte. *La somme du grand véhicule d'Asaṅga.* 2 vols. Publications de l'Institute Orientaliste de Louvain 8. Louvain: Université de Louvain, 1938; reprint, 1973.
English translation: John P. Keenan. *The Summary of the Great Vehicle by Bodhisattva Asaṅga: Translated from the Chinese of Paramārtha.* Berkeley, Calif.: Numata Center for Buddhist Translation and Research, 1992.

Atisha (*atiśa / atīśa*, 982-1054)

Compilation of All Pledges/ Collection of All Pledges
sarvasamayasaṃgraha
dam tshig thams cad bsdus pa
P4547, vol. 81

Bhāvaviveka (*legs ldan 'byed*, c. 500-570?)

Blaze of Reasoning / Commentary on the "Heart of the Middle": Blaze of Reasoning
madhyamakahṛdayavṛttitarkajvālā
dbu ma'i snying po'i 'grel pa rtog ge 'bar ba
P5256, vol. 96; Toh. 3856, vol. *dza*
Partial English translation (chap. 3, 1-136): Shōtarō Iida. *Reason and Emptiness.* Tokyo: Hokuseido, 1980.

Heart of the Middle
madhyamakahṛdayakārikā
dbu ma'i snying po'i tshig le'ur byas pa
P5255, vol. 96; Toh. 3855, vol. *dza*
Partial Sanskrit and Tibetan edition (chaps. 1-3): Annette L. Heitmann. *Textkritischer Beitrag zu Bhavyas Madhyamakahṛdayakārikā Kapitel 1-3.* Copenhagen: Videnskabsbutikkens Forlag, Kobenhavns Universitet, 1998.
Partial English translation (chap. 3, 1-136): Shōtarō Iida. *Reason and Emptiness.* Tokyo: Hokuseido, 1980.

Bo-dong Chok-lay-nam-gyel (*bo dong phyogs las rnam rgyal*, 1376-1451)

Presentation of the General Tantra Sets
rgyud sde spyi'i rnam gzhag
Encyclopedia Tibetica: The Collected Works of Bo-doṅ Paṇ-chen rnam-rgyal, vol. 24. New Delhi: Tibet House, 1969-1981.

Buddhaguhya (*sangs rgyas gsang ba*, eighth century)

Commentary on the "Concentration Continuation Tantra"
dhyānottarapaṭalaṭīkā
bsam gtan phyi ma rim par phye ba rgya cher bshad pa
P3495, vol. 78

Condensation of the Questions of Subāhu Tantra
subhāhuparipṛcchānāmatantrapiṇḍārtha
dpung bzang gis zhus pa'i rgyud kyi bsdus pa'i don
P3496, vol. 78; Toh. 2671

Condensation of the Vairocanābhisaṃbodhi
vairocanābhisaṃbodhitantrapiṇḍārtha
rnam par snang mdzad mngon par rdzogs par byang chub pa'i rgyud kyi bsdus pa'i don
P3486, vol. 77; Toh. 2662
Extensive Commentary on the Vajravidāraṇī Retention: Precious Illumination
vajravidāraṇī[*or* vidāraṇā]nāmadhāraṇīṭīkāratnābhāsvarā
rdo rje rnam par 'joms pa zhes bya ba'i bzungs kyi rgya cher 'grel pa rin po che gsal ba
P3504, vol. 78
Stages of the Path of Magical Emanation
mārgavyūha
sgyu 'phrul lam rim / lam rnam par bkod pa
P4736, vol. 83; rnying ma bka' ma rgyas pa, vol. 23
Buddhajñānapāda (*sangs rgyas ye shes*)
Engaging in the Means of Self-Achievement
ātmasādhanāvatāra
bdag sgrub pa la 'jug pa
P2723, vol. 65
Great Sacred Word
dvikramatattvabhāvanā-nāma-mukhāgama
rim pa gnyis pa'i de kho na nyid sgom pa zhes bya ba'i zhal gyi lung
P2716, vol. 65
Or: mukhāgama
zhal gyi lung
P2717, vol. 65
Bu-tön Rin-chen-drup (*bu ston rin chen grub*, 1290-1364)
Condensed Presentation of the General Tantra Sets: Key Opening the Door to the Precious Treasury of Tantra Sets
rgyud sde spyi'i rnam par gzhag pa rgyud sde rin po che'i gter sgo 'byed pa'i lde mig
Collected Works, vol. 14, 845.1-859.1. Śata Piṭaka No. 54. New Delhi: International Academy of Indian Culture, 1969.
Extensive Presentation of the General Tantra Sets: Ornament Beautifying the Precious Tantra Sets
rgyud sde spyi'i rnam par gzhag pa: rgyud sde rin po che'i mdzes rgyan
Collected Works, vol. 15, 6.1-32.5. Śata Piṭaka No. 54. New Delhi: International Academy of Indian Culture, 1969
Medium-Length Presentation of the General Tantra Sets: Illuminating the Secrets of All Tantra Sets
rgyud sde spyi'i rnam par gzhag pa rgyud sde thams cad kyi gsang ba gsal bar byed pa
Collected Works, vol. 15, 614.7-641.7. Śata Piṭaka No. 54. New Delhi: International Academy of Indian Culture, 1969
Chandrakīrti (*candrakīrti, zla ba grags pa*, seventh century)
[Auto]commentary on the "Supplement to (Nāgārjuna's) 'Treatise on the Middle'"
madhaymakāvatārabhāṣya
dbu ma la 'jug pa'i bshad pa / dbu ma la 'jug pa'i rang 'grel
P5263, vol. 98. Also: Dharmsala, India: Council of Religious and Cultural Affairs, 1968.
Tibetan: Louis de La Vallée Poussin. *Madhyamakāvatāra par Candrakīrti*. Bibliotheca Buddhica 9. Osnabrück, Germany: Biblio Verlag, 1970.
English translation: C. W. Huntington, Jr. *The Emptiness of Emptiness: An Introduction to Early Indian Mādhyamika*, 147-195. Honolulu: University of Hawaii Press, 1989.
French translation (up to chap. 6, stanza 165): Louis de La Vallée Poussin. *Muséon* 8 (1907): 249-317; *Muséon* 11 (1910): 271-358; *Muséon* 12 (1911): 235-328.
German translation (chap. 6, stanzas 166-226): Helmut Tauscher. *Candrakīrti-Madhyamakāvatāraḥ und Madhyamakāvatārabhāṣyam*. Vienna: Arbeitskreis für Tibetische und Buddhistische Studien, Universität Wien, 1981.

Clear Lamp Commentary on the "Guhyasamāja"
pradīpodyotananāmaṭīkā
sgron ma gsal bar byed pa zhes bya ba'i rgya cher bshad pa
P2650, vol. 60
Clear Words, Commentary on (Nāgārjuna's) "Treatise on the Middle"
mūlamadhyamakavṛttiprasannapadā
dbu ma rtsa ba'i 'grel pa tshig gsal ba
P5260, vol. 98. Also: Dharmsala, India: Tibetan Cultural Printing Press, 1968.
Sanskrit: Louis de La Vallée Poussin. *Mūlamadhyamakakārikās de Nāgārjuna avec la Prasannapadā commentaire de Candrakīrti*. Bibliotheca Buddhica 4. Osnabrück, Germany: Biblio Verlag, 1970.
English translation (chap. 1, 25): T. Stcherbatsky. *Conception of Buddhist Nirvāṇa*, 77-222. Leningrad: Office of the Academy of Sciences of the USSR, 1927; rev. reprint, Delhi: Motilal Banarsidass, 1978.
English translation (chap. 2): Jeffrey Hopkins. "Analysis of Coming and Going." Dharmsala, India: Library of Tibetan Works and Archives, 1974.
Partial English translation: Mervyn Sprung. *Lucid Exposition of the Middle Way: The Essential Chapters from the Prasannapadā of Candrakīrti translated from the Sanskrit*. London: Routledge, 1979; Boulder, Colo.: Prajñā Press, 1979.
French translation (chapters 2-4, 6-9, 11, 23, 24, 26, 28): Jacques May. *Prasannapadā Madhyamaka-vṛtti, douze chapitres traduits du sanscrit et du tibétain*. Paris: Adrien-Maisonneuve, 1959.
French translation (chapters 18-22): J. W. de Jong. *Cinq chapitres de la Prasannapadā*. Paris: Geuthner, 1949.
German translation (chap. 5, 12-26): Stanislaw Schayer. *Ausgewählte Kapitel aus der Prasannapadā*. Krakow: Naktadem Polskiej Akademji Umiejetnosci, 1931.
German translation (chap. 10): Stanislaw Schayer. "Feuer und Brennstoff." *Rocznik Orjentalistyczny* 7 (1931): 26-52.
Ornament for Clear Realization [of Guhyasamāja]
guhyasamājābhisamayālaṃkāravṛtti
gsang ba 'dus pa'i mngon par rtogs pa'i rgyan gyi 'grel pa
P2681, vol. 62
Supplement to (Nāgārjuna's) "Treatise on the Middle"
madhyamakāvatāra
dbu ma la 'jug pa
P5261, P5262, vol. 98
Tibetan: Louis de La Vallée Poussin. *Madhyamakāvatāra par Candrakīrti*. Bibliotheca Buddhica 9. Osnabrück, Germany: Biblio Verlag, 1970.
English translation (chaps. 1-5): Jeffrey Hopkins. *Compassion in Tibetan Buddhism*. London: Rider, 1980; reprint, Ithaca, N.Y.: Snow Lion Publications, 1980.
English translation (chap. 6): Stephen Batchelor. *Echoes of Voidness* by Geshé Rabten, 47-92. London: Wisdom Publications, 1983.
See also references under Chandrakīrti's *[Auto]commentary on the "Supplement."*
Dharmakīrti (*chos kyi grags pa*, seventh century)
Seven Treatises on Valid Cognition
1. *Analysis of Relations*
sambandhaparīkṣā
'brel pa brtag pa
P5713, vol. 130
2. *Ascertainment of Prime Cognition*
pramāṇaviniścaya
tshad ma rnam par nges pa

P5710, vol. 130

3. *Commentary on (Dignāga's) "Compilation of Prime Cognition"*
pramāṇavārttikakārikā
tshad ma rnam 'grel gyi tshig le'ur byas pa
P5709, vol. 130. Also: Sarnath, India: Pleasure of Elegant Sayings Press, 1974.
Sanskrit: Dwarikadas Shastri. *Pramāṇavārttika of Āchārya Dharmakīrtti*. Varanasi, India: Bauddha Bharati, 1968. Also, Yūsho Miyasaka. "Pramāṇavarttika-Kārikā (Sanskrit and Tibetan)," *Acta Indologica* 2 (1971-1972): 1-206. Also, (chap. 1 and autocommentary) Raniero Gnoli. *The Pramāṇavārttikam of Dharmakīrti: The First Chapter with the Autocommentary*. Rome: Istituto Italiano per il Medio ed Estremo Oriente, 1960.
English translation (chap. 2): Masatoshi Nagatomi. "A Study of Dharmakīrti's Pramāṇavarttika: An English Translation and Annotation of the Pramāṇavarttika, Book I." Ph.D. diss., Harvard University, 1957.
English translation (chap. 4, stanzas 1-148): Tom J.F. Tillemans. *Dharmakīrti's Pramāṇavārttika: An Annotated Translation of the Fourth Chapter (parārthānumāna)*, vol. 1. Vienna: Verlag der Österreichischen Akademie der Wissenschaften, 2000.

4. *Drop of Reasoning*
nyāyabinduprakaraṇa
rigs pa'i thigs pa zhes bya ba'i rab tu byed pa
P5711, vol. 130
English translation: Th. Stcherbatsky. *Buddhist Logic*. New York: Dover Publications, 1962.

5. *Drop of Reasons*
hetubindunāmaprakaraṇa
gtan tshigs kyi thigs pa zhes bya ba rab tu byed pa
P5712, vol. 130

6. *Principles of Debate*
vādanyāya
rtsod pa'i rigs pa
P5715, vol. 130

7. *Proof of Other Continuums*
saṃtānāntarasiddhināmaprakaraṇa
rgyud gzhan grub pa zhes bya ba'i rab tu byed pa
P5716, vol. 130

Dül-dzin-drak-pa-gyel-tsen (*'dul 'dzin grags pa rgyal mtshan*, 1374-1434)
Presentation of the General Rites of Action and Performance Tantra and Their Application to the Three Lineages, Set Down by Dül-dzin According to the Foremost [Tsong-kha-pa's] Practice
bya spyod kyi spyi'i cho ga'i rnam par bzhag pa rigs gsum la sbyor tshul rje'i phyag bzhes bzhin 'dul ba 'dzin pas bkod pa
Collected Works of Rje Tsoṅ-kha-pa Blo-bzaṅ-grags-pa, vol. 17 (*na*). Delhi: Ngawang Gelek, 1975. Also: Delhi: Guru Deva, 1979.

Gung-tang Kön-chok-ten-pay-drön-may (*gung thang dkon mchog bstan pa'i sgron me*, 1762-1823)
Difficult Points / Beginnings of a Commentary on the Difficult Points of (Tsong-kha-pa's) "Differentiating the Interpretable and the Definitive": Quintessence of "The Essence of Eloquence"
drang nges rnam 'byed kyi dka' 'grel rtsom 'phro legs bshad snying po'i yang snying
Sarnath, India: Guru Deva, no date. Also: New Delhi: Ngawang Gelek Demo, 1975.

Haribhadra (*seng ge bzang po*, late eighth century)
Illumination of the Eight Thousand Stanza Perfection of Wisdom Sūtra
āryāṣṭasāhasrikāprajñāpāramitāvyākhyānābhisamayālaṃkārāloka-nāma
'phags pa shes rab kyi pha rol tu phyin pa brgyad stong pa'i bshad pa mngon par rtogs pa'i rgyan gyi snang ba zhes bya ba
P5189, vol. 90

Sanskrit: Unrai Wogihara. *Abhisamayālaṃkārālokā Prajñā-pāramitā-vyākhyā, The Work of Haribhadra.* 7 vols. Tokyo: Toyo Bunko, 1932-1935; reprint, Tokyo: Sankibo Buddhist Book Store, 1973; and P. L. Vaidya. *Aṣṭasāhasrika Prajñāpāramitā, with Haribhadra's Commentary called Ālokā.* Buddhist Sanskrit Texts 4. Darbhanga, India: Mithila Institute, 1960.

English translation: E. Conze. *The Perfection of Wisdom in Eight Thousand Lines & Its Verse Summary.* Bolinas, Calif.: Four Seasons Foundation, 1973.

Hundred Means of Achievement

sgrub thabs brgya rtsa

P4127-4220, vol. 80; Toh. 3306-3309

Jam-yang-shay-pa (*'jam dbyangs bzhad pa*, 1648–1721)

Great Exposition of the Concentrations and Formless Absorptions / Treatise on the Presentations of the Concentrative and Formless Absorptions, Adornment Beautifying the Subduer's Teaching, Ocean of Scripture and Reasoning, Delighting the Fortunate

bsam gzugs chen mo/bsam gzugs kyi snyoms 'jug rnams gyi rnam par bzhag pa'i bstan bcos thub bstan mdzes rgyan lung dang rigs pa'i rgya mtsho skal bzang dga' byed

Folio printing in India; no publication data.

Also: The Collected Works of 'Jam-dbyaṅs-bzad-pa'i-rdo-rje: Reproduced from Prints from the Bkra-sis-'khyil Blocks, vol. 12. New Delhi: Ngawang Gelek Demo, 1974.

Great Exposition of Tenets / Explanation of "Tenets": Sun of the Land of Samantabhadra Brilliantly Illuminating All of Our Own and Others' Tenets and the Meaning of the Profound [Emptiness], Ocean of Scripture and Reasoning Fulfilling All Hopes of All Beings

grub mtha' chen mo / grub mtha'i rnam bshad rang gzhan grub mtha' kun dang zab don mchog tu gsal ba kun bzang zhing gi nyi ma lung rigs rgya mtsho skye dgu'i re ba kun skong

Edition cited: Musoorie, India: Dalama, 1962. Also: *Collected Works of 'Jam-dbyaṅs-bźad-pa'i-rdo-rje,* vol. 14 (entire). New Delhi: Ngawang Gelek Demo, 1973. Also: Mundgod, India: Drepung Gomang Library, 1999.

English translation (entire root text and edited portions of the autocommentary and Nga-wang-pel-den's *Annotations*): Jeffrey Hopkins. *Maps of the Profound: Jam-yang-shay-ba's Great Exposition of Buddhist and Non-Buddhist Views on the Nature of Reality.* Ithaca, N.Y.: Snow Lion Publications, 2003.

English translation (beginning of the chapter on the Consequence School): Jeffrey Hopkins. *Meditation on Emptiness,* 581-697. London: Wisdom Publications, 1983; rev. ed., Boston: Wisdom Publications, 1996.

Jang-kya Röl-pay-dor-jay (*lcang skya rol pa'i rdo rje*, 1717-1786)

Presentations of Tenets / Clear Exposition of the Presentations of Tenets: Beautiful Ornament for the Meru of the Subduer's Teaching

grub mtha'i rnam bzhag / grub pa'i mtha'i rnam par bzhag pa gsal bar bshad pa thub bstan lhun po'i mdzes rgyan

Edition cited: Varanasi, India: Pleasure of Elegant Sayings Printing Press, 1970. Also: Lokesh Chandra, ed. *Buddhist Philosophical Systems of Lcaṅ-skya Rol-pahi Rdo-rje.* Śatapiṭaka Series (Indo-Asian Literatures), vol. 233. New Delhi: International Academy of Indian Culture, 1977. Also: An edition published by gam car phan bde legs bshad gling grva tshang dang rgyud rnying slar gso tshogs pa, 1982.

English translation of Sautrāntika chapter: Anne C. Klein. *Knowing, Naming, and Negation,* 115-196. Ithaca, N.Y.: Snow Lion Publications, 1988. Commentary on this: Anne C. Klein. *Knowledge and Liberation: A Buddhist Epistemological Analysis in Support of Transformative Religious Experience.* Ithaca, N.Y.: Snow Lion Publications, 1986.

English translation of Svātantrika chapter: Donald S. Lopez, Jr. *A Study of Svātantrika,* 243-386. Ithaca, N.Y.: Snow Lion Publications, 1986.

English translation of part of Prāsaṅgika chapter: Jeffrey Hopkins. *Emptiness Yoga: The*

Tibetan Middle Way, 355-428. Ithaca, N.Y.: Snow Lion Publications, 1983.
Jñānākara
Introduction to Mantra / Introduction to Secret Mantra
mantrāvatāra
gsang sngags la 'jug pa
P4541, vol. 81
Jñānashrī
Eradicating the Two Extremes with respect to the Vajra Vehicle
vajrayānakoṭidvayāpoha
rdo rje theg pa'i mtha' gnyis sel ba
P4537, vol. 81
Ke-drup Ge-lek-pel-sang (*mkhas grub dge legs dpal bzang*, 1385-1438)
Extensive Explanation of the Format of the General Tantra Sets
rgyud sde spyi'i rnam par bzhag pa rgyas par bshad pa
Collected Works of the Lord Mkhas-grub rje dge-legs-dpal-bzaṅ-po, vol. 8, 443-630. New Delhi: Guru Deva, 1980. Also: Collected Works of Mkhas-grub dge-legs dpal, vol. 11, 215-368. New Delhi: Ngawang Gelek Demo, 1983.
Edited and translated by Ferdinand D. Lessing and Alex Wayman. *Mkhas Grub Rje's Fundamentals of the Buddhist Tantras.* The Hague: Mouton, 1968; reprint, Delhi: Motilal Banarsidass, 1978.
How to Practice the Two Stages of the Path of the Glorious Kālachakra: Quick Entry to the Path of Great Bliss
dpal dus kyi 'khor lo'i lam rim pa gnyis ji ltar nyams su len pa'i tshul bde ba chen po'i lam du myur du 'jug pa
Collected Works of Rgyal-tshab Dar-ma-rin-chen, vol. 1, 89-203. Delhi: Guru Deva, 1982. Also: Collected Works of Rgyal-tshab Dar-ma-rin-chen, vol. 1. Delhi: Ngawang Gelek Demo, 1981.
Kel-sang-gya-tso, Seventh Dalai Lama (*bskal bzang rgya mtsho*, 1708-1757)
Explanation of the Mandala Rite of the Glorious Guhyasamāja Akṣhobhyavajra: Illumination Brilliantly Clarifying the Principles of the Meaning of Initiation: Sacred Word of Vajrasattva
dpal gsang ba 'dus pa mi bskyod rdo rje'i dkyil 'khor gyi cho ga'i rnam par bshad pa dbang don de nyid yang gsal snang ba rdo rje sems dpa'i zhal lung
New Delhi: Tanzin Kunga, 1972
Kṛṣhṇachārin (*nag po pa*)
Illumination of the Secret Principles
guhyatattvaprakāśa
gsang ba'i de kho na nyid gsal ba
P2167, vol. 51
Long-chen-rap-jam (*klong chen rab 'byams / klong chen dri med 'od zer*, 1308-1363)
Precious Treasury of Tenets: Illuminating the Meaning of All Vehicles
theg pa mtha' dag gi don gsal bar byed pa grub pa'i mtha' rin po che'i mdzod
Gangtok, Sikkim: Dodrup Chen Rinpoche, 1969[?]
English translation: Albion Moonlight Butters. "The Doxographical Genius of Kun mkhyen kLong chen rab 'byams pa." Ph.D. diss., Columbia University, 2006, 298-707.
Precious Treasury of the Supreme Vehicle
theg pa'i mchog rin po che'i mdzod
Gangtok, Sikkim: Dodrup Chen Rinpoche, 1969[?].
Long-döl Nga-wang-lo-sang (*klong rdol ngag dbang blo bzang*, 1719-1794)
Terminology Arising in Secret Mantra, the Scriptural Collections of the Knowledge Bearers
gsang sngags rig pa 'dzin pa'i sde snod las byung ba'i ming gi grang
The Collected Works of Longdol Lama, Part 1, 87-170. New Delhi: International Academy of Indian Culture, 1973.

Lo-sang-chö-kyi-gyel-tsen, First Paṇ-chen Lama (*blo bzang chos kyi rgyal mtshan*, 1567?-1662)
Presentation of the General Teaching and the Four Tantra Sets, Based on Notes
bstan pa spyi dang rgyud sde'i bzhi'i rnam bzhag zin bris su byas pa
Collected Works, vol. 4, 10.1-45.3. New Delhi: Gurudeva, 1973.

Maitreya (*byams pa*)

Five Doctrines of Maitreya

1. *Sublime Continuum of the Great Vehicle / Treatise on the Later Scriptures of the Great Vehicle*
mahāyānottaratantraśāstra
theg pa chen po rgyud bla ma'i bstan bcos
P5525, vol. 108
Sanskrit: E. H. Johnston (and T. Chowdhury). *The Ratnagotravibhāga Mahāyānottaratantra-śāstra.* Patna, India: Bihar Research Society, 1950.
English translation: E. Obermiller. "Sublime Science of the Great Vehicle to Salvation." *Acta Orientalia* 9 (1931): 81-306. Also: J. Takasaki. *A Study on the Ratnagotravibhāga.* Serie Orientale Roma 33. Rome: Istituto Italiano per il Medio ed Estremo Oriente, 1966.

2. *Differentiation of Phenomena and Noumenon*
dharmadharmatāvibhaṅga
chos dang chos nyid rnam par 'byed pa
P5523, vol. 108
Edited Tibetan: Jōshō Nozawa. "The *Dharmadharmatāvibhaṅga* and the *Dharmadharmatāvibhaṅgavṛtti,* Tibetan Texts, Edited and Collated, Based upon the Peking and Derge Editions." In *Studies in Indology and Buddhology: Presented in Honour of Professor Susumu Yamaguchi on the Occasion of his Sixtieth Birthday,* edited by Gadjin M. Nagao and Jōshō Nozawa. Kyoto: Hozokan, 1955.
English translation: John Younghan Cha. "A Study of the *Dharmadharmatāvibhāga:* An Analysis of the Religious Philosophy of the Yogācāra, Together with an Annotated Translation of Vasubandhu's Commentary." Ph.D. diss., Northwestern University, 1996.
English translation: Jim Scott. *Maitreya's Distinguishing Phenomena and Pure Being with Commentary by Mipham.* Ithaca, N.Y.: Snow Lion Publications, 2004.

3. *Differentiation of the Middle and the Extremes*
madhyāntavibhaṅga
dbus dang mtha' rnam par 'byed pa
P5522, vol. 108
Sanskrit: Gadjin M. Nagao. *Madhyāntavibhāga-bhāṣya.* Tokyo: Suzuki Research Foundation, 1964. Also: Ramchandra Pandeya. *Madhyānta-vibhāga-śāstra.* Delhi: Motilal Banarsidass, 1971.
English translation: Stefan Anacker. *Seven Works of Vasubandhu.* Delhi: Motilal Banarsidass, 1984. Also, of chapter 1: Thomas A. Kochumuttom. *A Buddhist Doctrine of Experience.* Delhi: Motilal Banarsidass, 1982. Also, of chapter 1: Th. Stcherbatsky. *Madhyāntavibhāga, Discourse on Discrimination between Middle and Extremes Ascribed to Bodhisattva Maitreya and Commented by Vasubandhu and Sthiramati.* Bibliotheca Buddhica 30 (1936). Osnabrück, Germany: Biblio Verlag, 1970; reprint, Calcutta: Indian Studies Past and Present, 1971. Also, of chapter 1: David Lasar Friedmann. *Sthiramati, Madhyāntavibhāgaṭīkā: Analysis of the Middle Path and the Extremes.* Utrecht, Netherlands: Rijksuniversiteit te Leiden, 1937.

4. *Ornament for Clear Realization*
abhisamayālaṃkāra
mngon par rtogs pa'i rgyan
P5184, vol. 88
Sanskrit: Th. Stcherbatsky and E. Obermiller, eds. *Abhisamayālaṃkāra-Prajñāpāramitā-Upadeśa-Śāstra.* Bibliotheca Buddhica 23. Osnabrück, Germany: Biblio Verlag, 1970.

English translation: Edward Conze. *Abhisamayālaṃkāra.* Serie Orientale Roma 6. Rome: Istituto Italiano per il Medio ed Estremo Oriente, 1954.

5. *Ornament for the Great Vehicle Sūtras*
mahāyānasūtrālaṃkāra
theg pa chen po'i mdo sde rgyan gyi tshig le'ur byas pa
P5521, vol. 108
Sanskrit: Sitansusekhar Bagchi. *Mahāyāna-Sūtrālaṃkāraḥ of Asaṅga* [with Vasubandhu's commentary]. Buddhist Sanskrit Texts 13. Darbhanga, India: Mithila Institute, 1970.
Sanskrit text and translation into French: Sylvain Lévi. *Mahāyānasūtrālaṃkāra, exposé de la doctrine du grand véhicule selon le système Yogācāra.* Bibliothèque de l'École des Hautes Études. 2 vols. Paris: Libraire Honoré Champion, 1907, 1911.
Sanskrit text and translation into English: Surekha Vijay Limaye. *Mahāyānasūtrālaṃkāra by Asaṅga.* Bibliotheca Indo-Buddhica Series 94. Delhi: Sri Satguru, 1992.
English translation: L. Jamspal et al. *The Universal Vehicle Discourse Literature.* Editor-in-chief, Robert A.F. Thurman. New York: American Institute of Buddhist Studies, Columbia University, 2004.

Mātṛceta and Dignāga (*phyogs kyi glang po,* sixth century)
Interwoven Praise
miśrakastotra
dpel mar bstod pa
P2041, vol. 46; Toh. 1150

Nāgabodhi (*klu byang*)
Clear Meaning Commentary on (Nāgārjuna's) "Five Stages"
pañcakramaṭīkāmaṇimālā
rim pa lnga pa'i bshad pa nor bu'i phreng ba
P2697, vol. 62

Nāgārjuna (*klu sgrub,* first to second century, C.E.)
Five Stages
pañcakrama
rim pa lnga pa
P2667, vol. 61
Sanskrit: Katsumi Mimaki and Tōru Tomabechi. *Pañcakrama.* Bibliotheca Codicum Asiaticorum 8. Tokyo: Centre for East Asian Cultural Studies for UNESCO, 1994.
English translation of the introductory stanzas: Alex Wayman, *Yoga of the Guhyasamājatantra.* Delhi: Motilal Banarsidass, 1977.
Praise of the Element of Attributes
dharmadhātustotra
chos kyi dbyings su bstod pa
P2010, vol. 46; Toh. 1118, vol. ka
Praise of the Non-Conceptual
*nirvikalpastava
rnam par mi rtog pa la bstod pa
[?]

Six Collections of Reasonings

1. *Precious Garland of Advice for the King*
rājaparikathāratnāvalī
rgyal po la gtam bya ba rin po che'i phreng ba
P5658, vol. 129
Sanskrit, Tibetan, and Chinese: Michael Hahn. *Nāgārjuna's Ratnāvalī,* vol. 1. *The Basic Texts (Sanskrit, Tibetan, and Chinese).* Bonn: Indica et Tibetica Verlag, 1982.
English translation: Jeffrey Hopkins. *Buddhist Advice for Living and Liberation: Nāgārjuna's Precious Garland,* 94-164. Ithaca, N.Y.: Snow Lion Publications, 1998. Supersedes that

in: Nāgārjuna and the Seventh Dalai Lama. *The Precious Garland and the Song of the Four Mindfulnesses,* translated by Jeffrey Hopkins, 17-93. London: George Allen and Unwin, 1975; New York: Harper and Row, 1975; reprint, in H.H. the Dalai Lama, Tenzin Gyatso. *The Buddhism of Tibet.* London: George Allen and Unwin, 1983; reprint, Ithaca, N.Y.: Snow Lion Publications, 1987.

English translation: John Dunne and Sara McClintock. *The Precious Garland: An Epistle to a King.* Boston: Wisdom Publications, 1997.

English translation of chap. 1, 1-77: Giuseppe Tucci. "The *Ratnāvalī* of Nāgārjuna." *Journal of the Royal Asiatic Society* (1934): 307-324; reprint, Giuseppe Tucci. *Opera Minora,* II. Rome: Giovanni Bardi Editore, 1971, 321-366. Chap. 2, 1-46; chap. 4, 1-100: Giuseppe Tucci. "The *Ratnāvalī* of Nāgārjuna." *Journal of the Royal Asiatic Society* (1936): 237-252, 423-435.

Japanese translation: Uryūzu Ryushin. *Butten II, Sekai Koten Bungaku Zenshu,* 7 (July, 1965): 349-372. Edited by Nakamura Hajime. Tokyo: Chikuma Shobō. Also: Uryūzu Ryushin. *Daijō Butten* 14 (1974): 231-316. *Ryūju Ronshū.* Edited by Kajiyama Yuichi and Uryūzu Ryushin. Tokyo: Chūōkōronsha.

Danish translation: Christian Lindtner. *Nagarjuna, Juvelkaeden og andre skrifter.* Copenhagen, 1980.

2. *Refutation of Objections*
   vigrahavyāvartanīkārikā
   rtsod pa bzlog pa'i tshig le'ur byas pa
   P5228, vol. 95
   Edited Tibetan and Sanskrit: Christian Lindtner. *Nagarjuniana,* 70-86. Indiske Studier 4. Copenhagen: Akademisk Forlag, 1982.
   Edited Sanskrit and English translation: K. Bhattacharya, E. H. Johnston, and A. Kunst. *The Dialectical Method of Nāgārjuna.* New Delhi: Motilal Banarsidass, 1978.
   English translation from the Chinese: G. Tucci. *Pre-Diṅnāga Buddhist Texts on Logic from Chinese Sources.* Gaekwad's Oriental Series 49. Baroda, India: Oriental Institute, 1929.
   French translation: S. Yamaguchi. "Traité de Nāgārjuna pour écarter les vaines discussion (Vigrahavyāvartanī) traduit et annoté." *Journal Asiatique* 215 (1929): 1-86.
3. *Seventy Stanzas on Emptiness*
   śūnyatāsaptatikārikā
   stong pa nyid bdun cu pa'i tshig le'ur byas pa
   P5227, vol. 95
   Edited Tibetan and English translation: Christian Lindtner. *Nagarjuniana,* 34-69. Indiske Studier 4. Copenhagen: Akademisk Forlag, 1982.
   English translation: David Ross Komito. *Nāgārjuna's "Seventy Stanzas": A Buddhist Psychology of Emptiness.* Ithaca, N.Y.: Snow Lion Publications, 1987.
4. *Sixty Stanzas of Reasoning*
   yuktiṣaṣṭikākārikā
   rigs pa drug cu pa'i tshig le'ur byas pa
   P5225, vol. 95
   Edited Tibetan with Sanskrit fragments and English translation: Christian Lindtner. *Nagarjuniana,* 100-119. Indiske Studier 4. Copenhagen: Akademisk Forlag, 1982.
5. *Treatise Called the Finely Woven*
   vaidalyasūtranāma
   zhib mo rnam par 'thag pa zhes bya ba'i mdo
   P5226, vol. 95
   Tibetan text and English translation: Fernando Tola and Carmen Dragonetti. *Nāgārjuna's Refutation of Logic (Nyāya) Vaidalyaprakaraṇa.* Delhi: Motilal Banarsidass, 1995.
6. *Treatise on the Middle / Fundamental Treatise on the Middle, Called "Wisdom"*
   madhyamakaśāstra / prajñānāmamūlamadhyamakakārikā

dbu ma'i bstan bcos / dbu ma rtsa ba'i tshig le'ur byas pa shes rab ces bya ba
P5224, vol. 95
Edited Sanskrit: J. W. de Jong. *Nāgārjuna, Mūlamadhyamakakārikāḥ*. Madras, India: Adyar Library and Research Centre, 1977; reprint, Wheaton, Ill.: Theosophical Publishing House, c. 1977. Also: Christian Lindtner. *Nāgārjuna's Filosofiske Vaerker*, 177-215. Indiske Studier 2. Copenhagen: Akademisk Forlag, 1982.
English translation: Frederick Streng. *Emptiness: A Study in Religious Meaning*. Nashville, Tenn.: Abingdon Press, 1967. Also: Kenneth Inada. *Nāgārjuna: A Translation of His Mūlamadhyamakakārikā*. Tokyo: Hokuseido Press, 1970. Also: David J. Kalupahana. *Nāgārjuna: The Philosophy of the Middle Way*. Albany, N.Y.: State University of New York Press, 1986. Also: Jay L. Garfield. *The Fundamental Wisdom of the Middle Way*. New York: Oxford University Press, 1995.
Italian translation: R. Gnoli. *Nāgārjuna: Madhyamaka Kārikā, Le stanze del cammino di mezzo*. Enciclopedia di autori classici 61. Turin, Italy: P. Boringhieri, 1961.
Danish translation: Christian Lindtner. *Nāgārjuna's Filosofiske Vaerker*, 67-135. Indiske Studier 2. Copenhagen: Akademisk Forlag, 1982.

Means of Achievement of the Retention of the Thousand-Armed Avalokiteshvara
sahasrabhujāvalokiteśvarasādhana
spyan ras gzigs dbang phyug phyag stong sgrub thabs
P3555, vol. 79

Nga-wang-ke-drup (*ngag dbang mkhas grub*, 1779-1838)
Presentation of Death, Intermediate State, and Rebirth
skye shi bar do'i rnam bzhag
Collected Works of Ṅag-dbaṅ-mkhas-grub, Kyai-rdor Mkhan-po of Urga, vol. 1, 459-474. Leh, Ladakh: S. Tashigangpa, 1973.

Nga-wang-lo-sang-gya-tso (*ngag dbang blo bzang rgya mtsho*, Fifth Dalai Lama, 1617-1682)
Instructions on the Stages of the Path to Enlightenment: Sacred Word of Mañjushrī
byang chub lam gyi rim pa'i 'khrid yig 'jam pa'i dbyangs kyi zhal lung
Thimphu, Bhutan: kun bzang stobs rgyal, 1976.
English translation of the "Perfection of Wisdom Chapter": Jeffrey Hopkins. "Practice of Emptiness." Dharmsala: Library of Tibetan Works and Archives, 1974.

Nga-wang-pel-den (*ngag dbang dpal ldan*, b. 1797), also known as Pel-den-chö-jay (*dpal ldan chos rje*)
Presentation of the Grounds and Paths of the Four Great Secret Tantra Sets: Illumination of the Texts of Tantra
gsang chen rgyud sde bzhi'i sa lam gyi rnam bzhag rgyud gzhung gsal byed
rgyud smad par khang edition, no other data

Ocean of Means of Achievement
sādhanasāgara
sgrub thabs rgya mtsho
P4221-4466, vols. 80-81; Toh. 3400-3644

One Hundred and Fifty Means of Achievement
phyed dang nyis brgya pa
P3964-4126, vol. 80; Toh. 3143-3304

Padma-kar-po (*pad ma dkar po*, 1527-1592)
Presentation of the General Tantra Sets: Captivating the Wise
rgyud sde spyi'i rnam gzhag mkhas pa'i yid 'phrog
Collected Works of Kun-mkhyen Padma-dkar-po, vol. 11, 251-334. Darjeeling, India: Kargyud Sungrab Nyamso Khang, 1973-1974.

Paṇ-chen Sö-nam-drak-pa (*paṇ chen bsod nams grags pa*, 1478-1554)
Presentation of the General Tantra Sets: Captivating the Minds of the Fortunate
rgyud sde spyi'i rnam par bzhag pa skal bzang gi yid 'phrog

Dharmsala, India: Library of Tibetan Works and Archives, 1975

English translation: Panchen Sonam Dragpa, *Overview of Buddhist Tantra,* trans. by Martin J Boord and Losang Norbu Tsonawa. Dharmsala, India: Library of Tibetan Works and Archives, 1996.

Puṇḍarīka, Kalkī (*rigs ldan pad ma dkar po*)

Great Commentary on the "Kālachakra Tantra": Stainless Light

vimalaprabhānāmamūlatantrānusāriṇīdvādaśasāhasrikālaghukālacakratantrarājaṭīkā

bsdus pa'i rgyud kyi rgyal po dus kyi 'khor lo'i 'grel bshad rtsa ba'i rgyud kyi rjes su 'jug pa stong phrag bcu gnyis pa dri ma med pa'i 'od ces bya ba

P2064, vol. 46

English translation (chapter 1): John Newman. *The Outer Wheel of Time: Vajrayāna Buddhist Cosmology in the Kālacakra Tantra.* Ann Arbor, MI: University Microfilms International, 1987.

English translation and Mongolian text (chapter 2): Vesna Acimovic Wallace. *The Inner* Kālacakratantra: *A Buddhist Tantric View of the Individual.* 2 vols. PhD diss., University of California at Berkeley, 1995; and *Kālacakratantra: The Chapter on the Individual together with the Vimalaprabhā.* New York: American Institute of Buddhist Studies, 2004.

Ratnākarashānti (*rin chen 'byung gnas zhi ba*)

Commentary on (Dīpaṅkarabhadra's) "Rite of the Guhyasamāja Maṇḍala" / Commentary on (Dīpaṅkarabhadra's) "Four Hundred and Fifty"

guhyasamājamaṇḍalavidhiṭīkā

dpal gsang ba 'dus pa'i dkyil 'khor gyi cho ga'i 'grel pa

P2734, vol. 65

Commentary on the "All Secret Tantra"

sarvarahasyanibandharahasyapradīpa

thams cad gsang ba'i bshad sbyar gsang ba'i sgron ma

P3450, vol. 76

Handful of Flowers, Explanation of the Guhyasamāja Tantra

kusumāñjaliguhyasamājanibandha

gsang ba 'dus pa'i bshad sbyar snyim pa'i me tog

P2714, vol. 64

Presentation of the Three Vehicles

triyānavyavasthāna

theg pa gsum rnam par bzhag pa

P4535, vol. 81

Ratnarakṣhita

Commentary on the Difficult Points of the Saṃvarodaya Tantra

saṃvarodayamahātantrarājasyapadminīnāmapañjikā

sdom pa 'byung ba'i rgyud kyi rgyal po chen po'i dka' 'grel padma can

P2137, vol. 51

Sa-kya Paṇḍita (*sa skya paṇḍita kun dga' rgyal mtshan,* 1182-1251)

Differentiation of the Three Vows

sdom gsum rab dbye/ sdom pa gsum gyi rab tu dbye ba'i sdom gsum rang mchan 'khrul med

New Delhi: Pal-lden Sa-kya'i Sung-rab Book Publication, 1985.

English translation: Jared Douglas Rhoton. *A Clear Differentiation of the Three Codes: Essential Distinctions among the Individual Liberation, Great Vehicle, and Tantric Systems: the Sdom gsum rab dbye and Six Letters.* Albany: State University of New York Press, 2002.

Shākyamitra (*shākya'i bshes gnyen*)

Commentary on (Āryadeva's) "Lamp Compendium for Practice"

caryāmelāyanapradīpanāmaṭīkā

spyod pa bsdus pa'i sgron ma shes bya ba rgya cher bshad pa

P2703, vol. 62
Shāntideva (*zhi ba lha*, eighth century)
Engaging in the Bodhisattva Deeds
bodhi[sattva]caryāvatāra
byang chub sems dpa'i spyod pa la 'jug pa
Toh. 3871, *dbu ma*, vol. *la*
Sanskrit: P. L. Vaidya. *Bodhicaryāvatāra*. Buddhist Sanskrit Texts 12. Darbhanga, India: Mithila Institute, 1988.
Sanskrit and Tibetan: Vidhushekara Bhattacharya. *Bodhicaryāvatāra*. Bibliotheca Indica, 280. Calcutta: Asiatic Society, 1960.
Sanskrit and Tibetan with Hindi translation: Rāmaśaṃkara Tripāthī, ed. *Bodhicaryāvatāra*. Bauddha-Himālaya-Granthamālā, 8. Leh, Ladākh: Central Institute of Buddhist Studies, 1989.
English translation: Stephen Batchelor. *A Guide to the Bodhisattva's Way of Life*. Dharmsala, India: Library of Tibetan Works and Archives, 1979. Also: Marion Matics. *Entering the Path of Enlightenment*. New York: Macmillan, 1970. Also: Kate Crosby and Andrew Skilton. *The Bodhicaryāvatāra*. Oxford: Oxford University Press, 1996. Also: Padmakara Translation Group. *The Way of the Bodhisattva*. Boston: Shambhala, 1997. Also: Vesna A. Wallace and B. Alan Wallace. *A Guide to the Bodhisattva Way of Life*. Ithaca, N.Y.: Snow Lion Publications, 1997.
Contemporary commentary by H.H. the Dalai Lama, Tenzin Gyatso. *Transcendent Wisdom*. Ithaca, N.Y.: Snow Lion Publications, 1988. Also: H.H. the Dalai Lama, Tenzin Gyatso. *A Flash of Lightning in the Dark of the Night*. Boston: Shambhala, 1994.
Shākyamitra (*shākya'i bshes gnyen*)
Ornament of Kosala
kosalālaṃkāratattvasaṃgrahaṭīkā
de kho na nyid bsdus pa'i rgya cher bshad pa ko sa la'i rgyan
P3326, vols. 70-71; D2503, vol. *yi*.
Shraddhākaravarma
Introduction to the Meaning of the Highest Yoga Tantras
yogānuttaratantrārthāvatārasaṃgraha
rnal 'byor bla med pa'i rgyud kyi don la 'jug pa bsdus pa
P4536, vol. 81; Toh. 3713
Shrīdhara
Commentary on the Difficult Points of the "Yamāri Tantra": Innate Illumination
yamāritantrapañjikāsahajāloka
gshin rje gshed kyi rgyud kyi dka' 'grel lhan cig skyes pa'i snang ba
P2781, vol. 66
Sö-nam-tzay-mo (*bsod nams rtse mo*, 1142-1182)
Presentation of the General Tantra Sets
rgyud sde spyi'i rnam par gzhag pa
Gangtok, 'Bras-ljongs-sa-ngor-chos-tshogs, 1969
Tripiṭakamāla
Lamp for the Three Modes
nayatrayapradīpa
tshul gsum gyi sgron ma
Toh. 3707; Dharma vol. 62
Tsong-kha-pa Lo-sang-drak-pa (*tsong kha pa blo bzang grags pa*, 1357-1419)
Explanation of (Nāgārjuna's) "Treatise on the Middle": Ocean of Reasoning / Great Commentary on (Nāgārjuna's) "Treatise on the Middle"
dbu ma rtsa ba'i tshig le'ur byas pa shes rab ces bya ba'i rnam bshad rigs pa'i rgya mtsho / rtsa shes ṭik chen

P6153, vol. 156. Also: Sarnath, India: Pleasure of Elegant Sayings Printing Press, n.d. Also: *rJe tsong kha pa'i gsung dbu ma'i lta ba'i skor,* vols. 1-2. Sarnath, India: Pleasure of Elegant Sayings Press, 1975. Also: Delhi: Ngawang Gelek, 1975. Also: Delhi: Guru Deva, 1979.

English translation (chap. 2): Jeffrey Hopkins. *Ocean of Reasoning.* Dharmsala, India: Library of Tibetan Works and Archives, 1974.

Great Exposition of the Stages of Secret Mantra / The Stages of the Path to a Conqueror and Pervasive Master, a Great Vajradhara: Revealing All Secret Topics

sngags rim chen mo / rgyal ba khyab bdag rdo rje 'chang chen po'i lam gyi rim pa gsang ba kun gyi gnad rnam par phye ba

P6210, vol. 161. Also: Delhi: Ngawang Gelek, 1975. Also: Delhi: Guru Deva, 1979.

English translation (chap. 1): H.H. the Dalai Lama, Tsong-kha-pa, and Jeffrey Hopkins. *Tantra in Tibet.* London: George Allen and Unwin, 1977; reprint, with minor corrections, Ithaca, N.Y.: Snow Lion Publications, 1987.

English translation (chaps. 2-3): H.H. the Dalai Lama, Tsong-kha-pa, and Jeffrey Hopkins. *The Yoga of Tibet.* London: George Allen and Unwin, 1981; reprinted as *Deity Yoga.* Ithaca, N.Y.: Snow Lion Publications, 1987.

English translation (chap. 4): H.H. the Dalai Lama, Dzong-ka-ba, and Jeffrey Hopkins. *Yoga Tantra: Paths to Magical Feats.* Ithaca, N.Y.: Snow Lion Publications, 2005.

Great Exposition of the Stages of the Path / Stages of the Path to Enlightenment Thoroughly Teaching All the Stages of Practice of the Three Types of Beings

lam rim chen mo / skyes bu gsum gyi nyams su blang ba'i rim pa thams cad tshang bar ston pa'i byang chub lam gyi rim pa

P6001, vol. 152. Also: Dharmsala, India: Tibetan Cultural Printing Press, 1964. Also: Delhi: Ngawang Gelek, 1975. Also: Delhi: Guru Deva, 1979.

English translation: Tsong-kha-pa. *The Great Treatise on the Stages of the Path to Enlightenment.* 3 vols. Trans. and ed. Joshua W. C. Cutler and Guy Newland. Ithaca, N.Y.: Snow Lion Publications, 2000-2004.

English translation of the part on the excessively broad object of negation: Elizabeth Napper. *Dependent-Arising and Emptiness,* 153-215. London: Wisdom Publications, 1989.

English translation of the parts on calm abiding and special insight: Alex Wayman. *Calming the Mind and Discerning the Real,* 81-431. New York: Columbia University Press, 1978; reprint, New Delhi: Motilal Banarsidass, 1979.

Extensive Explanation of (Chandrakīrti's) "Supplement to (Nāgārjuna's) 'Treatise on the Middle'": Illumination of the Thought

dbu ma la 'jug pa'i rgya cher bshad pa dgongs pa rab gsal

P6143, vol. 154. Also: Sarnath, India: Pleasure of Elegant Sayings Press, 1973. Also: Delhi: Ngawang Gelek, 1975. Also: Delhi: Guru Deva, 1979.

English translation (chapters 1-5): Jeffrey Hopkins. *Compassion in Tibetan Buddhism,* 93-230. Ithaca, N.Y.: Snow Lion Publications, 1980.

English translation (chap. 6, stanzas 1-7): Jeffrey Hopkins and Anne C. Klein. *Path to the Middle: Madhyamaka Philosophy in Tibet: The Oral Scholarship of Kensur Yeshay Tupden,* by Anne C. Klein, 147-183, 252-271. Albany, N.Y.: State University of New York Press, 1994.

Medium-Length Exposition of the Stages of the Path / Small Exposition of the Stages of the Path to Enlightenment

lam rim 'bring / lam rim chung ngu / skyes bu gsum gyi nyams su blang ba'i byang chub lam gyi rim pa

P6002, vols. 152-153. Also: Dharmsala, India: Tibetan Cultural Printing Press, 1968. Also: Mundgod, India: dga' ldan shar rtse, n.d. (includes outline of topics by Trijang Rinbochay). Also: Delhi: Ngawang Gelek, 1975. Also: Delhi: Guru Deva, 1979.

English translation of the section on special insight: Jeffrey Hopkins. *Tsong-kha-pa's Final*

Exposition of Wisdom. Ithaca, N.Y.: Snow Lion Publications, 2008. Also: Robert Thurman. "The Middle Transcendent Insight." *Life and Teachings of Tsong Khapa,* 108-185. Dharmsala, India: Library of Tibetan Works and Archives, 1982.

Quintessential Instructions on the King of Tantras, the Glorious Guhyasamāja: Lamp Thoroughly Illuminating the Five Stages

rgyud kyi rgyal po dpal gsang ba 'dus pa'i man ngag rim pa lnga rab tu gsal ba'i sgron me

Varanasi: 1969

Treatise Differentiating the Interpretable and the Definitive: The Essence of Eloquence

drang ba dang nges pa'i don rnam par phye ba'i bstan bcos legs bshad snying po

Editions: see the preface to my critical edition, *Emptiness in the Mind-Only School of Buddhism,* 355. Also: Ye shes thabs mkhas. *shar tsong kha pa blo bzang grags pas mdzad pa'i drang ba dang nges pa'i don rnam par phye ba'i bstan bcos legs bshad snying po.* Tā la'i bla ma'i 'phags bod, vol. 22. Varanasi, India: vāṇa dbus bod kyi ches mtho'i gtsug lag slob gnyer khang, 1997.

English translation: Prologue and Mind-Only section, *Emptiness in the Mind-Only School of Buddhism, Dynamic Responses to Dzong-ka-ba's* The Essence of Eloquence, volume 1. Berkeley: University of California Press, 1999; Delhi: Munshiram Manoharlal, 2000. Also: Robert A. F. Thurman. *Tsong Khapa's Speech of Gold in the Essence of True Eloquence,* 185-385. Princeton, N.J.: Princeton University Press, 1984.

Chinese translation: Venerable Fa Zun. "Bian Liao Yi Bu Liao Yi Shuo Cang Lun." In *Xi Zang Fo Jiao Jiao Yi Lun Ji,* 2, 159-276. Taipei: Da Sheng Wen Hua Chu Ban She, 1979.

Vajragarbha (*rdo rje snying po*)

Commentary on the Condensation of the Hevajra Tantra

hevajrapiṇḍārthaṭīkā

kye'i rdo rje bsdus pa'i don gyi rgya cher 'grel pa

P2310, vol. 53

Vajrapāṇi (*phyag na rdo rje,* born 1017)

Quintessential Instructions on the Stages of the Guru Transmission

guruparaṃparakramopadeśa

bla ma brgyud pa'i rim pa'i man ngag

P4539, vol. 81

Varabodhi (*byang chub mchog/ ye shes mchog*)

Condensed Means of Achievement of Susiddhi/ Clear Realization of Susiddhi

susiddhikarasādhanasaṃgraha

legs par grub par byed pa'i sgrub pa'i thabs bsdus pa

P3890, vol. 79

Vasubandhu (*dbyig gnyen,* fl. 360)

Eight Prakaraṇa Treatises

1. *Commentary on (Maitreya's) "Differentiation of the Middle and the Extremes"*

madhyāntavibhāgaṭīkā

dbus dang mtha' rnam par 'byed pa'i 'grel pa / dbus mtha'i 'grel pa

P5528, vol. 108

Sanskrit: Gadjin M. Nagao. *Madhyāntavibhāga-bhāṣya.* Tokyo: Suzuki Research Foundation, 1964. Also: Ramchandra Pandeya. *Madhyānta-vibhāga-śāstra.* Delhi: Motilal Banarsidass, 1971.

English translation: Stefan Anacker. *Seven Works of Vasubandhu.* Delhi: Motilal Banarsidass, 1984. Also: Thomas A. Kochumuttom. *A Buddhist Doctrine of Experience.* Delhi: Motilal Banarsidass, 1982. Also, of chapter 1: Th. Stcherbatsky. *Madhyāntavibhāga: Discourse on Discrimination between Middle and Extremes Ascribed to Bodhisattva Maitreya and Commented by Vasubandhu and Sthiramati.* Bibliotheca Buddhica 30 (1936). Osnabrück, Germany: Biblio Verlag, 1970; reprint, Calcutta: Indian Studies Past and Present, 1971.

Also, of chapter 1: David Lasar Friedmann, *Sthiramati, Madhyāntavibhāgaṭīkā: Analysis of the Middle Path and the Extremes.* Utrecht, Netherlands: Rijksuniversiteit te Leiden, 1937.

2. *Explanation of (Maitreya's) "Ornament for the Great Vehicle Sūtras"*
   sūtrālaṃkārābhāṣya
   mdo sde'i rgyan gyi bshad pa
   P5527, vol. 108
   Sanskrit: S. Bagchi. *Mahāyāna-Sūtrālaṃkāra of Asaṅga* [with Vasubandhu's commentary]. Buddhist Sanskrit Texts 13. Darbhanga, India: Mithila Institute, 1970.
   Sanskrit and translation into French: Sylvain Lévi. *Mahāyānasūtrālaṃkāra, exposé de la doctrine du grand véhicule selon le système Yogācāra.* 2 vols. Paris: Libraire Honoré Champion, 1907, 1911.
   English translation: L. Jamspal et al. *The Universal Vehicle Discourse Literature.* Editor-in-chief, Robert A.F. Thurman. New York: American Institute of Buddhist Studies, Columbia University, 2004.
3. *Principles of Explanation*
   vyākhyayukti
   rnam par bshad pa'i rigs pa
   P5562, vol. 113
4. *The Thirty / Treatise on Cognition-Only in Thirty Stanzas*
   triṃśikākārikā / sarvavijñānamātradeśakatriṃśakakārikā
   sum cu pa'i tshig le'ur byas pa / thams cad rnam rig tsam du ston pa sum cu pa'i tshig le'ur byas pa
   P5556, vol. 113
   Sanskrit: Sylvain Lévi. *Vijñaptimātratāsiddhi / Deux traités de Vasubandhu: Viṃśatikā (La Vingtaine) et Triṃsikā (La Trentaine).* Bibliothèque de l'École des Hautes Études. Paris: Libraire Honoré Champion, 1925. Also: K. N. Chatterjee. *Vijñapti-Mātratā-Siddhi (with Sthiramati's Commentary).* Varanasi, India: Kishor Vidya Niketan, 1980.
   English translation: Stefan Anacker. *Seven Works of Vasubandhu.* Delhi: Motilal Banarsidass, 1984. Also: Thomas A. Kochumuttom. *A Buddhist Doctrine of Experience.* Delhi: Motilal Banarsidass, 1982.
5. *Treasury of Manifest Knowledge*
   abhidharmakośakārikā
   chos mngon pa'i mdzod kyi tshig le'ur byas pa
   P5590, vol. 115
   Sanskrit: Swami Dwarikadas Shastri. *Abhidharmakośa & Bhāṣya of Ācārya Vasubandhu with Sphuṭārtha Commentary of Ācārya Yaśomitra.* Bauddha Bharati Series 5. Banaras, India: Bauddha Bharati, 1970. Also: P. Pradhan. *Abhidharmakośabhāṣyam of Vasubandhu.* Patna, India: Jayaswal Research Institute, 1975.
   French translation: Louis de La Vallée Poussin. *L'Abhidharmakośa de Vasubandhu.* 6 vols. Brussels: Institut Belge des Hautes Études Chinoises, 1971.
   English translation of the French: Leo M. Pruden. *Abhidharmakośabhāṣyam.* 4 vols. Berkeley, Calif.: Asian Humanities Press, 1988.
6. *The Twenty*
   viṃśatikā / viṃśikākārikā
   nyi shu pa'i tshig le'ur byas pa
   P5557, vol. 113
   Sanskrit: Sylvain Lévi. *Vijñaptimātratāsiddhi / Deux traités de Vasubandhu: Viṃśatikā (La Vingtaine) et Triṃsikā (La Trentaine).* Bibliotheque de l'École des Hautes Études. Paris: Libraire Honoré Champion, 1925.
   English translation: Stefan Anacker. *Seven Works of Vasubandhu.* Delhi: Motilal Banarsidass, 1984. Also: Thomas A. Kochumuttom. *A Buddhist Doctrine of Experience.* Delhi: Mo-

tilal Banarsidass, 1982.
English translation (stanzas 1-10): Gregory A. Hillis. "An Introduction and Translation of Vinītadeva's Explanation of the First Ten Stanzas of [Vasubandhu's] Commentary on His 'Twenty Stanzas,' with Appended Glossary of Technical Terms." M.A. thesis, University of Virginia, 1993.

7. *Work on Achieving Actions*
karmasiddhiprakaraṇa
las grub pa'i rab tu byed pa
P5563, vol. 113
French translation (chap. 17): É. Lamotte. "Le Traité de l'acte de Vasubandhu, Karmasiddhiprakaraṇa." *Mélanges Chinois et Bouddhiques* 4 (1936): 265-288.

8. *Work on the Five Aggregates*
pañcaskandhaprakaraṇa
phung po lnga'i rab tu byed pa
P5560, vol. 113

Vinayadatta (*'dul bas byin*)
Rite of the Great Illusion Maṇḍala
gurūpadeśanāmamahāmāyāmaṇḍalopāyika
sgyu 'phrul chen mo'i dkyil 'khor gyi cho ga bla ma'i zhal snga'i man ngag
P2517, vol. 57; Toh. 1645

Yang-jen-ga-way-lo-drö, A-kya-yong-dzin (*dbyangs can dga' ba'i blo gros, a khya yongs 'dzin,* c. 1750)
Lamp Thoroughly Illuminating the Presentation of the Three Basic Bodies
gzhi'i sku gsum gyi rnam gzhag rab gsal sgron me
Collected Works of A-kya Yongs-'dzin, vol. 1. New Delhi: Lama Guru Deva 1971. Also: Delhi: Dalama, Iron Dog year. Also: Nang-bstan-shes-rig-'dzin-skyong slob-gnyer-khang, n.d.
English translation: Lati Rinbochay and Jeffrey Hopkins. *Death, Intermediate State and Rebirth in Tibetan Buddhism.* London: Rider, 1980; Ithaca, N.Y.: Snow Lion Publications, 1980.

Ye-shay-gyel-tsen, Tsay-chok-ling-yong-dzin (*ye shes rgyal mtshan, tshe mchog gling yongs 'dzin,* 1713-1793)
Illumination of the Meaning of Action Tantra
bya rgyud don gsal
Collected Works of Tshe-mchog-gling Ye-shes-rgyal-mtshan, vol. 9. New Delhi: Tibet House, 1976.

3. Other Works

Eliade, Mircea. *Patañjali and Yoga.* Trans. by C.L. Markmann. New York: Funk and Wagnalls, 1969.

Evans-Wentz, W.Y., compiled and edited. *The Tibetan Book of the Dead.* London: Oxford University Press, 1960.

Guenther, Herbert V. "Buddhism in Tibet," in M. Eliade, ed., *Encyclopedia of Religion,* vol. 2. New York: Macmillan, 1986.

——. *The Jewel Ornament of Liberation by sGam-po-pa.* London: Rider, 1963; rpt. Berkeley: Shambhala, 1971.

——. *Tibetan Buddhism Without Mystification.* Leiden: Brill, 1966.

His Holiness the Dalai Lama. *How to Expand Love: Widening the Circle of Loving Relationships,* trans. and ed. by Jeffrey Hopkins. New York: Atria Books/Simon and Schuster, 2005.

——. *How to See Yourself As You Really Are.* Translated and edited by Jeffrey Hopkins. New York: Atria Books/Simon and Schuster, 2007.

——. *The Dalai Lama at Harvard.* Ithaca, N.Y.: Snow Lion Publications, 1989. Jeffrey Hopkins, trans. and ed.

His Holiness the Dalai Lama, Tenzin Gyatso, and Jeffrey Hopkins. *The Kālachakra Tantra: Rite of Initiation for the Stage of Generation.* London: Wisdom Publications, 1985; 2nd rev. ed., 1989.

Hopkins, Jeffrey. *Absorption In No External World: 170 Issues in Mind-Only Buddhism, Dynamic Responses to Dzong-ka-ba's* The Essence of Eloquence, Volume 3. Ithaca, N.Y.: Snow Lion Publications, 2005.

——. *Emptiness in the Mind-Only School of Buddhism, Dynamic Responses to Dzong-ka-ba's* The Essence of Eloquence, Volume 1. Berkeley: University of California Press, 1999; Delhi: Munshiram Manoharlal, 2000.

——. *Maps of the Profound: Jam-yang-shay-ba's Great Exposition of Buddhist and Non-Buddhist Views on the Nature of Reality.* Ithaca, N.Y.: Snow Lion Publications, 2003.

——. *Meditation on Emptiness.* London: Wisdom Publications, 1983; rev. ed., Boston, Ma.: Wisdom Publications, 1996.

——. *Reflections on Reality: The Three Natures and Non-Natures in the Mind-Only School, Dynamic Responses to Dzong-ka-ba's* The Essence of Eloquence, Volume 2. Berkeley: University of California Press, 2002.

——. *The Tantric Distinction.* London: Wisdom Publications, 1984.

——. "The Ultimate Deity In Action Tantra and Jung's Warning Against Identifying With the Deity," *Buddhist-Christian Studies* 5 (1985): 159-172.

Joshi, L. M. "Facets of Jaina Religiousness in Comparative Light," L. D. Series 85 [Ahmedabad: L. D. Institute of Indology, May 1981], 53-58.

Jung, Carl G. *The Collected Works of C. G. Jung.* Princeton, N.J.: Princeton University Press, 1971; second printing, 1974.

Kuhn, Thomas. *The Structure of Scientific Revolutions.* Second edition; Chicago: University of Chicago Press, 1970.

Küng, Hans. *Theology for the Third Millennium: An Ecumenical View.* New York: Doubleday, 1988.

Lati Rinbochay, Denma Lochö Rinbochay, Leah Zahler, and Jeffrey Hopkins. *Meditative States in Tibetan Buddhism.* London: Wisdom Publications, 1983; rev. ed., Boston: Wisdom Publications, 1997.

Lodrö, Gedün. *Calm Abiding and Special Insight.* Ithaca, N.Y.: Snow Lion Publications, 1998.

Mi-pam-gya-tso. *Fundamental Mind: The Nyingma View of the Great Completeness* with practical commentary by Khetsun Sangbo Rinbochay. Trans. and ed. by Jeffrey Hopkins. Ithaca, N.Y.: Snow Lion Publications, 2006.

Rabten, Geshe. *The Life and Teachings of Geshe Rabten.* Trans. and ed. by Alan Wallace. London: George Allen and Unwin, 1982.

Sangpo, Khetsun. *Tantric Practice in Nyingma.* Trans. and ed. by Jeffrey Hopkins. London: Rider, 1982; reprint, Ithaca, N.Y.: Snow Lion Publications, 1983.

Sopa, Geshe Lhundup and Jeffrey Hopkins. *Cutting Through Appearances: The Practice and Theory of Tibetan Buddhism.* Ithaca, N.Y.: Snow Lion Publications, 1989.

Index